THE LIFE AND TIMES OF A HOOSIER JUDGE

JOHN LEWIS NIBLACK

ISBN 978-0-9831994-2-7

Cover Photo: Niblack store about 1908: Martha, Herman, John and (front) Griffith

Hawthorne Publishing
15601 Oak Road
Carmel, Indiana 46033
317-867-5183
www.Hawthornepub.com

TABLE OF CONTENTS

PREFACE TO THE SECOND EDITION

At the time of the publication of this second edition of his memoirs, in 2012, Indiana's John L. Niblack has been gone for twenty-five years.

His reputation as a leading jurist in the state of Indiana as well as one of its most interesting citizens has been modestly growing since his passing. That he led the Republican ticket in Marion County as Superior and Circuit Judge in the 1940s and 1950s, voted into office by citizens who valued his reputation as "a good judge" is recalled, as is his work as newspaper reporter on a nationally known crime case. My dad's description of the D.C. Stephenson Ku Klux Klan trial in the mid 1920s is still cited as the principle source of personal and accurate reportage by such authors as William Lutholtz, author of *Grand Dragon: D.C. Stephenson and the Ku Klux Klan.*

Niblack helped win the Pulitzer Prize for *The Indianapolis Times* for his coverage of the trial that sent the Klan's potentate to prison for over twenty years and broke up its sinister hold on the state of Indiana. Later, on the bench he was known for his sometimes humorous, often sardonic style as he listened to lawyers rambling on in boring detail in front of him. He himself, however, seemed most proud of being part of a group that helped found Indianapolis' Citizens School Committee to guarantee wide, non-partisan and diverse representation for guidance of the schools in the city and his leadership in the city's remarkable public golf courses.

John L. Niblack's biography is in the *Encyclopedia of Indianapolis.* His comments and photo are part of the Gallery of Famous Hoosiers at the Indiana State Library. Surely his book has also enhanced his reputation.

But most of all, as his other daughter Susan Niblack Goldsmith says, "My dad was a child of the soil of southern Indiana, a man who honored the sturdy pioneer stock from which he sprang. Judge Niblack was known for his quick wit and sense of humor and he genuinely liked "folks," as he called them. He was a man who stopped in the road to find out what his neighbors thought. He never lost that common touch. After he went to Indiana University to study law, his subsequent career as a lawyer, judge, and engaged public citizen brought him respect and recognition. He was a man of integrity and honesty."

It is in a spirit of appreciation for small-town values that this new edition of his much-loved biography *Life and Times of a Hoosier Judge* is being reintroduced to the public. The text of the memoir remains untouched, but we have added new photos and letters at the close of the book to honor Wheatland, Indiana, the town in which he grew up and which he never left in spirit.   Nancy Niblack Baxter, Senior Editor

JOHN L. NIBLACK
Judge, Marion Circuit
19th Indiana Judicial Circuit

INTRODUCTION

We have it on the authority of no less eminent a man of letters than the celebrated Dr. Samuel Johnson that the life worth writing about should be composed by the man who lived it. Such autobiographies challenge the interest of readers from many points of view: they enable the author to set down and estimate his personal achievements; they offer instruction and example to others, especially younger people; and they bring pleasure and information to those interested not only in the writer himself, but in the personalities and events of which he makes a record. Such are the standards for a well written life.

Examined by these criteria, the autobiography of the distinguished jurist whose story is told here will win both popular and critical acclaim. He writes from the eminence of mature years, aided by a Phi Beta Kappa intellect. His years of successful experience as a journalist reveal themselves in these pages by his capacity to observe carefully and to record accurately events of historic importance. In many of these he was himself a principal actor.

The Honorable John Lewis Niblack, presiding judge of the Circuit Court of Marion County, is a man bred in bone and blood of pioneer Indiana stock. Remote ancestors fought in the Indian Wars. His maternal grandfather John McClure enlisted as a teenager in the Fourteenth Indiana Infantry Regiment in the War Between the States, fighting in such storied battles as Chancellorsville and Gettysburg. Returning to Indiana in 1865, he farmed the family land, married, and ultimately undertook to rear the orphanned grandson who is the subject of this book.

There is an Horatio Alger quality to the Judge's career: farmboy, school-teacher, journalist, lawyer, prosecutor, legislator, and judge. He was graduated by Indiana University as bachelor of arts *cum laude* in 1922, where he was contemporary with Charles Halleck, Ernie Pyle, and Hoagy Carmichael. In 1931 he married Miss Margaret Wood of Sullivan. The marriage was blessed with two daughters, now Mrs. Arthur Baxter and Mrs. Linn Goldsmith. Upon the demise of his wife, the Judge married Mrs. Mildred Bacon of Washington, Indiana, widow of William F. Bacon. He has been President of the Central Indiana Contract Bridge League and for over forty years an official of the United States Golf Association for Public Links Affairs in Indiana.

Early on he developed an abiding interest in the political and social affairs of Indiana: as journalist or as prosecutor he acted important roles in the trials of the famous and the infamous, including those of McCray, Jackson, and Stephenson; as State Senator he helped to write laws which he was later to interpret from the Benches of Municipal, Superior, and Circuit Courts. For over thirty years he has made decisions which affect the lives and the institutions of Indiana citizens.

Now, putting black on white is not easy where one man fulfills the dual roles of author and subject. To this demanding task Judge Niblack has brought the necessary qualifications: accurate command of facts; organized chronology; exceptional skill in selection of material, including anecdote and quotation; delightful humor; earthy narration of earthy matters; and vivid memory. The book reveals the life and mind of a man who loves his native State, one deeply concerned with its people and their ways, dedicated to the ancient virtues of enterprise and industry.

This volume presents more than an account of a busy and useful life. It is American history.

George P. Rice, Jr.
Member of the Indiana Bar
Professor of Speech in Butler University

DEDICATION

I dedicate this book to the memory of Hannah Chute Poor, Grandmother Niblack's grandmother, who came down from Massachusetts in 1818 and, after the death of her husband, reared eight children in a lonely cabin in the forest in Orange Valley, Jackson county; to John Niblack, Jr., a great grandfather, who left Kentucky in 1817 with his rifle and Bible which I now own to escape the evil and degrading institution of slavery; to the girl who became his wife, Martha Hargrave, who came riding North out of North Carolina with her parents in 1818 to the free soil of Indiana for the same reason; to Daniel McClure, an ancestor, who was the first clerk of the first Protestant church in the Indiana Territory, an Anti-slavery and Anti-rum church, who first saw Vincennes in 1779 as a soldier with General George Rogers Clark; to Jonathan Purcell, my mother's double-great grandfather, who brought seventeen slaves from Virginia for the purpose of giving them their freedom; to Grandfather John R. McClure who answered Lincoln's call in 1861 to further the cause of union and freedom; to my God-fearing father, John Hargrave Niblack, who by precept and example, instilled into his children morality and patriotism; and last but not least to William H. Remy, prosecuting attorney of Marion county, Indiana, the Nemesis of the Ku Klux Klan in the Roaring Twenties, under whom I served as deputy.

Indiana is the greatest, the most American state in the Union. Southern Indiana, where I was born, was formed of three parts Dixie emigrants to one part New Englander. The Southerners brought a happy-go-lucky love of life. The Yankees brought a notion of thrift and enterprise, and a new England conscience, which is one that does not keep a sinner from doing anything, merely keeps him or her from enjoying it. All these are now dust to dust but once were Hoosiers who helped mold our destiny—especially mine.

JOHN S. NIBLACK

Life in a Country Town

I was born in a sleepy little Southwestern Indiana town down in the Pocket just east of Vincennes, in Knox County—the oldest city and the oldest county in the State. The time was at the close of the 19th Century—the Golden Age of the United States, despite its outside privies, coal-burning steam engines, kerosene lamps, and whalebone corsets.

One of the main reasons for my debut there in the Wabash country was that Danny McClure, a third great-grandfather, had been a soldier of the Revolution with General George Rogers Clark at the capture of Fort Sackville at Vincennes, and its British Commander, General Francis Hamilton, the "hair buyer," in 1779. Having survived the February march across the water-logged prairies of Illinois and the rest of it, Daniel, a Presbyterian Scotch-Irish lad from Londonderry, Ulster, returned to Knox County in 1802, where he was given 400 acres of rolling prairie as a war bonus, and bought 400 more for $1.25 an acre. It is now worth $700.00 an acre.

Wheatland had two dusty main streets and four hundred residents, with one-half as many dogs. Ninety of us were colored folk—not Negroes or Blacks, or Afro-Americans—and everybody in town got along fine. We were all self-supporting Americans. In fact, some of the colored people were more American than the rest of us, as old Uncle Tobe Granger, the patriarch head of the large clan, was one-quarter Creek Indian and his good wife, Aunt Fanny, was half white on her mother's side. Mrs. Sarah Colbert, a fast friend of Grandma Niblack, was fond of relating about her Cherokee blood. She was about half white, too. Uncle Tobe's son, "Old" Sam, was my boss one summer while I was in college and got a vacation job on the B & O Railroad laying steel on the section. The seventeen colored men were 100% Republican and one, Mr. George Horn, had been one of Lincoln's Boys in Blue. The colored folks had their own grade school and Baptist Church in their quarter of town, but they attended the one High School after a Republican Trustee was elected in 1895. Aunt Crit Horn was the only Methodist in the crowd, and she attended our Methodist Church whenever she felt like it.

Inserting here a little history in re race relations, ancestor Dan McClure and Mrs. William Henry Harrison, wife of the Indiana Territorial Governor at Vincennes, founded the first Protestant Church in Indiana, the Knox County Indiana Presbyterian Church, in 1806, and its membership roll of 1812 shows whites, Indians and Negroes all as full members. Daniel was its first and only secretary of the Quarterly Session until his death on Christmas Eve 1825.

Indiana was part of the Northwest Territory captured by Clark and, under Thomas Jefferson's Ordinance of 1787, was the only part of the United States that never allowed slavery. After 1865, all colored men over 21 could and did vote in this state without literacy tests, poll tax receipts, or other harassment.

At the turn of the century small country towns in Southern Indiana had no water works, no inside plumbing, no sewer systems, no electricity, no central heating, no cement sidewalks, and mostly dirt streets, though maybe the main street had recently been covered with gravel, which largely did away with mud but left the dust. However, there wasn't one automobile in all Wheatland to raise the dust in 1900, though there were a few in 1910. Horse drawn buggies and carriages didn't stir it up much, except when a couple of young bloods got in a race. Every nineteen-year old farm boy had to have a good horse and buggy, mainly for squiring the girls to ice cream socials and oyster suppers, or for Sunday afternoon drives.

There weren't any street lamps in Wheatland, and at about 9:00 or 10:00 P.M., depending on the season, it would get still as death. When the moon was down and it was cloudy, you really couldn't see your hand before you. I went out in our chicken yard one dark night, and accidentally stepped on our old black cat, which let out a frightful scream and scared me half to death. It seemed like I leaped ten feet straight up.

We also lacked the privileges of paying Federal and State income taxes and of supporting a Public Welfare system. There were no Social Security deductions; in fact, there was no Social Security

2

system except working and saving. Women couldn't vote. All of this has been changed now, but I can't see that we are any better off or happier, despite our automobiles and inside toilets.

People were afraid of the dark. That was the time when houses burned down, robbers came, rape was committed, and ghosts walked. A great many folks were superstitious and believed in the supernatural. The "Woman in Black" was a night time terror to us small fry and a lot of grown-ups, too. Ever so often some restless soul, suffering from insomnia or a full bladder, would peer out into the pale moonlight and imagine he or she saw the "Woman in Black" staring from under the cowl of her black grave clothes. It was a bad omen. Someone was due to die in the neighborhood within a year. Next day the bloodcurdling tale would go all over town. The "Woman in Black" always walked across yards, never in the street.

Another bad omen was for someone to carry a spade through the house, as again it portended death within a year. The only way it could be corrected, and maybe not even then, was immediately to carry it back through the house in the reverse direction. I frightened my first stepmother, a fine woman if there ever was one, almost into a fit when I marched through the house with a spade one day, and incidentally myself also when I learned the ill fortune I had unwittingly invited on our home. When she died suddenly from a ruptured tube within a couple of years, in my childish ignorance I blamed myself until I finally learned better.

A strange dog which would come and howl under a window at night also chilled the blood, as it likewise was a "token" of an early death on the premises. To this day when I am half awake late at night the mournful howling of a distant dog will send a shiver down my spine, and I still don't like to walk under a ladder or sit down with twelve others.

It was also bad luck to count the number of carriages and buggies in a funeral train, and many a person in that time would turn right around and go back home or wherever he started from if a black cat crossed his path. If there was an unexplained knocking or tapping on the roof or wall at night, it was the dead come calling for someone in the house. A peculiar kind of moaning wind around the eaves at night was nothing else than the wailing of babies who

3

unfortunately had died before baptism. In common with Abraham Lincoln, who was a Southern Indiana boy, many believed in warnings from dreams. Lincoln said that many times before a large event in his life he would dream he was on a large ship sailing rapidly away from the shore. He told his cabinet of this dream a few days before he was shot on Good Friday, April 14, 1865.

My good Methodist father, John H. Niblack (Hargrave for his grandmother), whom we four children always called "Pop" had quit a good job as dispatcher on the B & O Railroad to clerk in the family general store, owned by my grandmother Niblack, so we were always a little impecunious. The reason was, Pop wouldn't work on Sunday, as required by the Railroad. I am sure he could have been at least a division Superintendent with a fine salary, but I am glad he didn't stay on the Railroad as I might not have been here; at least, I might not have been me.

Pop was the Sunday School Superintendent at our church for as long as I could remember, succeeding his father, Sanford, who had been a co-founder with his wife in 1859. Grandpa in his old days would sit in a big easy chair at one side just below the choir, in the "Amen Corner," during sermons and in Thursday night prayer meetings, and he could roll out a sonorous "Amen." On cold nights he had a shawl around his shoulders. In my childish way, I thought he and grandma were that old when they started the church fifty years before, but fifty years does not seem such a long time now.

4

Home Life

In the days of our Pagan ancestors, when the South wind blew and the Spring Equinox arrived, they celebrated the demise of winter with festivals, fertility rites, and pilgrimages. When the robins returned to Wheatland in my youth, there were no fertility rites, at least not in public, but the housewife girded up her loins, hitched up her skirts and became the High Priestess of Spring House Cleaning. The sound of the rug beater was heard in the land, and how we teenagers dreaded it.

Put a rug beater in the hands of a fourteen year old adolescent boy and set him to beating a dusty carpet in the warm sunshine when the crows were calling from the woodlands and the tadpoles were frolicking in Possum Branch, our town creek, and you had the most miserable urchin on earth. Extreme lassitude would overcome us boys until we barely could lift our arms. And the carpets seemed to hold tons of dust.

Mama might be the High Priestess, but we were the unhappy Acolytes who helped bring spring in, and we swung the rug beater instead of an incense burner.

Our house had a kitchen, dining room, parlor, and a bedroom downstairs, with a hall and two bedrooms upstairs. The kitchen was considered very up to date, with a coal burning range which had an oven and a reservoir on one end for heating water. In addition there was also a coal oil stove. There was a storage closet and a large pantry at one side. For ablutions before meals there was a wash pan on a stand and a roller towel with a bucket of water at hand.

The dining room and bedroom downstairs had a coal burning Round Oak stove for heat, and they could make it mighty comfortable on a winter day. Grandma Niblack had a base burner in her living room which used "hard coal" (anthracite) and made a fine steady heat. It had a lot of little mica isinglass windows around the upper

5

part which let a cheerful ruddy glow shine through. It made a very little smoke or ashes—quite a luxury. You had only to fill the hopper once a day whereas our coal stoves had to be stoked about every hour.

Our "parlor" with its sea shells, family Bible, red plush sofa and bookcase had a grate. The two rooms upstairs had no stoves and in winter we dressed and undressed down in Pop's bedroom. On a cold night it took some doing to get warm in bed upstairs. Real cold nights I have heated a brick and wrapped it in a towel to put at my feet. It was just as bad to get up on a winter morning. My brother Herman often wished that the bed would be as warm at night as when we had to get up in the morning and vice versa.

One time when I was about fourteen, I read in the "Youth's Companion," long a genteel weekly for children of genteel people— or people who thought they were—about the virtues of a cold bath on arising. I almost put myself in the grave by carrying buckets of water upstairs one January and taking cold baths for eight or ten days. It was necessary to break a skim of ice before pouring the water in the bowl and my teeth would chatter. I gave it up readily just before I nearly got pneumonia. I don't know why I was so silly, as I never liked to bathe in my youth any more than the old folks made me.

On Saturday afternoon, winter and summer, every one had a bath whether he needed it or not. Summer days we would take a large galvanized tin wash tub and pump about a foot of water in it and let it set in the sun until warm, and then bathe in the wood-house or summer kitchen. In winter the tub was used in the kitchen and generally all three of us boys used the same water. One of the younger boys had to go last from then on after it was accidentally discovered he couldn't resist peeing in the warm bath water while bathing. We didn't know how long this had been going on before it was found out. I guess we got as clean one way as the other.

In cleaning house we started by moving all the furniture out of one room. Then Mama would pull the tacks out of the wall-to-wall carpet which had been tacked down a year before in yard wide stips. The dusty carpets were trundled outdoors and hung over the clothes line and beaten clean, while the dust got in the beaters' eyes, noses, and lungs. The dirty straw or newspapers used for padding was gathered up and taken out and burned. The floor was swept, dusted, mopped and dried, and the windows washed inside and out. Then came a trip to a neighboring straw stack with a sheet, and new fresh straw was brought in and spread on the floor. The revived carpet, cleaned, sunned and aired, would be spread and the tack hammer, aided by the carpet stretcher, would put the tacks in again about half an inch to an inch apart. The furniture then would be brought back in from the other rooms.

Alas! Then it was the turn of the other rooms. We got all done eventually, though it was a rare spring when one of us didn't get a smart crack on the rear with the rug beater as a sort of added ingredient, or booster, to our languid efforts. I have had nightmares wherein I dreamed I could hardly raise my arms to strike a feeble blow against some ruffian, and that is exactly how we felt when facing that dusty carpet in the warm sunshine.

One other task that unnerved the village youth who wasn't old enough to have a job involved the new-fangled washing machine, a labor saver for the housewife, but not for me and my younger brothers, Herman and Griffith, in their turn. The device had attached to one side a large upright wheel with a hand grip, and I was the motor which caused the wheel to revolve which churned the clothes. This was a regular Monday morning ceremony that kept me out of mischief most of the day. We generally got done before school in the winter or noon in summer, but I didn't feel too much like raising Hell the rest of the day.

Come to think of it, we all had chores that city kids never heard of. In the morning one child would take a large slop jar and make the rounds of the bedrooms, carefully pulling a chamber pot from under each bed and dumping the contents in the receptacle. Then the slop jar would be emptied in the outhouse, and all the utensils washed out and replaced. The outhouse sat back somewhere behind the woodshed with a screen of hollyhocks or sun flowers in front, known as "privy flowers." A Sears and Roebuck or Butlers catalogue took the place of squeezable tissue.

We had an uncle, Dr. Earl Niblack, who had graduated from the School of Medicine at Michigan University in 1893, and he lived in the metropolis of Terre Haute, a city of 30,000, and boasted an inside toilet. He said it was no wonder people in small towns and the country were constipated so much in winter, as it took a hero to go to the outside John when it was five degrees above zero and a chill wind blew.

Except in summer, another chore each morning was to take the ashes out of each stove and carry them outdoors. Then coal buckets had to be filled in the woodhouse and brought in and set behind each stove. A bunch of kindling had to be split each night and brought in and set beside the kitchen stove along with a bucket of corn cobs, so Pop could start a fire in the kitchen range for breakfast.

For breakfast on winter mornings we would have oatmeal which had been semi-cooked all night, or buckwheat or cornmeal pancakes, or maybe fried salt mackerel which came from New England in little wooden kegs. I thought it was great food. One time after I was married we had some salt mackerel for breakfast and it didn't taste at all as I remembered. We also ate pickled pork, fried, which was pure sow belly, fat with no lean, put down in brine. When fried crisp, it was good. We also ate a lot of mush and milk, and fried mush with fried eggs.

Another chore was to feed and water the chickens twice a day and gather the eggs after school. Twice a day, morning and evening, one child took a tin bucket with a lid on it and a nickel in it, and went up to Mr. John Overbay's farm house on the edge of town, exchanging the empty bucket for its mate which had a quart of warm milk in it, setting on his back porch with numerous other like buckets.

We also had to mow the yard, hoe the garden, and "bug" the potatoes by knocking the red Colorado potato bettle larvae into a tin can with some coal oil in it. Child labor was cheaper than arsenic.

The girls would wash the dishes and dry them, help with the beds, the washing, ironing, sweeping, and the babies. In our house, we boys got to dry the dishes after supper, which was at night. Dinner was always at noon. Incidentally, in Southern Indiana, when a person said "this evening" he meant anytime after noon until dark, which was "tonight."

8

Most houses in country towns had a large yard and room for a kitchen garden, chicken house, and maybe a barn for the horse, if you were a village tycoon such as a banker, station agent, merchant, or such. Some folks kept a cow and others a few hogs.

On hot, humid nights in August when there was no breeze and people sweat and slapped mosquitoes, sometimes the privies, hog pens, and barns would all get to stinking. Talk about modern pollution! Someone would groan: "Them durn privies are stinking again."

Speaking of language down home, three-fourths of our end of the State was settled up from Dixie: Virginia, Kentucky, North Carolina, and Tennessee, and the pioneers brought along the speech.

Lincoln, who lived and grew up about forty or fifty miles from my home town used Southern Indiana dialect I was familiar with in my youth. He would say "Marthy" for "Martha", and "Mishawaky" for "Mishawaka".

"I reckon" and "over yonder" were common usage. "Airy" and "nairy" meant "any" and "none". I have heard a farm hand say, "Have you got airy match?" and the answer was "No, I hain't got nairy one." Goods were either "homemade" or "boughten." The housewife would "redd up" the bed instead of "making it" (which after all was just as peculiar). An old timer would say "over thar" for "over there," and "Whar is it?"

No one in his right mind would say," I am not going" instead of "I ain't going," unless he was positively, absolutely, not going. As for me, I never could understand why "ain't" was counted as ignorant talk, when "don't," "won't" and "can't" became proper.

A friend of mine who taught a one-room country school in that era dwelt on the impropriety of saying "ain't." One day in recitation a pupil used the forbidden word.

"Oh! Oh! What is wrong here, class?" the teacher asked.

One little boy held up his hand and said, "Teacher, there hain't no such word as 'ain't.'"

In this respect, I call to mind a story Ralph Gates, former Governor of Indiana, liked to tell. He said that onetime while on his way to a political meeting in Southern Indiana he stopped to ask directions from a grizzled old Hoosier who was sitting on a bench in front of a crossroad store.

"Can you tell me where Stodger Junction is?" Mr. Gates asked.

The old man spit out some tobacco juice and replied: "Podner, don't move nary God dam inch and you're right in the middle of hit!"

The General Store

The old Buffalo Trace from Louisville, Kentucky, to Vincennes ran right through our town. In fact, it was the main street. It had been carved out by the buffalo in their migrations, used by the Indians, and the earliest settlers came along it. The Trace ran northwest through Wheatland, and Grandma's store was on the south side just before it crossed the B. & O. railroad. Across the street was Charley Qualls' Saloon, which some of our good church folks called a "Gambling Hell."

One time when I was a small lad, Pop and I were going to the store, walking down the railroad, and there were some playing cards lying on the track by the saloon. One of them was the ace of spades. "You see those things there, son?" Pop asked me, "they are playing cards and men use them to gamble their wages away so their children go hungry. They are instruments of the Devil and I want you never to touch them." With that he took me by the hand, and we made a big detour around the cards as an object lesson in avoiding vice.

Little did he imagine that years later his son would be State President of the Indiana Contract Bridge League and always happy to find the ace of spades in his hand. Son also dabbled some in 25¢ limit poker in later life.

One night Pop was going home from the store and was about half a block up the street when the door of Qualls' Saloon burst open, and out sped Rube Steffey, a bow-legged young farmer from north of town, a cousin of our livery stable Steffey. Rube was about five feet five and always wore a large floppy Stetson hat. Mr. Qualls was standing in the open door firing a revolver at Rube, with the bullets knocking dust all around him. Pop said that Rube, whose little legs almost ran circles around each other, finally dodged behind the same building where Pop was hiding.

Fanning himself with his big hat, he announced, "By God, I

11

may not be much of a fighter, but I sure am about the best little runner around these parts!"

Mr. Qualls' Saloon caught fire one night in 1919, and the wind blew the flames into our store, which soon burnt down, too. Pop and Uncle Herman Niblack had bought Grandma out a couple years before and were finally making some money, but the store was full of a big stock bought at War inflated values and we only had a small pre-war insurance, so Pop's finances again were at a low ebb, or worse than that.

The store was established by my great-grandfather, Thomas Jefferson Brooks of Mt. Pleasant, Indiana, now Loogootee. Mr. Brooks was a native of Cambridge, Massachusetts, where his family had lived since 1636; he was a keel-boat man running from Pittsburgh to New Orleans when he first came over the mountains. He was a merchant up there in the Martin County hills just east of us, and every year ran flat boats loaded with pork and whisky down the White river to the Wabash and on down to New Orleans.

Grandpa Sanford Niblack had been born in Dubois County, Indiana, just across the river, where his father John was an Andrew Jackson Democrat. He also was a politician who had surveyed the County lines in 1818 and built the log Court house and jail, and he was the first Judge of the Common Pleas Court. His son went as a clerk to Mr. Brooks, and finding that the old man was frugal with wages, decided that the best way to advance was to marry his daughter Susan, who was agreeable. Thomas J. set his new son-in-law up in a branch store at Wheatland when the new railroad went through. Everything was new—railroad, town, store, and newly-weds. Grandpa didn't turn out too well as a store proprietor, as he was too trusting and extended credit to a lot of dead beats, so he had to go through bankruptcy, and Grandma took over the store.

Grandpa did better as a sire. He begot ten children, eight of whom lived to a ripe old age. Two died in infancy from "summer complaint." In the 19th century, if a couple only lost one-fifth of their get in infancy, they were a great success.

I can see the old store yet, a two-story affair, painted red, with a big warehouse at one side and a salt house and a poultry house back of it. The village pump was on the other side under huge

12

cottonwood trees, with hitching racks for farmers' teams on all sides. "S.B. Niblack & Sons" was the name painted across the front standing for Susan B. Niblack and sons. Inside was the usual merchandise sold by a general country store in the Gay Nineties and early 1900's: canned and dried groceries of all kinds; barrels of pickles, pickled pork, sorghum molasses, white navy beans and soda crackers; kegs of salt mackerel and boxes of dried peaches, apricots, and prunes.

There was whole grain coffee in packages. If the customer wanted it ground, we opened the package and put it through a hand grinder. Most people took it home and ground it in a small wooden coffee mill which had a little drawer to pull out when full of ground coffee. The store even kept raw coffee beans for old timers who insisted they could get a better flavor by doing the roasting themselves.

In the warehouse was a large tank of "coal oil" (kerosene) and the usual purchase was a gallon for ten cents, with a small potato stuck on the spout as a stopper. All kinds of rope, crocks, tinware, stove pipe, and sacks of flour were kept in the store room. A lot of fine big rats also haunted its environs and the store kept two big cats to ride herd on them.

Grandma kept a large stock of candy, featuring chocolate drops, marshmallows, licorice whips, gum drops, hore hound strips, coconut bars, red hots and red striped peppermint sticks. When a credit customer paid his bill on Saturday night, he was given a peppermint stick for each child in the family.

Every so often some country boy would be hired as a new clerk, and invariably his first question was "Mr. Niblack, you care if I eat some candy?"

"Pshaw, eat all you want," was the answer.

"All I want?" the boy would ask incredulously.

The new hand would eat about a pound and a half the first day, some the next day and in a week he wouldn't go near the candy case except to wait on a customer. Maybe when opening a bucket of a new kind of candy he would eat one piece.

Grandma kept everything for the hunter except guns; shot gun shells and rifle and revolver cartridges, bulk gun powder, lead bars for muzzle loaders, and all sizes of lead shot for reloading shells.

Buggy whips, black snake whips (large ones for cattle and mules) farm clothes, shoes, boots, nails of all sizes in kegs, screws, hammers, axes, hatchets, you name it, Niblack and Sons had it.

On the west side of the store was the 'dry goods" section, with bolts of calico, ginghams, red flannel, linen, flannelette, silk and other cloth; dress shoes and stockings, O.N.T. thread (Our New Thread) of all colors and strength, and ribbons of all widths and colors.

Back behind was salt house where barrels of coarse salt were sold, likewise block salt for setting out in the pastures for the cattle to lick. The store sold hams, flitches of bacon, and canned salmon. We also had a large stock of canned pumpkin, called "punkin" by a true Hoosier, and other vegetables and fruits, Black pepper, nutmeg—whole or grated, and other spices were there ready for the housewife.

In the center of the main store was a large tall iron heating stove surrounded by sand about an inch deep contained by a little metal strip, so the loafers and others could spit their tobacco juice in the sand instead of on the stove or base boards. Many a grave debate was had around the stove the year around, though of course there was no fire in it except in cold weather.

One of the store's regular loafers was a gentleman of leisure who occasionally did odd jobs, by the name of George Jones. George had spent a life time fathering eight children and growing a large handle-bar moustache, which was his pride and joy. His wife, Miss Mindy, took in washing and sewing, and she was tolerant of George.

"Poor George, I guess he was just born tired," she used to say.

Anyway, my Uncle Bill Niblack, who worked in the store when he was not out West trying to locate a ranch in Montana, or up in Michigan for his hay fever, liked to fool around with scissors and knives, sharpening or honing them. One day he was honing some shears while Mr. Jones was gravely droning on about the sins of the Republican Party (he was a 100% Democrat) when Uncle Bill reached out, seized one end of the famous moustache and with one move—snipped it off.

For once in his life poor George was galvanized into action.

"By God! I'll take my trade summers else," he bellowed angrily, as he stamped out.

Pop as a young man carried a .32 caliber revolver at night in the store, and it nearly cost him his life. One evening about 10:00 P.M. a couple of swamp angels from out toward Montour's Pond knocked on the door just after closing time and wanted to see some shoes.

Pop unlocked and let them in. He stooped down behind the counter to get some shoes, and when he raised up they had a pistol on him and one said:

"Johnny, we've come for what you got. Put up your hands.'"

Pop said, "Oh, no you don't!" and reached for his weapon and started firing, knocking the coal oil lamp off on the floor. The robbers shot him through the chest and fled. Pop beat out the flames with his bloody shirt, and staggered to the doctor. He finally recovered, as the bullet missed his heart about half an inch. I used to look at the bullet holes in the old store, and I also on occasion was allowed to feel the bullet which lodged in his back about half an inch under the skin. I don't know why he never had it cut out, but he carried it to his grave fifty-two years later.

This event took place a year before he was married. If the robbers' aim had been a half inch to the left, someone else would have written this piece.

The old General Store in Southern Indiana did a large barter trade. Farmers' wives would bring in two or three pounds of yellow butter, or a few dozen eggs to trade on groceries. The men often brought a couple bushels of onions or potatoes. If they brought more than they bought they received a "due bill"—no cash—good for future purchases.

The old time Country General Store is no more—gone with the local passenger train, outside plumbing, ankle length skirts for women, and detachable celluloid collars for men.

15

Funerals

Funerals were quite an event in 1900, although not so much as the big city Irish Wake. All funerals were held at church. The decedent was kept at home, in the parlor, without benefit of embalming, and folks "sat up" with the corpse, mainly to see that all went well. I think this custom originated in early times when there were no screens on the windows and they had to be kept open in warm weather. I have heard my grandmother tell how when she was young, the watchers were sitting up with a corpse one time when they heard a cat coming in the distance, howling and getting nearer and nearer until a big black cat jumped through the window and up on the corpse's chest as it lay in the coffin, and it had to be broomed out of the house. Also, there was a fear in those days of grave robbers or body snatchers, for sales to Medical Schools.

The body of the son of one President and father of another, Scott Harrison, was snatched and only recovered from the University of Cincinnati just before it was to be dissected.

When the coffin was carried out of the church, the church bell began to toll and kept up its dismal dirge until the funeral procession was out of sight or reached the grave. If the funeral was at a country church, the bell began to toll when the hearse, leading the procession, came in sight.

While the body lay in state at home, a black or purple crepe wreath adorned the front door, and also at a man's place of business. A widow wore "Widows Weeds"; black dress, hat, veil and gloves, for a year, at least, in mourning. The adult male survivors wore a black arm band for a month or longer.

Hearses were horse drawn, generally by two black horses. There might be a few bouquets of flowers, if it were spring or summer, but small towns and rural areas were not equipped to furnish much of a floral tribute at funerals. The neighbors took over the cooking and brought in food for the family and relatives

16

who came "from off." Potato salad, meat loaf, baked ham, cakes and pies were common items.

My maternal grandfather, John R. McClure, was a Civil War Veteran, a private for three years with the 14th Indiana Infantry Volunteers, and liked to talk over the war with other old soldiers. This got him in trouble once with grandma about a funeral. They lived on a large farm over in Palmyra Township toward Vincennes.

One time they were attending the last rites of a prominent farmer and Grandpa insisted on riding in the buggy with another veteran, whom I shall call Mr. Jones, so they could talk over Gettysburg and Chancellorsville as the funeral procession wound over the hills and hollows to the Upper Indiana Church. Processions in those days were at a sober and seemly pace, with the horses walking. Nobody in the Gay Nineties was rushed to the tomb at forty miles an hour, as happens nowadays.

Perforce, Grandma was given the reins to drive our old Nelly, and had as her companion Mrs. Beck Jones, the other gentleman's wife, both ladies dressed soberly in their voluminous black dresses and small pincushion hats befitting to a funeral. As the procession went along, Mrs. Jones was seized with bowel pains resulting from an overdose of Carter's Little Liver Pills, a fairly strong laxative she had taken the night before in an unguarded moment. Even years later Grandma still smarted from the subsequent events and held them against Grandpa.

"Drat the luck! John caused it all—(which was a little off the mark) just so crazy to ride with another old soldier. That's all he thinks about, is that old war and going to reunions," she said later. "There we were, toward the head of the procession, and Beck had to get out and squat in the fence corner and hist up her dress, and me sitting there to one side in the old buggy, red-faced as a sunset, while all those buggies and carriages passed by, and people gawking and snickering behind their hands. I tell you, that John McClure, if I'd a had him then, I'd have wrung his neck! And I thought that procession never would end."

Grandpa's own funeral caused his descendants a little excitement. The good old man had nearly been carried off by an ounce Minié ball at the Battle of the Wilderness at the age of 22, but

17

lived to be 81, surviving Grandma about four months. They had been married 56 years and were in fairly good health when the old lady had fourteen teeth pulled one day, which caused her death a week later. Grandpa was a lost soul, and just laid down and died. The doctor told me, "If you don't get that old man out of bed, he's going to die."

"Grandpa," I said, "You got to get out of bed or you are going to pass on, the doctor said."

"Well, Johnnie, your Maw is over there and I want to go over there and join her, I can hear her calling me," he replied. He always called her "Maw" to us, as they helped raise me and my sister after our Mother died.

He got up for a while, but went back down again, and his lungs filled up and he died—hypostatic pneumonia, or something like that.

Grandpa was lying in state in the main bedroom of his old house, with the Civil War regimental flag on his coffin the night before the funeral. It was a drizzly, rainy night in late March, 1923. Brother Herman and I were "sitting up," half dozing, in the next room—the dining room, and my sister and Aunts and Uncles were all in bed on beyond, sound asleep. The old family clock struck three.

All of a sudden there was a knocking on the outside wall of the house "Knock! Knock! Knock!" just below the ceiling, about where the rooms joined. It was like someone knocking on a door. I sat straight up wide awake now, and glanced at Herm. He was wide awake, too. I said:

"Did you hear anything?"

"I thought I heard a knock," he replied, "But maybe I was dreaming."

Well, we listened. Nothing more, except the rain gently dripping from the eaves and we subsided, and tried to get comfortable again.

Then—"Knock! Knock! Knock!" it came again, and we both were a little scared, though both were grown young men. My hair sort of started to rise.

"You suppose that's Grandma come calling for Grandpap"? I asked Herm.

"Oh, shut up! I'm scared enough now," he replied.

"I'll look in here and see if he is still in his coffin," I said, not too joyfully, and peeped around the corner. There was Grandpa lying peacefully in death, his hands folded in his last sleep. Then we opened the side door and looked out. Nothing, just the rain, and the wind sighing in a big tree off a piece.

We heard the knocking once more along about 5:00 A.M., and we didn't need any coffee to keep us awake. The night wore on, and was I glad to see the folks about 6:00 A.M.! They made all manner of fun at us when we told our story, and Uncle Lew thought we had been drinking, though we hadn't had a drop.

Well, I went on back to Indianapolis after the funeral that afternoon, and Herman went on back to his job. Sister Martha, Aunt Fanny, Uncle Lew, Uncle Alf and Aunt Mayme remained to divide the heirlooms that night, and got in a quarrel about the dishes. As Chancellor Kent or some famous lawyer once said:

"You never know a man until you divide an inheritance with him," and he should have added "or her." They were in the same bedroom where the coffin had stood.

All of a sudden, they heard the knocking up on the wall exactly where we did. A frozen silence came over the crowd, Aunt Fanny told me later. Some one said, "My God! You suppose that is Paw this time?"

Anyway, Martha said that everything was sweetness and light from then on, and instead of quarrelling, each heir was insisting that the other heirs make first choice.

Uncle Lew bought the old house, and he said that knocking was never heard again.

The obituary, or biography, of the decedent was always read or spoken at a person's funeral, and it always mercifully omitted mention of any human frailties, coming down hard on good points. One time down in the hills of southern Indiana they were having the funeral of a village ne'er-do-well, in fact he was a little worse than that. The preacher was laying it on pretty thick about the good man's good traits, when the widow, who was sitting in the

19

front row, whispered to the oldest boy, "Johnny, take a good look at that coffin and see if that really is your pap in there!"

A male quartet was generally called on to render an old time sacred song or two. Pop sang a fine baritone, and officiated in many a quartet at many a funeral. He once told me when he was old "It seems like I have sung at a thousand funerals. The worst thing about getting old is that I have buried nearly all my friends."

"In the Sweet Bye and Bye" was a favorite funeral song. "We shall meet on that beautiful shore," went the sad refrain.

They also sang, "Jesus Lover of my Soul," "In the Garden," "Lead Kindly Light," or "Rock of Ages," to the accompaniment of the church organ. You don't hear such songs now at funerals. In fact, funerals don't amount to much any more. Just a preacher uttering a few quiet platitudes. Most people don't attend funerals nowadays. They go the night before and "pay their respects," sign the book, and leave.

I attended my first funeral two weeks before my third birthday when my mother died at the birth of brother Herm. About all I remember was that Pop lifted me and my twin sister Martha up in his arms and showed us our mother lying in her coffin in the parlor of our house, and I also remember wrestling with Uncle Frank McClure in the carriage on the way to the graveyard.

Poor Pop had a mighty sorrowful time, burying his first two wives, both good women who died young.

The Railroad

In the Gay Nineties and early 1900's the main artery of life in a small town was the railroad, in our case the Baltimore and Ohio, extending from St. Louis to Washington, D. C., Baltimore, and New York City. It had been put through in 1859 just in time to help President Lincoln save the nation by providing fast transport for the Midwestern farm boys whose muskets broke the back of the Great Rebellion, and for supplies from the same region, forming a vital link between the Father of Waters and the Eastern seaboard. The main line was single track, but there was a long side track for passing and other loading tracks and switches.

Daily, except Sunday, ten passenger trains went through Wheatland, five each way. Four were locals which stopped to disgorge "drummers" as we called traveling salesmen, with their trunks and sample cases, and to pick up local citizens who wished to go into the County Seats a few miles in each direction. The other six were mail trains, with diners and Pullmans, and they didn't stop— "fast trains," we called them. You could hear No. 2, east bound at 1:00 P.M., whistling for the crossing as she topped the Graveyard Hill west of town and everybody stood spellbound as she rushed by at seventy miles an hour, the deep whistle going full blast, bell ringing and black smoke pouring out as the sweating fireman shoveled in the coal, while all the dogs barked and ran or howled, and the dust flew from the crossings. The mail car door would open, and a mail man would kick out the mail pouch, at the same time extending an iron crook to sweep in the bag of outgoing mail suspended on a post.

"Boy, she sure would cut one Hell of a swath if she was going sideways" was a common joke.

For those passengers who didn't use the dining car, No. 2 would stop twenty minutes at Vincennes at the Union Depot Hotel. You could hear her coming with a hollow roar over the Wabash River bridge and around the bend at Second Street, and as she rolled to a

21

stop, old blind John Moore would start fiddling at top speed "The Ballad of Sam Bass" or "Turkey in the Straw," with his tincup handy for alms. A Negro in a white cap and apron would beat a huge gong just outside the door of the restaurant and passengers in their brown derbies and maxi-skirts would pour madly out of the day coaches and rush into the restaurant while the conductor bawled "Vincennes! Twenty minutes for lunch." Five minutes warning was given with two sharp toots of the whistle, and the train would start to roll very slowly to allow the last laggard to run out, sandwich in hand, and jump aboard.

The freight trains had soprano whistles, and when heavily loaded they had a time making it up the Graveyard Hill. At night you could hear them "Chuff! Chuff!" slower and slower until you would think they were going to stall and stop entirely. It would almost give me nightmares and I would cover my ears, as it sounded exactly like a person dying, whom I had heard. Usually the train would make it, but if not, the crew would uncouple, put half on the side track and go back after the rest. Sometimes in the still of the night in the summertime when I would hear the distant thin wail of a freight train, I would think maybe it was a mosquito.

One still summer night we were awakened by a frightful bawling of a lot of cattle. Mr. John Overbay's herd of forty steers had broken out of his pasture and wandered through town out into the railroad cut between the village graveyard and Mr. Boltinghouse's farm. There an eastbound freight plowed into them, killing many, wounding other, and derailing the engine and some cars.

The frantic bellowing of the maimed and dying cattle, as well as the terrified survivors, made my hair stand on end as the sound floated in on the night breeze, especially as I heard Pop say it was out by the graveyard.

Such wrecks were not uncommon, giving rise to many a law suit which was decided generally in favor of the farmer by a jury of farmers. The railroad generally settled out of court for as little as possible.

The local freight came each morning and switched cars for an hour or so, as nothing "from off" was delivered by truck. It would pick up a carload of hogs, or cattle, cars of grain from the three elevators, twelve or fourteen flats of coal from the mine, and leave some empty cars on the siding in their place. It might also leave a car of lumber at Simpson's Lumber Yard, or some box cars on the siding with good for local merchants, to be transported by Sol Harbin in his dray wagon, which was drawn by mules.

We boys became experts on how the train crew could make a "flying cut," or a "saw by," or how to use a push pole when the engine was on one track and the car on another. A "flying cut" was a tricky maneuver used when the engine was pulling a couple of cars or so and they had to be put into a switch ahead of the engine. The engineer would back up quite a piece, then go forward at ten miles an hour, slow down before he got to the switch, and then give her full throttle while the brakeman on the engine's rear undid the coupling. This created a gap between the engine and cars, and after the engine passed the switch, the other brakeman threw the switch and the cars would roll into the siding. A "saw by" was used when two freight trains going in opposite directions had to pass each other, and both were longer than the passing side track. Some rainy day you can sit down and figure it out, as it is too long an action to describe here.

Small town boys also became expert in "hopping" freights and passenger trains. We learned by watching the trainmen gracefully grasp the curved handrail as the rear end of the caboose swept by and swing himself up on to the step. We also learned how to detrain while it was rambling at a good speed. I could walk along the tops of the swaying boxcars and jump across the intervals in between. We were a nuisance to the crews, who tried to keep us off.

It was dangerous. A farm lad from out Pond Ditch way, Bert Wheeler, fell under the wheels one Saturday night and had both legs cut off. Another time I rode the local freight six miles west to Frichton, dressed in my Sunday best, going to township school institute. I was eighteen years old. To my dismay, the train didn't stop, so I got down on the step to let go, when the fireman and head brakeman leaned out and made frantic signals they were going to stop. I didn't understand, so jumped, and turned somersaults for twenty feet, but wasn't injured. Then I noticed to my horror there were new railroad ties scattered along in the weeds on the right-of-way. I just happened to not hit any, or my brains would have been splattered around. I sure didn't act that day like I had any brains though, as a country school teacher. I could have ridden over on No. 5, the accommodation passenger train, for fifteen cents. I was a little shook that day at institute, and didn't hear much of the program. It was one of several harebrained escapes from death I brought on myself in my early days.

Many a Wheatland boy got a job on the Railroad. Pop and Uncle Willie and several others hung around the station until they learned the Morse Code and became telegraphers. My father never passed the station to his dying day at 85 years but what he would stop and read the messages. I would ask him what the instruments were saying. Other local youths became firemen, engineers, brakemen, baggage smashers or railway mail clerks, while eight or ten local men worked on the section, laying steel or tamping ties.

The summer I worked on the section I got $3.00 a day for ten hours, more than I got teaching school. I learned to pump the hand car up the Graveyard Hill as the sun got low and I learned never to go to the toilet at home, but always on the company's time. It was an unwritten rule. I also learned how to play poker at the section house, though I didn't let Pop know about it, even if I had been to Normal School.

All of this is changed now. Gone is the station with its chattering telegraph instruments. Gone are the local accommodation trains. Where folks in Wheatland in 1910 who wanted to go to Bicknell, nine miles north, had to take the B & O into Vincennes, fourteen miles away, and then take the Indianapolis and Vincennes Railroad and go another fourteen miles northeast, using up half a day, now in their automobiles they reach Bicknell in fifteen minutes over the paved road. Also gone are the passenger mail trains, with their diners, Pullmans, and travelling post offices.

Vanished is the local freight train as everything comes in by truck, and everything goes out the same way—peaches, grain, hogs, timber, or what have you. The railroad still does good business with its overland freight, but the section gang has been reduced to one track walker. As a result you hear of frequent train pile-ups; false economy, I call it. The railroads are taxed heavily to subsidize the airlines and truck highways. Times have changed.

Gone also are the huge steam engines with their mellow whistles —road hogs, the old time railroader called them—which used to pant and snort and blow off steam as they lay at a station. Now two or three efficient Diesels yank 130 cars up the Graveyard Hill like it wasn't there. The coal mine is gone, and a whole lot of the town is gone, too, vanished into the mists of yesteryears.

Sex Education

While I received my religious education at the Methodist Church and at family prayer meeting each Sunday night at home when we all got down on our knees while Pop prayed for us, the community, State and Nation, a lively boy in a small country town in Southern Indiana in the early 1900's had a multitude of other learnings thrust upon him, bginning at a very early age. Life then was only one generation removed from the Civil War, and a couple more from Indian days and people of the small towns and farms as a whole were rather earthy and fundamental. Language in a whole lot of homes was not too delicate, and folks were apt to use the Anglo-Saxon four letter words for natural functions and parts, rather than politely mentioning an initial letter, such as "P" for "piss," or even further, "going to the bathroom." A lot of their great-grandchildren now in college have turned the wheel full cycle.

However, my grandmother Niblack was a descendant of Boston Brahmans and had been East in her youth to a Female Seminary, and she had reared her eight children not to use four letter words. All of her tribe spoke in refined fashion of "using the pot" or "going to the privy" while many things such as pregnancy were not mentioned at all in mixed company. In this latter connection, I have overheard an old lady state, "Well, he's got her pregnant again," as if rape had been committed.

Sex was no mystery to the boys and girls, even of pre-school age. They watched the chickens, dogs, and cattle copulate and knew full well why the cow was taken to the bull. If their parents didn't explain, an older child would, in detail, generally out behind the barn. I received my earliest sex eduction at about age five from an older boy age seven. The way he explained it, your papa and mama had sex relations when they wanted a baby, and in about five or ten minutes, Lo and Behold! the baby would pop out like a Jack-in-the-box. It seemed like a pretty clever idea to me, and I felt vastly

26

superior that I didn't believe that the Doctor brought babies in his black satchel.

At a little later age, say eleven or twelve, I was allowed to sneak in the back door of Steffey's livery stable and sales barn to witness the performances of Mr. Steffey's stallion and jackass in helping farmers get colts. The barn had a sign right above the breeding pole which read: "Service price $15.00. Foal guaranteed to stand and suck." The breeding pole was a large pole about eight inches in diameter and twelve feet long set on two posts about four or five feet high, so that the stallion could be on one side and the mare on the other while they courted and bit each other and whinnied until everybody was warmed up and then the pole would be removed. Sometimes there was a horrible anti-climax for the stallion, or "stud" as Mr. Steffey called him. If the farmer wanted a mule colt, the services of a male ass or jack was required. Now, the jack would just about come up to the big mare's belly and she would have nothing, not anything, to do with Mr. Jack unless blind with passion, so Mr. Steffey would let the big stallion tease the mare a while and then lead him back to his box stall where he would trumpet with rage and jealousy and kick resounding blows on the boards while the mare was led into a pit and the jackass performed for the farmer.

Mr. Steffey tried half-heartedly to keep us kids out, but we got in anyway. Whenever we would see a farmer driving into town in his buggy and leading a mare, we would all run to the sales barn, and so would a lot of men loafers. It was free entertainment and quite educational. I always felt a twing of sympathy for the stallion when the jackass had the last say. The reason for this dual performance was that a crossbreed between a horse and an ass is sterile, though a very fine work animal. It is as big as its mother, and is stronger than a full-blooded horse. It is also apt to be an ornery cuss. A United States Senator once said of the mule, "He has no pride of ancestry and no hope of posterity." The jackass had a powerful voice, and after he performed in the pit, he would rear back and bray in long drawn out "Hee-Haws" that could be heard all over town, which only aggravated the stallion's sufferings.

One time we had different entertainment with an animal. A wandering Italian brought an European brown bear to Wheatland

and had him perform for us yokels. It was the first bear I had ever seen. The Italian had him on a leash that was attached to a halter on the bear's head. He rolled over, danced on his hind legs and begged from the crowd. Then came the climax. A long rope was attached to the leash and the Italian led old bear to a tall telegraph pole by the Railroad.

"Climba the pole, Bear" said the owner. Mr. Bear sat down with all four legs around the pole, and closed his eyes.

"Climba the pole, Bear!" the owner urged again sternly.

Old Bear was tired, I guess, and refused until the Italian bellowed again and gave him a kick, whereupon old Bruin went up about ten feet and halted despite shouts, prayers, and oaths.

"Climba the God damn pole, Bear, or I keel you! Climba the God damn pole, Bear!" screamed the owner, and producing his long walking staff which had a sharp end, evidently prepared in advance for such an emergency, the Italian briskly pushed and jabbed the unfortunate creature in his fundament, whereupon he shinnied up the pole to the top in a hurry. There he rested for about ten minutes while the owner yanked on the rope and pleaded, "Coma down, Bear! Coma down now!" Old Bear finally slid down, and the Italian went up and patted him and offered him a tidbit, whereupon the disgruntled animal let out a mighty roar and swung his big head at the Italian as if to say, "To Hell with you!"

The Italian then passed the hat, took up a few dimes, and ambled on out of town down the railroad, headed for Washington, the next county seat east, leading his chum.

Our town Fire Department was the bucket brigade, consisting of half-dressed citizens who had been aroused by the dreadful cry of "Fire! Fire!" We would run out and see the red glow against the night (nearly all fires happened at night) and hear someone say "It's the West elevator" or whatever. The building always burned down despite the futile efforts to save it, though one time they did save the new three holer privy Mr. Hedrick had built back of his old frame store which burned down one night. Four men picked it up and carried it away, and a few minutes later Mart Brown, a farmer from the edge of town, was running with two buckets of water and unwittingly stepped off into the uncovered cement vault

28

which was about half full of water, etc. You never saw a madder man in you life when he was fished out.

Another time, this in the afternoon, the uptown barber shop caught on fire, and Mrs. Horace Jones, who lived acress the street, came out in her front yard and screamed "Fire Fire! Why don't someone holler 'Fire!' " You could have heard her a mile.

Men were handing buckets of water up a ladder and throwing the empty ones down, when one empty lit on the head of one of my uncles, rendering him unconscious.

When the East elevator burned down the second time, "Little Doc" Lytten, the village wit, remarked, "Well, I guess those mice have gone to carrying matches again."

Education, Coal Mines, and Fisticuffs

Before World War I there were seven one-room country schools in our township, and the colored grade school and the High School in town. There is not a school in the entire township now. Everybody rides the yellow bus, some twenty to thirty miles a day, down to South Knox, a consolidated school.

Apraw was the name of one country school, called after the Indian name for a ford over White River. The Bottom School was located in the river bottoms and enjoyed a recess in time of flood. Then there was the Shake Rag School below town, origin of name forgotten by my time, where I won a township spelling match. Others were named after farmers who donated land.

There was an elementary school of four rooms for town children in the same red brick building built in 1908 where we forty-five high school students attended. There were seven graduates in my senior class. Our High School leaned toward solid learning, such as three years of Latin; four years of English (including Shakespeare); algebra; plane and solid geometry, and physics. History (Ancient, English and American) was a must, as was botany. Music was taught by an accomplished young lady, and my knowledge of classical music came when the entire High School was drilled in singing parts of the Tales of Hoffman and other selections.

Drop-outs were encouraged in Wheatland. To get into High School you had to pass a stiff written examination administered by the County Superintendent of Schools. A student was required to be either in the recitation room or studying in the assembly room. If you didn't get passing grades you were flunked, and eventually let go to enter the stream of industry or get married, or whatever.

Times were a little crude, as the Grade teachers enforced discipline with the hickory or oak stick. I had one very fine dedicated Grade School teacher, Miss Nanny Dunn, who was born without a right hand. She was a good looking gal about five foot seven, who could and did knock the wind out of many a hulking youth with a

30

straight right jab to the solar plexus with her stub, which was fitted ideally for such a tactic. Miss Nanny would not tolerate pulling the girls' hair in class, or mixing chewing gum in it, or whispering, note writing, or paper wad throwing, a common diversion. A favorite minor punishment she dished out was to stand on one foot a while, and she also laid on the gad after school, as I can testify. Sometimes she would smack the knuckles of your hand with a ruler.

Due to the death of my mother when I was three years old, my twin sister Martha and I got our first education in a one-room country school while living with our maternal grandparents. We both sat in one double seat, as did other small children. There is one advantage to a child going to school with older children, be it eight grades or two. You listen to the older classes and learn by osmosis. Also on the playground one rapidly finds his niche in the pecking order and learns a lot about how to adjust with society. One time when I was in the third grade, a big boy about fourteen years old in the fourth grade named Walter was having trouble at the blackboard with "long" division. I already knew it, though the third grade had not progressed beyond "short" division.

"You ought to be ashamed, Walter, not to know this. I'll bet the third grade knows how," said the teacher. "Johnny, come up here and show Walter how to do long division."

In an ill-advised moment, I marched up to the board, took the chalk and gave a triumphant demonstration. Alas! At recess Walter kicked my fanny all over the school yard and punched my nose in rage and humiliation.

"I'll learn ye to make a fool out of me, you God Dam little brat," he hollered.

Walter never spoke truer words. I have never forgotten that if you want to make a bitter enemy, just humiliate a person in public. Walter really "learned" me, even though his grammar was not too good.

I might add that a year or two later, Walter went to work in the coal mine, and in a fit of rage stuck a pick in a mule's hip, so it had to be destroyed. The mine boss, Tom Harris, fired him, but his father, a digger in the mine, promptly started a strike.

31

"Pour out your water, boys, they can't treat poor Walter like that jest on account of some dam mule," he said.

The miners poured out their drinking water and came up. That's what they called a wild cat strike; pouring out the drinking water. In two or three days Tom had to rehire Walter and the coal started coming up again. The Coal Miners' Union was strong, even in 1910. Walter's father could earn $12.00 a day, so he only worked two or three days a week, and then went fishing. Poor people had poor ways, Pop always said.

Sqeaking of mining, I spent one winter in Coalmont, Indiana, in a big mine field of deep shaft mines. Work was very irregular, and if your mine was to work the next day, at 8:00 P.M., its whistle would blow. On winter nights you could hear the mine whistles near and far reverberating over the hills and hollows and each miner knew his own. Most of them lived in "row" houses near the mine with outside privies, bought goods at the company store on charge, and were desperately poor, as work was spotty. They had large families and drank lots of whiskey. Also they were overcharged at the store. However, once a miner, always a miner, despite the risk. They enjoyed the cool, even temperature, short hours and good pay when they did work, and you couldn't have hired a miner to do any other kind of work at double his pay.

Wheatland was on the edge of the Southern Indiana soft coal district and the miners' sons and the others of us formed opposing clans or gangs, sort of over-lapping and co-mingling at times, it is true, but we had our differences. One time, when I was a Junior in High School, I was in Willard Hedricks Drug Store, a common headquarters for all the boys in town to loaf in, when a miner's son named Oscar, a chunky lad of sixteen, accompanied by his fifteen year old brother and a third boy, came up and said "Niblack, we're going to get you Saturday night at the oyster supper."

In alarm I asked "What for?"

"Well, you bastard, you told Willard we slugged his slot machine," was the reply. Mr. Hedrick kept a one-armed bandit for our amusement and his own profit of nickels. I denied the charge.

"Well, you better stay home," they said.

A lot of folks heard the challenge. I never had heard of "High

Noon," as Western movies had not yet been invented, but I knew exactly how the fellow in the ballad felt who said, "I gotta go out there and meet him or lie a coward in my grave." I didn't feel so good.

Saturday I made a pair of knucks out of an inch thick oak board, went up to the hall, sat down at a table and despite no appetite, ordered a bowl of oyster soup, which cost fifteen cents and was made by the ladies of the Rebekah Lodge. Oscar tapped me on the shoulder and said, "We want to see you downstairs."

I got up in a very dismal frame of mind, marched out first and as I got outside, I sidestepped over so my back was to the wall and fitted my hand on my knucks behind me. A lot of people streamed down to see the fight. The three boys faced me and began to curse me, when all of a sudden I hit young Oscar on the point of the chin as hard as I could, believing with Napoleon that the best defense was a good offense, and he went out like a light. The next crack sent his brother down, and I got the third kid down, grabbed his hair and was pounding his head up and down on the cement walk when somebody hit me on the left arm with an empty beer bottle nearly breaking it, he being the second brother. I had to get up and start fighting him again, bare handed this time, and about then the boys' father, a hulking coal miner, started to swing on me, but was restrained by the village Doctor, Doc Woods, who was also a big man.

"It's a boy's fight, Gus. Your boys started it. Now let them alone," he said.

By this time I had the field to myself, and went home with my sore arm, a big lump on my forehead, and some dirty torn clothes.

I had other fights before and after that, single combats, where I won some and lost some, but I wasn't bothered too much around there after that. I still carry a scar in my left eyebrow which I got when I was in the Eight Grade, when Louis Snider hit me with a metal dinner bucket. Boy! That sure ended that fight, as I went home with blood streaming down my chin and all over a white blouse, which in the custom of the times, was tied with a draw string around my waist. We also wore knickerbocker pants till we began to shave, which in my case was sixteen, somewhat late.

33

Notable Characters

In common with other small towns in the Midwest, Wheatland had its share of "characters," such as Mr. John Overbay, our town milkman, who once licked a cat's bottom, thereby pocketing five dollars. John was loafing one rainy day in Mr. Curt Sechrist's butcher shop when the store cat bent her neck and washed her fundament with her tongue, as all cats will do.

"John, I'll bet you $5.00 you couldn't do that," said Mr. Sechrist.

"I'll take that bet," replied the farmer. He walked over picked up Pussy, raised her tail, and gave her three or four good swipes with his tongue. Curt paid off.

Occasionally a Medicine Man would appear in our town in his horse drawn camper. I remember one such who was accompanied by an Indian dressed in what he thought was native redskin attire —principally a fringed buckskin shirt and feathered head dress. In the afternoon the Indian passed out hand bills advertising a medicine show—free.

About dark the show began, lighted by a flaring gasoline torch hung on the camper. The Medicine Man played on the banjo and sang some ditties. One of them went: "While she was chasing her boy round the room, She was chasing her boy round the room."

"Now folks this is a mighty good song," he said. "I'll sing the second verse."

"Second verse: While she was chasing her boy round the room,

"She was chasing her boy round the room."

He repeated this about five times, and finally said, "You want to hear the rest of it?", but we all yelled "No."

Then he announced the Indian would do a war dance.

"Chief Rain in the Face here was one of Chief Sitting Bull's main assistants and took part in the Battle with General Custer," he said. "He will now perform the War dance of the Sioux which the Indians did the night before the massacre."

34

He beat a tom-tom while the Chief gyrated around and let out some falsetto screams while popping himself on the mouth with his hand. Next came the spiel wherein he extolled his "Magic Indian Tonic"—a 1910 Geritol.

"This here bottle of Magic Indian Tonic will cure what ails you" was the gist of the story. He was a good salesman.

"In the morning when you first wake up, do you feel like you sure could sleep another hour? Along about 11:00, just before noon, do you want to quit work and go eat some food? Late in the evening do you feel kinda weak and wore out and you just can't work any more till supper? Ah! my friends, you sure have the symptoms! Yes, indeed! Your sure have the symptoms. You are on the downward path"—and much more.

"Well, this Magic Indian Tonic is made from roots and yerbs of the field and forest according to a secret recipe handed down from an old Indian Medicine man and it will cure you, and maybe save you from an early grave: Only one Dollar, just one Dollar."

Mr. Overbay said, "By God, that is exactly the way I feel. Gimme a bottle!"

I suppose the faker sold ten or fifteen bottles. I learned later in life that the basis of all such cure-alls was about 80% alcohol.

Speaking of that, Old Aunt Mary Anderson, a leader in the Temperance movement which put the country dry a few years later in 1919, bought a patent medicine by the dozen bottles and swore by it. She said a couple of tablespoonfuls before breakfast and supper made her feel so good. When someone let her in on the awful truth that it contained more methyl alcohol than most whiskey, she had the hired man take it out to the barn with orders to pour it out. Unfortunately, she told him why, and he wound up roaring drunk.

Maybe Mr. Overbay wasn't fooled so much after all, as he liked a nip now and then, and had been around a long time. One time he was getting shaved by Skeet Scott, one of our town barbers, who would go on a spree once in a while, and Skeet accidentally drew a little blood with his straight razor.

"Well, now then that's the trouble with drinking whiskey, dern your hide, Skeet," said the farmer angrily.

"Yes, I notice it makes the skin tender," was the meek rejoinder.

35

We had a town drunk who played the fiddle. When he had too much booze on a Saturday night, which was often in the summer time, he would get down in the ditch and play his fiddle. When we kids passed by on our way to Sunday School, we would stop and watch him a few minutes.

My father, the Sunday School Superintendent, never drank, swore, or used tobacco. He was a tee-totaler, and a leader in the Anti-Saloon League with Mrs. Anderson. However, Pop kept a quart of whiskey for medicinal purposes on the top shelf of the pantry and if anyone, including himself, was getting a cold, or "grippe" as we called the Flu, they would give them a "hot toddy."

One time, about two years since it had been used, Pop got out the nearly full bottle to make a remedy for some one of us, and its contents instead of being red were almost pale as water, much to his consternation. It developed that Aunt Crit Horn, our esteemed fellow Methodist and one of our colored folks who did our ironing, also believed in the medicinal powers of good whiskey and would take a sup now and then of Pop's whiskey, carefully refilling the bottle with water to the same level so as not to hurt anyone's feelings.

Aunt Crit, who said she had been named after a grandparent, Governor John J. Crittenden, of Kentucky, having been born on his plantation before the Civil War, also liked to "dip snuff." You take a twig and chew one end out to a brush, put the snuff on it, then place it between your gum and cheek and let the other end protrude from your mouth. That was the only form of tobacco on which I never got sick. Snuff also came as a tobacco dust.

There was a gentleman of our community who owned two or three farms. Occasionally he would make a tour of his places, and would stay overnight at one in particular where there was a rather comely "hired girl" who was not too "slow" in the parlance of the times. Though Grandpa Jones—as good a name as any—was about fifty years old, he liked to sneak into the gal's bedroom for a midnight touch of romance, as the lady was generally willing.

One evening he arrived after supper, and the folks forget to tell him the hired girl had gone home on a visit, and her room had been lent for the night to a bearded young Jewish pack peddler.

Along about midnight, Mr. Jones crept into the bed where he supposed his paramour was, and in an unfortunate maneuver, instead of caressing a soft check his hand encountered a hairy set of whiskers. The terrified owner imagined he was about to be robbed or murdered, and screamed for help at the top of his voice, while pummelling poor Grandpa Jones lustily, who fought back. They both wound up on the floor under the overturned bed, but luckily people ran in with lights and assisted each party to escape the others clutches. The incident caused a lot of merriment, but is not discussed in detail by Mr. Jones' posterity.

In the early days there was a man in the next township named William Bruce, a Scout in the War against Tecumseh. He had fifteen children, and his wife died about then, whereupon he took a second wife, a young one. She bore him ten more babies. The town was named Bruceville after the old Scout.

When Mr. Bruce got well up in years, he wrote a little piece about himself, and his memory not being so good, he stated that he thought his fourteenth child was a girl, but he wasn't sure.

"I believe she was a girl, and I think she married a man named Hodgen. Anyway, they went out west over the Oregon Trail and I never heard any more of them," he said.

Pop's second wife, Miss Anna Scroggin, of Bruceville, was a descendant of Captain Bruce, and consequently my half-brother, Griffith, her son, is a scion of a noted Indian fighter and champion sire. He is now an editor of the Indianapolis News.

There was an elderly gentleman named Traub who sold organs, which were foot pump musical instruments, to farmers for their daughters. He toured the county in a covered one-horse spring wagon with a sample organ on behind, protected by a canvas cover. Mr. Traub was noteworthy because he wore, in hottest summer weather, red flannel underwear, heavy clothes, an overcoat, and heavy hat and gloves.

"What will keep the cold out will keep out the heat," was his staunch statement to all arguments.

Such men were not too rare, in former times.

Then there was Aunt Sairy (Sarah) Steen, for whose family the township was named. An epidemic of typhoid hit Wheatland in the 1880's. Several people died, and many others were desperately sick. My father had it as a young man, and had to learn to walk again after he recovered. About then some young doctor advanced the theory that typhoid fever was caused by germs in drinking water.

Mrs. Steen stoutly declared that her surface well was uncontaminated.

"There aint no tyoids in my well," she said, "My water is just as clear as it can be."

Be that as it may, it is no wonder people caught the disease. Window screens were unknown or primitive. The discharge from the bowels and bladder of the sick was dumped in the outside outhouse, whence it seeped into the surface wells. Also, flies would crawl around in the privy vaults and then walk around on a diner's piece of pie or other food.

Wheatland had three village doctors, M.D.'s, at that time, where it now has none. A favorite prescription of the doctors then was a round of calomel. Calomel was based on a mercury compound, and would give the hapless sufferer a belly ache, a diarrhea, and a griping of the fundament. As if this were not enough, the Doctor would order a final dose, Epsom Salts, a most nauseous physic, bitter as gall. If the calomel didn't make you forget your original sickness, the salts would cause you to forget both.

Too much calomel would "salivate" a person's teeth—cause them to fall out. One of our housekeepers, after my mother's death, had lost her teeth that way in Arkansas, she said.

Mrs. James Prather, wife of the President of a Vincennes bank, told recently about her father, Doc Robinson, one of our three medics. She found some of his records, which went something like this:

"First day: called on patient. Prescribed a round of calomel."

"Second day: Visited patient. No better, prescribed another round of calomel."

"Fourth day: Patient worse. Prescribed more calomel."

"Seventh day: Patient dead."

Another of our M.D.'s wasn't too careful about cleanliness in his office. His cat slept on his operating table, and his instruments laid around unsterilized some times. My brother Herman was opening a box in our general store as a young man, when a splinter flew into his eye, right in front of the pupil. Old Doc fooled around with it with his tools, it became infected and Herm lost the sight of his one eye for the next fifty years.

There was a farmer who lived down south of town in the White River bottoms below the Shake Rag Schoolhouse, whom I will call Ben Simpson, which was not his real name, but it will do. Ben liked to come in town on Saturday and trade at our store, then oft times he would put in the evening at Quall's Saloon. Pop as a young man slept upstairs in the store as a guard. He said that one Saturday night he heard a fumbling at the back door on the porch, and heard Ben's voice saying:

"Mary! Oh, Mary! I'm home. Open up, Mary, and let me in."

Pop found Ben sound asleep on the back porch in the hot August sunshine about 8:00 A.M. the next morning. He had taken off his shoes and used his blue denim shirt as a pillow.

Old Ben came in the store one day and said," I et seven eggs and six dodgers of sausage for breakfast today, I did, and so I did!"

Another time he said, "Mary makes light bread biscuits for me three times a day. By God! I would just as soon lay down on the floor and open my mouth and let the sunshine in as eat that there boughten bread."

Ben also expressed his views on divorce.

"I hear tell how over there at Vincennes they're having divorces, just cain't seem to keep their wimmin' satisfied no more. Hell! The way to handle a woman is to keep her knocked up [pregnant] give her plenty of hard work and one dress a year, and I'll guarantee she won't cause no trouble."

Another farmer from below town, who had a big family, was on a jury at the County Seat trying a rape case. He came home over the weekend when the case went over until Monday. Later he described an experiment:

"The testimony by this woman was that the man just got her down on the bed and plumb screwed her by force, no weapons. I just told my wife, 'Isabel, just get on that bed, and I'm going to rape you, and you just try to keep me away!' By George, you know, I wrastled that woman a half hour and I never could get to her."

"Hell! I went back over there and voted for acquittal."

I sort of doubted the part about thirty minutes, as I figured Isabel would be a willing partner after about five minutes. They had had eight or nine children in fifteen years.

JOHN AND MARTHA NIBLACK
Age Three—Wheatland, Indiana

JOHN H. NIBLACK AND FAMILY—1908

Left to right: Herman, Martha, John L., stepmother Anna; front: Griffith, now an Editor on the Indianapolis *News*.

WHEATLAND, INDIANA, SENIOR CLASS, 1915
Left to right: William Sechrist, Howard Niblack, Alta Prather, Mafair Prather, Olive Root, Bernice Abbott, Frances Root, and the author (Bernice moved away in mid-winter).

Harvesting gang, 1920, on the lone prairie, western Kansas. The author is the fourth man from the left.

ROBINSON COUNTRY SCHOOL, 1915

WORLD WAR II POLICE COURT JUDGE
Fort Harrison Provost Marshall Stewart (right)

Tobacco

When Columbus discovered America in 1492, the American Redskins from Montezuma, Lord of all the Aztec Empire, down to the squalid Digger Indian, were puffing away at their tobacco pipes. Four Hundred year later, in Southern Indiana, their pale face replacements were not only smoking tobacco in pipes, they were inhaling cigarette and cigar smoke, chewing and swallowing the leaf, and sticking it up their noses to make themselves sneeze. Tobacco is a member of the Nightshade plant family which includes the poisonous Belladonna and it contains its own poison drug, nicotine, which is lethal if enough is taken.

I poisoned myself on plug tobacco, Granger rough-cut twist, pipe tobacco, cigars and cigarettes numerous times and oft, but I was born with some determination, and I stuck with them all until I conquered. I guess my motto was "I shall overcome," but I near puked my socks off ten or twelve times doing so. All my chums had the same experiences.

Three such episodes will suffice to illustrate how we small town boys proved we were manly enough to use tobacco. I had tried corn silk cigarettes, which burnt my tongue, dried mullin leaves, cubeb berries, and the seed pods of catalpa trees. Then one day I got some Granger Twist, (pure natural tobacco leaf) some newspaper and matches, and with my cousin Howard Niblack and another boy crawled under a rick of fence posts which had been set up to dry. We were all about ten years old. We made ourselves some huge cigarettes and smoked them furiously. It was a pretty evil tasting and evil smelling combination—printers ink and nicotine—and we repented our sins, alas! too late. I have never bothered Granger Twist since.

A few years later I went in Grandma's General Store, and there was a sample of chewing tobacco lying in a shelf: "Peachy Plug" with a picture of a ripe red and yellow peach on it. I imagined it would taste like a delicious ripe peach, and I slipped it in my pocket. Then Howard and I, the two Nicholson boys, and Denny Weaver all went swimming out to the old swimming hole in Possum branch, on Bob Nicholson's farm. We all undressed, took a big chew of Peachy and dove in. We spit and chewed and swallowed and told each other how good it was, and took a second chew. Very shortly the paddling and gay talk simmered down, and silently one by one we crawled out and put on our overalls and shirts and straw hats (the three pieces of clothing small boys wore then in the summer— no shoes). We all strung out for home through the adjoining wheat field, which was full of shocks of cut wheat. Every one of us soon was draped over a wheat shock, victims of nicotine poisoning, tossing his cookies in a big way. I never even thanked Grandma for treating us to such a pleasant outing. I don't believe I even mentioned it to her.

Another time I was fooling around the store, and someone gave me two White Owl cigars, or I thought he did. Anyway I took them home, and got up in the window of our summer kitchen, hung my feet out into the alley, and smoked a cigar and a half. It was about 11:00 A.M. All of a sudden I fell out in the alley—you guessed it —here I was again, nicotine poisoning. I laid there about an hour wishing I would die and afraid I wouldn't, when all of a sudden I heard Pop hollering.

"John, Oh, John! Come on, son. It's time for dinner!"

I thought "Oh, my Lord! What'll I do now?" Pop was a mild mannered man, a good Christian, but he had read the entire Bible through several times, and he had not missed King Solomon's admonition "Spare the Rod and Spoil the Child." My two brothers and I were never spoiled. Pop didn't believe in using tobacco, though he sold it for Grandma in the store.

Proving there is a lot of substance in Mary Baker Eddy's teachings, and also demonstrating the power of mind over matter, I got up, marched into the house, pale and green as my face was, sat down and ate a fair dinner (lunch nowadays). I even made a little polite conversation, and no one was the wiser.

It also proves up another of Solomon's sayings, "As a dog returns to his vomit, so shall a fool return to his folly." King

42

Solomon had observed 3,000 years ago what I have seen farm dogs do often. They eat some carrion, it makes them sick, and they throw it up. Then Old Towser will lie down and rest a while until he feels better, all the time keeping an eye on his vomit. After a bit he will go and eat it again, and repeat the up-chuck. Sometimes a dog will do this three or four times.

Anyhow, I never thought Solomon was the wisest man who ever lived, despite his sayings. No man in his right mind would have 1,000 wives unless he took in washings. Still, he had one thing in his favor that most men don't have. If the girls got too restless, he was Commander-in-Chief of the armed forces and he could send in a regiment of Marines to quiet them down.

Getting back to nicotine, plug tobacco, such as Star or Horseshoe or Dipper, was a big item of sale in Grandma's old store. Each plug had a little tin star, horsehoe or dipper on it. This was chewing tobacco, although quite a few farmers of economical bent would save the cud and let it dry out on the living room mantel or some such safe place and then smoke it in a corn cob pipe.

Plugs came in boxes, in strips about a foot long, two and a half inches wide and one-half inch thick, which could be, and were, cut into three inch lengths by our tobacco cutter, a sort of guillotine operated by a lever. The plugs were made of shredded and pressed tobacco leaf evidently mixed with some mild syrup or licorice juice as they were moist inside and solid.

We also sold other chewing tobacco in small pouches. It was of flakes of moist tobacco, loose leaf, with the same sweetish flavor as plug. Two favorite names were Mail Pouch and Red Man.

Incidentally, the emblems and certificates or coupons that came with tobacco were like modern green stamps and were good for merchandise at St. Louis, Missouri. I saved up some I got from men, or loose ones in the boxes, and got a good kodak camera one time. Another time I got a .32 revolver, not too good a fire-arm, but sufficient to shoot our old cow, Brindle, in the hip. Though the bullet didn't go in too deep, it made old Brindle bawl lustily and buck and jumped all over her fenced-in lot which she shared with our chickens. It was a pure accident caused by a ricochet bullet during target practice.

The accident didn't help her milk flow any either and neither did the time she pulled the end of her tail off when going in the barn and the wind blew the door shut on her rear extremity. All that, plus the fact that when I took her to pasture, I sometimes rode on her back, or made her run if I was in a hurry, sort of dried up her flow, as a milk cow is supposed to lead a serene life. Poor Pop finally sold the unfortunate bossy in disgust, allowing she was a might poor producer.

Grandma's store also sold cigars and pipe smoking tobacco in tins, such as "Prince Albert" and "Velvet," but no cigarettes, which she called "coffin nails." However, we sold the "making"—"Bull Durham" or "Dukes Mixture—" being ground up tobacco in little sacks with yellow drawstrings and a packet of thin rice cigarette papers attached to each stack. With these you rolled your own, gave it a lick of spit with your tongue, scratched a match on the seat of your pants, and were in business. Some experts flicked the match with a thumb nail, and some could roll a neat cigarette with fingers of one hand. An accomplished trick of tobacco chewers was to hold the quid in one side of their mouth and drink water or what not down the other.

About every public place, except a church, had a spittoon, or "gobboon," as some called them: Fraternity houses, Lodge halls, railroad stations, stores, bowling alleys, etc, were equipped with cuspidors (another name) and they were generally full. Likewise the floor spaces about such receptacles were copiously splattered with the "ambeer," as it was known, and a fire place was a favorite receptacle, too. Charles Dickens in his travels in America in the mid 19th century was plenty disgusted. He said every American male gobbled tobacco every waking moment and spit all over the floor, stoves, and anything in sight. It was not quite that bad by 1910, but it was bad enough. I once saw a man in Wheatland open a screen door of a restaurant and inadvertantly deluge a passer-by with a copious shower of tobacco juice.

My children's grandfather, Judge Walter F. Wood, of the Sullivan County, Indiana, Circuit Court, had been raised on a farm down on Indian Prairie. He always arose at 5:30 A.M., and the first thing he did was reach for his pants, pull out a plug of Star and

44

bite off a good large chew. After working this over for about forty-five minutes, he would be ready for a good hearty breakfast of sausage and eggs.

As for me, I continued to smoke cigarettes like a chimney until I was forty-four years old, despite my father's oft repeated warnings. So did my two brothers. One day I quit. I was at a political meeting in Wayne township and lit a cigarette, then realized the end of my tongue was sore and had been some time.

"Oh! Oh! Cancer!" I thought, so I threw the cigarette and my package out in the aisle, and have never smoked since—though occasionally I dream I am smoking, and then asking myself why after all these years. I had no trouble at all quitting, as I began to gain weight. I had kept myself at 130 pounds, almost a skeleton, because nicotine destroyed my appetite, as it does for some folks. I went up to 180 pounds in a year and a half simply because I began to eat well.

I was like Mark Twain, who said quitting smoking was the easiest thing he ever did,

"I've done it hundreds of times," he said.

However, I only quit once. I discovered Pop had been right all along.

Business Man at Eleven

When I was eleven years old I accepted my first regular paying job. I became a cow boy. Mr. Charlie Nicholson, the village Postmaster, hired me to drive his cow, Old Maud, to pasture and back each day. It was exactly one mile from Maud's town stable to the pasture gate on Mr. Nicholson's farm. For the two mile trip each day I got five cents. At the end of each month Mr. Nicholson gave me a bright silver dollar and a half dollar.

It was a nice job. From early spring to late fall old Maud and I would wander down the alley, take the street down to the Old Buffalo Trace and follow it to the farm. I generally took my sling shot and would improve my aim by practicing on tin cans, birds, or other objects along the way. This job lasted two summers, and came to an abrupt end one day when Mr. Nicholson observed me riding peacefully home on Old Maud, bare back.

About the same time I became a news boy, selling the Cincinnati Post, a daily paper, at one cent a copy. It came in the afternoon, and I had about twenty customers. One-half cent was the profit on each sale. On this route I learned lessons in merchandising. Mr. John Nuckols, one of our colored citizens and the town handy man, got into me for 29¢. I stopped his paper, and finally collected the whole sum. John wouldn't pay the whole 29¢ at once, but every time I saw him down town I would say "Mr. Nuckols, give me a penny" and most of the time he would. He was reinstated as a customer again, but thereafter his credit limit was one week.

I also put up Five Dollars security with the Curtis Publishing Company of Philadelphia to be their agent for the Saturday Evening Post. I paid two and one-half cents for each copy and sold it for a nickel. The front cover page said "Founded by William Penn. Circulation 25,000." It later went over a million before the company went bankrupt.

The Post came on Thursday by mail and I would peddle my

regular route of anywhere from 18 to 30 customers. The Post each year held subscription contests, and quite frequently the main prize was a Shetland Pony and carriage, which had one seat facing forward and one to the rear, according to its picture. Annually this would excite boys throughout the nation, but, alas, I never even won a "handsome pencil set," another prize. The lucky winner always lived in Texas or some far off place and to read the account, he evidently sold about everybody in his county.

I used to go down to the B. & O. depot at noon and go through the two accommodation trains hawking my extras, often selling one or two to the drummers. I liked this part, as it gave me a chance to wait until the train started up before swinging gracefully off the step, a la best brakeman style, or so I thought.

I finally gave up the Post route, and took on the Indianapolis News, which sold for two cents each, thus doubling my profit.

Pop encouraged me to open a bank account in Mr. Prather's Bank, "The Farmers and Merchants Bank of Wheatland, Indiana," with my cow money. So each pay day I would put one dollar in the bank, and keep the half dollar to spend. Fifteen cents of this would go for a Saturday afternoon of roller skating at Mr. A. C. Nicholson's roller rink—a converted warehouse.

A. C. was one of nine Nicholson men, brothers or first cousins, who were the village tycoons. They owned farms, mostly inherited, on the lush rolling prairie around Wheatland, had promoted the first railroad coal mine, laid out the town cemetery and sold lots, and operated the Postoffice, a hardware store, a grocery store, and the upper drug store, among other things. They rode out on Sundays in shiny two seated carriages, that is, until they brought the first automobile to town. I can remember Lytton Nicholson (nicknamed "Barney" for Barney Oldfield, a 1910 race driver), a fourth generation scion, taking some of us high school friends to Vincennes in the Haynes with its air cooled engine, and on the return trip the word was passed back "Hold on tight! We're going to try to go 50 miles an hour!" This we did to my consternation, as it was a gravel road with bumpy bridges and right angle turns every now and then.

47

When I was about 14 years old, I read how to make a "hot bed" to raise garden plants from seed early in the spring, so I went into that business for three or four years, raising mango, cabbage, and tomato plants, which sold for ten cents a dozen, and found plenty of buyers.

To make a hot bed, one dug a place in the ground about two feet deep, as long and wide as wanted, then covered it with a frame made of white muslin, slanted to shed rain and hinged for opening. The next step was to take the family wheel barrow and trundle some fresh horse manure from Mr. John Buntin's livery barn, two blocks away, and fill the excavation about a foot deep with it, then shovel in a foot of soil. The manure would start heating in a few days and keep the bed warm in the cold days of March and April. The muslin top frame would be laid back on warm days to let the sun or rain in.

There was another source of income which I operated for several years from about the time I was in the Seventh Grade—selling squabs, young pigeons, to the Union Depot Hotel twelve miles away in Vincennes. The B. & O. Railroad from St. Louis to Cincinnati, the I. & V. from Indianapolis, the Evansville and Terre Haute Railroad, and the Big Four from Illinois, all converged there. Mr. Ed Watson ran a big brick hotel and restaurant at the junction.

The loft of our small empty barn was converted into a pigeon loft, replete with self feeders full of grain, a watering can, nest boxes and small doors with landing steps for the pigeons to use when they were let out, which was most of the time so they could scuff up their own food.

In addition to the squabs I raised, the surrounding farmers allowed me to search their barns for young pigeons, quite often successfully. Many nests were just under the eaves on the inside of the walls, and easy to get at. However, other pairs built their nests in the cupola set high in the middle of the peaked barn roof. These were hard to get to, but I developed a technique of crawling up underneath a rafter like a giant sloth. I could hook my small hands in the spaces between the cross pieces laid on the rafters, push with my bare toes in similar spaces and go right up. The young birds

48

would go in my cap, which I would clench with my teeth as we went back down.

This was a comfortable operation when the huge barn lofts were full or half full of hay, but on occasion in an empty barn, I have looked down sixty feet to the planks below and wished I were safely down. If I had fallen every bone in my body would have been broken. The other boys who went with me sometimes wouldn't climb the rafters, or couldn't.

I sure didn't have very good sense as I look back on it. Once in a while after I was grown I used to dream about those empty barns and wake up sweating.

The squabs were shipped in boxes on the B. & O. to Mr. Watson when I had a dozen or two. He paid twenty-five cents a pair, and his menu showed "Philadelphia Squab Dinner—$1.00—Full Course Dinner." Probably "Wheatland Squab Dinner" would not have been so good.

This contract was lost by cheating. One time I only had 23 squabs, so I slipped in one old bird. A little later I slipped in three old ones. Now squabs were tender, plump morsels just before they left the nest. A good one weighed twelve ounces or so, and their meat was white. An old pigeon was tough. His breast meat was black, and it was something like eating a boiled rubber boot heel.

After the second or third fraud, I received a letter from Proprietor Watson enclosing his check for 21 birds, and stating my services or wares were no longer needed, as some drummer (traveling man) had raised Hell about his "squab."

I am happy to relate that I got right on No. 5 train and went down to see Mr. Watson, and by promising to lead a virtuous life and absolutely, positively, never to slip in any more old pigeons, I was re-instated, on probation as it were. I kept the faith.

I had a wire attached to some sliding panels on the pigeons' feeder which I could pull to allow the birds to feed. It was a sort of Rube Goldberg contraption, as the wire ran on pulleys and around bends, across the chicken lot, through the wood house and to the back porch, so I didn't have to go clear down to the barn and up in the loft if it rained, or anything. I spent a day and a half trying to rig up a running water fountain for the pigeons out of an old coal oil stove tank and some feeder pipe which curled down, around and up to empty into the top of the tank again, as I imagined that the tank holding much more water than the pipe would cause it to circulate. Much to my dismay, the water would rise no higher in the slender pipe than its level in the tank, so I gave up on what I had fondly imagined was to be a real nice invention.

Another time the Methodist Church sexton resigned, so Pop got me on at fifty cents a week to sweep out, ring the bell for services, dust the seats, and stoke the stove in winter (the preacher who lived next door would start the fire). This only lasted about eight months as my services were not too satisfactory, except I did a very fine job of ringing the church bell, which I would have done for nothing.

My lack of attention to the dust cloth was my downfall, as Aunt Liz Dunn complained that her Sunday percale dress got soiled.

Incidentally, Mrs. Dunn lived to a ripe old age and never tired of telling, in public, when I would go back to Wheatland on a visit, of how she assisted the doctor at my birth.

"I put the first dydee on you, Judge," she would remark as we shook hands after church.

She also told me that after I was born the doctor said, "Nope! Wait a minute! There's another one coming!" And it was my twin sister.

"She only weighed about four pounds," said Mrs. Dunn, "and the doctor says 'Just lay that little girl on the sofa there. She looks pretty puny and I don't think she's going to make it.'"

I told my sister Martha, now Mrs. Leland Schuster of Hastings, Nebraska, about this one time, and she felt sorry for the new born girl.

"Oh! That poor little thing," she said, before realizing that it was she.

Pop named the new twins John and Martha, for his grandparents, Judge John Niblack and his wife, Martha, early pioneers of Dubois County.

Two other sources of income added to my spending money and

bank account. In our garden plot I raised prize tomatoes—Ponderosas and Baltimores—and peddled them over town at ten cents a dozen. Then each fall and winter while I was in the eighth grade and high school I would trap fur bearing varmints—skunk, possum, muskrat and rabbits. This was a common endeavor for many farm and small town boys in those days.

The principal and most profitable catch was the muskrat, which lived around creeks and rivers. I would catch ten to twenty-five in the fall and early winter, until I tired of the arduous work of getting up at 4:00 A.M. in the dark, running the trap line, messing around in the cold water (the traps had to be set out in the water so the hapless muskrat would drown and not gnaw off his leg to escape) and lugging them home, after which I had to skin them and stretch the skins on a board to dry out. I once got $1.05 for one dark muskrat pelt, though the average price was from thirty-five cents to seventy-five cents.

I got $5.00 for one star skunk, all black except a white patch on his head. I also was excused from school the day it was caught. I dressed and sold the rabbits for ten cents each. One time I got thirteen rabbits with my .22 rifle and old dog Jack after a snow in the night. We had to make two trips to town to bring them in.

At various times Grandma Niblack paid me thirty-five cents a week to carry in her hard coal for her base burner, and set it on the back porch, and also to go the one block up the hill from her house to Mr. John Overbay's house to get the milk.

All in all, I had plenty of my own money after I was eleven. I had a bank account and spending money in my pocket. One fall when I was 13 Pop had me buy myself a nice new wool knickerbocker suit for $4.50 and a pair of school shoes for $1.50. I was dressed in style. I believe Pop got $15.00 a week for clerking in the store, when he could have been making three times that much on the railroad where he started out as a telegrapher. A farm laborer then got a dollar a day and free rent and garden space.

On several occasions, while in high school, Mr. John Buntin, the livery stable owner, gave me $1.50 to drive a drummer and his sample cases to Monroe City, Verne and on to Vincennes. Monroe

City and Verne were two towns in the county which had no railroad, but used our station. It was a thirty-two mile trip.

Mr. Buntin was of Quaker ancestry. However, the only trace of that religion he showed was when he became angry and swore.

"God damn thee! Thou art a liar!," I heard him tell a fellow once.

Other boys in Wheatland had similar experiences in being financially independent. It was a rare privilege, as it brought in some money and kept us occupied when we might have gotten into mischief. God knows we found enough spare time as it was for the latter endeavor.

Juvenile Delinquent

Looking back on it, I believe if I and my youthful peers in Wheatland, before World War I, were boys now we would almost be counted juvenile delinquents. Seems like most of us resembled Dr. Jekyll and Mr. Hyde—we were good and bad. We'd piously go to church, and mean it, and then cut up and get into mischief—often just for the Hell of it.

A boy in his progress from a one-celled creature in his mother to a responsible man goes through the whole evolution of the human race. At the age of three or four, he is an innocent pre-dawn man without any sense of right or wrong. A few years later he is a cave-man hunter, stalking the fat mama robin red-breast and the unsuspecting sparrow and killing them in cold blood with his sling shot or BB gun to satisfy a primeval hunting instinct. Approaching puberty, he becomes a gangster—a member of a gang—prone to horseplay, sex talk, vandalism and fighting. Violation of the law or breaking rules seemed like high adventure. In modern days some of this is satisfied by identifying with Boy Scout troops, Boys Clubs, Little Leagues, or high school athletics as player or loyal rooter.

In our little town we boys had Mr. Willard Hedrick as our mentor or club leader—a term that would have surprised him. Willard ran the drug store and ice cream parlor, with side lines of tobacco, stationery and other notions. The upper floor was Hedrick's Hall, wherein were held the weekly flicker movies, dances (round and square), basketball games, and oyster suppers. He also had a slot machine—the old familiar one-armed bandit with its cherries, lemons, plums, and so forth, which now and then spewed out trade tokens. He also had a large side room equipped with benches where all of us boys could loaf, scuffle, and tell outrageous stories. We could also play the slot machine and buy cokes and ice cream. Willard drew the line at fighting inside the store. The slot was illegal, but our county sheriff was understanding in such matters after he talked to Willard and saw that we boys needed innocent diversion to keep us out of trouble.

I became a counterfeiter at the age of ten by coining lead nickels for the slot machine, sneaking a strip of soft lead from Grandma's General Store (stealing, really), cutting it in chunks and for a die using hammer and pocket knife, with one of Uncle Sam's genuine nickels as a model. Sometimes I was careless and my lead nickels would be too thick or not round enough. Some of the other boys followed my example.

I was pretty artful and cunning abut it, as Willard was a suspicious old boy and mighty hard to fool, and he had been known to give a lad a good boot in the rear with a number eleven shoe if detected cheating at the slot—to teach him good morals.

My system was pretty good though. I would take some real nickels and a few homemade slugs and wait until Mr. Hedrick went out in his warehouse room to "spike" a coke for Roy Falls, our village barber, or Uncle Willie Niblack (our township had a saloon, but Roy and Uncle Willie and kindred bons vivants liked a wee drop now and then for a snake bite or a bad cold and couldn't afford to be seen entering the grog-shop). (Uncle Willie had the first yellow wheeled buggy and first high wheeled bicycle in Wheatland, Doc Lytten told me once.) I would feed in a nickel or two and then start the slugs, until I heard Willard returning, when I would nonchalantly play a last nickel or a bonafide token and check out.

If a lead slug stuck and stopped the machine, I fled out the door lickety-split before Mr. Hedrick got back.

Along about the time we were sophomores and juniors in high school, we began to have chicken roasts on weekends, though the chickens were not roasted but stewed in a bucket. The first order of business was to steal a couple of fowls, generally from a parent or a relative of one of the gang, though not always. We all had a little spending money, mostly earned at odd jobs, but buying a chicken was out. Then we would build a bonfire, dress the game and cook it. Someone by pre-arrangement brought the bucket, another some salt, a third a loaf of bread and a fourth a jug of drink-

54

ing water or a coffee pot. We would eat, drink and be merry, sometimes along the railroad and sometimes behind the Christian Church, which was the last building in town on the old Bicknell Road, and rather secluded. We would wind up making the night hideous, singing "Sweet Adeline," "Down by the Old Mill Stream," "The Old Rugged Cross," "Wandering Boy Come Home," and other selections. One we liked real well started out: "In a lonely graveyard, many miles away, Lies my Dear Old Mother in the cold, cold clay." It was a real tear-jerker.

We came a cropper on this business which nearly got us into the Indiana Reform School. We got caught! Uncle Tom Greene had sent off and bought a blooded pedigreed Plymouth Rock rooster (that is what we called a male). Seven of us "borrowed" the unfortunate fowl one evening and ate him up. We were doubly careless in not stealing from a relative and in not noticing the band on the old rooster's leg. He was tough but we ate him.

The next day Tom missed his prize chicken and, happening to live near the church, he went down and found the bones with its band. No fool, Uncle Tom inquired around and very shortly had the names of all seven of us. One of them was a boy I fined many years later for annoying a widow about unrequited love, when I was police judge in Indianapolis. Denny Weaver and the Nicholson cousins, Hugh and Charles, were in the crew. Mr. Green howled to high heaven and to our parents that we were going to be arrested, taken before Squire Curt Wheeler and bound over to Circuit Judge Orlando Cobb at Vincennes, if he were not made whole, and at once, and in a big way.

Now Judge Cobb had just sent a boy from Monroe City to the Boys' School until he should be 21 for stealing turkeys, and were we in a fright! Tom allowed his rooster had cost him $15.00 plus express (really $5.00), and that he was entitled to $25.00 additional to soothe his pain and suffering and mental anguish at the loss of such a dear companion. We paid off like a slot machine—and willingly. There were no more chicken roasts, at least by our crowd.

Another crime I committed, though I was only about eleven or twelve, was when I vandalized an empty house. I had a sling shot,

55

homemade, with a fork I cut out of a maple tree and large rubber bands. I laid in a good pocketful of round pebbles from the railroad and went out to shoot song birds. I killed an innocent red-headed woodpecker which was about half tame and looked around for more worlds to conquer. Going up the alley back of Mr. Charley Nicholson's house I took a couple of shots at his pet tom cat, but missed, and then saw this empty house. I lay in the weeds where no one could see me and shot out five windows. This caused me a large fright, as I knew Pop would wear out a stick on me if it got out, and I lived in terror for some weeks. That was the last of that business, too, though I never told anyone about it until now.

Another time we went over in Daviess County and stole watermelons, although we could have bought huge ones at ten cents a piece. This was when I was a senior in high school. We went in an auto owned by Mr. William Prather, president of our town bank, and driven by his son, John, who is now president of the bank at Loogootee, Indiana. Two or three others went along. We got separated in the dark and I arrived at the designated melon patch first. It was about three-fourths of a mile off the road. Soon I heard the others coming, talking in subdued tones so as not to wake the farmer. For a joke, I reared up, threw some big clods and yelled in a changed voice', "Get to Hell out of here before I shoot."

There was a startled silence, and then it sounded like a herd of cattle rushing away. In no time flat, the car lights came on and away they went to Wheatland—five miles away, forgetting all about poor old innocent Niblack. I had to walk home, and got about half way before my buddies remembered I had been along and came sneaking back after me.

Speaking of watermelons, about that time we engaged in interstate theft one night, a Federal offense, by stealing prize melons out of a box car while the train was stopped in Wheatland. One boy got inside through a little open window in the end of the car and handed them out to another who stood on the coupling. He handed them to the third boy who placed them in a ditch. I guess we got ten or eleven before she began to roll out. A year and a day in Atlanta Federal Prison was the penalty if caught.

56

Among some other deeds I am sorry to relate, when I was a freshman in high school, I carved my initials, "J.L.N.," in a big way along the edge of a new teakwood table the township trustee had bought for a laboratory room. Almost every school boy in the grades, especially in the one-room country schools, had a yen to leave his mark for posterity by using his pocketknife on his seat and desk, set out in Whittier's poem:

"The warping floor, the battered seats with jack-
knife's carved initial."

Our good superintendent, Mr. J. B. Leas, however, took a dim view of high school students defacing a valuable new table, especially a student dumb enough to sign his work. He was pretty good at psychology and made me suffer three days and nights by telling me privately that at 4:00 P.M. next Friday he wanted to see me in the laboratory about an important matter he had discovered in there. He was a barrel-chested fellow and I was sort of a runt until almost through high school, and I repented my sins heartily. On Friday I wore two pairs of pants to school firmly expecting a good walloping; in fact, J.B. threatened me with one as we edged around the table during our conference. I kept it between him and me. Finally, Mr. Leas let me off with a promise that I would hire Mr. Ed Meuser, the village carpenter, to plane out the offending autograph, which cost me five dollars, again financed by my paper route.

After that I reserved my initial carving for telephone poles and the front of the depot, and Mr. Sechrist's butcher shop, both of which were finished in soft pine. Mr. Sechrist didn't like it either, and would blank out my initials every time he found them, much to my disgust. He never said anything though, just outlasted me.

I got some deserved retribution another time, one summer, from my faithful old yaller dog, Jack, my hunting, play and boyhood companion. I loved old Jack, but one day I thought it would be fun to throw him in a bumble bee's nest we found in Mr. Bob Nicholson's field, the one by the old swimming hole. Jack trustingly came when I called him over, and I picked him up (he weighed about sixty pounds) and dropped him in the nest, then ran away laughing to see him snapping at the angry bees. I changed my tune in a hurry. Poor soul, he ran to his master for protection, ran between my legs and knocked me down, while all the time I was screaming "Get away, Jack! Go home! Beat it!"

A couple of the bumble bees got inside my shirt, and stung me five or six times, as they don't shoot their wad on one sting, as do honey bees. Boy, was I sore.

Some years later, when I enlisted in the Navy and went away to World War I, old Jack got to acting strangely, wouldn't eat much and so on, and Pop had him shot on the advice of our colored handy man, John Nuckols, who theorized that he was going mad. I never saw him any more, only his grave.

I believe these were about all of the crimes and misdemeanors we committed, though I think some of the older teenagers now and then were guilty of a little more or less innocent assault and battery with intent to rape while grappling with their high school dates. Maybe it was mostly wrestling with intent to gratify sexual desires. Anyhow, it most generally was unsuccessful, though not always, as by common report some of the Wheatland girls would diddle just a little if properly approached.

Now and then a "Wood's Colt" made its appearance, to everyone's scandal. This term was a hang-over from pioneer days for a bastard, arising from the fact that occasionally a mare would get pregnant by some unknown horse out in the woods. I am glad to state that we are more virtuous now, as there have been no bastards born in Indiana since 1941, by courtesy of the legislature, which decreed that they should be called "children born out of wedlock," in deference to the tender feelings of welfare mothers.

Down on the Farm

Modern city dwellers have no idea how life was lived on a Hoosier farm prior to World War I. The farmer was a rugged individualist, and he had never heard of public welfare. Like Abraham Lincoln's character, it was, "Root Hog or Die!" Oh, there was the county poor farm for aged men or women who were childless and too sick to work, generally a dingy, dirty, smelly brick building.

My mother, Nannie J. McClure, was born on the 175-acre farm of her father over in Palmyra Township, six miles from Wheatland. When she died at the age of thirty, my twin sister and I went to live with Grandpa and Grandma McClure where we got our first education in a one-room country school. The farm was five miles from Vincennes, and was part of lands that had been in ancestral hands since 1802. Grandpa was born there, too.

Southern Indiana farms were self sustaining units in 1900. Hand power and horse power (or mule) made the wheels go round. The more children the better, as they were an economic asset rather than a liability. The boys helped with the farm work and the girls the house work: Gardening, soap making, milking, churning (to make butter), berry picking, canning, preserving, washing, ironing, mending clothes, chicken raising, and last but not least, baby tending as new ones appeared. A good healthy daughter as a first or second child was a prize asset on such a farm, ranked right after a good bull. In fact, if no sons arrived to bless the household, an older daughter or two early learned to handle a team in the fields.

In the fall came hog killing time, or "butchering." Six to ten corn-fattened shoats or barrows (castrated males) of around two hundred pounds were dispatched by Grandpa with a well placed rifle bullet between the eyes. Grandpa had been one of Lincoln's "Boys in Blue" in the great war between the states, enlisting at age 19, in the 14th Indiana Volunteer Infantry, the first three year

59

regiment from the state. He was the head of a menage of a wife, three sons, three daughters, two hired men, a hired girl, and a Civil War pension of $50.00 a month, and about the only work I ever knew him to do was to man the rifle at hog killing time, mainly, I think, to demonstrate he had not lost the skill he had as a sharp shooter at Antietam, the Wilderness, and other hot spots.

Grandma McClure, whose maiden name was Purcell, was born on the adjoining farm west. She sometimes got fed up with Grandpa's idolatry of President Lincoln, the Republican Party, and the Grand Army of the Republic.

"Your Grandpa learned to 'soldier' in the war," she told me once, "and he and all the other old soldiers have 'soldiered' ever since. I don't think he's done a lick of work since 1865. Just run around to any reunion inside of 300 miles."

You would have thought she didn't like "John R." as he was known, but she was secretly very proud of him, and they lived happily together fifty-six years.

Grandpa always retorted that very few farm families had it so good, so why should he get out in the fields?

"By Dad Burn!" he would say, "I done my duty by the country and everybody, and now it's their turn. Beside, not everybody got an ounce Minnie ball through their body at the Battle of the Wilderness and lived to come home and raise a fine family like this and keep them in style!"

Grandfather once told me that right after the War, he and two other veterans, all about 21 or 22 years old, got in a horse and buggy, with a jug of whisky, and drove up toward Bicknell ostensibly seeking work. They stopped at one farm and much to their consternation the owner offered them jobs of clearing woods at seventy-five cents a day, fine wages then.

"Oh, My God! 'Tain't near enough!" they said, and hurriedly drove away.

When the hogs were dead, their hair was removed by scalding water heated in a huge outdoor iron kettle; they were then gutted and cut up. Intestines were cleaned and stuffed with sausage made to the farm wife's own secret recipe, maybe handed down from her

60

mother. The prowess of many such good women in mixing their sage and other herbs and flavorings and seasonings into the newly ground pork was well known and their sausages were mighty tasty on a cold winter morning.

Hams and bacon were smoked over a hickory fire in the smoke house, a small side building. Lard from the fat was rendered and canned. Some folks would butcher a half grown steer now and then, but not many, as it was harder to keep than hog meat. There were no deep freezers then.

In this connection, my Aunt Fanny once related how one of her mother's Purcell cousins, a substantial farmer who would take a drink if properly urged, went "to town" one hot summer Saturday with a load of wheat and had the misfortune to get somewhat drunk while there. He swapped most of his wheat money for two sides of beef, which he proudly brought home to his unhappy wife and three buxom daughters, who had to pitch in and furiously can beef all Saturday night and Sunday. Nobody, least of all the culprit, ever knew where he got two sides of fresh beef in the summer time.

Our farm raised corn, wheat, and hay—clover, timothy or alfalfa. Clover and alfalfa were legumes and had bacteria on their roots which took nitrogen from the air and fixed it in the soil. Nitrogen is one of the best fertilizers there is, so those crops did double duty. Soybeans and cow peas are also legumes. Farmers nowdays buy liquid nitrogen by the tank full.

A prime source, and about the only one, of fertilizer was horse and cattle manure, also containing nitrogen. Soil wears out if not fertilized, and raises mighty puny crops, if any.

Farmers in those days kept horses and mules for machine power, and these animals raised their own food. Their exhaust went back to enrich the soil. Their replacement, the tractor, has to have its feed bought in town, and its exhaust vanishes in the air, adding to pollution.

The old time Indiana farm sold enough grain, hay, and meat on the hoof, steers or hogs, to pay the taxes and buy other necessities. The horse power farmer didn't need to raise so much, and he was more independent of labor unions, implement salesmen and fertilizer manufacturers. The Mennonites and Dunkards are still doing very well under the old system.

"Boughten" goods were not needed much on the farm after the Civil War for some time, but by the time of World War I most farmers had turned largely to the town stores for their clothing, shoes, and dress goods. However, my Grandmother made most of her own soap out of lye and fat. She also made the lye by letting water drip through wood ashes. The lye was clear and looked just like water, but if it got in your mouth it created burns that would not heal, so farm women had to be careful with it. A neighbor boy of six or seven one day mistook a glass of lye for water and drank about half of it. He lived three or four years in torment before he died a lingering death.

Grandma also plucked feathers from chickens and geese and made feather beds and pillows, which were very comforting on a cold winter night in our old un-modern farm house which was set on a hill with huge old pine trees in the front yard. I have lain on one such thick feather bed while covered with another thin one in addition to blankets and listened contentedly to the northwest wind sighing through the pines and the snow flakes hissing against the window panes. It would be below freezing in the room, as there was only a large fire place with the fire banked for the night.

Many years after Grandpa and Grandma passed away, my Aunt Fannie, Mrs. Frances McClure Hynes, who also lived here in Indianapolis, brought up from the old farm house a feather bed and gave it to me. She had got the farm after the old folks died. She said, "Maw made this seventy-five years ago and I want you to have it."

Well, I had no particular use for a feather bed, but it was the vehicle that caused me to engage in a little idle philosophy on uncertainty of life and how little chickens or men know of their future.

I told Aunt, "I'll bet those chickens down on the farm there little dreamed that seventy-five years later parts of their bodies would be carted away 125 miles to furnish a bed for a fellow to lie on who hadn't even been born then."

Maybe man has about as little idea of the real future as those fowls.

Along this line, one time I had a lively colony of ants back of my garage in Indianapolis on Carvel Avenue, and I used to bend over them and watch their busy activities, workers going and coming with food, warriors ready to rush out and repel enemies, nurses frantically to carry the babies away from danger, and somewhere a Queen Mother down below heading up things—all a well ordered society—working together in more harmony than some human societies I knew. These folks were organized, self sufficient, and, I suppose, thought they were the highest form of creation. Yet they had little conception of who I was, no knowledge at all that there was a Monon Railroad a block away running to Chicago, and they had never heard of that city, the world, or the stars beyond.

Man thinks he is pretty smart, too, and believes that he is the highest form of creation. Yet he can't even tell you how high it is straight up or when Time began or whether it will ever end.

Grandma and other farm wives made their own bread, good solid homemade loaves set to rise with a yeast culture often carried over from mother to daughter. Once a week was baking day, and a good thick slice of hot bread with butter and sugar on it was the delicious reward of good little children. Soda or baking powder biscuits were common fare, as well as light bread biscuits. Grandma's only fault as a cook was her soda biscuits. She thought if a little soda was good, a lot was better, so they never rose much.

In pioneer days people made their own dyes, juice from walnut hulls furnishing a lasting brown for homespun clothes. Grandma didn't make homespun, but she knew how to make dyes. One Easter she colored some eggs with yellow extracted from onion skin, red from poke berry, and for green she gathered some green blades of winter wheat.

The industrious farm wives raised turkeys and chickens, hundreds of the latter. Barred Plymouth Rock chickens were the most common, being a dual purpose fowl—good for eggs and eating both.

In the spring, summer, and fall the common Sunday noon dinner was chicken, fried, stewed with dumplings, or roasted. That was when relatives, friends or the preacher, and family came to dinner. Along with the chicken went a groaning table of vegetables, gravy, pies, cakes and fruit.

Just before dinner would come the "fly drive." In the early days farm houses were poorly equipped with ill fitting screens at the best. With stables, hog pens and chicken houses and consequent manure piles close to the house, there were swarms of house flies in attendance all day long in numbers the present generation can not imagine. They made themselves at home in the house, too, especially where there were small children running in and out all day long.

Just prior to the meal everyone handy would seize rolled up newspapers and "shoo fly" sticks made of strips of thick paper tied to a stick, and in the manner of native beaters driving game for hunters, we would all get in the back of the room while one stood ready to open the screen door, and really rush the startled insects out the door with a mighty flailing.

Grandma also hung sticky fly paper from the ceiling in long thin strips and spread sheets of it on tables and around. These trapped many of the unwary pests, whose futile buzzing would fill the air. We also had wire fly traps baited with sugar water which would catch quarts of flies, and there were fly swatters on every hand with which we killed many more. However, no matter how many we slew there were plenty to take their place in the front line, like Russian peons sent into battle by the Czar.

The farmer's wife took the sour cream and churned it until butter formed. She also made clabber cheese, or cottage cheese. With butter and eggs she was ready to barter with the grocer when she went to town on Saturday. Some times a huckster wagon, or traveling grocery, came along, drawn by two horses. The proprietor had a large coop on the back in which to put chickens he took in trade.

The chickens were raised by a hen laying a clutch of about twelve or fifteen eggs, and then setting on them twenty-one days while running a fever of two or three degrees. The hen laid one egg a day, but it would not start to incubate until the nest was full and "setting" began. During this time the old hen was apt to be mighty short tempered and querulous, giving rise to the old saying "As cross as a setting hen." Also, she had no time for romance, and I have seen an unwary male, the "rooster," take out after a setting hen who was off the nest for refreshment, only to his great surprise to find himself in a furious battle instead of a thrilling love chase.

The turkey hen would steal away to the fence rows or woods to make a nest and in time come up with a brood of striped young. The old Tom turkey, or "Gobbler," was about as lascivious and sex-hungry as any modern hippie is supposed to be, and in the absence of his wives (he was a polygamist) he would rape an unsuspecting chicken, often with fatal results, as the twenty pound Tom would trample her flat as a pancake while giving vent to his passion. One of us kids would holler "Grandma! Oh, Grandma! Old Tom has got a chicken down again," and out would run Grandma with her broom and knock him silly.

"Drat that old fool! I just ought to kill him right now," she would say.

One time we asked Grandma why the old rooster chased the hens around till they squatted down, and then jumped on them, and wallowed them around.

"Oh, that's just to make the eggs round," she told us, which satisfied our childish minds as a perfectly natural thing. Eggs were round, and evidently something caused them to be that way. Children are not too critical.

One time when I was about five, Grandpa and I were going in to Vincennes in the buggy behind old Nelly, the family driving horse. Nelly lifted her tail, and let loose a bowel movement, concluding by causing her fundament to wink and curl in and out some, which fascinated me no end.

"Grandpa, what makes old Nelly's ass hole go in and out like that?" I asked. On the farm then men and boys invariably used the Anglo-Saxon words for natural functions and parts.

"Well, Johnny, that is nature. That's just nature," he replied, and that was a perfect answer as far as I was concerned.

In re old Nelly, one time Grandpa and Grandma got all dressed up and took me and sister Mart to the carnival in town. We were dressed up, too. All four of us rode in the buggy, which had only

65

one seat. Driving into the grounds we passed an elephant, and Nelly saw and smelled him. Ordinarily the most gentle of beasts, Nelly stood up on her hind legs in fright and began to whinny and paw the air, scaring me no end.

"Let's go home, Grandpa," I begged, as he soothed Nelly down. "Let's go home right away!"

"Well, no, let's stay and you can see the elephant again," he said.

"I don't wanna see no elephant. I can see one in a book much better," I implored, but we stayed a while anyway.

My Aunt Fanny (Frances, for her mother) age 18, and Uncle Frank, age 21, were living at home when we arrived. One day for fun, they turpentined Old Trip, one of our two farm dogs. He was a big, black, short-haired dog with a trusting nature, which caused him some sorrow that day. Turpentining dogs or tying a tin can with rocks in it to their tails was a form of simple amusement in early days for people who had too much time on their hands.

"Here Trip! Here Trip! Nice doggy! Want a piece of bread?" said Aunt Fanny, holding out her hand to the unsuspecting animal, who trotted up to her. She held his head and fed and petted him while Uncle Frank busied himself by lifting old Trip's tail and scouring his fundament roughly with a corn cob previously soaked in turpentine. Now turpentine has a startling effect on mucous membrane, to wit, a keen burning sensation sets in soon after it is applied.

Old Trip stood patiently a little bit, then turned his head and glanced apprehensively at his rear to see if perchance a bee or something was around. A look of horror came over his face, he jerked loose, let out a howl and sat down on the ground to rub his hind end. Then he disappeared around the corner of the house sitting down while running furiously with his front legs, and faded away up the lane, sending back mournful howls. Aunt and Uncle thought it was about the funniest thing they ever saw, and screamed with laughter, while sister and I looked on in astonishment at the whole performance.

Old Trip finally came home, but he never allowed anyone to

hand feed him again to the day of his death.

Two important members of the household on the McClure farm were Bill Eccles and Harve Smith, the "hired hands." They lived in a small room at the end of a porch on the rear of the house. Harve was about fifty years old and Bill somewhat older. I don't know if they ever took a bath. I don't believe they did. Sister and I would peep in their room once in a while when they were out and sniff the aroma, which was a little gamey and musty, to say the least.

The hired man was an institution on early farms, an equal who ate at the table with the family and was at home in the living room after supper on winter evenings. On such occasions Grandma would bring up a crock of red winesap apples from the cellar, and everyone, including Harve and Bill, would eat one before retiring.

"An apple a day keeps the doctor away," she would say.

Small talk on the events of the day, some gossip heard at church or school, or reminiscences of Gettysburg or the Battle of Cheat Mountain would pass a pleasant half hour or more, while the flames crackled in the wood-burning fireplace.

One time Grandma told about a panther, or mountain lion, which jumped out of a tree when she and her younger brother, Deck, were on the way to school and killed the family dog which was going along with them. This was at the head of our lane, when she was nine years old, which would make it 1851. The children ran home.

"We had heard this panther howling in the night on the big hill up back of our house," she said. "It sounded just like a woman sobbing out there in the dark forest."

The reason everyone gathered in the living room was that it was the only room in the house that was warm, as the fires in the kitchen range and dining room stove were allowed to go out after supper. When I first read Whittier's "Snow Bound," I recognized a familiar scene.

"Uncle" Harve and "Uncle" Bill, as we children called them, usually cleared out on Saturday afternoons, going down to the County seat. Harve went in for a weekend on the town, jousting with John Barleycorn and whatever else he could afford on his six dollar cash a week. What Mr. Eccles did I never learned. Harve finally died in the poor house when he got old and sick and helpless.

Old Bill Eccles was of a different stripe. I learned later from the folks that his grandfather was a remittance man, or a younger son of an English lord. Seems like his grandfather had a carriage and horses with silver spangled harness and that Bill had attended Asbury College, now DePauw University. It didn't take, as Bill never married, and lost his ambition somewhere. He was also sexton of the Upper Indiana Presbyterian Church, where Grandpa was a deacon, and made a few extra dollars a year mowing the cemetery and keeping it spick and span. Grandpa said Bill knew who was buried in every grave. It was too bad he didn't plat it out, as his knowledge died with him. Many graves now contain unknown decedents, as markers are gone.

This church was about a mile and a half from our farm, and it was the first Protestant church in Indiana. It was integrated as the membership roll of 1812 showed Whites, Indians, and Negroes.

Man's Work—Boy's Pay

When I was 16, I went to work on the farm of my uncle, Curt McClure, my mother's cousin, who also had two or three hired men beside me. The senior hand lived on the farm in a tenant house, with his wife and five children, and received $1.00 cash a day, free rent, land for a garden plot and chicken yard; the use of a milk cow, feed for a hog and chickens, and use of a driving horse to go to town on Saturday. A single man received $1.00 a day with board and room at the Big House. I, being a boy, was paid fifty cents a day with board and room. The hours were not too bad though, as I never had to get up before 4:00 A.M. on summer mornings, and always got in bed by 8:30 P.M.

I did what they used to say down home was a "man's work for a boy's wages." Whenever the two grown hired men shocked a shock of wheat, they saw to it that I shocked one also. When one plowed a row of corn behind a team of mules, I plowed another behind two other mules. The correct term was a "span" of mules, as horses were a "team." Both kinds were taught to turn right when the driver hollered "Gee!" and to turn left on "Haw!"

Right before World War I, a span of good mules was worth about $500.00, and should stand about 17 "hands" high, a hand being a measurement based on a man's hand, even as a foot is based on his foot length, an inch on the first joint of his thumb and a yard on the length of his arm.

Uncle used to go up in the hills and buy baby weanling mules by the dozen, and put them to pasture until they were three years old. The males were castrated. When grown they would be "broke" to harness and to work and sold. He kept an old mare horse in the pasture with them who was their leader and boss. Wherever she went, the mules would go. If they didn't obey orders, or got "uppity," the old mare would bite them or make their ribs pop with resounding kicks.

Every morning at 4:00 A. M. we would arise and each would

get his particular span of mules brushed, harnessed, and fed the first thing. The harness was pretty heavy and the mule didn't like to have it put on, especially if he had a collar sore on top of his neck. The collar fastened around the neck and it was heavy padded leather to which were attached the tugs, thick leather and iron strips. These ran back to hook to the plow or wagon. Then there was the one piece bridle and bit. The latter was of iron, and went in the old mule's mouth and over his tongue and stuck out each side. The guide lines were attached to it and ran back to the driver's hands. When he pulled on the right one the animal turned right, and vice versa. On chilly mornings the iron would be cold, and mister mule would resist taking the bit until you whacked his teeth right smartly with it.

All this harness was anchored in place with a wide belly band, or belt running down the under the belly, where it was buckled. It had to be tight. This also applied to a saddle on a riding horse. The horse didn't like a tight belly band either, and when you started to pull it tight, the animal had learned to take a deep breath and hold it while the band was cinched. However, the farmer had also learned the trick and would pull it tight as he could until the poor beast could wait no longer and had to exhale; then would come the final tightening.

Mules were sort of mean, some of them, and a little treacherous. Uncle had a fine big gray mule named Jess which lived in style in a box stall on Sundays. One time Jess pinned Uncle against the wall when he went in the stall by leaning against him. I suppose this was in revenge for some ancient wrongs, real or fancied, and it caused Uncle some pain. He had one heck of a time getting loose, but he finally did, whereupon he got part of a broken boom pole, and whacked old Jess a dozen or fifteen mighty blows on the head and gave him a good cussing.

I said, "Uncle, look out, or you're going to knock that mule's eyes out, and he's worth $250.00."

"By God, that's just exactly what I'm trying to do," said Uncle, who was a red-headed former college football player and a mighty man of valor. He was the hardest working man I ever knew and expected his help to keep up. He was a fair man though, and good company. However, when he got angry the fur flew, and it was said he could lick any cop in Vincennes if he had a drink or two.

I mind one time he and I were milking. We milked three or four cows each morning before breakfast, and then slopped 200 hogs. Uncle was milking a Jersey heifer, whom we called "Babe" after a young damsel in the neighborhood who would bestow her favors on the farm boys on occasion, and who had big liquid brown eyes also.

Babe hadn't got too used to having people fool around with her udders and teats, —the cow that is— and she was pretty ticklish this day. First she swatted Uncle four or five times in the eyes with her tail, stepped on his foot, kicked him on the leg, and finally gave a snort and stepped in the half-filled milk pail. That did it!

Uncle grabbed a fence rail and beat the unfortunate Babe on the back some mightly blows, calling her every thing but a lady. Ker—whack! and Babe would grunt and bellow and try to jump the fence, which I myself hastily did. Again I expostulated:

"Look out, Uncle, you'll break that cow's back!"

"Just what I aim to do," he roared. "I'll teach the son-of-a-bitch to step on my corns!"

Babe didn't let down much milk for about a week or two and I had to be her milkmaid thereafter, for whenever she saw Uncle, she looked for the nearest exit.

The hired man was something else again in the life of teen age farm boys. He taught them four letter words they never had heard of before, expounded the joys of houses of prostitution in detail, and generally rounded out their education. I imbibed my first alcohol, beer, under the apt guidance of Oss, our senior hired man.

One hot August afternoon when it was about 95° above, he and I took a load of hay into the city, and was it warm up there in the sun during the two and one-half hour ride! We got mighty thirsty. Oss dwelt on the delights of cold beer until I fancied it was something better than lemonade or cold spring water—probably about the most delicious drink every heard of. Oss sneaked me in the back door of DeJean's saloon on Third Street, and ordered me a big nickel stein of beer, more than a pint.

Parched and dry as I was, I promptly took a great big swig and just as promptly spit it all out involuntarily on the floor, as it tasted

71

more like Epsom salts, mixed with urine, than the honey from Hymettus I had imagined. However, I stuck with it and had two more just to show I was a man. I was about half drunk when we got home.

Oss was a card! He could suck raw eggs, much to my great admiration. He would find one in the manger, open one end and pour in some salt from the barn salt barrel, and down she would go at one gulp.

"God! That's good!" he would say. "Make a man of yuh! Puts lead in your pencil!"

Then I would try it, but the white was too slick and slimy, reminding me of nothing except the strings of snot that used to hang out of school kids' noses on cold days. Up it would come in about fifteen seconds—just pure imagination, as I have since eaten many a raw egg beaten up in milk.

Uncle was a scientific farmer for those days. He kept a herd of registered black Angus cattle which furnished much manure for his two farms, and he rotated his crops with clover, alfalfa and cow peas to enrich the soil. In the summer of 1917, he had one hundred acres of wheat in one field which I helped shock. It made thirty-three bushels to the acre, which was not bad considering the average yield in Indiana was less than twenty and in Kansas, the Wheat State it was only twelve. He sold it for $2.18 a bushel, three times what it formerly brought, and declared, "The hour of the farmer has come." It had come, but it went away in the great depression of 1921.

Uncle's son, Thornton, who left the farm to become President of the University of Rhode Island, tells a tale about an event that made up his mind. He said he was instructed to plow some corn one hot July day, and to rest the mules under a big shade tree if they got too warm.

"Here's a scythe, and while the mules are resting, you can mow the weeds along the fence row," was a final instruction.

The story is probably apocryphal, but it illustrates how hard boys were expected to work down on the farm.

Wheat harvest was a special event on the farm, and it involved the use of the first automatic farm machinery, the harvester, or "binder" and the steam threshing outfit.

Along in September we would plow the field and plant the

wheat kernels saved from the last crop. Indiana grew "winter wheat" as contrasted to "spring wheat" grown on the Great Plains. It grew and stayed green all winter, frost and snow having no effect on it. By the Fourth of July in Southern Indiana wheat was ripe in yellow golden stalks about two or two and a half feet high, each with a head of thirty or more kernels.

I helped "cut wheat" by following the binder, a mowing machine which cut it and tied it in bundles and spewed them out in rows. We would grab the bundles and prop them upright against each other, heads up, about ten or twelve in a bunch, with a couple of bundles laid sideways on top to shed rain.

As a small boy not old enough to work, I have run down and caught many a young rabbit which darted out of the wheat ahead of the binder. They would let out pitiful squalls when finally grabbed, but this did not prevent the boy from placing the foot on the unfortunate bunny's head and pulling it off so it would be properly bled. Young rabbits made mighty good eating along with mashed potatoes and rabbit gravy.

As has been observed before, civilization is based on the charnel house or slaughter pen where our lesser cousins meet their end—a rather bloody business all around.

I knew a lady who once went on a conducted tour of a modern packing house and witnessed squealing hogs trundling by hanging by their hind feet while a butcher slit each throat expertly. At the end of the tour she was offered a free pound of bacon, which she indignantly refused. She remained a vegetarian for eight years afterward.

After the wheat dried out in the shock came threshing time—a co-operative affair. Farmers would form a threshing ring, and buy a threshing outfit consisting of a large separator, a steam engine, a water tank and coal wagon. The engine would pull the outfit from farm to farm at about two miles an hour. On arrival, it would place the separator on the designated spot and be turned so the front end would face the separator. The engine then was thrown out of gear and its heavy pulley wheel thrown into gear. A huge belt about ten inches wide and thirty feet long ran from the engine to a similar pulley on the separator.

73

This was a large machine into which was fed the bundled wheat straw with the kernels still attached. It knocked and shook loose the kernels which went down and out one pipe while the straw was blown out through another.

Each farmer in the ring furnished a man driving a team and hay rack wagon, or he might send a man with a pitch fork, whose job was to go into the field and pitched the bundles onto wagons. The driver would stack them neatly in interlocking rows about six or eight feet high and drive off to the separator while the pitcher loaded another empty wagon. The wheat bundles would be tossed heads first into the maw of the separator. The dust, smoke and flying chaff, plus the rumble and roar of the machinery and the puffing of the engine made quite an impression on city cousins.

The women folk put on a co-operative dinner at each stand. Ice was brought from town for lemonade and ice tea. The fatted capon was fried, plus ham. New peas, new potatoes, green onions, lettuce and beans decked the groaning board, and pies and cakes topped things off. Hot coffee was a must.

I travelled with a team for Uncle around the ring. I remember once at Mr. Decker's farm the lady of the house stuck her head in from the kitchen and queried her daughter:

"Ethel, have they all be coffeyed?"

"Yes, Maw, they've all been coffeyed," was the dutiful reply.

I could load about as pretty a load of wheat as any one. There was an art to it. You went around and around the wagon surface, which had no sides on it, building tier by tier, and balancing the load. If one was slipshod and fell off enroute to the separator, especially where it would block a lane or gate, the driver suffered dire shame, disgrace, and humiliation, and maybe a few well directed curses from the host farmer.

Raising corn, Indian Maize, was a pleasant task. First you plowed the field. Taking a stance on one edge you fixed your eye straight across to a post or tree, set the plow point at ready and hollered "Giddap!" You never took your eye off the object, and when you got across, on turning around there was a straight line. If by chance you had looked away, there was a crook in the line.

When the corn was up five or six inches, we began to "plow"

it—cultivate it, they call it now. Your team and the cultivator, which had a seat for the driver, straddled the row, and two or three small plows went along each side of the corn plants plowing up or turning under the small weeds. This was easy work. I have sat on the cultivator on a balmy June morning plowing corn under the sun and blue sky and listening to the meadow larks singing from an adjacent hay field, or a Bob White calling from a fence row and known perfect peace and contentment such as I have never known since in the city. Not a care, or ache, or pain in the world.

On one such summer morning, far beyond the eastern horizon across the ocean, Kaiser Wilhelm launched his panzer divisions across Belgium in a move which would affect me and all my generation, as well as future ones, for all time to come. America would never be the same after World War I. The Age of Innocence in the United States of America would be gone.

All the farm boys of suitable age wanted to join up and go to war. A war song of that vintage went like this:

"How you gonna keep them down on the farm
After they've seen Paree?"

Another had these lines:

"Goodby, Maw! Goodby, Paw!
Goodby mule with your old Hee Haw!
I may not know what the war's about
But I'll bet, by gosh, that I'll soon find out!"

And a lot of Midwest farm boys soon found out. They marched down to the troop ships to the tune of "Over There!" Many of them are still there, in Flanders Field, where poppies grow, under the rows of white crosses.

Early Day Basketball in Southern Indiana

When Dr. Naismith invented the game of basketball in the Y.M.C.A. at Boston in the early nineties, he thought up a game which has had almost as much influence on the history of America as the invention of the internal combustion gasoline engine. The good Doctor nailed a peach basket up at each end of the gym with the open end up, ten feet above the floor and he designed a pneumatic basketball to go into the basket.

This became a very popular game, and early spread throughout the nation. It got to Indiana, I imagine, along in the late nineties or early 1900's. At least they were playing it in Wheatland, Indiana, a little town of 400 people where I was born and spent most of my youth, about the year 1908, according to my earliest memory. I believe the game was first played in the Hoosier State in Montgomery County, of which Crawfordsville is the County Seat, and also the site of Wabash College. Maybe it started at Wabash. I do know that the Y.M.C.A. was the carrier of the basketball germ that infected the whole nation.

Basketball as we first knew it in Southern Indiana, around Vincennes, Washington, and Bicknell, was rather primitive. The early games were played outdoors on the clay courts and the light was furnished at night by flaming gasoline torches. The players got large beams and set them in the ground and constructed wooden backboards and had the local blacksmith make some iron hoops. They had gotten their description of the courts and the standards from somebody who evidently gave them a proper description. The goals were ten feet above the ground as they were in the beginning and as they still are. There were no nets on the hoops. I do not know at what time or by whom the idea was conceived of using nets to aid the referee in deciding whether the ball has passed through the goal. The ages have produced other unsung heroes.

Enthused by watching the High School players perform there on the clay courts in Wheatland, some of us 8th grade boys got up a

Wheatland Kid Team. We furnished our own uniforms which were rather nondescript to say the least. One of the boys, Hank Watjen, played in rubber boots.

We had three games with Kid Teams from out of town. We played one game with the boys from Bruceville who came down in an old Brush automobile, four or five riding in the car and towing the other two on bicycles. They had a ball about the size of a muskmelon while we had a ball about one-eighth oversize. We had sent to Butler Brothers, a mail order house in St. Louis, and bought our ball, which cost $3.00. When we found out it was oversize, we had our hoops altered to fit. We had a great game that day. We played one half of the game with their ball and the other half with ours. I do not remember who won.

We played home and home games with the boys from Bicknell, a town nine miles away. Most of them were coal miners' sons and a pretty rough bunch. We went to Bicknell in the town dray wagon owned by Mr. Sol Harbin, who took us up there for nothing. We had a good time going and coming. We played in an abandoned outdoor Nickelodeon, which had a cinder floor. A Nickeldodeon was an outdoor enclosed area without any roof where the proprietor showed primitive movies, or "flickers," for a nickel admission. I remember Hank clunking around mightly lively in his rubber boots. I had tennis shoes. We came back in the old dray wagon, singing "Down by the Old Mill Stream."

My chief recollection of these two Bicknell games was of a husky boy named Parrish, wht outweighed me about fifteen pounds. He insisted on getting behind me, laying his arms over my shoulders and leaning his weight upon me. I sure got tired of being ridden around the basketball court by that fellow.

We got into High School and we played High School basketball, largely the same crowd. In those days they had the center jump and the team that had the tallest center generally was most successful. One boy would play back-guard and he would stay back underneath the net with the opposing forward. The running guard got over the floor in rather lively fashion, while the center roamed up and down quite a bit. The stationary forward played under our goal and the running forward went out to meet the center and run-

77

ning guard. There wasn't much dribbling in those days, in fact, hardly any in the very early days. However, on our team we had a very good dribbler which was quite a phenomenon as many teams did not have one.

The boys in those days were not nearly as tall as they are now and our center was about five foot nine and a half inches tall. I was about five foot seven and weighed about one hundred ten pounds. Our stationary forward, "Wim" Sechrest, the local butcher's son, was about five foot eight and weighed two hundred ninety-eight pounds. However, our running guard, as I said, was a young fellow named Lawrence Litton, who was very expert on dribbling. One of our forwards, John Weaver, was one of the most expert players in whole Southern Indiana; in fact, he could have made a Big Ten basketball player if he had decided to stay in college. He had a dead eye on the goal, and whenever he shot, it went through about half the time. He went up to I.U. at Bloomington for a while but he yearned for the flesh pots of Wheatland and came home, where he became rather well off financially dabbling in oil wells, whereas some of the rest of us who finished college didn't do nearly so well.

All the time I was playing, we never played in an inside gym except once: That was when we went to Oaktown, a town about eighteen miles away. They played in the basement of the schoolhouse. It was a very fine thing, I thought. They had some bleachers along the side where the spectators sat. They weren't very fond of us, as I remember. I got underneath the bleachers one time to get the ball and some lady poked me in the back with an umbrella. Well, they beat us 41 to 20, and to add insult to injury, they ran us out of town. I remember a bunch of local yokels chasing us down the street to our Model T Fords and one of them hit our Principal, Mr. Crawford, in the back with a brick which caused him quite a bit of pain and some black and blue places on his back.

We did have some cheers. The girls would stand along the side of the court and cheer. I remember one cheer that our Professor, J. B. Leas, got up for us that went like this:

Hump! Stump! Flump a Diddle!
Erah Boom, Rig Doom, Jig Doom!

Body Mody Kyro, Eroh Myroe!
Sis! Boom! Baw!
Wheatland High School
RAH! RAH! RAH."

And there was another we yelled:

Give them the ax
Give them the ax
Give them the ax
WHERE?
Right in the neck
Right in the neck
Right in the neck
THERE!

Sometimes when we had a game scheduled on Saturday afternoon or Saturday night during basketball season in September or October, the game would have to be called on account of rain.

We didn't have a coach. We didn't have many plays, although our High School principal thought up a few simple ones for us and outlined them on a piece of paper. As I remember the gist of them was that our center would tap the ball to the running guard, he would throw it to one of us forwards, and we would throw it in the goal. This, unfortunately, did not always work out as our center was so short that he hardly ever got the tap, and this resulted in somebody else executing the plays. We weren't too successful, but we had a lot of fun.

After I was graduated from High School, I taught in a one-room country school around there and I became coach, chauffeur, and the referee for our Wheatland High School basketball team. They were a little bit better than the team I played on. They got to play in some inside gyms. I know we went over to Monroe City to play our deadly rivals of four miles away, and they played inside in an old skating rink, with the hoops attached to the wall at each end.

In those days the teams furnished the referee for each half, and I was referee for our half of the game. The spectators were standing along the side, and I remember once when I hollered, "Foul on

Monroe City," some big farmer standing there doubled up his fist right by me and said, "What did you say?"

I said, "Foul on Wheatland."

They weren't going to catch me in any kind of a trap like that. There at Monroe City they had a little fellow about five foot six who had learned to run up the wall; he would take a run at it, put his foot on it and go almost up to the goal. I thought this was a pretty clever device at the time and it enabled Monroe City to beat our Wheatland boys by a rather good score.

Now Monroe City, Wheatland, and other hamlets of Southern Knox County have been consolidated into one large High School, and it is on a par with Vincennes, the County Seat. There used to be eleven High Schools in the County tournament, but now there are three. Vincennes used to handle us farm boys with one hand, as it were, but those days are long gone.

Later on that year we went to Washington to play. We went in two Model T touring cars. There was snow on the ground and it was very cold. To get the car started, I had to pour three gallons of hot water in the radiator and pour hot water over the carburetor. In those days nobody thought of using alcohol in the radiator. We got in and away we went! I had to stick my head out of the side curtains beause the windshield got frosted up and we could not see where we were going without looking through the side.

By this time our team had gotten an inside hall up over Hedricks Drug Store, which had a stage at one end and a coal burning stove along the side. It was thought quite a feat to throw the opposing players on the sharp edge of the stage so as to sort of disable them for the rest of the game, a trick which is not too uncommon now, if it can be worked. Also, they thought it a great feat if they could run somebody on the opposing team into the hot stove. Needless to say, this game in early Indiana was no place for mollycoddles or milquetoasts. I might add, when our team went to the surroundings towns, we were paid off in kind and came home with many a bruise. The home team really had the advantage, what with the crowds, the physical accoutrements, and everything else.

The rules were about the same in those days as now to a large extent. There was not supposed to be physical contact, but there was an awful lot of it. The main foul was two on one. The person who was fouled did not have to shoot the foul shot, so each team had their expert marksman shoot the goals. This was changed later on so that the player fouled had to shoot his own fouls. There was no expulsion for committing more than five personal fouls, and there was no one-and-one foul shot. A foul was a foul.

Speaking of roughness, Doctor Kenneth Craft, who lives here in Indianapolis, told me that in 1908 he was a student at I.U., and he and another medical student were sttting along the side lines when the Purdue team came down to Bloomington to play I.U. The famous All American football player, "Catchy" Oliphant, a Linton, Indiana boy, was on the Purdue team. These medical students were sitting right along the edge of the floor in the old wooden gymnasium and I guess somebody had been harassing Oliphant a little bit. Anyhow, the ball came over by the late Dr. William Doeppers and it fell in his lap. Oliphant ran over, grabbed the ball, and without a word gave him a stiff right fist in the left eye, knocking the poor lad flat. He had to have two leeches applied to his bruise to reduce the swelling. That was quite a remedy in those days, to have a leech suck out bad blood.

Yes, there was quite a bit of roughness in the way the game was played in the early days. Quite frequently there would be a fist fight between some players on the corner of the floor, and the spectators sometimes had a fight amongst themselves. The rooters of one team often fought the rooters of another, and sometimes the players and the rooters got into a fight. The referee generally managed to get out pretty fast after the game was over, looking over his shoulder. I have been informed this is not too uncommon in the modern day and age of basketball, and that the rivalry is still pretty hot, although the boys play in slicked up gyms on big floors in front of ten to fifteen thousand people with fine uniforms and expert coaches and trainers and what have you.

When I got to Indiana University in 1919, basketball had settled down some, and they had a pretty good game out of it. Bloomington had just won the State High School Basketball Tournament the year before. The State Basketball Tournament originated in Bloomington at Indiana University. One day the Booster Club was sitting around there in 1910, and the boys tried to think up something to publicize Indiana University. One of them came up with the idea of having a State Basketball Tournament of the best High School teams. So, in 1911 they invited the leading basketball teams of the High Schools over the State to come down and play off the tournament, which they did. Then they got to playing by congressional districts with the winner coming down and it evolved into the "Sweet Sixteen " system whereby sixteen district winners came to the State Finals.

This was a very successful situation, and we had the tournament down there until 1921, when it was taken to Purdue for one year, then to Indianapolis at the "Cow Barn" of the State Fairground, and eventually wound up at Butler University.

I was walking across the campus in the Spring of 1920, and some student said, "Let's go over to the gym and see the basketball game."

"What game is that?", I asked.

"It is the Semi-finals of the State High School basketball Tournament," he replied, "and Anderson and Franklin are going to play at 11 :00 o'clock."

So we went over and got up in the gallery, —just as simple as that—no tickets, no admission, and watched Franklin play Anderson. That was the Franklin "Wonder Five" headed by the famous "Fuzzy" Vandiver; two other players' names were Lyle Gant and Burl Friddle, as I remember. These teams came down to the State Finals and stayed at the various fraternity houses at no expense to themselves.

We watched this game and along about four or five minutes before it ended, Franklin was ahead somewhat, I think maybe 19 to 16 or 17, something like that, because in the early days there was very little scoring. This boy, Burl Friddle, who was later a famous coach and won the basketball Championship, both at Washington, Indiana, and at Fort Wayne, Indiana, with his High School teams, was over in the corner of the floor and had a held ball, or jump ball, with a red-haired boy from Anderson, who was four inches shorter than Friddle. Friddle at that time showed evidence of having a good basketball brain. The referee would throw the ball

82

up and Friddle would catch it and hold it up, out and away until they had another held ball, or another jump. This went on for four minutes until the game was over; consequently, Franklin won.

I might add they won the State Final that year and won it three years in a row. They are the only team that has ever done that.

This episode caused a new rule to be passed shortly thereafter by the State High School Athletic Association: That you couldn't catch a jump ball when it was thrown up at center or on a held ball, as we used to call it. You had to tap it away. Prior to this time, you could catch it and look around and see what you wanted to do with it.

Well, those days are gone.

Gone are the clay courts where we played outside.

Gone are the flaming gasoline torches that furnished our light.

Gone are the Model-T Fords with the side-curtains that we looked out of while driving through the snow.

And gone are most of the players I played with, most of them dead of old age.

However, I am sure the modern players don't have any more fun than we did in the old days.

A Country School Teacher at Age 18

At the age of 17 plus, I was graduated from High School in a class of 7. The entire High School had 45 pupils.

Following custom, I decided to teach school. A High School graduate in 1915 could go to Teachers College at Terre Haute, study 90 days, and get a certificate that he was a qualified educator, whether he was or not. Also, you could be paid as much as $2.50 a day, which was not bad, considering that a farm laborer drew $1.00 a day and board.

So I went to Terre Haute with my bicycle and rode it back and forth from my uncle's home to Normal School. There the educational hierarchy ordained that my prep course to teach a country school should include Vergil's Aeneid, Ancient Greek history, Chaucer, the science and development of arithmetic and observation of public school teaching. The local schools being closed for the summer vacation, we did our observation from a book.

Terre Haute, then as more recently, was a wide open town and houses of prositution filled the streets just west of the small campus. Some of our more worldly budding teachers enhanced their education by occasional visits to the girls who could hang out their upstairs windows and beckon as we left class, but I had been shown a medical book by my Methodist father before I left home wherein was depicted in startling color and detail the sores and stages of horrible decay of fellows who strayed from the straight and narrow path, suffering from various venereal diseases denominated Blue Ball, Shanker, Clapp and Syphilis. I would not have entered such a house for $1,000. However, I did venture one well chaperoned moonlight boat dance on the Wabash River with other students.

Thus equipped mentally and socially broadened, after 90 days, I was duly appointed by the Township Trustee to teach at the Robinson School, located about five miles north of Wheatland. It was a nice new one-room brick school house, with a hot air coal furnace underneath—the first modern country school in our township. It

84

was not too modern at that as it had outhouses, one for the boys and one for the girls, and a pump for drinking water with the common tincup chained to it. There was also a vestibule, and a school bell up above which I rang every school day at 8:00 A.M. for the first Bell. The school was set in a pleasant grove of oak and hickory trees, of which more a little later. My pay was $2.40 a day, plus a nickel a day for building the fire.

The school was in a district half coal mining and half farming. On opening day, I rang the bell, and saw 36 sturdy young Americans trudging across the hills and hollows to enroll. They ranged in age from Richard, six years old, to some boys and girls of 15 and 16. There were 8 grades. Richard was alone in the beginners class. I asked him, "Richard, do you know your letters?" He replied, "No, that is what I come to school to learn." I said, "Can you count?" and he said in his little piping voice, "I can count to 10."

All of a sudden my throat got tight, as I thought "My word, how are Vergil and Chaucer going to help me now?" Then I remembered how I had started out in a one room country school twelve years before and how the teacher taught his beginners. So I drew capital letters on the blackboard, and had Richard learn their names, and then small type, and then script letters later on; and with a primitive system of phonics I invented (probably as old as 700 B.C. when the Greeks taught the children that "A" was for Alpha and "B" for Beta) by spring Richard could read and write. The last time I saw him he was a substantial gray haired farmer of the community.

As I looked over the school that first morning, I was not too confident. I gazed at the three large girls in the 8th grade, and wondered if I could prepare them for the County Examination next spring, which all pupils desiring to enter High School would have to pass. In those days children were required to attend school only until they were fourteen years of age, and the authorities did not worry about "drop outs." In fact, they encouraged it. If you did not pass the entrance exam or if you failed in your grades, or would not study, or became incorrigible, your education ended abruptly and you were "expelled," and you entered the stream of commerce, industry, farming, or marriage at a much earlier age than now. Education was reserved for those who desired it, and not for those reluctant or unequipped youths who had to have it thrust upon them or into them. No child was promoted as a matter of course and the fellow who later would become the village moron was kept in the 2nd and 3rd grade two or three years and then released to his folks.

On that first morning I also gazed into the faces of three big boys in the 7th grade. One out-weighted me by ten pounds. I was a late developer physically, and at that time weighed about 118 pounds and was 5' 7" tall, although I grew more later. I knew these boys had "run out" a lady teacher the preceding year and had promised me the same treatment, according to the grapevine.

Well, we all got along pretty well the first month and a half. I had 8 classes to instruct in six hours, each with about five subjects. We had a recitation bench in the front of the room where each class took its turn, averaging about eight minutes a class. I would examine each pupil briefly to see if he or she had the lesson, commend the diligent, admonish the lax, and assign the next day's lesson in that subject. Maybe I might explain a tough problem or two. I might add that graduates of the old one room country school had to "learn" their education, dig it out themselves, thus putting into practice a sort of true University style of education—though modified sometimes by a request to stay in at recess or after school to do a little extra studying—as much punishment for me as the hapless pupil.

I did have a little trouble teaching two new fangled required courses—Manual Training for the boys and Domestic Science for the girls. We had no equipment for either except a broom, so we studied, rather briefly, text books on the matter which I bought. Anyhow, the girls knew more about the broom than I did.

I kept discipline pretty well, as I always believed in it, and kept whispering and throwing paper wads to a minimum, helped along by giving a 3rd grade boy named Freddie a spanking over my knee for violating the rules persistently. The next day Freddie handed me a note from his mother that I should not "lay hands" on him any more, or his coal miner father would come over and "lay hands" on me. I wrote her a note that I was sending Freddie home to stay until he brought her or the father over to the school to see me and to promise he would behave. Our correspondence ended the next day when Freddie showed up alone, but with a note stating he would behave and mind the teacher.

I kept waiting for the larger boys to carry out their threat, and I worried some about it. There came an early snow, and at the evening recess three small girls came in and tearfully reported that Rex, Frank, and Woody had knocked them off their sleds, and when they said they were going to tell the teacher, the boys pulled their hair, and said, "Tell him! We're going to run him out any way." I did not mention anything about it and dismissed school as if all were well, although I knew, and all the pupils knew I knew, that a crisis was at hand. The three large boys glanced at me askance as they filed out at 4:00 P.M., and made little effort to conceal their smirks.

That evening I climbed up in an oak tree and cut three stout gads about five feet long long and thicker than my thumb. As an after thought, I cut off a stunted hickory limb about two foot long and two or three inches thick. The next morning as all were seated I made a short speech to the effect that in lieu of opening exercises and singing "America" and reciting the Lord's Prayer, as we did each morning, I was going to have a little exercise on discipline.

I spoke on the value of education and the value of discipline and good behavior, and then pointed out that three boys had been bad the day before and would have to be punished. I asked them if they were guilty, and one said, "Yes, what do you think you can do about it?"

I said, "I can do plenty. See these oak switches? I am going to make an example of all three of you here and now. I will show you who is the master of this school. Frank, you are the biggest, come on up here and take off your coat.'

Frank slouched down in his seat and said, "I ain't a-comin' and you can't make me, can he, fellers?"—looking at his two buddies.

That did it! I dropped the switch, grabbed up the short club from under my desk, and shouted, "You come up here this second, or I will come back there and knock your fool head off. Move!" As I started toward him, the young fellow jumped up, his face white as a sheet and said, "I'm a-comin', I'm a-comin'," and I wore the switch out on his back. Then I got another one and said to the oldest and toughest boy, "Rex, your turn," and he gave in also and took his switching. By this time I had the victory, so I said to the third boy, "Woody, you are the smallest and I am not going to whip you. You go home to your Mother and tell her what you all did and what has happened. You will stay home until I give you permission to return."

I made a short speech to all the pupils then, begging their pardon for having to conduct a public flogging, but stating that all must follow the rules and behave themselves, as there were more limbs on the oaks outside. I never had one minute of trouble with any pupil, including the three boys, after that. I might add that in later life, Rex, the ring leader, was shot and killed while pulling a robbery in Detroit. The other two wound up in later life as prosperous and hard working farmers, leaders in the community.

Such a public whipping or spanking—according to one's size— was not uncommon in the Hoosier Grade Schools of fifty years ago. I received more than one myself as I was a rather mischievous boy, although I always had my lesson.

Old time country one-room schools back there many years ago, before my time, were apt to be a tough assignment on teachers, as one can gather from reading "The Hoosier Schoolmaster" by Eggleston. My father-in-law, Walter F. Wood, Sullivan, Indiana, which is down in the Wabash River Valley pocket in Southern Indiana, was born in 1878, out on Indian Prairie southeast of the city. He once told me that along in December a bunch of big boys from a neighboring rural school, the Mud Creek school, came by one day with their teacher, a man, in tow as a captive.

"He won't promise to give us enough of a treat at Christmas," they said, "So we are taking him over to Big Pond to duck him. Get your teacher and come along."

Wood said they went along, though not taking their own teacher. When they arrived at the pond, the big boys, really young men, got their teacher down to the water's edge, and asked, "Now, how many sticks of pepermint candy are you going to give us on Christmas?"

"One stick apiece is all I can afford," the hapless fellow replied.
"Not enough! Duck him, boys," the leader shouted.
"I'll give two sticks," the teacher yelled.
"Not enough! Throw him in", said the leader.

"I'll give three sticks apiece," the poor fellow screamed, as he faced the ice cold water.

"That's better, Mr. Jones. That'll do," the boy told him, and away they all went. Wood though it was a bit of expected horse-play customary to the season, though the teacher would have been ducked if he didn't come up to demands.

Generally on Friday afternoons we had a spelling match after recess. The older children would line up and I would give out the words. When a word was missed, the loser sat down, and by elimination the winner was found. It was not always the same student, either.

On special Friday nights some country school would advertise spelling match for all comers, adults or students. When I was in the Eighth Grade, one night I walked two and a half miles down to the Shake Rag School below Wheatland and was lucky enough to emerge as winner.

Once during this year, I was reported to the Trustee by an old maid who watched me through a telescope from her farm home across the swale. Being somewhat boyish myself, on quite a few occasions at noon I would take all the larger boys, some 12 or 15, and would track rabbits in the snow, or run across country, or play ball. Sometimes we would forget, and the noon recess would stretch out to two hours, while the girls and small boys played in or around the schoolhouse. The Trustee asked me about it, and I admitted my derelictions.

"How are the children doing with their studies?" he inquired.

"They are all doing very well," I replied.

"Well," he said, "You seem to know how to keep a school, at least they haven't run you out yet. Maybe, if you go out to track rabbits with the boys you can hunt out west of the school where old Aunt Clary can't see you!" I was a little more careful after that.

I had one startling experience that unnerved me quite a bit. One afternoon one of the boys raised his hand and asked, "Can I borrow Johnny's knife to sharpen—?" and made motions on his finger as if sharpening a pencil. Then he had an epileptic fit, throwing back his head and howling, then falling over and foaming at the mouth while beating his feet on the floor in convulsions. This was my first ex-

89

perience with such an affair, and in the quietness of a school room, it was quite a shock to me and to the other children, though the unfortunate boy couldn't help it. I dismissed classes then and there.

When the boy came back to school, I was uneasy, always expecting another fit, so that I went to see the Trustee, and I told him I would have to quit if the boy stayed in school. He sent me to talk to the mother and she assured me, "He just has those spells when the moon is full, and I'll keep him at home during those times." So I went back, feeling somewhat relieved.

Sure enough, however, the poor fellow had a second attack in school. I looked at the calendar, and the moon wasn't even half full. So the Trustee excused him the rest of the year. I am glad to say the lad outgrew it, or got some medicine, or both, and later became a successful business man, but for many a year I would have an occasional nightmare about the episodes.

Well, the year ended. Richard could read and write. The three Eighth Grade girls passed the County High School entrance exam with flying colors. All the other children received their promotions without exceptions, as there were no dummies in that school; they had studied faithfully, with a little duress here and there.

At noon on the last day of school, much to my surprise, the parents gathered for a covered dish dinner. We ate and sang; some of the children gave recitations which they had memorized, and then we had a spelling match. One father, speaking for all parents, thanked me for my services and asked me to request the Trustee to send me back the next fall to their school.

I did not return.

I was placed in the town school, somewhat of a promotion, and I never saw many of those 36 children or their parents again.

I have always had a warm spot in my heart for that old one-room country school, where I rang the bell, made the fire, heard the recitations, put down a rebellion, hunted rabbits, and played Andy over with the pupils. There I had learned how to make a living, how to take charge of people and guide them, and there I had changed from a boy to a man.

I never passed by that school, after it was abandoned and as long as it stood, but that I thought of Whittier's poem.

"Still sits the schoolhouse by the road,
A ragged beggar sleeping.
Around it still the sumac grows
And blackberry vines are creeping.
Long years ago a winter's sun
Shone over it at setting,
Lit up its western window panes
And low eaves icy fretting."

A gray-haired man in a distant city still can see that picture in his memory.

Off to College

When I entered college in the fall of 1917, I didn't know much about college, and less about college fraternities. I had attended a little State Normal School one summer for 90 days while I lived with my uncle, and that was very much like a super High School.

In 1917, I was determined I would volunteer for World War I, but failed my test for the 5th U. S. Marines, as being too light, although I ate a dozen bananas and drank a quart of milk before being weighed. My maternal grandfather, a veteran of the 14th Indiana Volunteers and the Army of the Potomac, insisted I go to college instead of War.

"War is no place for boys," he said. I had lived with him some years as a small boy and had listened to his War stories.

"Grandpa, I've heard you tell many a time about Pickett's charge at Gettysburg and fighting the Louisiana Tigers in the Battle of the Wilderness, and how exciting it all was when the cannons roared, and the Rebels gave the rebel yell, and so on," I told him. "Well, son," he said, "if I took a butcher knife right in this room and ran it in your belly, you would be in an awful mess. I have seen men die like that on the battlefield and it hurts a lot. Maybe I stuck a couple with a bayonet myself. Maybe I never told you how I had dystentery all one summer and got down to 100 pounds," he replied.

"I'll give you $50.00 now and $30.00 a month and you go on up to Purdue. I don't want you going up to that Godless place at Bloomington—that Indiana University."

Grandpa's name was John R. McClure and his ancestors were Scotch-Irish Presbyterians out of Londerry, Ireland. He was a fundamentalist and believed with John Knox and Calvin in predestination, and that struggle as you might, your fate was pre-determined. However, he was a little canny also, and tempered his belief enough to see that I would not be needlessly exposed to the wiles of the Devil

92

which he believed cavorted about the I.U. campus and caused sinning and socialism up there at Bloomington. This was shortly after Wendell Willkie had headed up the young Socialist and Freethinkers Club at I.U.

I took grandpa up on his offer, as I couldn't get in the War anyhow, though it fretted me no end to hear the recruiting bands pay," "Over There" and "Goodby Mule With Your Old Hee-haw" and to see the other boys off at the depot, with the flags waving and the girls weeping.

So one fall day I got on the B & O accommodation train with a suit case full of new underwear and two pairs of heavy cotton flannel pajamas and other wear and headed for college. I had duly qualified at Purdue and my tuition of $75.00 a semester had been taken care of by the County Commissioner who annually had two such scholarships at both State Universities.

I transferred to the north bound Monon Railroad at Mitchell and at many stations we picked up boys bound for college. They were all bright young fellows and pretty cheerful although a few had hayseed sticking out of their hair as I did. The Monon had an unique character. It was the only railroad that lay entirely in Indiana, started at one penitentiary, ended at another, and served four colleges in between: Wabash, Depauw, Indiana University, and Purdue. The State Reformatory was at its south end in Jeffersonville, and the State Prison at the north end at Michigan City.

A young fellow named Wible got on at Bedford, and sat down with me, and we talked quite a bit. He was going to Purdue, too, and had a rush date with some fraternities, he said, and wanted to know if I had some, too. I said, "No," as I had very little idea what a college fraternity was. He wised me up some on fraternities and colleges. It seemed like most of the boys in our car had bids. As we neared Lafayette where the University was located, Wible told me, "Here is a written recommendation to such and such a fraternity. It's quite the thing to belong. I'll introduce you also to the boys who are coming down to meet me."

As we approached the Wabash River and slowed up for the station, excitement started to mount and everybody got ready, combed his hair, adjusted his tie, and brushed off the cinders to make a good

93

appearance. I did the same, thinking "I'm sure glad I found out about all this. I'll just look calm and easy when they invite me to go along." However, it didn't work out well. My friend disappeared some way in the crowd. Other collegiate looking youths grabbed the new comers by the hand with cries of welcome, but no one at all noticed young Niblack in his new pegged top trousers, or even spoke to him. Well, away they all went, the train pulled out, and there I still stood, not exactly like a simpleton with my hand stretched out in greeting with no one there, but feeling exactly like that.

There was an old man sitting on a bench there, chewing tobacco, so I said, "How do you get to Purdue?" He said, "Go down to the end of the platform yonder, go one block and catch a street car and go across the river."

Soon I arrived at the campus, found the registration office, and this time I was the center of attraction from three or four young fellows who were soliciting new members for their boarding clubs. They were students who each managed boarding houses near the campus for indigent ladies, and got their board and room free in return. I liked the looks of a blond boy named Gerald Moore, and he sure made me welcome. He carried my suit case to Mrs. McClintock's boarding house for "genteel young men—no rowdies allowed" on Grant Street. There I stayed some time. I can hardly believe this myself now, but it is true, that I paid at the rate of $3.50 a week for a nice shared room and two meals a day—breakfast and supper. I had a room mate from Bippus, Indiana, who was helping finance his education by working for a pig raiser beyond town at 10¢ an hour.

I was entered in the Agriculture College, and was assigned to a block or section with 35 other budding future farmers of America. I was dedicated to be an Orchardist on Grandpa's 175 acres, but turned out to be a Judge. Abie Gordner became a highly successful life insurance agent in Indianapolis. Duke Patrick got a law degree at Michigan and became the first attorney in Washington, D. C. on radio and later T.V. regulation. A fellow named Cunningham became a professional wrestler, and another boy wound up as an oil man. Ray Meade became owner of a large construction company. I suppose some of the others went on and became farmers.

We all, as a group, attended the same classes, from 8:00 A.M. until 4:00 P.M., five days a week, but only from 8:00 A.M. to 12:00 noon on Saturday. Purdue, in those days, (the fall of 1917) did not believe in the University system whereby you were on your own. You were force fed, supervised, coached, and urged on, a good deal like the little High School where I had graduated. A student got 15 hours credit a week in this fashion: one hour recitation counted one hour credit, two hours of lecture counted one hour, three hours of laboratory counted one hour. We spent 37 hours each week under the eye of the professor or instructor. Laboratory work, as in chemistry or stock judging, was closely supervised and no monkeying around allowed.

There were different colleges, or degrees, at Purdue, such as Agriculture, Pharmacy, Civil Engineering, and so forth. All freshman were known as "Rhinies," and had to wear at all times out doors little green skull caps with different colored buttons on top. We Agriculture freshies had yellow buttons, Pharmacy had brown and Mechanical Engineering had purple buttons, I remember.

I got signed up in Chemistry, which I never had taken in High School, English, Stock Judging, Chicken Coop designing, (really mechanical drawing) Botany, Zoology, which included heredity, and some other subjects I can't remember. Chemistry was almost my Waterloo. In High School I never took a book home at night. My forte was reading, writing, and language, and I could easily learn things like that in school. Chemistry was different. At the end of six weeks the Professor gave an exam and I got a mark of 24. I was lost.

I hardly knew the difference between H_2O and heavy water. My plight somewhat resembled that of the college football star who flunked his chemistry and was thrown off the team the week before the "big" game. His coach implored the chemistry teacher to give him a special exam, and see if he could pass, and thus be able to play. The professor said, "Well, I will. If he makes 50%, I'll pass him." The boy passed, and joined the team and made the winning touchdown. Later, at the faculty club, the coach cautiously inquired of the teacher, "Say, I don't want to know too much about it, but how in the world did Howard, dumb as he is, pass the exam?" "I just gave

95

him two questions", the instructor replied, the first was 'What color is blue litmus' and he answered, 'Pink', and that was wrong. Then I asked him, 'What H^2O stood for', and he said, 'I don't know', and that was correct, so he got a grade of 50%."

Then I decided to do something about it, and for the first time in my life I got down and studied my lessons—really worked at it. I went back to the beginning, and started all over and learned each step thoroughly, and got caught up to the class. At the midterm exam I got a "100." Chemistry is like geometry or building a house. You lay the foundation thoroughly, piece by piece, and build on up from there. You can't start in mid-air.

All this time I thought about joining a fraternity. I had got it into my head it was the thing to do, that the upper crust belonged. That was not exactly true, but the frats had big imposing houses on the bluff overlooking the Wabash Valley. Also, there were many fraternity pledges in my section, all proudly wearing their pledge pins in their coat lapel, and I felt left out. I knew you couldn't ask to join a fraternity, but there were more ways to kill a cat beside choking it to death on cream, I had heard.

I discovered that a top-notch rooming house, a little higher priced one run by a lady named Mrs. Reed, was occupied mostly by fraternity pledges for whom there as no room in their houses. I went over to get a room, but the lady said they were full. I told her to put my name on the waiting list in case somebody flunked or died. Little did I think—

That mid November, Purdue went down to Bloomington to play football at Indiana University, a deadly rival. The Friday night before the game a lot of us went down and got on a Monon freight and rode down in style, though we didn'g get much sleep and it was fairly chilly. We thought we were going to win as we were favored. Purdue had a coach who was part Indian and he liked a nip of the fire water now and then. At our pep rally that week, he had a couple of shots of the old bug juice, and, thus inspired, gave us good news. "I have got their captain and star back and center disqualified by the conference as professionals," he told us cheering students, "and it's a cinch, we'll win big." At that time a lot of good college athletes did a lot of moonlighting for hire with semi-pro or pro-teams under assumed names. It was commonly known as a practice, but under a sort of unwritten gentlemen's agreement, no coach was supposed to squeal on another college.

Illustrating what spirit can do, the only upshot of such disqualification was to anger the I.U. team, and they beat us 37 to 0, substitutes and all. Then their student body started a snake dance on old Jordan Field, which wound up in chasing our outnumbered group to the Railroad depot. The schools broke off athletic relations over this business, and everybody hated everybody more than ever. I. U. boys spoke derisively of Purdue as a "Cow College."

A boy from Purdue named Kent was riding our train going down to I.U. that Friday night, and in some way fell between the cars and was killed. I knew him, and I knew he roomed at this place I spoke of, so I rushed over there and got his room, sharing it with a young fellow from Seymour named Shepherd, who happened to be pledged to the Sigma Nu Fraternity. We became fast friends. He was in the Civil Engineering school and wore a red button on his cap. I was making good grades, mostly A's, and I took care to let Shep see my papers and reports. Fraternities were always on the look out for good athletes or good students. It wasn't long before I was invited over for dinner, given a pledge pin—a little round brass button with a coiled serpent with a red eye on it—and moved into the Sigma Nu house. At the time that fraternity was one of the Big Four College Fraternities, along with Sigma Chi and a couple of others.

I got in the house before Christmas and liked it real well. There were 29 of us, all four classes. Freshman were "hazed" some and made to stay in their place. They had to learn to take it if they wanted to be initiated, and we all did. It was the old theory that you must learn to obey before you are able to command. The freshies cleaned the house, fired the furnace, washed windows, carried out the ashes, acted as call boy in the morning while firing the furnace at 4:00 A.M., mowed the lawn in season, and ran errands for the three upper classes.

The house manager made a weekly list of those chores and who drew what detail. In addition, they had a lot of good stout paddles, about 2 1/2 feet long, 4 inches wide and one-half inch thick, with a good hand grip on one end, around the house and we Rhinies got paddled on our behinds with many a stout lick. At the least infraction of the rules, or sometimes just for the hell of it you would hear "Bend over, Rhinie" and ker whack, you had it. I got toughened up to where it didn't really hurt much, and sometimes us freshmen, in quiet times when things were too dull, would swap licks to see who could hit the hardest or endure the most. I have seen the upper classmen do the same with each other. Young men and teenage boys enjoy rough physical stuff and like to display their prowess and fortitude. Fraternity life then, when Chapters were small and closely knit, exemplified the gang spirit that seems to be born in boys. Everyone knew the others by their first names, and had a sense of great pride in being one and belonging.

The House was a nice large three story stucco building sitting on a bluff overlooking the Wabash Valley and its famed river, up which my Grandfather's Grandfather had trudged in 1811 as a soldier of the Indiana Territorial Militia under General Harrison to battle with Tecumseh's Red-skins at the battle of Tippecanoe. About 150 of those American soldiers were sleeping their last sleep at Battleground just north of our fraternity.

We ate on the first floor and had lounges and living rooms there. Two, three, or four boys each shared a study room on the second floor where we lived, and studied, dressed and undressed. We slept in double decker bunks in the floored attic, or dorm, and I want to tell you that heavy flannelette pajamas over your underwear and a lot of blankets on top felt mighty good at night when the snow flakes would drift in the open windows on the north wind. The winter of 1917-18 was the coldest ever experienced in Indiana.

One Saturday morning in January or February, it got to 26° below zero. I had on my green Rhinie stocking cap with its yellow botton, and in a walk, or rather run, a few blocks to the campus the lower lobes of my ears froze but they soon thawed out when I got inside and rubbed them with snow. There was also a lot of deep snow that war winter.

The master of our domicile was a senior Agriculture student whose name was Derrick, "Bull" by nickname. All of us freshmen addressed him reverently as "Mr." Derrick. In company with all our seniors, he enjoyed the privilege of wearing the senior cords, or corduroy pants, embellished by pen and ink names of girl friends and others. His word was law, as indeed was the word of any initiated man, including the hated Sophomores. Having just been released from the serfdom of being freshman, they really enjoyed laying on the paddle and in otherwise throwing their weight about. In later life Derrick became a valued client of mine when I practiced law.

Just before Christmas, the powers of the fraternity decided to decorate the house with a Christmas tree. Half of us freshmen were detailed as a scouting party to go out and locate a nice evergreen, which we did. We went up Happy Hollow, up the river, and spotted a trim cedar in a woods. The other freshmen were then sent one night to bring it in. They left about midnight. It was snowing and cold, and the lads cut the trip short by stopping in a grave yard and chopping down a good size cedar, which they dragged home and stowed in our garage.

Unfortunately, it quit snowing about that time, and they left quite a trail. I was on the house detail that week of getting up at 4:00 A.M. firing the furnace and awakening the others according to the times they marked against their names on the call board.

Along about 7:00 A. M. here came the caretaker of the cemetery in a horse and buggy, and with him a minion of the law, a constable he had aroused. They triumphantly found the tree in the garage and gave some loud knocks on the door, while the law man hollered "Open in the name of the law!" They couldn't have raised more hue and cry if they had discovered a body which was the corpus delicti of a murder.

I opened the door and asked what they wanted.

"Who's in charge here? See that there tree there? It's been stolen, cut right off the head of a grave, and somebody's going to jail or pay up or both. Who's in charge here?", the constable asked.

"Mr. Derrick, the commander," I said.

"Well, young feller, you just march right in there and fetch him out this minute," he told me.

I didn't hesitate one second. The law might be fearsome, but it had no terrors for me like getting Mister Derrick out of the downy one hour before his call time. I would have rather have faced the Devil himself.

"Mister, if you want to have Mr. Derrick waked up, you do it yourself," I said.

"Just show me to him," was the answer.

I escorted them upstairs to the dorm, pointed out the sleeping "Bull" and fled. What happened up there I don't know, but before long I saw five startled freshmen under arrest and being told to be in the Squire's Court at 10:00 A.M., all without benefit of warrant

Warrant or no warrant, nobody went to jail, but it cost each of us $5.00 a piece, or $150.00, what with the Squire's fees, constables fees, and a whopping sum for the outraged owner of the tree, which, by the way, he confiscated and took away with him. Seems like college boys in those days were always getting in trouble, especially if they got caught.

Speaking of paddling, it was all a part of the game, and most freshmen didn't resent it too much. I remember one peaceful Sunday afternoon I was down in the big sunny front room reading a book, and Preach Prather, a senior was dozing on a sofa in front of the grate fire. He was feeling sort of puny, in other words, ailing a little. He roused up, and asked me to get him a glass of water so he could take a pill. I went to the kitchen, and by mistake, turned on the hot water, so just for the Hell of it, I couldn't resist taking Preach a glass of nice hot water, though I knew I was inviting disaster. He put the pill in his mouth, reached for the glass and took a hasty swig. I almost doubled up laughing at his surprised expression which soon changed to annoyance, and he called out to Al Heine, our football letter man: "Al, hit this sap a couple of good ones for me. Burn his ass good. I'm too weak to do it justice."

Al complied with a vim, and the end of the paddle broke off and went hurtling past my ear, so I got off with only one crack—still laughing.

Shortly after this event, a tight fisted uncle found out the Grandpa was sharing his Civil War pension with me, and made the old man cut it out, and made me sign a promissory note for what I already had received. Thus ended, at mid term, my college career at Purdue —"Where the Wabash spreads her Valley."

I was glad to leave, anyway, as I now had a good excuse to go to the War, if I could get in, which I eventually did by tricking Uncle Sam as to my age.

World War I

"The Minstrel Boy to the war has gone
In the ranks of death you'll find him,
His father's sword he has girded on,
And his wild harp slung behind him."

When the bugles blew for war early in 1917, I, like the Minstrel Boy, went to war. However, I did not take my wild harp as my musical ability at that time consisted of playing a few sashays on the mouth organ and some tunes on the mandolin. Likewise, I never was found in the ranks of death as I did not get out of the United States. In fact, I got in the Naval Aviation and my war record was rather short and inglorious. I never saw the ocean and I never got in the air. I spent my time at Great Lakes in Chicago. I might say, in later years when I ran for public office, I did not run upon my war record.

I was in my teens when Woodrow Wilson ran for a second term as President upon a platform of "Peace and Prosperity, he kept us out of war." A month after he was inauguarated he had Congress declare war on Germany and we joined World War I.

It was an exciting time for the United States. Like most other American boys, I was anxious to join and go over there. Although I did not make it into the armed services until the summer of 1918, I really tried to get in shortly after the war was declared.

One day I was plowing with a walking plow in a field where there were a lot of stumps. Along shortly before noon, I ran the plow into a stump and broke one of the tugs with which we harnessed the mules. I unhitched the mules and took them to the barn and went in the house for dinner. At that time we had dinner at noon on the farm. While resting on the floor after dinner reading the Indianapolis News, I saw an article that said 2800 men were wanted for land service in France by the Marine Corp. At that time they were getting up the 5th and 6th Marines. Thereupon I never went back to get the plow out of the stump, and as far as I know, it is still there today.

The next day, in company with another farm boy named Earl Robinson who lived just outside of Wheatland, I went to Indianapolis and took an examination for this special Corp of the Marines. Unfortunately, I was too light, as at that time I was about 5' 8" and weighed about 120 pounds, or something like that. I couldn't make it, although the second day before I went back to be reweighed I drank a quart of milk and ate seven or eight bananas, I was still too light and was rejected. Earl went ahead and was accepted, and became a member of the 5th Marines, went overseas and had his left foot shot off at the Battle of Belleau Wood. I have always been thankful I was a little light for the Marine Corp at that time, as in the many years that have elapsed since World War I, I have seen too many old veterans lying around in the hospitals without legs or other wise maimed and incapacitated, and they are forgotten by the general public.

To make a long story short, Grandpa and my father talked me out of trying to enlist so I went to Purdue University that fall of '17 on some money that Grandpa shared with me from his Civil War pension. This financing gave out about the middle of the second semester, as I have related elsewhere, and left me free to return to Wheatland, whereupon I began to try to get in the war again.

About this time they organized a National Guard Unit in Vincennes. Some of the boys tried to get me to join, saying, "under the Constitution of the United States, they can't send us out of the country. We will have a grand ole time riding about the country being a National Guard. We can't go over there." I said, "That is not what I want. I want to go over there where the action is and fight the Huns." Consequence was I didn't join that unit. They were taken to Mineola, Long Island, sworn in and put in the Rainbow Division and sent across ten days after being sworn in. They were in the second Battle of Marne and all around over there and came home quite the heroes, and I never made it across to the field of battle.

However, early in the summer of 1918, I found out a way to get

102

into the armed services. I was not registered for the draft and did not have to go but I went up to Indianapolis and joined the Navy. I learned from somebody that if you were too light, the Navy would accept you by knocking off five pounds for each year you were under 20. I told them I was two years younger than I was which allowed me to weigh in ten pounds lighter; also, in the several months in between my attempt to get in the Marines I had gained a few pounds so now I was accepted by the Navy. I saw my discharge over at the State House one day many years after I got out of the Navy and I could not for a moment remember why I was listed as two years younger than I really was until I remembered I had lowered my age two years.

The branch I was put in was Landman for Machinists' Mate Aviation. They sent me to Chicago in mid-summer of 1918 to Great Lakes. I remember that a boy from Wheatland, Ernest Dillion, who is now a rather prominent lawyer in Indianapolis, went along with me; also two boys from Vincennes, Earl McClure, later a Postmaster there, and "Spots" Horn, were in my outfit.

We got up to Chicago late in the evening and bedded down in some straw between two barracks at Camp Boone where we took our boot training. The next morning we were lined up to get our uniforms and had various inoculations and were told what to do and how to talk. I remember the Petty Officer who spoke to us seemed to me to be a very old "salt" himself. He had his white hat tipped over one eye and he said, "Now when I say "pipe up' I mean "speak up,' and when I say 'pipe down,' I mean 'shut up' and so on and you will just have to learn the sea talk around here, that is all there is to it." I was under the impression he probably had been in the Navy for years, but I found out later on he had been in about three months.

I was then transferred to Camp Dewey where I put in a lot of my rookie time the rest of the summer and early fall. I remember we lived in wooden barracks and were given a hammock as part of our outfit. Everybody had to learn to sleep in a hammock. It was something like trying to ride a bicycle. Many an unlucky recruit fell out of the hammock in his sleep. One boy broke his toe and has since drawn a pension for "wounded in action," I suppose that is what you would term it. I soon learned to sleep in the hammock very peacefully and got to where I liked it very much. In fact, when I went home on furlough at Thanksgiving I could hardly sleep in the bed because it was so straight and my back was used to being bent when I was asleep. Our hammocks were slung about five feet off the floor.

Our life consisted mainly of getting up at 5:00 A.M., when they blew the bugle, getting dressed, and out on the street taking calisthenics for about a half an hour and the daily dozen somebody had invented by this time. Then we all went to breakfast when they had the breakfast call. After that we drilled or did "make work" because there was not much for us to do around there. I have seen four husky sailors soberly carring a twelve-foot two by four timber up the street about half a mile, and later gravely carrying it back again, slowly pacing along like pall-bearers. It was an easy way to get out of work that some rookie had thought up. Uncle Sam had not been prepared for such an influx of recruits. However, they gave us all rifles and duffel bags for our clothes and we learned how to wash our clothes. I could take a bucket of cold water, a bar of salt water soap and wash all my clothes and press them myself by stretching them out and then rolling them into a tight roll and tying tightly, and then I could wash my hair and take a bath, all in one bucket of water.

We put in a lot of time in infantry drills, "Squads Right, Squads Left, Squads Right About," and soforth. I had a big advantage over the other boys on this propositon as I had a semester and a half of R.O.T.C. at Purdue and had learned this sort of drill which was in vogue at this time. It was the same as it had been in the Civil War and for many years thereafter. I had been a Sergeant in R.O.T.C. at Purdue.

We also did a lot of "make work" as I said before to keep us busy. One time we were going to build a new ball diamond. There was a slight hill on some of the vacant territory around the camp, and one day they marched our company over there, along with some other companies to start building the ball diamond. We had to wheel some dirt off this hill and spread it out over some place else. We marched over there in style. The officer said, "Company Halt! Right Face! Attention! At Ease!"

104

Then the Fatigue Officer who was in charge of us—a Petty Officer with about a second or third class rating, I suppose, said, "Is there anybody here that knows how to drive a Ford?" Well, immediately quite a few of us held up our hands. I had visions of driving one of those little Gray Fords that I had seen driven around the station. Then he said, "All youse guys that can drive a Ford take one step forward." I stepped forward along with some other eager beavers and taking one look at us, he said, "All right, boys, grab one of them wheelbarrows right over there." Much to my horror, we saw about forty wheelbarrows sitting over there so we all grabbed a wheelbarrow. And then he said, "Now you push them over here and you other boys here take a shovel apiece and get over there on the hill. When they bring the wheelbarrows over, you load them up; and you fellows with the wheelbarrows take them way over yonder and dump out the dirt to be spread and come back and get another load. This is what we are going to do all day."

I thought, "This is terrible," but there was nothing else to do, so away we went with our wheelbarrows. There were about forty of us with wheelbarrows and about four hundred that had shovels. We would drive our wheelbarrows up to the elevation where they were shoveling and in about three seconds the wheelbarrow was full. It was a hot July day, and I had to trundle the thing about three or four hundred yards, and I soon got up a sweat. I thought to myself, "Boy! This is something, what can I do now?"

Well, there was a young fellow in my company from West Virginia. He was a fine sort of fellow but a little slow thinker. About the fifth round I made, I saw him and said, "Hey Jack, come here a minute." He said, "What do you want, Jack?" I said, "Would you hold this wheelbarrow for me a minute, I have to go over here behind a tree and answer a call of nature." "Sho, sho, I'll do that for you," he said. "By the way," I said, "let me have a shovel as I don't want to be caught without anything in my hand." He said, "Okay, take it with you." So I went over and got behind a tree and watched. Pretty soon here came the Fatigue Officer and I heard him say, "Come on, Jack, get that wheelbarrow moving." The poor fellow said, "This ain't my wheelbarrow. It belongs to—hey, where is he? Where did he go?" He looked all around for me and said,

"This ain't my wheelbarrow." The Fatigue Officer says, "It belongs to Uncle Sam and you get going with it." The last I saw of him, away went my friend, Jack, wheeling a wheelbarrow full of dirt. I slipped over with my shovel and got in the shoveling gang and every time he came around the rest of the day I would be busy looking the other way. He saw me once and he said, "Come on, Jack, take your wheelbarrow back." I said, "What the Hell is wrong with you, Jack, it don't belong to me, it belongs to Uncle Sam," and about that time the Officer came by and made him get going again.

I never volunteered but one other time, and I should have known better then. About a month or so later, they lined us up one morning and said, "We want twenty-four volunteers for Special Detail." I had visions this time of being sent as one of a squad that went around on War Bond sales drive that they had been sending around to St. Louis and Cincinnati and other places to stimulate the citizenry to buy War Bonds, even as they do today during the Wars.

Well, anyhow, I kept hollering, "Take me, Captain Monahan, take me." So they named off twenty-three of them and I insisted, so he said, "All right, Niblack, step forward."

He made three Squads out of us—eight to a Squad—so we turned Squads Left, and marched on over to the Armory where there was a landing cannon left over from the War of 1898, I suppose. The wheels were about six foot high and it was a thousand pound landing cannon. The Officer said, "All right, boys, grab the toggles, we are going to have a little special drill. Each company in the regiment is to furnish one of these landing cannons and we are going to have a review here in about three weeks from now and the Rear Admiral from somewhere is coming over here and we are going to have an inspection to see who can do it the best." Well, there I was. I thought "This thing is pretty bad."

This cannon had two long ropes attached to it then toggles across the rope that you pulled, so I thought "I will get as far away from it as I can." Four of us got on the front end and four of the heaviest guys got on the back end on two little short ropes to hold it back to keep it from running away down hill. We ran through the August sun up and down hill with that dern thing for about two and a half weeks. It turned out that when we went across this big field that everybody and the cannons had to be in line, so then naturally the first four men, of which I was one, had to be in line with the next company's front men. Consequently, the only ones pulling were we four men and in addition we had to yank those four hanging on behind.

Well, I never got so tired of anything in my life but we finally got through with it, and after that I never did volunteer for anything.

I got in a mess one night about three o'clock in the morning. I was sound asleep and here came the Officer of the Day (I don't know why they didn't call him Officer of the Night) with two or three aides clattering in the back end of our barracks, making an unholy racket, and woke me up and I suppose several others. I got about half awake and not realizing what was going on, hollered out in a big voice, "What the Hell is going on down there? Can't you let a man sleep? We don't get enough sleep in the Navy anyhow. Who in the Hell are you down there?"

There was a startled silence from the Officer of the Day and the two or three aides accompanying him and he said, "Who said that? Pipe right up now. Come on, who said that? It is going to be bad on you if you don't speak up." Nobody said anything, and I wished I hadn't and that I was back home in Wheatland about that time.

Well, he got himself a slat or barrel stave or something and started up the barracks. Our company was all sleeping in the hammocks in two rows and he started on the outside row, hitting each hammock right in the bottom where the man's setter was hanging down and giving it a big crack, he would ask, "Did you tell the Officer of the Day to go to Hell?" "No, sir. No, sir," was the reply. Then he would go to the second man and wake him up if he wasn't already awake and give him a big whack and ask, "Did you tell the Officer of the Day to go to Hell?" "No, sir. No, sir," was the answer. Then the Officer said, "I had better find out who it was or I will get this whole company up and run them up and down the street double time until I find out who it was." He was sure throwing his weight around.

He got up to about 15 and he only had about 45 more to go before he started to turn the bend. I though "I had better speak up because I'm sure going to be in bad with this company if they all have to get out of here and take that punishment." So I spoke up and said, "It was me, sir, it was me." He ran down there and hit me a crack under the hammock and the aide said, "Get out of there, Jack. Get out of there. Get your clothes on. Get your clothes on. Get your duffel bag and rifle." He took me out in the company street and he said, "See that sentry down at that end of the street and that one down at the other end of the Street? You double time up and down there until they have reveille in the morning."

So I got down and got dressed, and he stood and watched me double time up and down there in a jog-trot. After a while he went away somewhere and I cheated on him. After that I just walked back and forth between sentries. They didn't care; they weren't going to tell on me, anyhow. That duffel bag with all my clothes and shoes weighed about forty or fifty pounds, it seemed like to me anyhow, and that rifle was pretty heavy.

After that I never spoke up no matter what happened.

I think the only other trouble I had was when I refused to wash the clothes of the officer who was in charge of our particular company. He was a non-commissioned officer, too, a CPO or something like that. He called me in one day and said, "Niblack, here are my dirty clothes. I want you to wash them." Being an independent young American, I said, "You can wash them yourself. I didn't join this Navy to wash anybody's clothes. I am going overseas and going to do some fighting." Well, I think as the result of that, he backed off. He knew I didn't have to wash his clothes but later he put me on Kitchen Police and assigned me to the Cook, on some pretext or other, which was very fortunate for me because in the Navy there is a saying "If the cook starves, he is a fool." So when the officers or anybody had steaks, the cook had the best steak and I, as the cook's assistant, had second best. We also had new peaches, watermelon, and anything else that came along. I was sorry when that detail ended.

Although we weren't found in the ranks of death as The Minstrel Boy was, death did invade our Camp. We had about 45,000 boys in training there at Great Lakes and one day they brought in some recruits from Boston and put them in tents next to our barracks. They had the Spanish Flu, as some of them had been overseas and came back with the disease. Before it was through, about four thousand young men died at Great Lakes, which was approximately ten percent. This was a somewhat heavier ratio of deaths than many combat companies had overseas. I know I used to watch every morning a switch engine come and take away two or three cars of coffins with young men who died of the Spanish Flu.

It was in September of 1918 that they sent these corpses all over the United States. I don't know whether that spread the disease or not, but anyway, there is where it started, at Great Lakes.

They had such a shortage of nurses that I was assigned to the hospital and they made some emergency hospitals out of given barracks. The disease seemed to effect the boys' lungs. They would get sick, have a fever, and have a hemorrhage of the lungs, a lot of black blood would gush out, and they would be dead very shortly. I know that we took as good care of them as we could. It never effected me. It seemed to me it was the heavier set and fleshier boys that succumbed to this, and as I said, I was skinny and wiry at the time, and it didn't bother me a bit.

I learned all the bugle calls, the call for reveille to get up, and the call for food: "Porky, Porky, Porky, not a strip of lean! Soupy, Soupy, Soupy, not a single bean!" Then the taps at night, "Sleep, go to sleep; Go to sleep . . . ." I learned them all and I know them to this day. They all have different tunes, of course, for different things. I especially liked the tune for pay day. Uncle Sam paid me the magnificent sum of one dollar a day and deducted for my clothes; like, a blue blouse was six dollars, and a pair of pants was six dollars. We had our blues, which I liked very much; we had white summer clothes and hats; we had our pea jacket and our white leggings and black shoes. We got all dressed up every so often and would go down in Chicago, where we had a great time.

I remember during the World Series, in 1918, I was going along the street there just shortly after noon and a fellow in a Haynes Sport automobile drove up and said, "Jack, where are you going?" I said, "Nowhere." He said, "How would you like to go out to the ball game?" I said, "What game is on?" He said, "The World Series and I got an extra ticket." The Chicago people were very hospitable to sailors at Great Lakes and the soldiers at Fort Sheridan. He said, "Get in and we will go." I got in and we went out to the ball park. He had two seats right behind the catcher and Lo! and Behold! Who was playing but Chicago and Boston, and who was pitching for Boston but Babe Ruth. It was the only time I ever saw him play. They won 1-0. Babe Ruth was a left handed pitcher, and he was such a good batter that they finally made a fielder out of him.

We were invited to many breakfasts and dinners and to stay all night in Oak Park and Wilmette and other places with most anybody who was trying to entertain soldiers and sailors.

I remember one night about midnight I was downtown getting ready to go back and here come two or three girls and a couple of fellows and one lady, a young gal named Elsie Popp, had on a red dress and red hat, and she said, "Come on, Jack, we need one more fellow to fill the party." So I went out for an all night party with plenty of beer and had an awful good time. I wrote to that girl two or three times after the War as she was a real nice girl. We danced and drank beer and at dawn I went back to Great Lakes, after having a very good time. I have never seen any of them since.

The day of the Armistice we were all given a pass down to Chicago. I want to tell you—I never have seen anything like it in all my life. A City of three or four million people went absolutely stark raving crazy and they would run up and down the street. All the saloons were open then as prohibition had not come in yet. I saw somebody that got a white horse into a Bar on Madison Avenue and the horse was astraddle the bar the last I saw of it. They had a real celebration in Chicago that night and I guess they had it in the rest of the country, too. Anyway, it was some two or three days before we got over our headaches up at Great Lakes.

After I got through at Camp Dewey they put me in an Aviation Regiment over to the 15th Regiment along with other boys, and there we took our training for Naval Aviation. Uncle Sam as usual was unprepared for War and he had hardly any planes at all, though I believe they cut down some spruce trees out in Washington getting ready to make some new planes.

They trained me to be a Machine Gunner on a bomber. They

didn't have any bombers but did have a Lewis machine gun so I studied the machine gun and got so I could take it apart and assemble it in the dark or blindfolded, and we practiced that on the range and elsewhere. I thought I could do pretty good with the machine gun, and I guess I could at that time.

When we got over with the 15th Regiment at our new quarters, they asked for volunteers who could drill a company. A little Italian fellow from Chicago said he could do it, so he was backing up and giving us forward march and then he gave us Squads Left, which would have been all right but unfortunately he was turned around, so he marched us all into the company barracks and the clothes lines and there we were up against the wall. At this time the CPO who was in charge said, "Fall out everybody and reform on the street. Does anyboy else want to try it?"

I said, "I can do it, sir." So I just gave them forward march up and down the street and squads right about, consequently I was made a Platoon Commander and they gave me a sword. There were one hundred twenty men in a company and I was given charge of sixty men in Platoon B. I gave them close order drills, and we passed in review over at the Main Station many times. I led my Platoon with my "cheese knife" and marched to John Philip Sousa's Band. It was quite a thrilling moment to be a part of twenty-five thousand sailors marching in review, all in harmony with the playing of the Stars and Stripes Forever, or some other tune.

I kept trying to get out of Great Lakes and go on the ocean or go somewhere else to see some action. I even had my father write to the Commanding Officer of our Regiment to have me transferred. I got called in about that as they were annoyed because I was raising so much trouble to get out of here. I couldn't help it because I wanted to go. Later when the War was over, everybody got to go home except me. When the Commander of the whole Company left, they made me Company Commander and left me there with dwindling ranks.

Finally, I went over to the Main Station along late in February or early March. I wanted to see Rear Admiral Moffat. I didn't have any pass to go there either, but I went. I said to the attache in the outer office, "I want to see Rear Admiral Moffat," who was in charge of the Station. He said, "What do you want over here? You are just a Second Class Gunner's Mate. Have you got a message or anything?" I said, "No, but I got an uncle, Rear Admiral Niblack, in the Navy and I want out of this place."

So he took me in to see Rear Admiral Moffat and I told him who I was and about my uncle. He wasn't my uncle—I lied about that—he was my father's first cousin from Vincennes and he was a graduate of Annapolis and he was in the War and was a Rear Admiral over in Europe at that time, so I was made welcome to say the least. The next day I was on my way home on the train. I went back to Wheatland and got there early in March.

Thus ended my War career.

It was a great experience. I never helped save the nation or anything like that. In fact, I would have been better off and the country would have been better off if I had been home helping to raise some corn and pigs for the armed services.

However, I have a lot of fond memories of that time. I especially liked the time when we went to bed, lights out at 9:00 o'clock P.M. I would lie in my hammock and through the still of the night, I could hear the bugle playing taps. It really was a mournful and desolate call as I knew those notes had been played over the graves and at the funerals of thousands upon thousands of American soldier and sailor boys.

Wheat Harvest

In the spring of 1920, at the end of my Sophomore year at Indiana University, about 35 of us students went to Kansas to work in the wheat harvest. I believe there were eight of us from the Sigma Nu Fraternity House. We intended to earn some money for the coming year's schooling and to have a little fun and adventure as well. Before I got back home, I had a belly full and more of both the latter activities.

Some one had written to the County Agricultural Agent in Larned, Kansas, and he replied, "Come on out, the pay is good." The Midwest farm boom was still on following World War I. We all met in St. Louis and went in a body to Larned, a town of 2500, on the Santa Fe Railroad. There we put up in a small hotel and waited, as we were about ten days ahead of the harvest.

Our particular group of Sigma Nus included a football tackle and a guard from Englewood High School in Chicago; two halfbacks from Evansville and one from Fortville: Gene Thomas who was a four-letter man at Indiana University. In 1926 he coached the Marion, Indiana, Giants to a High School State Basketball Championship and later wound up as President of a College in Michigan. There was also with us Frank Hanny, star end on the 1920 football team who scored a touchdown against Notre Dame in 1920 when they beat us 13 to 10 out at Washington Park in Indianapolis. Incidentally, Frank jarred the famous George Gipp so hard that the latter suffered a couple of broken ribs and never amounted to so much afterwards. I won $25.00 on the game, betting on odds.

Being short on money and long on appetite we thought up various schemes to eat. Some of the boys were musically inclined and had brought a few instruments along so they borrowed some more, organized a band, and gave a dance. The rest of us sold tickets and squired the native girls to the merry-making—thus combining business with pleasure.

Some of our athletes joined the local semi-pro baseball team and

113

played for $10.00 a Sunday, thereby losing their amateur standing. It was a good thing for them the Big Ten did not know it. Some of the rest of us toiled at "make work" public jobs, sweeping streets, mowing park grass, and so forth, at thirty cents (30¢) an hour paid by the City Chamber of Commerce which wanted to keep labor available. All in all, we fared well.

Finally, the harvest rolled north from Oklahoma and we became employed. I went eleven miles out in the country with a farmer named Ralph Hoar who had settled on the wide prairie out there, moving from Salem in Southern Indiana, not too far from my home in Wheatland. The pay was $7.00 a day, all you could eat, and a nice bed to sleep in. I had spent some years back home on a farm and was an old hand at harvesting and threshing bundle wheat. This however, was spring wheat and was not cut by a binder and bound in sheaves and shocked as at home. It was "headed."

The header was a machine with teeth and a conveyor belt which was pushed, not pulled, into the standing wheat, snipping off the heads and about six to ten inches of straw and throwing them into a big wagon that was driven along side. When full the wagon went to a site where two parallel stacks were being made, each about thirty feet long, eight feet wide, ten feet high, and about six feet apart. Here the heads were dumped out and trampled into a compact straw stack to await the steam threshing rig.

I drove one of the wagons for seven days and enjoyed it. The Kansas air was fresh and the meadow larks sang, and I ate hugely. I enjoyed watching the jack rabbits jump and run. They were new to me and I thought they looked like small donkeys.

The average yield of wheat in Kansas at that time was twelve bushels an acre, quite a surprise to me as the winter wheat we grew in Indiana averaged eighteen or twenty bushels per acre and we had one field back home that made thirty-three bushels an acre.

Well, I got through there and went back to town and got a job on a threshing outfit at the same rate of pay, $7.00 a day, board and room, only the room turned out this time to be a quilt in the hay mow of a big barn. The thresher had a 20-horsepower Case threshing engine, a separator machine run by a big belt from his engine, a water tank, and a cook shack. He carried his own crew, which included me, five other pitchers or forkeys, and a cook.

His separator was a big machine on four wheels that engulfed the wheat thrown into its maw, and spit the kernels down one pipe and the straw out another. He would back it up to the opening between two stacks, put on an extension conveyor belt running the length of the stacks, rig up his belt, give a toot of the engine and away we would start and continue without stopping until both stacks were gone.

There were three men on each stack. I was with two big Swedes, about 200 pounds each. I weighed about 130 and was five foot ten inches tall. I was light but wiry and tough. The two Swedes knew I was a tenderfoot, so they each took one end of the stack and left me the middle. They each managed to take down the ends, being careful to not get too close to the end to fall off. That was about all they did, so I found myself in charge of about one-half of the entire stack, and that first morning I almost killed myself trying to keep up. The wheat was matted and hard to get up and I was not heavy enough to break it loose by weight alone, so it was real wearing on me. I soon smarted up to where I insisted we rotate positions, but I was really too light for the work. I had threshed bundle wheat in Indiana, but this was the hardest work I ever did, or have done.

I'll say one thing, I got up a marvelous appetite. I could and did at noontime eat a pound of meat, big potatoes at two bites, and an onion as big as a hen's egg in a few chews. I slept soundly at night, lying up in the old barn with the other "hands," listening while the west wind which swept over the Kansas prairies all day and all night made the boards creak.

The first night I was about asleep when I smelt something dead under the hay. I finally said to my Swede friends, "Hey, there's a dead rat under this hay!" One of them lying close by said, "Aw now! That's shoost my feet. They always smell like dead rats when I take mine shoes off." I thought to myself, "You ought to sleep in your shoes," and I took my quilt and moved to the other end of the barn.

Well, I lasted four days and then it rained. We got in the barn and played poker—no limit. I had played a little catch-as-catch-can poker in the United States Navy in 1918 and when I worked with the boys the summer before laying steel on the B & O Railroad. I had refined my game a little at the Sigma Nu and other fraternity houses on week end nights at Bloomington, so I was silly enough to get in the game. I had my $49.00 on me, and never dreamed of losing it. Well, along after about half an hour, I was about even when the pot was opened for $5.00, the game being straight draw poker. I had the two black kings, so I stayed. I put in my $5.00 and three others stayed. I was first under the gun, so I said, "I'll take three" and I got them. I picked them up and saw two kings. I almost said, "Hey, I've picked up my discard," but didn't and then saw they were the two red kings. They got around to the dealer, who didn't draw any—just put down the deck. Well, the opener at my left checked (in those days we played "check the nuts" or you can raise after checking and not betting). This was before women got hold of the game and made deuces and what have you "wild." The engineer, who was the dealer, said, "I'll bet $10.00." Well, I thought I had him, and I got so excited the old stuff got up in my throat, and I said, "I'll raise you $10.00," only much to my horror, I heard my voice saying, "I'll call that," and then I had to throw in $10.00, and we spread our hands. He had a heart flush— not straight—and I won. He said, "Thanks, Boy, I would have gone as high as a Hundred Dollars more on this flush, I believe." I sure kicked myself, but I never told my good old Methodist father about this episode.

When I had left home my father advised me to stay away from whisky, wild women, and gambling with strangers. It was real good advice, and I sometimes wished I had followed it. He also advised against tobacco. Pop never had any of those bad habits, although he told me that once he had tasted beer in Jasper, Indiana, when he was a traveling man, and a prospective customer thrust it upon him. I believe this bothered him the rest of his days. If there ever was a Christian man, my father was one.

Well, it rained again the next day and again we couldn't thresh. I was happy because I was about all in. I had lost ten pounds I couldn't spare. The man was going to Larned for supplies and I said, "Well, I'll just go in, too. I'm quitting, because it's too hard for me," and so we parted the best of friends, he thinking how I had saved him $100.00, I guess.

I got back to our hotel and found some of the other boys there. They had had enough, as most of them didn't know the front end of a mule from the rear. In fact, we kidded Bud McCaw, all conference football guard from Chicago, when it was reported he tried to put the crupper on the harness into a mule's mouth instead of around its tail where it belonged.

I then went out and had a date with a young village siren I had met at our first dance and had a few dates with. She gave me a bit of news that upset me a little. She burst out crying and said, "You seduced me and I am pregnant." This was sure news to me in more ways than one, as I had never seduced her, although I will state that being young and vigorous just such a pleasing thought had crossed my mind several times when I was with her, as she was real shapely, though not so terribly pretty. In fact, I had no sex relations at all with her, seductive or otherwise, and I was sure, even then, that a person couldn't get pregnant otherwise. One of our gang did marry a local girl and stayed there permanently. I don't know if my girl friend knew of this and wanted to get married or was really pregnant by someone else. I never waited to find out. I went back to the hotel and rounded up the gang and said, "Well, you've been wanting to go bumming out to Colorado Springs, let's go right away!" One said, "Well, what changed your mind? I thought you were against it." I said, "Well, I've got a sudden yearning to climb Pike's Peak. My father walked up it in 1888 on the 4th of July, and he says it is a great experience." Anyhow, I never heard any more about my threatened fatherhood.

So we all sent our money and clothes home the next day and took off riding blind baggage on a Santa Fe passenger train, heading West. There were three or four of us. All I had was my dungarees, a red bandana handkerchief, one suit of underwear, two socks, two shoes, and a harvester's straw hat. I had them all on.

On the second morning we pulled into Kinsley, Kansas, just after daybreak. As the train stopped at the station we all jumped off (our usual routine) and ran out in a corn field across the tracks. There were thirteen of us debouched thusly. I don't know when or

117

where all the others got on. As per plans, when the train started up I ran out of the corn and jumped on the back of the engine tender, not noticing my buddies heads still sticking out of the corn, watching with horror as a Santa Fe Railroad "Bull" ran along side of me. He said, "Come on, Jack, get off," and I replied, "You go to Hell, I'm going to see Pike's Peak." I thought he was another hobo. He said, "I'll Pike's Peak you! I said Get off!" and he pulled a .45 revolver and waved it under my nose. I got off right now and he arrested me and put me under the town bandstand (which served as a jail) with some other worthies who were arrested, too.

After a while he came and let me out and asked my story and then said, "Well, you better go back East to College. You boys are traveling in mighty fast company. That crosseyed feller in there who was with you on the train is wanted in Texas for murder," and he let me go.

I soon found my buddies and they wanted to go on, but I had some doubts. There was a big long freight train standing on the side track headed East. It had two engines on it and just then the lead engineer blew the "high ball" to go—two longs and two shorts —and she began to roll out. All of a sudden I got powerful homesick and ran and jumped in an empty watermelon car with straw on the floor. I sat in the door and waved goodby to my college buddies until they faded away in the distance. I later learned they went out to Colorado and went up the mountain. It seems like I have always been a lone wolf and generally in the minority.

We rolled on across the prairies all day. I hadn't had anything to eat since breakfast the day before and powerful hungry. It was real nice lying there on the straw and watching the fields and farm houses and little towns slide by. In the afternoon I saw a pair of legs hanging over my door. When we stopped somewhere, the man came to see me. He was the brakeman, a real nice fellow. He, too, asked me what I was doing and I told him. He said I could ride on into Hutchinson, Kansas, but then I'd have to get off— there were too many bums—as he put it.

We got there about 5:00 P.M. and I hit a couple of back doors to get a hand-out, but my technique was faulty and I did no good. I just couldn't plain out ask for food, so at one place I asked if they needed their grass cut and at another if they needed any wood split for their fire place. I think both matrons thought I was slightly addled, as it was mid July and the grass was burnt up out there and fire places were not being used much, seeing the daily temperature was 95 or 100 degrees above zero.

Next, I went over to the Y.M.C.A. and asked to take a shower. I was hot and dirty and had cinders and dust in my hair. The man said it would be twenty-five cents. I told him I didn't have any money. He said, "Have you been a harvester? If so, you can shower for a dime." I said, "Brother, when you're broke a dime is as big as a quarter or a thousand dollars, so come on, that water is running in there and give me a shower." He refused, and I cancelled my subcription to the College Y.M.C.A. when I got back to the campus.

I decided then I had better go back to work, as everybody seemed adamant about money. I never had realized until then how it was to be starving and penniless, and I mean: No money at all. I went over to a restaurant by the railroad yards and asked the proprietor if he had any dishes he wanted washed or any work whereby I could get some food. He said, "Yeah, there's a lot of dirty dishes back there. You wash 'em and I'll feed you."

Then he looked at me and asked, "When did you eat last?" and I replied, "Yesterday morning." It was about 8:00 P.M. then. He said, "Hey, Gene, give this feller all he wants to eat and let him work afterwards." So I got a plate and took half of a chicken, then a lot of roast pork beside and made do with some other stuff and coffee and milk and pie. I can't remember ever eating so much at one time in all my life! I washed up a few dishes (there weren't many) wrapped two big doughnuts in my bandana and went over to the freight depot. There I got up on a baggage truck, rolled up my dungaree jacket for a pillow, put my hat over my eyes and slept like a log until the sun came up. I was covered with dew and also with cement dust which evidently had been left on the truck from some prior loading. I ate the doughnuts for breakfast. I felt real good. I have often thought since, while enduring insomnia in a nice bed, that perhaps I should be on that cement truck out in the dew and maybe I could sleep.

I asked someone where I could get a job and he directed me

119

to the Morton Salt Works there. They took me on as a laborer, loading block salt into box cars. My pay was $4.00 a day, and at night I slept in a straw stack of baled straw beside the plant. The company was unaware of this transaction. They used the straw to pad the salt blocks when I was not using it to sleep in. I would get on top of the stack and build a little cave out of the straw bales and sleep back in it snug and warm. I ate in the company cafeteria. I worked there six days and drew down $14.00, as the rest was deducted for food. I was the only English speaking worker except the boss. The others were Mexicans, and there in six days, I learned to like the Spanish language. I tried out my college Spanish on them and found it worked, although they often corrected my pronunciation. After that I made Spanish a hobby and for many years I have been able to read and speak it, though people have to speak very slowly if I am to hear it right.

I learned there that next to food and drink soap is the next best thing. I was getting pretty "gamey" by this time, rather dirty and smelly. I got about one-half cake of soap out of a rest room and went down to the Arkansas River which in winter carried huge floods but now a trickle of water three feet wide on a sandy bed. I took off all my clothes, took a bath, washed my hair, and washed all of my clothes, spread them on some bush willows to dry. I felt much better. When I got to Missouri, I borrowed a razor once a week and shaved.

I left there and went on East. I bought a ticket out of Kansas City, Missouri; as it was such a large city I did not know how to get through its railroad yards on the bum, and I was afraid I would get hurt. My destination was Lees Summit, Missouri, just east of Kansas City and right next to Independence, Missouri, home of President Harry S. Truman. I left on the midnight express and mail train of the Missouri, Pacific Railroad—a train of about fourteen cars with two big passenger engines pulling. I alighted at Lees Summit, a small town, and waited in the dark until the train started up, and made my run for the blind baggage and got on. However, the train men evidently had been watching, and they immediately stopped the train and shooed me off, then started up again. I seemed to have bad luck with passenger trains.

I was pretty stubborn in those days and ran and got on again, and I will say this : Those fellows stopped that big train again and the brakeman and conductor ran me up the street about one hundred fifty yards until they got out of wind and went back. I probably am one of the few hoboes who ever had so much honor and attention paid him by so many devoted men.

I took the hint, for I wasn't too dumb. After the last Pullman rolled by, I stood in the middle of the track and watched the three red tailights fade away in the distance while the steam engine whistle blew faintly for a road crossing miles away. Then all was silent as a tomb, and about as dark. Somewhere far off a dog howled, and I felt a little lonely and unloved, but I shook myself and looked for a place to sleep. I found a nice warm bed for the rest of the night in a box car on the siding, about half filled with new baled clover hay— any farm boy will tell you that new cut clover heats up nicely.

The next morning I had some breakfast at a little restaurant, and was sitting on the curb about 9:00 A.M. thinking up the day's program, if any, when a man drove up in his 1918 Ford and asked me if I wanted a job. I told him I wasn't sure I did, what kind of work and what did he pay?

He said, "Threshing wheat."

I inquired, "Bundle wheat or headed wheat? I've had enough of headed wheat," and he told me it was bundle wheat, that he would pay $5.00 a day with board and room for the rest of the summer. I made sure I didn't have to sleep in the barn, accepted the position, and away we went. I stayed with him six whole weeks to the day, and slept with his son, Guy Trimble, Jr., age 14, in a nice modern home. He was foreman of a 2,000 acre farm owned by an oil man named Thompson, of Kansas City, and his wife was a fine cook.

Well, threshing was in full swing, and he took me out to the site. There I was given a brand new pitch fork with a stout hickory handle, and assigned to a wagon with a local driver and team. We went out in the field, and I began to load. Now loading bundle wheat is child's play. The bundles weight eight to ten pounds and you just push over the shock and throw them up on the wagon one at a time.

About the third shock I pushed over, there was a huge rattle

121

snake exposed, blinking in the sun and all coiled up with his tail rattles, or buttons, going lickity-split and his tongue darting in and out. I never had seen a rattle snake before, nor heard one, but I had seen pictures of them, and knew they struck from a coiled position. Without any hesitation I swung one mighty blow with the fork from over my head, killing Mr. Snake and breaking the new hickory fork handle at one crack. He, or she, was six feet long, had seven rattles and a button of one on the end, was big around as my forearm, and was a beautiful diamond back specimen of upland rattler, a species of the pit viper and deadly poisonous.

I cut off his rattles, and then mopped my brow. I said to the local man who was driving the wagon, "My God, are there many of these around here?"

He replied, "Yeah, there's an old canyon over there about a mile away where there's thousands of snakes of all kinds," and added as a cheery after thought, "You better be keerful down there in them short weeds. Them rattlers generally go in pairs."

I said to him, "You get down here and pitch, and I'll load. I can load as pretty a load of wheat as you ever saw," but he wouldn't do it. I got the reserve fork from under the wagon, and we went on, me being mighty "keerful" indeed. I kept the rattles for some time as a trophy, but I do not now know what became of them.

I never saw any more rattlers there, except one dead one by an old stump, but I had one more snaky experience. Later in the summer, we were shocking oats that had been cut for two or three days, and as we went from one winrow to another, I picked up a stray bundle and was carrying it along when a big black bull snake stuck his head out of it right in my face. They are non-poisonous, but it startled me so, I let out a yell you could have heard for a mile and threw the bundle and Mr. Snake up in the air at least twenty feet. I sure was tired of snakes about then. I never did like them much, anyhow.

This farm was in the Jesse James country, and one of the old houses on it was the Cole Younger cabin, which Mr. Thompson had bought. Younger was one of Jesse's gang. The local fellow told me about it and then sang for my benefit part of the "Ballad of Jesse

James." All I can remember was a part which went something like this

> "Oh! the dirty little coward who shot Mr. Howard,
> Oh, he laid Jesse James in his grave.
> Poor Jesse had a wife who mourned him all her life
> And three children who were so brave.
> But that dirty little coward who shot Mr. Howard,
> Oh, he laid Jesse James in his grave."

Mr. Thompson had three or four Kentucky running horses, saddle horses, and five milk cows. He kept these five cows in a pasture of sixty or seventy acres, and every morning it was my job before breakfast to saddle a horse and drive up the cows and help the foreman milk the bossies. I was a pretty good rider, as back home on the Indiana farm I used to ride old Pete, our fine galloper, who was a "long loper." I would race around the pasture a while each morning on Mr. Thompson's running horse just for the thrill of it, with the morning breeze parting my hair. The horse liked it, too. One morning I became a jumper, involuntarily. I was running this horse at full gallop across a part of the pasture I hadn't been in, when all of a sudden my mount bunched up her feet some way, gave a might leap, and we soared over a dry ditch about fifteen feet wide and the same depth. Boy, after that we did our riding in known parts.

Summer fled. I never went to town that six weeks, just sent in a little money for chewing tobacco—plug tobacco, mostly "Star" or "Horseshoe." They had a rule against smoking around the barn or fields, so I quickly learned to satisfy my nicotine longing by "chewing." At that time I was smoking a pack of cigarettes or more a day. This chewing habit came in handy in later life when I would go fishing. I quit nicotine entirely in 1944.

Mr. Trimble gave me a check for $180.00 which I carried home with me. With the $77.00 I had sent home from Kansas I got back to Indiana University that fall with $257.00 cash and made it nicely through my Junior year with what I could borrow from the Wheatland Bank and earn by working at I.U.

123

Since then, once in a while across the many years, I have thought of the lonesome wail of that midnight mail train as it faded in the distance, leaving me standing in the night in a Missouri town where I didn't know one soul within 500 miles.

I never tried bumming again.

College High Jinks in the Roaring Twenties

To be young and healthy and in a Big Ten land grant college in the early 1920's—the "Roaring Twenties"—was quite a memorable experience. I was a freshman at Purdue in 1917, and after a year out for the Navy in 1918, to make the world safe for Democracy under President Wilson, I transferred to Indiana University at Bloomington in the fall of 1919 to study law.

It was the era of National Prohibition—a witches' brew—if there ever was one, with its bath tub gin, home brew beer and white mule bootleg whisky, the Charleston dance, the flapper with her mini-skirt hemline half way between her hips and her knees, which she painted with rouge; the coonskin coat, the Model T Ford, the Ku Klux Klan (which had its College Chapters), and a lot of other frills and fancies. In addition, the big colleges were small; Indiana University had 2,500 students where it now has 30,000, as an example.

College students had a large percentage of young World War I Veterans among them, most of whom were experienced in the ways and wiles of the world, including wine, women, and song, and they were two or three years older than the usual crowd of Freshmen and Sophmores—a rough and ready crew if there ever was one. Brother Vern Bell, an end on the football team, had been in the tank corp overseas. Bud McCaw and I had been in the Navy; Frank Hanny, another end, had been in Italy with the 332nd Infrantry; Bill Hill and Harold Hammond, of Hammond, Indiana, were army veterans, and Brother Ted Matthews had been in the Marines. There were others.

As might be expected, we had a lot of fun, engaged in lots of horseplay, and enjoyed life to the fullest. I can remember looking out my study room window at the Sigma Nu Fraternity House on 5th Street at the yellow harvest moon one evening and telling my roommate, "Boy, this is the life. I'll always remember this night." I was at peace with the world.

125

Before I get into the high jinks part of three years at old I.U., let me assure everyone, there was a lot of serious studying done. In the frat house we had compulsory study hall Sunday to Thursday inclusive for all freshmen, from 7:30 P.M. to 10:00 P.M. This was known as "quiet hours," and the study room was presided over by a Junior or Senior of serious mien with a paddle close at hand. Our professors and instructors were dedicated men and women, and none or very few were on research, as I remember. Even Dr. William Lowe Bryan, President of Indiana University in my time, at once an ascetic and a very human fellow, taught some classes in philosophy. We all knew him personally, some more and some less, as he mingled freely with the students, and now and then he would address the entire student body.

I remember on Saturday afternoon a great many of us were, seated in the old gymnasium listening to telegraph bulletins of our football game with Iowa—which had a fine team. We got beat 41 to 0, and "Prexy" Bryan was there, too, (he was a letter man in baseball in the 1880's at I.U.) and gave us a short talk. Among other things he told us that victory was not the only thing in the world and reminded us, that the Spartans at Thermopylae had won undying fame although they lost everything, including life.

"It's not whether you win or lose, but how you play the game," he said.

I do not know if that remark was original with him, but at the time I thought, "Jeez, our boys sure must have played the game terrible up there."

Being at a small college, about everybody knew a lot about everybody else, including "Prexy." When Dr. Bryan was married his name was William Bryan, but at the wedding he took his wife's maiden name of Lowe as his middle name. It was only fair, he said. It was also commonly reported, and widely belived, that "Prexy" and his wife had never consummated their marriage physically, that the good Doctor had stated that he had married a virgin and would not violate her body. Also it was reported that when he felt the pangs of love he would take an ice cold shower and thus subdue the Old Adam within himself. I do not know where our informants got their information, but I do know that Dr. Bryan was a gentle-

126

man, a fine scholar, and a good friend to thousands of I.U. students and a strict disciplinarian.

I helped get out the college paper, the Indiana Daily Student, along with Ernie Pyle, a later a noted War Correspondent; Charlie "Abe" Halleck, for 34 years Congressman from Indiana (and a Phi Beta Kappa); and some other budding journalists.

One day, unfortunately, a typographical error slipped into the paper, and the head line stated "Y.M.C.A. boys will be entertained by three trained hores and a dog." Doc Bryan got a final proof, rushed over in horror, stopped the press, and made us burn the whole edition.

Ah! Those good old innocent days, or prudish days, if you prefer! That was before this modern enlightened era wherein the College Kids of today with their beards get out the campus papers sprinkled with words describing the body functions of beast and man, or taking their Creator's name in vain. The campus troubles of today are spawned by their huge size. Students are faceless numbers in a cold, impersonal city of 30,000 strangers. Universities are suffering from Dinosauritis—uncontrollable growth.

Apropos of Ernie Pyle, he was a red-haired boy from Dana, Indiana, already starting to get bald, a lone wolf sort, and of a rather serious nature. He and President Bryan didn't see eye to eye about Ernie going with our baseball team on a tour of Japan in his senior year as a sort of war correspondent. Doc Bryan said "No," and meant it, and Ernie went, anyhow. When he got back Doc expelled him from the University, and he didn't get his sheepskin, as there was no Civil Liberties Union in those days to make College Presidents behave. I.U. was glad enough twenty years later to give him his degree, and now there is a magnificent hall of journalism on the campus proudly wearing the name of Ernie Pyle, the famed war correspondent. In 1960, I visited his grave in Punch Bowl Military Cemetery on Oahu, where he and 35,000 other American boys lie with the booming surf on the Pacific Ocean as their requiem.

In short, we had our serious side of life, and most students made their grades and passed into history as successful business men, doctors, politicians, attorneys, teacher, housewives, or what not. We even had five members from our house singing in the vested Choir of the First Methodist Church, and I can still remember such snatches as, "Here we sit by Babylon's wave, Where heathen hands have bound us, Far from Thee, Holy City, Far from Thee, Oh, Jerusalem," where I would come down hard on the bass.

When our classes had been attended, our studying done, and other amenities preserved, on weekends we would relax and cut loose a little, or a lot, as fancy and opportunity dictated.

One of the first functions to be attended to when school opened in September was to haze the freshmen as a whole and let them learn their place as inferiors in the collegiate world. Added to the woes of acute homesickness which invariably smote the Rhinies, this quite often was enough to completely unnerve some of the unfortunate wretches and cause them to reconsider a college career and take an early train home.

The Sophomores had a tradition of hair cutting for the newly-arrived freshies, the male ones, that is. Roving bands of Sophs armed with scissors and hand clippers would corner a newcomer and give him a hair cut. This generally was a complete job all over down to the roots. Sometimes however, an extra touch was provided in the case of a cherished hair do, say a fine curly head of hair, by clipping two swaths in the form of a cross, extending the entire length and breadth of the head and painting the shorn area with red or green paint. Sometimes Juniors and Seniors would join in the fun. We had one youth in our fraternity, one of those bubbling good-natured fellows who are born for disaster, who had his hair cut by the Sophs when he was a freshman, by the freshman when he was a Sophomore, and as a Junior the third time by an unidentified group.

After some days or weeks of this the Freshmen would begin to get smart and retaliate in kind on the Sophs, and as there were always some eager beaver leaders among the second-year men who went in for hair cutting in a big way, they were generally trapped somewhere and were sheared in revenge.

I can remember some of our Sigma Nu Sophs were in the forefront of this hair cutting one fall. We looked out one Saturday noon and the yard was filled with what looked like a lynchng party of some three or four hundred angry freshies, armed with scissors, shouting for several of us Sophomores. There were 16 of us in that class, twelve being war veterans, and most of us were in our house at the time. We all ran up in the dorm on the third floor which was accessible only by a narrow, steep stairs and an outside fire escape. We were armed with paddles and ball bats, and we repelled a charge up the stairs with some lusty head knocking. A big Rhinie led a line of others up the fire escape until he got about ten feet below where Brother Ted Matthews, of North Vernon, Indiana, was standing on the top platform of the fire escape tapping the railing with a heavy oak paddle. Ted who later was Circuit Court Judge at North Vernon, Indiana, had been a Lieutenant in the U. S. Maries overseas in the late war, and something about his demeanor caused the big freshie to stop.

"Go on up and get the bastards" the crowd down below yelled up to their leader. "Go on!"

He looked down at his buddies, took another look up, and called, "You can come on up here and get him yourselves, if you want him. I'm coming down!" Which he did.

St. Margaret's Episcopal Church was immediately across Grant Street from our house, and about this time big Ed Leonard, from Englewood High School in Chicago, a Sophomore, and a leader in hair clipping, was flushed out from a hiding place in the Church by some triumphant freshmen scouts who recognized him as an arch enemy who had helped scalp many a freshie. They set up a hue and cry, "Here's Leonard! He's one of them. Grab him." Ed stood not upon the order of his going but lit out in a dead lope up Kirkwood Avenue just ahead of a hundred boys in hot pursuit. Ed returned about supper time with all his hair, and said he had out ran all of them, though some lasted until beyond the cemetery at the west end of town. Maybe our cross-country coach should have signed him on. We sophs at the Sigma Nu House sort of let up on the hair business the rest of the autumn, as we could take a hint. Anyway, the open season on hair was about over for the year.

Freshmen were fair game for just about any jupe or hoax anybody could think up, and as most of them were just in new from the sticks and as green as grass, tney were easily fooled for a while. The Gentry Dog and Pony Show Circus wintered three miles below

Bloomington, our college town. One early fall day Big Bill Williams, from Evansville, a senior and later Juvenile Court Judge down there, came in about noon and said the elephants were having sexual intercourse (not his exact words) down at the circus headquarters, and by the graphic way he described the operation in all its interesting details and by stating the act would last for about one hour more, pretty soon there were some eleven curious freshmen running strung out in a line down to the grounds. It was all untrue, of course, and when the boys returned somewhat sheepishly later, they never heard the last of it. To this day the legend is enshrined in the annals of the Chapter, and the tale of how the hapless Rhinies ran three miles in vain to see elephants copulating is thought by old grads to be one of the best.

Another freshman, whom I shall denominate Sammy, (not his real name because he is one of my best friends and a highly successful business tycoon) was a somewhat credulous youth from a tiny southern Indiana town who, while fooling around the gymnasium, contracted a dandy case of "gym itch." This was a fungus skin ailment something like mange on a dog and is very painful and itchy. Unfortunately, it seats itself upon and around the victim's scrotum and between his legs, and causes a big red blotch and no end of trouble. The cure for it at the time was some sort of salve called "Blue Ointment" which I believe had a mercury base. This had to be smeared on the area, and when it began to burn a little, must be removed at once or it would scald the skin severely. Poor Sammy consulted some of our athletes, of which we had about twenty in the Chapter, and they told him they would cure him after dinner. Accordingly, late in the evening they got the trusting youth up in the northeast room, had him undress, except for a red "I" sweater somebody gave him for warmth, had him lie down on an old rain coat on his back and spread out his legs while a couple of artists copiously painted his scrotum, etc., with the blue ointment. When it began to burn, they assured him the cure was working nicely and told him to stand the pain and he would be cured. There must have been twenty-five of us in the room pretending to assist unfortunate Sammy, and despite his moans and lamentations, he was talked into leaving it on much too long. Finally, after he could stand it no more, he broke

130

from his captors and demanded a doctor. After some more delay a phone book was located and Sammy called the fraternity physician, Dr. Harris, a good-hearted man, but prone to swear on occasion. Old Doc's wife got him out of bed and Sammy gasped out, "Doc, you've got to come out here quick! I'm dying! I'm dying!"

"What's wrong? What's the matter?" asked the Doctor in alarm.

"Oh, I've got the gym itch and ——" but Sammy never got to finish.

"Well, damn it to Hell," bellowed the crusty doctor, "What do you mean getting me out of bed at midnight to tell me you are dying from gym itch? Just get some blue ointment and spread it on your balls and you'll be O.K. Now, Goodby!" and bang went the receiver.

More blue ointment was the last thing Sammy wanted or needed. He managed to scrape off most of the salve and to survive, but was powerful sore for quite a while. I will state that when his skin grew back the gym itch was indeed entirely gone.

Some one invented a game for the pledges called "Hot Hand." A cushion would be placed on a table and the freshman invited or ordered to bend over and hide his face in it; then some Sophomore would deal him a lusty crack with a paddle. By guessing what was hot, he was released.

"What's hot?" would be asked of the butt of the fun.

I remember we had a big freshman who had to play this game, and he answered "Fire."

"Nope! Give him another!" and the same question.

"Electricity," answered the victim.

"Wrong, once more! Think harder!" and bang.

"Steam!" bellowed the youth, who by this time should have guessed what was hot, to-wit, his rear.

"Once more! What's Hot?" and bang.

"Mary Jones!" yelled the freshman in desperation, naming a "college widow" who was pretty popular with the fast boys. A "college widow" was a type of town girl who had graduated and never married, but who continued to date oncoming generations. This was thought to be such a comical answer that the freshman was excused without further ordeal.

131

Freshmen sometimes took revenge on their tormentors. Once they gave twelve of us Sophomores some croton oil. Eight of us were football players, and we other four stayed out to watch the practice, so we had a late dinner. There were three of our freshies who worked as waiters, and they put a drop or two of croton oil on the point of each slab of apple pie we had for dessert. We all ate our pie except one, who smelt the oil and said "This pie is rancid." Bud McCaw, all-Conference guard and later a radio broadcaster, who had a tremendous appetite, said, "Let me have it, it's all right." So he had a double dose, and had to have Old Doc Harris called in. Shortly after eating all the toilet seats in the house were in full use, and the back yard had a half a dozen more woe begone Sophomores behind as many rose bushes. The pains did not strike Ed Leonard, the football tackle above mentioned, who was for many years an executive with Pittsburgh Plate Glass Company, until he had gotten into a borrowed formal dress suit and went over to the Alpha O. sorority house to a dance. Croton oil causes one to have continuing bearing down pains for quite a while, as I can testify, and poor Ed got on one of the girl's toilet stools in a half bath room and couldn't be pried off for nearly an hour, much to the dismay of different damsels who would open the door unwittingly.

Speaking of croton oil, a couple of years later some collegiate half-wits dumped a lot of it in the punch at the Blanket Hop, a formal dance held once a year in the gymnasium to finance "I" blankets for letter men. Ere long the same sudden dire pain struck beauty and chivalry alike, and some of the unfortunates never made it off the floor. It sure broke up a dance.

Most of us, especially the returned veterans, thought life was a pretty nice outing after barracks or battlefield and were not averse to "looking upon the wine when it was red" as the Prophet said 3,000 years ago in Holy Writ. We would also "look upon the mule when it was white"—the common name of bootleg whisky being "White Mule." This was in the early days of the "Noble Experiment"— National Prohibition.

People also brewed "Home Brew Beer." Dr. Lyons, head of chemisty department, was asked by a colleague to analyze some of his brew and the good Doctor was said to have reported, "I'm sorry to say, your horse has diabetes." Doc was rich from a baking power he invented.

Such bootleg whisky generally sold for about $8.00 a quart and due to a large percentage of fusel oil and high alcoholic content, it was liquid lightening. Too much fusel oil would make you deathly sick. Once eight of us bought a quart, and after drinking a swig, right away it would come up. I remember walking around the back yard saying, "By George, I'm not going to throw this up. It cost me a dollar." But I did. Probably saved my eye sight, as a lot of people went blind from bad mule.

Not all white mule was bad; in fact, some was pretty good, and a person could get up quite a glow. We had an annex to our house, four upstairs bedrooms which we rented in a house about a block away. One Saturday night I was at the Book Nook, a college soft drink emporium and eatery run by Nick the Greek, and in company with some kindred spirits we toasted our football team and about everything else we could think of. Shortly before midnight I departed for the annex, where I was to spend the night. I was a little woozy and somewhat unsure of directions but I made it upstairs okay, pulled off my shoes and pants and went to bed. The next morning, Sunday, I woke up about 6:00 A.M. in a strange bedroom, not in the annex at all. I got on my clothes, tiptoed down the stairs and out the door, and saw I was in the house next door to our annex. I have often wondered what the good lady of the house must have thought when she found someone had slept in her front bedroom. Thank God, they did away with Prohibition in 1933, and since then I have been a man of measured merriment. No more White Mule!

I suppose a lot of young fellows, college and non-college, experiment with the Demon John Barleycorn, and it is only by the grace of God, as Franklin said, that social drinkers don't become bums on skid row.

Another time the freshies took some revenge on our guard, Bud McCaw. Like all 20-year old athletes he had a huge appetite. Along about 10:00 P.M. Bud would tour the rooms looking for food, like if some Mother had sent a cake and son had not eaten it all and was careless in hiding it. A pre-medic got some menthol blue tablets at school, and the lads inserted some in three chocolate caramels, which

133

they left in the candy box in a drawer. Bud easily discovered and ate them all. Now this menthol blue has only one function as far as I know. It will turn your urine a brilliant robin-egg blue or green.

The next morning Brother McCaw stalked out of the dorm and into the head and in a moment the house was filled with his reverberating screams for his buddy Ed. He was urinating a beautiful green stream much to his unbelieving horror, not an unnatural emotion in anyone, I suspect, under like circumstances.

"Ed! Ed! Come quick! My God! I've got the clap, or syph or something! Oh, I just knew I never should have diddled that professor's daughter (not his exact word for it), and I used two rubbers at once, too. What'll I do?" Such a performance, plus the unexpected public confession, caused unbounded joy to the jokers who were lurking nearby and to the rest of us, too, when we hurried up and found out what was going on.

We had a house rule that anyone who brought liquor in the house would be fined $5.00, and if you came in drunk you were fined $1.00. The brothers would hide their stuff in the basement or in a small bottle in a pocket. There were some violations, of course.

In my Senior year I was elected President of the Chapter, or Commander as it was known, Sigma Nu having been founded at Virginia Military Institute. In the fall I had the honor of bestowing a pledge pin upon a rotund Sophomore who had done his freshman year at Illinois, where he had gone unpledged, whether by choice or necessity I do not know. Anyway we were glad to have him, as he was a cheerful fellow, and his father was a banker. The new pledge's name was Herman B Wells—no period after the "B." Hermie was a "brain," a quiet, deliberate sort of fellow, a good student, wise in counsel, and later he became President of Indiana University and National Regent of Sigma Nu's 125 Chapters.

At the time Hermie was quite the "College Joe." He had a huge raccoon skin coat, (it took a big one to fit over him) a flat hat, and other garb we wore in the early twenties, and drove a roadster, so he was plenty popular. He never broke the rules, so about twice a month I gave him a good solid crack with a paddle just to remind him he was a lowly pledge. Hermie was a little tender in the spot and would wince some, but he bore his ordeal with fortitude.

134

Along toward Christmas Hermie approached me and said, "Mr. Niblack, the fraternity has been so nice to me and the other pledges we'd like to give a nice party for everyone. We'll have cheeses, meats, near beer, punch and about everything you want, some Saturday night." After consulting some of the other elders of the Chapter, I granted pledge Wells his wish, and the Saturday night party was flung.

It was quite a success indeed, and I mean a howling success. In some manner Hermie and his crew got hold of two or three gallons of medical alcohol, mixed up a small tub of punch with it, and the fling-ding was on. It was the first and last time I ever saw forty men and boys tearing up a fraternity house. Our athletes roared and bellered, wrestled, upset the piano, tore the banisters off the stairs; someone threw a brass cuspidor from the den through a big window, and several members tossed their cookies in untoward spots. Even the Commander was about half-stewed. I'll say this, when Hermie saw how things were warming up, he and a couple other pledges faded away early into the night.

The next Monday night in our regular stated meeting, I announced that every man in the Chapter, including pledges and myself were each fined $5.00, and it was made a matter of record in our minutes in case the National Grand Regent or High Council of Sigma Nu got wind of the doings. Later, I verbally, and privately, instructed the treasurer to not put the fine in his monthly statement to the boys as I was a little hard up financially, and I thought some of the others were, too. That was the first fine I ever suspended. Neither President Bryan or National Headquarters ever raised any stink about it, the main reason being they never found out about it.

One item of freshman revenge happened when the pledges put some "Cow Itch" in the crotch of Brother Cecil Craig's pajamas. This was a chemical powder which caused intense itching and discomfort for some hours, especially if it got into crevices or close places. Cecil, called "Cocky" for short, was from Otwell in Southern Indiana and a third cousin of mine. He was awarded a Phi Beta Kappa key in mathematics and ended up as a noted Professor at Michigan University. Each study room or living room had a hand lavatory in it, and the last I saw of Cocky that evening before I went

135

to the dorm he was sitting naked up in the lavatory fratically splashing cold water on his affected areas. He had been there for an hour or so. Cocky later figured out that it was Big McCarthy, a pledge from Liberty, Indiana who had done him wrong, and the next night dumped three gallons of water into the unsuspecting fellow's mouth and face as he lay snoring on his back with his mouth wide open, nearly strangling McCarthy. Cecil got the wrong culprit at that, as it was Big Mac's cousin, Little Mac, later a prominent lawyer over in southeastern Indiana, who did it.

As I said, Craig got his Phi Beta Kappa key in mathematics; Brother Hiram Stonecipher, later president of the Union Title Abstract Company in Indianapolis, got his in Latin, and Brother Frank Whelcher earned his in chemistry, while I merely got mine in English and History. I always put my key away when around those three. As a matter of fact, I haven't seen my key for years. I early found out that with the key and a nickel you could get a cup of coffee most any place.

I will now describe how, in my Junior year at I.U., I slipped from the straight and narrow path a little, though at the time it didn't bother me any. There was a fellow around Bloomington who was not quite all there in the upper story, but he had a little money. His name was Deb, and he loved to play poker with the fraternity boys. He was a good player and would bring in a little drinking white mule to share with us as an inducement to let him join in. One Thanksgiving eve we had a little two-bit limit poker game at the house, as about everyone except me and a few others had gone home for the holiday. Deb came down, and we had a nice evening, except that I had $18.00 to use the next day in catching the early Monon down train for my father's home in Wheatland, in southern Indiana, and by a series of bad plays, and bad luck, I lost $17.25 of my kitty. Perforce, I spent a quiet Thanksgiving weekend in Bloomington with some of our athletes who lived far off, such as McCaw, Leonard, Frank Hanny, and a few others.

We had a pretty good time. Ed and Bud had a two-burner gas stove in the basement, and they had rigged up a little still out of some copper tubing and what not, and they distilled some "mule" out of some raisin mash they had been making in secret for some time with sugar purloined from the commissary. However, eating was our main problem.

We solved this by chipping in what we had and bought some canned goods, and Thanksgiving night we went up the alley just back of the First Methodist Church where I and a couple of brothers sang in the choir, and under my expert supervision, we lifted a Plymouth Rock rooster and three hens off their roost, so we had stewed chicken a plenty until the boys got back, though I will say the old rooster was powerful tough. There is an art to stealing chickens which I learned while in High School in our little country town. You pick out a place where there is no watch dog, and in the dark you very quietly go in the hen house, feel up along a chicken until you can squeeze his throat and shut off all noise. He will flop, of course, but other chickens think somebody is just falling off the roost. When you feel along a chicken in the dark, he believes it is another fowl crowding him a little, and may cluck a mild protest but won't squawk. Down home stealing watermelons or an occasional chicken for a chicken roast by boys was thought to be fun rather than larceny, at least by the gang. I might add that this was the last time I ever did any stealing.

One other time my poker playing, which I had learned one summer while laying steel on the B & O Railroad before I went into the Navy, got me in a little trouble at I.U.

We usually played on weekends, but one Wednesday night I got into a game at the Acacia Fraternity house sponsored by Ed Harris, who later was a wealthy real estate man and attorney in St. Petersburg, Florida. It lasted all night, until 7:00 A.M. I went home, drank two cups of coffee, washed and shaved and went to an 8:00 o'clock exam in American History under a grand old Professor, James Woodburn, who wore a snow white beard and was head of the History Department. I was perfectly fmiliar with American History as I had taught it two years in country grade schools, however I was so tired and sleepy I couldn't stay awake, let alone remember. I turned in my blue book and went home and slept. Later Professor Woodburn called me to his office and said, "Mr. Niblack, I am astounded that you flunked this test. What in the world happened? Why, look here how you left sentences half finished, and how some trail over two or three lines. I know you know this history."

I confessed all then and there, and you know what that kindly old man did? He tore up my exam paper and gave me another test a little later. I finished with "A+" in his course, which was as high as they went.

All my grades at I.U. were "superior," that is "A" or "B," except one three-hour class in advertising, presided over by a bald-headed instructor called "Sis" Bolser by us students, though not to his face. Sis took a dislike to me for some reason, probably because of my cocky attiude or know-it-all air which I sometimes had. Leonard and McCaw were in the class, and always sandwiched me in between them on the back row where their activities would not be so notorious. For example, on one written examination I was looking at the ceiling trying to think up a right answer, while both brothers waited expectantly with poised pencils, ready to copy my answer.

Finally McCaw whispered, "Come on, Nibby, get your answer down. We can't wait here all day." The sequel to all of this was I got three hours C+ credit, while my brothers, Ed and Bud, each made an "A." Sis was proud to have distinguished athletes in his class.

I must explain why we had so many athletes, and good ones, in our Chapter. In 1916 old I.U. was the football door mat of the Big Ten and Brother George Cook, a farm boy from Wheatland, Indiana, a wealthy alumnus of our Chapter and I.U. class of '96, and a former Grand Regent of Sigma Nu, decided to something about it. He recruited some twenty-five sterling players from northern Indiana and the Chicago area and sent them down. Our Chapter pledged about twelve, and gave the other fraternities the others, including Babe Pierce, our sterling center, who later was the first Tarzan of the movies. We soon attracted athletes of other sports. Cook had also caused "Jumbo" Stiehm, a famous Nebraska University coach, to come to I.U. as football coach. Stiehm used a board, or paddle, in practice to make linemen charge quickly. He was especially fond of smacking Brother Ed Leonard, our big Swede tackle from Chicago, on the rear as he hollered "charge." He thought Ed was a little lazy in practice.

Brother Cook also arranged for I.U. to go to Boston to play Harvard, then basking in its glory as the football power of the Gay Nineties and later. We all went over in a special Pullman hooked on the rear of the train. I say "we," because I went along as special non-paying guest of the team captain, full-back and punter, my roommate, Johnny Kyle of Gary, for many years after graduation the coach of Froebel High School up there. Two or three other non-athletes went, too. We would hide under the seats whenever the Pullman Conductor came in, which was twice a day. There is about a foot clearance under there, and the players would spread an overcoat over me and play cards on it during inspection. I sure couldn't get under Pullman seats nowadays, even if they had Pullmans. I weighed 129½ pounds at the time—pretty skinny.

This coach was a weirdo. He was a thinker and planner, but on this trip he out-thought himself and everyone else except Harvard. He told Kyle, "You will punt on the first down every time we get the ball the first half, while I study their play and find our their weakness." I doubt if ever there was a sillier football game played in the United States. I.U. never ran one play the entire first half, and while Jumbo was alerting himself on Harvard's frailties, they made three touchdowns and, of course, we had no points. It turned out their only weakness was inability to kick points on conversion, and they led 18 to 0 at intermission. It came on a big rain for the second half, and there was no more scoring, although we did a lot less punting.

In this connection, little Centre College of Kentucky, led by the famous Bo McMillin, later our most successful coach until John Pont and also coach of the pro Detroit Lions, came to play us in the fall of 1919. It was a rainy, drizzly day and old Jordan field was muddy. We led 3 to 0 until the fourth quarter by virtue of a drop kick field goal by Chick Mathias, our quarter back. In those days the football was rounder and drop kicks were easily made by an expert. Andy Gill, a Sigma Nu, made one of 55 yards in 1910 against Illinois.

Early in the fourth quarter the players' uniforms were heavy with mud and water. McMillin, their quarterback, called time out when Centre got the ball, went to the side lines and shucked off his football togs, revealing a tracksuit. He put on running shoes and on the next play danced away from our boys for a 60-yard touchdown. He did it again as soon as Centre got the ball again, and we lost 12 to 3. The irony of it was that Bo had come to I.U. in 1916 and asked Coach Stiehm for a grant-in-aid and wanted to play for I.U. Stiehm said he was too little. Bo later led his team to a 6 to 0 victory over Harvard, champions of the East.

Our athletes were on a subsidy plan whereby Cook and some others paid their room and board through the office of a local stone quarry company. It was a little sub rosa, I am afraid, but I am confident the statute of limitations has now run. Anyway, Michigan and Chicago and the other Western Conference powers did the same, I believe, although by this time they had cleaned it up and would not allow a good athlete from off somewhere to matriculate and play another four years under a different name, as was done in the 1880's and Gay Nineties.

The fund gave out suddenly when the depression of 1920 and '21 struck, and our Chapter got way behind on its mortgage. I was Treasurer that year, and made repeated trips down town to the Stone Company to no avail. Finally, we adopted a rule of "No pay on house bills, no eat." This I enforced with a ball bat by standing at the head of the stairs that led down to our basement dining room, physically separating the sheep from the goats. I never had to strike anyone, though I had a shouting match with Brother McCaw who was a hot-tempered Irishman and always hungry.

There were many other interesting things that happened while I was down there in the Roaring Twenties, but the above are some fair samples.

I will close by citing some of our college songs. We had a Sigma Nu song which we had inherited from our Chapter of the Gay Nineties, that set forth a lot of our ideas at the time—and may do so for the present generation:

"Bring out the old Golden Goblet
"With Sigma Nu upon it,
"And we'll open up another keg of beer.
For we all came to college
"But we didn't come for knowledge,
"So let's raise Hell while we're here!"

We had another song which expressed our joys and appreciation of a four year college career, free from responsibility and care. It went:

"Eenie Meenie Minie Moe
"So sings the heathen Chinee,
"Eins Zwei Drei Vier
"We'll be back next year,
"Oh, College Days, we'll sing your praise,
"One, two, three, four."

Newspaper Reporter

Times were hard in 1922 when I got my A.B. from Indiana University, as the Midwest farm depression was in full flower. I owed a lot of money I had borrowed to go to college. I was on a crutch from left leg badly burnt by boiling coffee at the Senior picnic, and I needed some eating money.

The venerable Thomas Adams, editor of the Vincennes, Indiana, Commercial, a Republican daily paper, offered me a job at $18.00 a week as reporter, because my grandfather Niblack had helped him start the paper back in the 1880's. It was the only job I could get, even with a cum laude sheepskin. Two years before I had gotten $7.00 a day and board and room on a wheat farm in Kansas and nobody even asked me if I had passed the third grade. Mr. Adams would not have given me this job if he had known my grandmother McClure was a Purcell, cousin of the elderly Royal Purcell, editor of the Democratic Vincennes Sun. They were bitter enemies.

After a few weeks in Vincennes, the Indianapolis Times offered me a job. They had gotten my name from the I.U. School of Journalism, where I had worked up to be Tuesday night editor on the Indiana Daily Student, the college newspaper. Scripps-Howard had just bought the Times and were hiring a bunch of college graduates to pump some new life into it. The managing editor of the Times was Mr. "Ungh-Ungh" Peters, a name the reporters gave him from a habit he had of grunting while talking.

I was pretty canny with Peters about my starting salary. He asked me what I was making at Vincennes, and my Methodist conscience has always hurt me a little, as I lied grievously. I said, "Twenty-five Dollars a week."

He wanted to know if I could live on that for a while and I was wary. I said, "How long? I owe $1750. debt from college, and it carries eight percent interest."

"Oh, till you make good," brother Peters replied.

"Well, how will I know when I make good?" I persisted.

"I suppose if you are not fired, Ungh! Ungh!, you may assume you have made good," he said.

I went to work at the Times on Meridian Street across from L. S. Ayres. The City Editor was Felix Bruner, a kindly, rotund fellow in his early 30's. He gave me a desk on which was an Oliver typewriter so old it looked like Horace Greeley might have used it in the Civil War. The third day I was there, Felix had Freddie, the dramatic and music critic, take me over to the Court House and introduce me around as the new Court House reporter for the Indianapolis Times. Freddie, who sang tenor and had long eye-lashes, had previously doubled as Court House man. He lived by himself in a nice apartment and was an excellent cook, occasionally throwing a big meal for a lot of us reporters.

I was a little dubious about my ability to cover a metropolitan beat such as that, and my confidence was not increased when I met the Honorable James A. Collins, presiding genius of Criminal Court, later a good friend and golfing companion of mine. Jim was the Boston-born son of English immigrants and he had come to Indiana in the '90's because of a disappointment in love back East. He had a red moustache and a crusty temper.

"So you will be the new Times reporter, huh?" he snorted. "Well, you better stay out of Criminal Court. I just recently sentenced Kilgallen, the City Editor of the Times, to ten days in jail for lying about me, and I don't want to see anybody from that dirty rag even coming in here."

I later learned that Kilgallen, the father of Dorothy Kilgallen, the late columnist, never waited to serve his term, but immediaely took off for Mexico City where he got a new job.

This was a fine introduction to a new job, and for a few days I stayed out of Criminal Court, until I mustered up courage and went in every day to the clerk's desk to see what was going on. I soon made myself at home in there and eventually got acquainted with Judge Collins, though he wouldn't let me come in his chambers nor give me any news. This annoyed me no end as my rival reporter from the Indianapolis News, Wayne Guthrie, had a key to the chambers and back door of the Court, and "scooped" me all the time. "Scoop" was a dirty word in the newspaper world. It meant that when one paper printed a story first, and without fail, the scoopee reporter heard a few salty words from his City Editor.

Wayne, who still writes a column on the News, was one of the most thorough and hard working reporters I ever knew. Unlike many of his colleages of the "Roaring Twenties," he didn't drink or swear, but he was a whiz at finding the news. Judge Collins would give him the Grand Jury reports and other news in advance and freeze me out.

This lasted until October, when one day I was in the Court idly listening to appeals from Police Court. There were 16 such appeals from bootlegging convictions, and I suddenly realized the State was losing nearly all, in one way or another. Some were dismissed because the witnesses didn't show up, a very common thing on appeals, as it was a practice of Police Court lawyers to get repeated postponements until witnesses would refuse to come to court any more. Two defendants were found not guilty because they were represented by Attorney Ira Holmes, the Republican County Election Commissioner, and Judge Collins was up for re-election in the next month on that party's ticket. No search warrant or faulty ones let some more guilty birds fly the coop; and two were thrown out because the liquid evidence had disappeared during the long wait on appeal.

I made careful notes and wrote the story. The headline the next day stated "Judge Collins convicts only one of sixteen bootleggers." I hung around the Court after lunch, and sure enough, here came E. S. Shumaker, State Superintendent of the Anti-Saloon League, and a mighty power to be feared in politics, as all good church people and tee-totalers received recommendations before each primary and fall election about what candidate was "wet" and who was "dry," as far as the Demon Rum was concerned, and the folks voted accordingly. Between the Ku Klux Klan and the Indiana Anti-Saloon League, many a politician developed ulcers and gray hairs in the early days of the 1920's.

Accompanied by the League attorney, Mr. Jesse Miles, Superintendent Shumaker went with Judge Collins into his chambers and the door was closed. Pretty soon I heard loud voices and table pounding from within, and then here came Judge Collins bursting out of his room, as the visitors left by the rear door. He spied me. "Johnny, what in the Hell are you doing to me?" he asked in a plaintive tone, his face red as a beet. "What do you mean, what am I doing?" I replied innocently. "Come in here," he said, and took me in his office for the first time I was ever there, and pointed to the Times lying on his desk where the minions of the W.C.T.U. had left it. "Now Johnny, this kind of stuff is going to beat me in November. It ain't right! Do you know what that fat-hipped old bastard Shumaker did? He threatened to blacklist me next week in all his bulletins to all the churches in this————town. What am I going to do? Why are you crucifying me?"

"Judge, let's call a truce. You quit scooping me all the time, and I'll lay off of you. Just treat me like Guthrie," I said.

Judge and I thereupon shook hands and he gave me a key to his back door, and we never had any more trouble. It was sort of unfair to the old boy at that, as in fifty percent of the appeals there was no search warrant, or somebody had drunk the evidence while the case lay in Court. Also, the Judge wasn't responsible for witnesses taking a powder under duress or for remuneration. The story was technically correct, however.

We had to report to the City Room at 7:00 A.M. and at noon, then back to the beat and we were free at 5;00 P.M., when the offices closed. I only had to work one-half day on Saturday, as the Courts shut up at noon.

Life was a lot simpler in Indianapolis in the early Twenties. I soon bought a second hand Model T Ford with some money loaned me by a young widow lady friend and kept it in the alley beside my rooming house on 16th Street. I drove it to work and then to the Courthouse, back and forth at noon and home at night as parking places were plentiful downtown. One time, however, going back after noon from the office, I had to double park and run in to cover a trial. I forgot about my Ford, and went home on the street car. The next morning there was my auto standing out in Alabama Street all by itself, not even a car between it and the curb.

There were wooden paving blocks on Meridian Street south of 16th Street, which was lined with large Elm trees and family residences from 14th Street north. In fact, Blythe Q. and Tommy Hendricks, two reporters, grand nephews of United States Senator Thomas Hendricks, lived at 1127 N. Meridian, and I had Thanksgiving dinner with them and their hospitable mother in 1922.

These paving blocks in wet weather would get slick as ice, from oil or tar in them, I suppose, and sometimes I could come up at a pretty good clip in the old coupe, turn the front wheels and slap on the brake, whereupon we would go into a spin and whirl around three or four times. Of course, you had to make sure no other traffic was around, but then traffic was usually very light, and the police didn't care. Anyhow, they were all on walking beats then.

Other new reporters were Alec "Spaz" Tolle and Dudley Smith from Indiana University, and Lee Miller and Don Hogate from DePauw. I found out from them that Peters started their salaries at whatever they said. Miller, later a big shot with Scripps-Howard in the East, came from the Kokomo Tribune, where he was getting $30.00 a week, but he started at $50.00 because he was a bigger liar than I, or maybe a little smarter.

Hogate and I became fast friends, and we roomed together at Mrs. Price's emporium at 22 West 16th Street, a genteel rooming house for gentlemen and ladies. Don was a brother of Casey Hogate who was a founding father of Sigma Delta Chi, the newsman's honorary college fraternity, and later Editor of the Wall Street Journal. They were from Danville, Indiana, where their father ran a paper. Don eventually made a fortune in advertising in the East, as did Don Hoover, whom I followed on the Courthouse beat. Hoover became president of Bozell and Jacobs in New York City.

When I went to work on the Times, some of my fellow reporters were Eugene Jepson Cadou, Sr., who became the "Dean of Political Writers," and stayed in harness until his death in 1969; William Lowell "Tubby" Toms, many years editor of "The Great Outdoors" column on the Indianapolis News; Walter Shead, later a Democratic politician; Blythe Q. Hendricks; Heze Clark, old time police reporter and wrestling coach, and Volney Fowler, City Hall reporter, soon promoted to City Editor.

Other newspaper reporters on the News were Tommy Hendricks, Blythe's brother; Walter "Watty" Watson, famed City Hall reporter, a graduate of Wabash College; Wayne Guthrie, Courthouse reporter; Bill Herschell, author of "Ain't God Good to Indiana;" C. Walter "Micky" McCarty, a police reporter; Kin Hubbard, editor of Abe Martin; and Leo Litz, a big country boy from Smithville, Indiana, a Navy veteran who later covered the atom bomb explosion in the Pacific. We were all brothers in the bond, though competitors for news. Litz, McCarty, Hubbard, and I had a golf foursome that played at Pleasant Run, near the Hubbard and Litz homes. The course occasionally sprouted white button mushrooms, and Kin loved to pick them and put them in his golf bag. One day he announced he had played the eighth hole in "seven strokes and nineteen mushrooms." It was a par four hole.

"Jep" Cadou was a character, as were most reporters. They were cynical and believed that eighty-five percent of public officials were crooked, or would be if properly tempted. There was no hero worship. Jep had attended Indiana University with Paul V. McNutt, a Governor of Indiana and later United States Commissioner over the Phillipines. Paul was a natty dresser, and always felt the importance of his office. When he returned from the Phillipines, he held a very dignified press conference in the Athletic Club, receiving the boys in his semi-formal outfit—dignified that is until Jep asked the first question:

"Hi, Paul! Is it true what they say about Chinese women?"

McNutt glared a second, then broke out laughing and replied, "How in the Hell would I know, Jep?" Whereupon everyone had a drink and things went off real well on an informal basis.

Horace Coats, of the Indianapolis Star, and Maurice Early, of the same paper, were co-founders of the Indianapolis Press Club in 1934, along with Cadou and some others. The locale was in the basement of Mike Hanrahan's Saloon in the first block of North Pennsylvania Street. It was a beer-drinking, poker-playing outfit, twenty-five cent limit. I was not a charter member, but joined in a few months as a "B" member (ex-newspaper man). After a while we moved up over the Pretzel Bell, a saloon on North Illinois Street, then to the Canary Cottage and eventually to the I.S.T.A. Building, where it is now. Many "C" members, business people, have since been admitted, and now if you were to toss your cookies on the floor

147

or start a poker game over there, you would be expelled immediately.

Our poker game was something else again—every Monday night and Saturday afternoon. Straight poker was automatically barred, and if you could think up a new game, like all aces wild, it would be named after the inventor. Walter Greenough, a Vice-president of the Fletcher Bank and former Star City Editor, was the presiding genius of the game and made all rules and cut each pot a quarter for the Club.

We also supported the Club by the one-armed bandit slot machines (common then to private clubs) until a member got under the influence and squandered his pay check one Saturday therein, whereupon the Board of Directors voted to return his money and abolished the slots. Anyhow, the late Mayor Al Feeney and I, as Police Judge, felt a little squeamish about playing poker in the presence of the machines and had been urging their removal.

Our poker game was discontinued many years ago, or rather, degenerated into a rubber bridge game at one-fifth cent a point. Cadou, Jimmy Doss, ex-City Editor of the Indianapolis Times; the Reverend Howard Lytle, of the Goodwill Industries; Tom Batchelor, Deputy Attorney General; Lee Whitehall, Attica, Indiana, attorney and former Grand Master of the Indiana Masons; and myself kept the game alive until younger generations took over, a far cry from the boisterous old poker game.

We had square dances and lots of things at the Club. We even put in a bar at the Canary Cottage. A wife saw it and remarked, "It won't work! No newspaper man ever bought himself a drink, let alone anyone else." That was cured soon by taking in "C" members. One time, Clark Gable, the movie star, came up for dinner, and during the evening had recourse to the men's room. Cadou had a large sign printed which he stuck on the wall, reading: "Clark Gable Urinated Here! This stall is not for common people!" (Urinated was not the exact word, but it will do.)

Newspaper reporters, just after World War I and during the "Noble Experiment" of National Prohibition were a wild and wooly bunch in the United States. The stage play "The Front Page" about Chicago newspaper men and city politicians was a caricature of true life with exaggeration, though not much in some respects. The Indianapolis boys were no exception.

There were several reasons for this: Most of us were young and unmarried, and many were veterans of World War I, where we had learned a few minor bad habits such as drinking and smoking. Misguided patriots kept mailing me cartons of cigarettes to the Navy until I became an addict. The hired man down on the farm had already taught me all the four-lettered words. All this was unknown to my very fine Methodist tee-totaler father. However, a little later in my career, his precept and example in my childhood steadied me down quite a bit.

Then, the "Noble Experiment" just naturally irritated newspaper men, a group of liberals, as a bind on their cherished American freedom. The late Heywood Brown, a great reporter in New York would say, "Come on, boys, let's strike a blow for freedom," and pull out his pocket flask.

Reporters gravitated around public offices and there were no greater violators of the prohibition law than public officials, with a few exceptions, such as William P. Evans and William H. Remy, successively Prosecuting Attorneys of Marion County. Reporters were given Christmas presents of cases of good contraband whiskey at the City Hall, State House, and other places, and on other occasions, too. Under the "Wright Bone Dry Law," it was a crime to manufacture, sell, give away, buy or receive intoxicating beverages.

Newspaper men also attained a sort of immunity from arrest and conviction of minor charges, such as drunk or speeding. They all knew the Mayor, Sheriff, Chief of Police, Traffic Judge, and other Judges, and all of the higher ranking police officers, or their buddies did. Many a reporter who got drunk or in a public brawl was hauled home in a police or sheriff's car with no charges filed. Even "Watty" the News reporter, who loved liquor but could not "hold it," as they say, and who couldn't count on his fingers and toes the times he was arrested and thrown in the cooler for fighting police, was never charged once, let alone tried in Court. He did get beaten up in the City jail bull pen several times by fellow prisoners who couldn't stand his insults. One time he nearly lost an eye.

Horace, the Roman poet, wrote "In vinum est veritas," (while

149

drunk the true nature shows). Watty, when tight, thought he was a second John L. Sullivan, though he only weighed about 120 pounds, and he also had a vile tongue at such times. He had company in the fraternity of other newsmen. Watty was an intimate of the Mayor, Lew Shank, and dug up more good news stories than any two of us.

The Court House was a four story limestone building built in 1870 to hold five courts and not paid for until 1928. It was situated on the south half of the block surrounded by Washington, Market, Delaware, and Alabama Streets, with the main entrance on Washington. There was a large tunnel under Washington Street connecting the basement floor with the jail, one block south. The Court House was too hot in the summer and too cold in the winter. It was plenty dirty and harbored more rats and cockroaches than any place in town except the City Market just across the Street. Ocasionally, a janitor would put out some rat poison, and if you have never smelled fifty dead rats decaying deep within walls, you have a treat coming. Winoes also slept in the basement in winter.

Here, then, was my beat.

The Times built a new home in 1923 on Maryland Street, just south of the State House, and we moved on a Saturday afternoon. We had a new Managing Editor, one Al Berman, from the Cincinnati Post. Al gave instructions that all reporters should stay and help move. We hung around until about 1:30 P.M., and no moving, so we took up a collection and sent an emissary down to the Hay Market bootlegger by Kingan's Meat factory, and he soon returned with half a gallon of gin. Under its warming influence, we became impatient. Hogate vowed he hadn't been hired as a moving man, and we asked Editor Berman what we were supposed to do in the moving. He said we could ride over and keep the Oliver typewriters from falling off the truck.

"Keep them from falling off? Hell's fire! We'll kick them off and maybe you'll get some new ones!" said Cadou, later INS editor for Indiana.

Just then the genius of the moving operation, Big Jess Pigman, foreman of the composing room, walked through. Berman said, "Jess, these reporters are getting impatient. What shall I tell them?

150

Jess glowered around at us, spit out a quid of chewing tobacco and roared, "Tell them to go to Hell!" and walked out.

"Come on, boys, let's go," said "Tubby," our State House reporter. So away we all went, and showed up next Monday at the new plant. We never heard any more about it.

Speaking of Criminal Court, one day I heard the Judge order the sale at public auction of an automobile, used by a convicted bootlegger in his business, the proceeds to go to the State according to law. I had heard this before. Later I got the Court's order Book, and found it was ordered sold on a certain date between 10:00 A.M. and 4;00 P.M., at the Coffin-Dodson garage near the Court House. George V. Coffin was the Republican County Chairman.

I got the case records on nine such affairs, and from the Sheriff's books it was discovered all nine cars had gone to Republican faithful party workers for a song. For example, Bill Garrabrant, custodian of the Court House and a Ward Chairman, bid in a rather new car at $50.00 privately.

I worked two weeks, and then sprung the story, one story a day for nine days. The next sale had been advertised in small print in an obscure newspaper as usual, but I included the notice in my last story. Three thousand people blocked Market Street in an effort to buy the car cheap, but it sold for nearly as much as the other nine together.

Incidentally, this caused poor Guthrie a big headache. He knew I was up to something and watched me look at the big books in the Sheriff's Office, and later I saw him going through them in a hopeless effort to see what I was doing.

I had to keep my nose to the grindstone every day, a full day, because of Wayne. I couldn't sneak off and play golf or go to a show on an afternoon, or I would get "scooped," and then bawled out. However, Guthrie did have one weakness—baseball. Now and then he and I would agree to go together out to the Indians' ball park on West Washington Street, leaving about 2:30 P.M. His City Editor never dreamed Wayne would do such a thing and mine couldn't catch me. We would ride out on an open air street car for a nickel.

The Times gained one good reporter, Ralph Brooks, who

151

muscled his way onto the staff. He wanted a job as reporter, but nobody would hire him. One Monday, he came in, hung up his hat and announced he was going to work there. Ralph sat there two weeks until the City Editor gave up, put him on as office boy at $8.00 per week, and after a couple of months, made him a reporter at $20.00 a week. He ended up as Editor of the Sunday Star magazine section after a long and successful career as a Court House reporter.

On holidays, even when our public offices were closed, we had to come in for half a day, and rewrite stories from the "Indianapolis Star," the morning paper. Of course, this was yesterday's stuff, but we cleverly would bring it up to date by a new "lead" or first paragraph, such as: "John Jones is in jail today, hoping to get bail, as he was arrested yesterday on a charge of forgery," or, "Mrs. John Smith is in the City Hospital today. Yesterday she gave birth to twins in a taxi-cab, with a policeman for midwife." I privately thought such phony leads were silly, but they were a "sine qua non" with Fowler. "No stale news on this paper" was his firm edict.

One Labor Day morning I had done all my share of the Sunday Star rewrites, except one, a story about the Reverend Charles H. Gunsolus, a local Spiritualist leader, having predicted the second coming of Christ in 1970. Somebody had already been over to the Haymarket, and I had had a couple of cups of coffee royal au gin (you should try it sometime), and I was inspired to play a practical joke on City Editor Fowler.

I blew up the story quite a bit, starting with the Reverend Gunsolus' prediction, and went on to relate that if Christ did come, he better detour around Indiana as he would be arrested for changing water into wine at the wedding feast at Cana and the Anti-Saloon League would see that he got six months in the pokey, (almost in those words). Also, that the Ku Klux Klan, then rampant in Hoosierdom, would very likely take a stern view of the matter, as he was a Jew, and ride him out of town on a rail, after tarring and feathering him.

I gravely laid it in the city desk basket, and waited for Fowler to explode as he read it before passing it to a copy reader. I waited and waited. Shortly after 10:00 A.M., press time, I got uneasy and asked him about the Reverend Gunsolus story. It developed that in an absent-minded moment he didn't read it, but had handed it to "Rip" White, a headline writer. Rip had been to Dayton, Ohio, over the weekend and had just gotten in for work without any sleep and with a nice hang-over. He had headed it up, sent it out, and the presses had started to roll.

My God!" screamed Fowler, "Stop the press! Niblack! And you, White! I'm going to fire you both! What will Mr. Shumaker (Anti-Saloon League) and the Klan think? And what is worse, what will Roy Howard (President of Scripps-Howard) think?"

I said, "Better fire yourself, too, for not reading it, Volney."

"You shut up and go home,"he replied, which I did. I never heard any more about if for some reason, and neither did Rip. It was a close call. I guess it never made the street.

Fowler decided one day to brighten our lives by having a staff conference each morning just before we left for our beats, with constructive criticism and suggestions. It turned out to very much like Dickens' School Master Squeers and his spelling class, where the child who spelled "horse" got to go feed the "horse," and the one who spelled "winder" got to wash the "winder." It didn't last long, but one day Volney himself thought up a "doosey."

"I want someone to go out to the poor farm and interview people as to how they got in the poor house," he said. In those days the poor house was our public welfare system, plus an occasional hand out from the Trustee, always at night to avoid shame. Times have sure changed!

He looked around the circle and fixed his eyes on me. "Nibby, you can have it. It'll be a good series."

"Now, Volney," I protested, "I got the whole Court House and it is a full time job. I can't do it."

"Just do it in your spare time," he said.

"Hell, that's about the nuttiest idea I ever heard you put out, Fowler, and you've had a lot of them. How would you like to be in the poor house, and have some snoopy young ass come and ask you how you got in there? Why, it would be awful!"

About a week later, Fowler said to me, "How are you coming along, Nibby, on the poor house stuff?"

"Damn it, Volney, I told you I couldn't do it. I just think it stinks. Now let someone else take it."

"Yes, you CAN, too, do it! Now get busy," he said.

Some five days later, he says, "Nib, where is the poor house copy?"

"Volney, damn the luck, I haven't been out there, and I'm not going. To hell with it, and you too," I replied.

"Niblack, this is Wednesday! Saturday is pay day, and if you haven't laid the first story of that series in my hands by then, it sure will be your last and I don't mean maybe," was the edict.

"Well, All right! *All right!* If you are going to be unreasonable, I'll go, but I bet they won't talk."

That afternoon about 2:30 I got in my old jalopy and went to the poor farm on Tibbs Avenue. I thought, "O.K., I'll just show old Volney these people won't talk." With that I marched up to a small old man sitting on a bench and barked, "Say, Mister, I'm a newspaper reporter and I've come to find out how you got in the poor house!"

"Well, sit down, young man, and I'll tell you all about it. It's a long story," he said, much to my great surprise.

I interviewed ten old people there, and they were more than willing to talk, and at length. No one had been interested in them for so long. I didn't use names. It was the best feature story I ever did. I entitled it "The House of the Living Dead." It started off with a quotation from the 3rd Chapter of the Book of Job, which describes man's last home, the tomb: "There the wicked cease from troubling, there the weary be at rest; the small and the great are there and the servant is free from his master."

The first old man was born in Cornwall, England, he said, and as a boy went to mind the race horses of some Lord or Duke. Being small, he became a jockey. He claimed he had ridden in the English Derby, and later came to America and raced on nearly all tracks east of the Mississippi. Getting older and heavier, he became a sulky racer, and finally, Father Time put him back to stable boy when he became old and feeble. He said he had made good money at racing, sometimes a lot, "I spent it all on wine, women and song, Bud," he said, "and I never was much at singing."

When he was old, he came here with the horses to the Grand Circuit at the State Fair one fall, and became ill. They took him out to the poor farm and here he was.

"Uncle, if you had it all to do over, would you do any different? Maybe save up something for your old age, or a time like this?" I asked him.

"Naw, can't say as I would. I get plenty to eat here, such as it is, plain food, nothing fancy. I got a nice cot up there in a warm room to sleep on when it rains or snows outside, and on sunny days I get out here and potter around the yard and smoke my pipe and read and think about the good times I used to have. Sometimes at night I dream I hear the roar of the crowds as we come down the stretch. After all, an old man don't need much. Old John D. Rockefeller can't do any more than I can, with all his money."

That was the story of nearly all: Get old, get sick, be penniless and no folks to care for you, and it was over the hill to the poor farm.

There was a law then that people could pay board and room for their aged parents and keep them in the poor house. The only one who refused to talk to me was an old bedridden man, a college graduate and a former professor at DePauw University, whose wealthy daughter here in Indianapolis had put him out there and was paying his bill.

"Just get right out of here," said the feeble old man, "I'm ashamed to be here, but I'm old and helpless."

One case I wrote up was of a squat, slightly bowlegged old fellow who said he had been a survivor of the United States 7th Cavalry Regiment which rode off under General Custer, Chief Yellow Hair, to its rendezvous with Death at the Battle of the Little Big Horn in June of 1876.

"Hee! Hee! I was in the headquarters stockade waiting court martial," he waid, "warn't I lucky?"

He had wandered the earth since then doing odd jobs, and had been in and out of jails. He loved whiskey, he said, and his only complaint about the poor house was that he didn't get it there.

"When I was young, I was a powerful feller, and I could drink a quart of whiskey without stopping," he said, and then added craftily, "If you don't believe it, just bring me a quart and I'll show you. Will you? I can still do'er!"

I didn't do it, as I thought it would kill him.

It was the Grand Jury's duty to inspect County Homes, and one day I went with the jurors down to Julietta, then called the "Marion County Asylum for the Insane." We had a good dinner with the Superintendent, a gray-haired man of fifty, and he told us it was the same as the inmates ate, which I doubted. Then we toured the building. It was distressing, as some lunatics were shouting from padded cells, though others were sitting and rocking peacefully in a big room, reading or playing cards.

We were going down a corridor, when the Superintendent said, "Now gentlemen, stoop down and run by this next cage. There is a lady school teacher from University Heights here who went crazy over sex. She is liable to throw a pot of urine out on you."

He explained she was a nymphomaniac and had gotten so bad she would run away and work free gratis in houses of prostitution in the red light district of Indianapolis, which in those days were chiefly along Capitol Avenue, Pine Street, and Court Street.

The Superintendent, the six jurors and I all stooped down and went running by. I stopped and looked back and there was a beautiful red-haired girl of 24 or 25 years standing at the bars. She beckoned to me, and as I saw she had nothing in her hand, I went back and talked to her.

Who are all these men and who are you?" she asked apparently normal in a lot of ways, though I sensed she seemed a little strange.

I told her.

"My!" she said. "You're a beautiful boy," and reached out and touched my hand. "Can't you get in here some way so we can visit?"

"Sister, I wouldn't mind if I could, but the Grand Jury wouldn't like it," I replied. "How come you're here?"

"Well, if that's the Grand Jury," she said, "I have a complaint to make about that old Superintendent. He owes me $12.00 for pleasure, and he won't pay me."

It was a good story, and I had no doubt it was true, but I couldn't use it. I never went back to an asylum for the mentally ill

156

after that.

In those days people were committed to the asylums by the Justice of Peace, often without any hearing or notice. I was in Superior Court, Room 3, one day in 1925, listening to a Habeas Corpus plea by a Spanish War veteran who was an inmate of the House of Seven Steeples, as we called the State Asylum on West Washington Street. The man, after some years, had somehow gotten hold of an attorney, Honorable Ira Holmes, who brought the action. The man testified he was sitting on his front porch one day and two constables came up and said,

"Come with us!"

"What for?", he asked.

"Well," they replied, "You're crazy and we have to take you away."

"You're crazy yourself," he said he told them. "I never have had a trial or anything."

They took him anyhow, though he was sane, and it was shown at the hearing that his second wife and her son had caused his commitment after a squabble, and they were enjoying his property and pension.

I wrote the story, incidentally scooping Guthrie, and we played it up. As a result, the Indiana Legislature of 1927 passed the Uniform Mental Health Act, divesting the Justice of Peace of all jurisdiction and placing exclusive power over inquests in Circuit or Superior Court, with compulsory notice to the patient, and a further requirement that the Court must appoint two qualified Medical Doctors to examine the person and report in writing to the Court before an inquest could be ordered.

During my years as a reporter I covered the trials of D. C. Stephenson, Grand Dragon of the Indiana Ku Klux Klan, for murder; of Warren T. McCray, Governor of Indiana, in Federal Court on charges of using the mails to defraud; and of John Thomas Shaw, a Negro, in a famous kidnapping-rape-murder case, who was first convicted by a jury and ordered to the electric chair, but found innocent by a later jury.

The last year or so I was on special assignment and feature writer. I had a real nice time, covering football for Tony Hinkle at

Butler, out in Irvington, and the dedication of the new Indiana University Stadium at the Purdue-I.U. game there, which wound up in a scoreless tie. At this event I had a telegrapher in the press box with me and dictated a running account direct to the Times. I also covered the State Amateur Golf Tourney at French Lick, a pleasant outing.

One day in late May, 1925, I had just gotten home when I got a telephone call from Fowler.

"Get on the train at once and go to Princeton, Indiana," he said. "There's been a tornado, and several hundred people are dead."

I got down there next morning. J. M. Moore, our photographer, went along. I hired a taxi and we traced the path of the twister twelve or fifteen miles, to Griffin, Indiana, on the Wabash River, where it entered the State. It was the biggest tornado ever to hit the Midwest, starting in Oklahoma, cutting across Illinois, Indiana and Ohio, and dying away over Pennsylvania. The sky rained paper, cornstalks, debris and dust for hours and days after the monster passed.

The trail wound over hill and dale, through woods, towns and fields, and was a quarter of a mile wide. It looked like the dry bed of a river. You could walk anywhere in Griffin, as only one wall of the brick school house was left standing. There were over 100 corpses in one morgue.

One old farmer told me, "I went down to the road to meet the school bus and get my small daughter. The sky was black as ink. We ran in the house and all laid down by the west wall. It turned pitch dark, and the Devil passed by in the middle of the storm. I saw him and smelt the smoke and brimstone. There was a roaring overhead like a thousand freight trains were passing over the roof. The house blew away, and when it got light and calmed a little, there were me and my wife on the floor, and the child gone. After a while I found her down in the orchard, about two hundred yards away, on some grass, safe and sound, and not a scratch."

I saw one ten acre woods of huge hickory trees all sheared off ten feet above the ground as if a giant scythe had done it at one fell swoop. Not far away was a farm house with the two outside walls of a downstairs corner room entirely gone, with the furniture still in place, and no other damage.

Three thousand white chickens the farmer had in a building behind the house were strewn for miles, up in trees and everywhere, a lot of them naked.

I became so engrossed in this mighty display of Nature's power that I flunked my assignment disgracefully, not sending in any story until too late for the home edition. This was partly due to the fact I kept going farther west all the time, not realizing the wires were all down way out in the country.

Now and then we reporters made a little extra money on raffles. Once before Thanksgiving, Watty came over from the City Hall, and he and I and the Star reporter raffled off a turkey. We sold $35.00 worth of tickets at twenty-five cents each, and on Wednesday we had the drawing in the Clerk's Office. Uncle Dan Jones, an elderly Negro in the Auditor's office, was the "unlucky" winner of the prize: An eight pound, aged hen turkey, that Watty got at City Market. It was the scrawniest and puniest bird I ever saw.

Uncle Dan told me later, "That was the toughest turkey I ever tried to eat. My wife cooked it three days off and on, about every way she could, but it never amounted to nothing."

We each made about $11.00 apiece clear.

One time I was down town on Saturday afternoon and here came Watty and his three year old son. "Say, Nib, where can we get a drink?" he asked.

"Well, I'm just going down to the Southside on Union Street and get a gallon of sacramental wine from a Rabbi friend of mine," I said, "So come on along."

I attempted to leave the boy in the automobile but he insisted, "I wanna go too, wanna see the bootlegger."

I said, "Shhhh! He's not a bootleger, he's a Rabbi and he can sell some wine legally—I think."

Anyway, we all three went up and I bought a gallon of good Tokay for $10.00, and Watty bought a quart.

My salary question at the Times was a problem. I had to live on $12.50 a week at first and send $12.50 to pay on my debt. I knew of a cafeteria under the Bankers Trust where you could get a pint of

159

baked beans for a dime, and many a time that, and a glass of water, made my supper. At first I walked a mile to work to save a nickle street car fare.

During the first three months I was there, I waited patiently for Mr. "Ungh-Ungh" Peters to raise my pay . It was in vain. Then I went to see him.

"I've come to tell you I've made good," I said.

"Ungh! What in the world?" he said frostily.

"Well, you told me if I wasn't fired I would know I made good, and here I am—haven't been fired."

"Now, Mr. Niblack," he said soothingly, "I know you're doing a good job, but the Times is just getting started, advertising is bad and Blah—blah—blah," the same old song and dance I was to hear many times.

I had a fraternity brother, Vic Mays of Pendleton, who had gone to New York and was in the publicity business. I wrote Vic and he got me a job as advance man for Charles Reign Scoville, the second leading evangelist in the United States then. I was to meet him in Walla Walla, Washington, on New Year's Day, and go with the tour down the coast and back east to Oklahoma, salary $200.00 a month and expenses. I signed a contract.

Along about the first of December, I marched into the office to see Mr. "Ungh-Ungh" again.

I'm leaving December 15," I said.

"Leaving, what for? Leaving, you can't do that. Who'll run the Court House?"

"I don't know. That's the least of my worries," I said. "Maybe you can take over on that yourself, but I'm long gone. You say you can't pay me any more here."

He wanted to know the details and I told him about the $200.00 a month, and expenses.

"Now what are you getting here?" he asked, and I told him, although he knew.

"Twenty-five, Ungh, Ungh?" he said. "Well, I'll give you thirty a week!" Big hearted Scripps-Howard!

"I'll take it!" I said. What a sap I was, but I had a new girl friend here. I have always thought it would have been a great experience. Poor Reverend Scoville! His plans were upset, and so was he. He threatened to sue me, but that would have been more than idle folly.

The next raise didn't cost me nearly as much, only about $2.50. I went in the office one Saturday afternoon with a bottle of gin, and was having a little libation at my desk, by myself, when the new Managing Editor, Berman, came in, and saw me. It turned out later that he was quite a lush, and he used to send the office boy down to the Haymarket each morning for a pint.

He came over and joined me, and I recognized the symptoms.

"Have a drink, Mr. Berman!"

"Don't care if I do, though I hardly ever use the stuff," he said. We got real palsy-walsy for two strangers. He'd only been there a few days.

"Nibby, ole boy, you're 'bout the best reporter on this sheet," he announced after a while. "I'm goin' raise your pay. What is it?"

I told him it was $30.00 a week.

"Be $35.00 now on," he said. I thanked him and left. Much to my surprise, the raise was there next pay day.

My salary went up to $65.00 by early in 1925, due to hard work and the fact I found a new gadget to get increases. The News City Editor got to offering me a job about each six months, but he never would offer any more than my Times salary.

"The prestige of working on the News is worth more than mere money," he would intone.

I was always careful to tell Fowler I was to be interviewed by the News for a job. When I would come back, he would ask:

"Well, what did you do? You going?" and lowering his voice, "How much did they offer you?"

"Now, Volney, I'm not going to tell you. You know I like it here," which I did, "and if you give me a raise I'll stay. Otherwise, I probably will go."

It worked every time, until after I covered the trial of D. C. Stephenson. I said, "I've got to have more money. I'm your head reporter (Tubby, Cadou, Hogate, Miller and others were long gone) and that's it. I got a law degree last June at night school and Mr. Remy has offered me a job as Deputy Prosecutor."

161

For fear that people might think I spent all my time roistering and drinking, I must inform you that in September of 1923, I entered Benjamin Harrison Night Law School, of which Federal Judge William Steckler is also a graduate. This was a two year course, ten months a year, five nights a week from 6:00 to 8:00 P.M.

I arose each week day at 6:00 A.M. and was at work by 7:00 A.M., and I don't mean 7:01. I got off at 5:00 P.M., had supper somewhere, and attended class from 6:00 to 8:00. I studied in a lawyer's office until 9:30 or 10:00 and went to bed at 11:00, slept seven hours and started all over again. Saturday was my day off for fun in the evening. I also had night assignment from the City Editor, say—once every ten days. I graduated in June 1925, LL.B.

Volney got in touch with the higher ups at Cleveland, and Scripps-Howard offered to send me East with their chain at a substantial salary increase, but I turned them down.

I told them I was born in Indiana, I liked it, and if I could arrange it, I would die on Hoosier soil. My grandparents, all eight great-grand parents and about ten double great-grandparents were all buried down yonder in Southern Indiana, near Vincennes, as well as six triple greats. I was Hoosier all the way through, and I believe that was the real reason I never went with the evangelist.

On January 1, 1926, I was sworn in as Deputy Prosecutor under William H. Remy, at a salary of $200.00 a month.

Thus ended my newspaper career.

McCray Trial

In 1920, Warren T. McCray, age 55, a millionaire farmer and cattle breeder from the fertile prairies of Newton County, was elected the 30th Governor of Indiana. He was owner of the finest Hereford cattle herd in the world. McCray was a kindly man who inspired great affection in friends, a devoted presiding elder in the Presbyterian Church of Kentland, Indiana, the faith of his Scotch-Irish fathers, and a stalwart Republican.

McCray served three years and four months as Governor and then spent the next three years and four months in the United States Prison at Atlanta, Georgia, convicted of issuing a million dollars worth of fraudulent promissory notes written by himself to himself, signed by himself using other names, endorsed on the back by himself and sold to 157 State banks which were depositories of State Funds. Chicago banks got some also.

He was found guilty by a jury in Federal District Court in Indianapolis, Indiana, on Monday, April 28, 1924, on thirteen counts of using the United States mails in a scheme to defraud in mailing out the notes. The jury deliberated thirteen minutes. It was one of the most remarkable trials in the history of the Hoosier State.

I was there as a newspaper reporter for the now defunct Indianapolis Times, a Scripps-Howard paper. Judge Albert B. Anderson, the presiding genius of the trial, and an autocrat, a sadist, and a mean old man if ever there was one on the Federal Bench, almost sent me to jail, too. Immediately after he snarled out the sentence in his high pitched nasal whine "Ten Thousand Dollar fine and ten years in the Atlanta Prison," I made a racket as I dashed for the door—which was locked.

McCray's administration ushered in the brawling "Roaring Twenties" when the flapper with her mini-skirt and rouged knees danced the Charleston to the tune of "Dardenella," "Margie," and "Somebody Stole my Gal." Another feature was a howling farm deflation which followed the end of World War I, and which bankrupted many a farmer in the Midwest—including the unfortunate Governor of Indiana.

McCray ran for nomination for Governor in the Republican Party primary election of May, 1920, with his political headquarters in Indianapolis. He was successful, and carried his own precinct by 170 votes to 30. The home folks turned out to welcome him as he returned on a Big Four train on May 7.

They met him at Earl Park, the railroad station six miles away, and a triumphal procession was held to Kentland, the county seat, where all stores and businesses were closed, and the town band played. At the head of the parade in an upholstered and gaily decorated float rode Brummel Fairfax, the famous red and white leader of the great McCray registered Hereford herd of 1500 bulls, cows and calves. He weighed a ton, and was valued at $100,000.00, or $50.00 a pound on the hoof. His proud owner rode second place. The picture of Brummel and McCray had figured prominently in the campaign. They were followed by a long line of floats and cars filled with cheering neighbors. Brummel was a grandson of Perfection Fairfax, founder of the herd.

Cattleman McCray kept most of his herd on a 2,000 acre tract he called his Orchard Lake Cattle Farm, although the lake was really only a large pond. It was located on the rich flat lands of Newton County, eight miles northeast of Kentland. One of Brummel's cousins (maybe a son) sold for $25,000 and another for $50,000. Another bull was named Lowden Fairfax, after Governor Frank Lowden of Illinois, a chum of McCray.

In 1915 at the Hoosier State Fair, McCray entered the Fairfaxes—papas, mamas and children—and they won 19 first place blue ribbons out of 21 Hereford events, including Grand Champion bull.

Two other Hoosiers made the 1915 State Fair headlines. A man of color from Indianapolis driving a horse named Rock of Ages challenged a street car loaded with fair goers to an impromptu race up Illinois Street. Two policemen on the car ordered the motorman to go at top speed and the driver was captured and arrested for fast driving, but only after Rock of Ages was winded.

Also, Mayor J. H. Mellet of Anderson got in a fight with a policeman and was fined for disorderly conduct over refusal to buy

164

a ticket to get into the fair. He gave an assumed name of "Frank Moore," Portland, Indiana, but the press smelled him out anyway. In 1919 McCray sold $436,000 worth of such animals at one public auction at his farm. He had a sales barn that seated 2,000 stock breeders amphitheater style. In 1920 another auction brought in $330,000. Three-fourths of such sales were paid for in promissory notes which McCray would sell at various banks at discount. When he was inaugurated, McCray was said to be worth $3,000,000. He owned 15,000 acres of land in four States and Canada and had been organizer and president of the National Cattle Breeders' Association. He made his first million by 1906, dealing in grain and in organizing a chain of grain elevators in northwestern Indiana, starting as a fifteen year old farm boy with a grade school education. In 1906, McCray bought five Hereford cows "with three calves at foot" to start his herd. There were 57 buildings on his place, and a news reporter driving out from Kentland in 1915 was awed by the sight of giant silos, barns, and water towers looming against the horizon. He described McCray's life as a "path lined with roses."

Mr. McCray lived on another farm nearby, a small affair of only 460 acres, his home place. He had married well, his bride being a sister of George Ade, the Hoosier author, whose name is enshrined in the Ross-Ade Football Bowl at Purdue. They had three children, daughters, Lucille and Marian, and a son, George Ade McCray.

After winning the 19 blue ribbons at the 1915 State Fair, cattleman McCray looked around for more worlds to conquer. He decided to enter Republican politics, and in 1916 ran in the Republican Primary (in those days there were primary elections for governor and other state officers) unsuccessfully against James P. Goodrich, a wily attorney and financial tycoon from Winchester, Indiana. Mr. Goodrich became the 29th Governor of Indiana, a fast friend in time of need to his hapless successor. At one time in 1923 he raised $300,000 from prominent Republicans to help Governor McCray in his distress.

The new Governor was inaugurated on Monday, January 10, 1921, at 10:00 o'clock A.M., when he appeared before the Indiana General Assembly accompanied by the outgoing Governor. The

Indiana Society of Chicago came down for the affair and many of the Republican elite of the state attended. However, some anxiety was expressed because Vice-President Thomas Marshall, also a former governor (but a Democrat) was not present though invited. McCray expressed the hope—a biennial one—that the legislature would "limit itself to bills of worth and forget hobbies, and would deal in quality, not quantity."

Then an unfortunate incident, a bad omen as it were, happened. As the august inaugural parade, led by the two governors, wound down the State House stairs from the Legislature to the Governor's office, Pete Tepoff, an Indianapolis policeman stationed on the middle landing with orders to permit no one to go up or down, spread out his arms and cried, "Halt!" The startled procession stopped in dismay until a superior officer was brought up who countermanded the order.

"How was I to know they was them? I never seen neither of 'em before," said officer Tepoff plaintively.

"It's a great day for us farmers," exclaimed State Senator Miles Furnas of Randolph County.

The new Governor shared the front page that day with "Devil Anse" Hatfield, a leader in the Hatfield-McCoy feud in which thirty-five men and one woman were slain. Anse was buried on Big Sandy Mountain in West Virginia while eleven surviving children and sixty-five other descendants mourned his peaceful passing at age 81. He was a Democrat.

Henry Abrams, a Hebrew legislator from Indianapolis, announced he would introduce a bill that would provide jail sentences for persons guilty of libelling the patriotism or reputation of any religious sect or member thereof. It was aimed at the Ku Klux Klan, just then getting a hold on the state.

Outside the State House a chill January wind blew. It was no colder than the winds of financial distress and deflation which started blowing across the farm heartland of America that winter. In 1920 farmers paid $5.00 a day plus board and room for men to harvest their wheat. In 1921, many let the wheat go uncut.

McCray was an energetic Governor whose administration was a good one, taken as a whole. He moved the State Reformatory for young men from its antiquated building at Jeffersonville to a new one at Pendleton with its modern buildings on thirty acres surrounded by a 30-foot high wall. It was a model prison.

The Legislature having proclaimed the yellow poplar tulip tree blossom the State Flower, the Governor dutifully planted a tulip tree on the south lawn of the State House in the presence of 100 nature lovers and school children. He made a speech for the occasion. He said it was the first tulip tree he had seen.

He got into high disfavor with the aging veterans of the Civil War when he vetoed a bill aimed at stopping the 500-mile auto race in Indianapolis on Decoration Day. Fifteen hundred survivors of Gettysburg and Shiloh threw their G.A.R. hats in the air and cheered after unanimously passing a resolution at the annual encampment at Muncie, in substance denouncing McCray as a scoundrel.

"I wanted to sign the bill into law but my conscience wouldn't let me, as attorneys said it was class legislation," he said. "Anyway, you can't legislate morals into people," he added piously.

Incidentally, it was said among the press that the bill had been introduced as a "shake-down" of the Speedway by the Honorable Ralph Updike, a Klan member of the Indiana General Assembly, and that it had gotten away from him when the G.A.R. got behind it. From that day on Lem Trotter, the Speedway "public relations" agent, saw to it that all our state law givers were copiously supplied with pagoda box seat tickets for the race. I used some in 1929 and 1931 when I was in the State Senate from Marion County, and no one has ever introduced such a bill again.

McCray imposed the first state gasoline tax and made Indiana a leader in paved roads, far ahead of surrounding states. He and Henry Ford took the state out of the mud.

During his term the state adopted an amendment to the Hoosier Constitution to allow women to vote and limited the ballot to citizens. Indiana has never had a literacy or poll tax test on the right to vote. His administration rewrote the teachers' retirement law on more generous terms. It built eighty-seven State buildings, many of them at the State Fair Grounds.

Governor McCray and family were the first to occupy the new Governor's Mansion situated on Fall Creek back of the Marrott

Hotel, which now uses the site as a parking lot. It was the scene of the elaborate wedding of his daughter Lucille to William P. Evans, a Phi Beta Kappa graduate of DePauw University and a brilliant young lawyer who was to have the sad duty of being prosecuting attorney of Marion County when his father-in-law's case of alleged embezzlement of $155,000 of state agricultural funds would come before the Grand Jury in 1923.

The new Governor was barely rid of the 1921 legislature when new woes began to assail him. He was going broke. His cattle empire was crumbling due to the farm depression of 1921. Not only were prices way down, but most farmers had no money to buy blooded cattle at any price. Some Fairfax bulls sold at prices of $75.00 to $175. He also had overexpanded in buying farm land, paying anywhere up to two, three or three hundred fifty dollars an acre for one-hundred dollar an acre land, secured by purchase price mortgages. Overhead, taxes, and mortgage payment began to ruin McCray financially.

He was not alone. Thousands of farmers were caught in the same trap. An uncle of mine, Curtis T. McClure, a leading farmer of Knox County, told me during the World War I inflation when wheat brought $2.25 a bushel: "The hour of the farmer has come." Uncle mortgaged his two farms to buy a couple hundred acres more of land at $275.00 an acre, land that shortly before had been valued at $100.00, and which later sold for fifty. Uncle wound up as custodian for the Vincennes banks, struggling valiantly, to the day of an untimely death ten years later, to get back on top.

Hoping and believing that the recession would soon end, and farm prices would boom again, McCray devised a plan to tide himself over until such a time. Using his credit and that of the State, he began borrowing money from banks on promissory notes which he said were received for sale of cattle. He wrote these notes himself, as he admitted on the witness stand in April, 1924. He also borrowed $155,000 from the State Agriculture Board and put it to use in his own bank account at Kentland.

McCray then, and in two courts, and as he was taken to prison, and to the day of his death in 1938, maintained, insisted, and believed that he had done no wrong.

168

"I had no intent to commit crime," he said, "and without intent there can be no crime!"

He evidently was a victim of self-hypnosis as the federal jury didn't believe his protestations, but looked at the substance. The jury evidently went on the old maxim of law that it is presumed a man intended to do what he did do, plus a mountain of evidence of forgery of notes.

Toward the summer of 1923 rumors began to go around the state that Governor McCray had embezzled $155,000 of State Agriculture Funds, that he was borrowing money from banks which were State depositories of tax money, and that he was bankrupt.

Hoping to quell the tumult, Governor McCray, on August 31, 1923, went before a meeting of his creditors in the Severin Hotel and submitted a trust agreement whereby he and Mrs. McCray would turn over everything they owned, 15,000 acres of rich land, all his herds and all personal property such as notes, bank stock, securities bond, and three automobiles, for satisfaction of his debts, his home farm alone excepted.

Governor McCray, among other things a member of the Chicago Board of Trade, a Vice-President of the Sawyer Grain Company, and President of the Discount and Deposit Bank of Kentland, Indiana, told the meeting:

"I have suffered from the deflation of farm values of the past three years and the fall in price of prize cattle, and I am unable to meet my obligations."

He said he did not know how much he owed but thought it was around two million dollars. The State Savings & Trust Company of Indianapolis was chosen as trustee.

On Saturday, September 22, Republican leaders, including State G.O.P. Chairman, Clyde Walb of LaGrange; United States Postmaster General, Harry New, a Hoosier; United States Senator James E. Watson of Rushville; ex-Governor Goodrich, and others met to ponder the matter. Walb wanted McCray to resign and if he should refuse, to have a special session of the Legislature called to impeach him.

"We are acting for the Republican voters," Walb declared.

Gotdrich and others demurred to such drastic action.

"Give the man a chance," they said, "Maybe he can straighten it all out. At least, let's wait a little and see."

McCray indignantly refused to resign.

"I have done no wrong, and I can explain everything," he said, "No group can sway me from my duty."

McCray closed his statement with an appeal to his friends "to believe in my integrity and stand by me in my effort to protect my creditors, my family and my good name."

Furthermore, the Governor was the only one who could call a special session of the Legislature, and he was not about to do so.

On this same date, Kee Goon, not long out of Canton, China, shot a hold-up man in the knee at his hand laundry at 16th and Illinois and bit off his left ear. Kee was shot through the belly, and they both rode to the hospital in the same ambulance.

Some friends, headed by ex-Governor Goodrich, raised $300,000 and repaid the State the $155,000 the Governor had borrowed from the State Agriculture Board and also some other debts.

Early in October, the Marion County Grand Jury began an investigation to the charges. McCray's new son-in-law, William P. Evans, an upright and conscientious young man, was in the unfortunate position of being elected Prosecuting Attorney of Marion County and hence in charge of the Grand Jury. He asked to step aside, and the Honorable James A. Collins of Criminal Court appointed two special prosecutors, Clarence W. Nichols and Eph Inman, both prominent local attorneys.

The United States Bankruptcy Court took hold of the matter on October 6, 1923, when three Fort Wayne banks filed a petition to have the Governor declared bankrupt. The Governor was ordered to file a list of his assets and liabilities, which he did. He also testified at the hearing on November 16th that he didn't know how much he owed exactly—that he had no record of bills payable. It was mostly to banks in Indiana and Chicago, altho he said he had borrowed $900.00 from the Kentland Cemetery Association. He testified he had signed names of his farm managers to promissory notes made out to himself and later made arrangements for them to approve the same.

The same week, Purdue and Northwestern, both winless,

fought it out for the cellar championship of the Big Ten—Purdue won 6 to 3. At the same time Wasbash College "cooked up some special plays" and defeated I.U. 23 to 6. Butler defeated the Haskell Indians, led by Chief Big Buffalo, 19 to 13. Haskell had another "red-skin" player named Petratovich. I. U. beat Purdue 3 to 0, the last game of the season.

Also, detectives in Chicago arrested a youth on charges of mayhem in chloroforming a university student and robbing him of his glands which were transplanted on an aging candy manufacturer who wanted to marry a 22 year old beauty.

The Governor transacted State business as usual until his conviction. On the day he testified at his bankruptcy hearing on November 16, he went back to the State House and declared the new Pendleton Reformatory open and directed all state judges to start sending prisoners there.

On November 30, 1923, the county grand jury indicted the Governor of Indiana on charges of embezzlement of the $155,000.00, whereupon his son-in-law, Prosecutor Evans, resigned, tendering his written resignation to his indicted father-in-law on December 8, 1923.

Later testimony revealed that on the same day the Indiana Ku Klux Klan officials headed by Grand Dragon D. C. Stephenson, offered the besieged Governor $10,000 in cash to appoint as Evans' successor a Klan lawyer, one James A. McDonald. McCray instead appointed William H. Remy, Evans' Chief Deputy, who was a violent foe of the Klan. Stephenson also offered McCray "absolute protection" from conviction on the criminal court charges.

"I have control of the county clerk's office, the two jury commissioners and the courts. I have the money. We have done it before and can do it now," was the substance of "Steve's" offer.

The emissary who carried Stephenson's $10,000 in cash into Governor McCray's office was the Honorable Ed Jackson, of New Castle, Secretary of State, who had been elected on the Klan ticket of 1922, and who was to be Stephenson's and the Klan's successful candidate for Governor in 1924 on the Republican ticket.

"You can take your money back to your office, Ed. I am astounded!" said the forlorn McCray when the money was shoved

171

under his nose in the Governor's office at the State House. "My fortune I struggled so hard to accumulate and to preserve, and my good name may be in ruins, but I will never surrender my integrity. Take your money and get out."

McCray also was indicted Frebruary 25, 1924, by a United States Grand Jury in the District Court at Indianapolis on charges of using the mails in a scheme to defraud and on charges of violating the national banking laws.

On St. Patrick day, March 17, 1924, Governor McCray went on trial in Marion Criminal Court in the old Court House before the Honorable Harry Chamberlin, Circuit Court Judge serving as Special Judge.

The Criminal Court Room was one of five original courts in the towered limestone Court House built in 1870. It had a 35 foot high ceiling on which appeared a huge painting done in colors of a court of Roman justice. Behind the judge's bench at one side was a large iron statue of blindfolded justice and at the other side, one of Chronos, old Father Time with his scythe. I never knew if the latter symbolized anything to guilty defendants or not. There was a large hole in a post behind the bench resulting from negligent twirling by a Deputy Prosecutor in a murder case of "Exhibit A," a .44 revolver.

Occasionally the room would be filled with the odor of rotting rats in the ancient walls, dead by a janitor's rat poison.

It took eight days and the examination of two hundred talesmen before a jury was selected. On March 27, the first witness was heard. On April 11, 1924, twenty five days after the trial started, after thirty-five ballots, the jury was discharged as hopelessly "hung" along about 7:00 P.M.

I covered the trial as reporter for the Times. Mr. McCray, a heavy set man about five feet, nine inches tall, eyed the jury anxiously all during the trial. From the stand he repeatedly told the jury he had no intent to embezzle the $155,000.00; that he had always intended to pay it back, and that in fact, it had been repaid.

After being discharged, a juror said that the final ballot stood 8 to 4 for a finding of guilty. However, as we left the Court House in the dark, the Governor, grasping at straws, took me by the sleeve

172

and said, "Now, it was 7 to 5 for acquittal at first. Remember that, and put it in the paper."

This cleared the deck for action in Federal Court, where the case was on the docket for 9:00 A.M. Monday, April 21, 1924, ten days later.

Promptly at that hour we gathered in the third floor Court Room, with its stained glass windows, where Judge William Steckler now presides. "We" were: newspaper reporters; Defendant McCray and his attorneys, the Honorable James Noel, a trustee of Purdue University, and the noted firm of Ruckelshaus and Ryan; Homer Elliott of Martinsville, a silvery haired attorney of the old school, the United States District Attorney, together with his assistants; and the United States Marshall and 400 spectators—a standing room only crowd which jammed the Court. There were as many more outside in the halls.

High over all on his bench in front, like the seventh avenging angel sitting on his cloud, sat the Honorable Albert B. Anderson in his black robes, eyeing the defendant malevolently and smacking mental lips over the feast to come. The United States through its thrice potent and duly appointed judge would show the world how to put the Governor of a great State in his place—and speedily.

"Close the doors, and lock them, and have the United States Marines from the recruiting office patrol the corridors," decreed the Judge, and the trial began.

"Gentlemen, I want to get this trial over with as speedily as possible," stated the Judge, obviously referring to the long trial in Criminal Court.

"Fill the jury box, Mr. Marshal."

Seventy-five prominent men from all parts of the State were present as a venire, but only 28 were questioned. The Judge frequently urged both sides to speed up.

"Gentlemen, let's move on, we're wasting time," he admonished sharply.

In one hour and fifty minutes twelve good men and true were selected and sworn in as never having heard of the case and having no opinions as to guilt or innocence, or if they had heard of it, still had no opinions, who thought they could give both the United States and the defendant a fair trial.

There were five farmers on the jury, three merchants, one insurance salesman, one street railway executive, one real estate dealer and one securities salesman.

We reporters were not given a table or any special consideration other than we were allowed in the Court room and were given seats in the front row.

Here might be a good place to speak a few words about the presiding Judge.

The Honorable Albert Barnes Anderson was born February 10, 1857, near Zionsville, Indiana, in the next county to his Court room. He attended Wabash College and was admitted to practice law in 1882, at Crawfordsville, Indiana, where he served a term as elected Prosecuting Attorney.

On December 18, 1902, he was appointed by President Theodore Roosevelt as Judge of the only United States District Court in Indiana. He held the post until he resigned in June of 1929. He died April 27, 1938.

Anderson was a typical Federal Judge, appointed for life or good behavior, and the only way he could be removed was by a vote of two-thirds of the United States Senate. Consequently, he was lord of all he surveyed and brooked no opposition to his Court room, least of all from a defendant or his attorneys.

Judge was a tall, lean man, aged 67 years at the time, and he enjoyed playing cat and mouse with trembling defendants. I suspect he would have died of apoplexy if confronted by the "Chicago Seven" and their antics. I imagine, however, Attorney Kunstler and his clients never would have finished their trial because of being in jail for direct contempt of Court as often as they got out on bond and entered the Court room again.

I was present in the Judge's Court in the fall of 1922, when he tried a coal miner from Bicknell, Indiana, for contempt of Court. There was a nation-wide strike called by John L. Lewis, the Miners' Union President, which began in March that year and lasted through the fall. Judge Anderson issued an injunction that strikers could not cross a certain line, and a guard said, "You can't come here," to the defendant.

"Who says I can't?" inquired the man.

"Judge Anderson up at Indianapolis, that's who," was the answer.

"To Hell with that old Son-of-a-Bitch. I'll go where I please," said the miner.

For that and some other infractions, the man was arrested and the next morning put on the 7:00 A.M. Indianapolis and Vincennes passenger train for Indianapolis to see the Judge. The Miners' local phoned a firm of young attorneys, Asa J. Smith and Thomas Garvin, to defend their man.

He went on trial at 2:00 P.M. on that same day.

The guard took the stand and related the above offense just about as I have stated it.

"The Government rests," said the District Attorney.

The defendant said he was sorry.

"Anybody got anything to say about this case?" queried Judge Anderson, who was sitting screwed around sideways on the bench.

"Your Honor, may it please the Court, I'd like to say—" begun young Smith.

"May what please the Court?" snarled Anderson, swinging round in his chair and fixing the attorney with a bilious eye. "I'll have you know this man called his Honor a Son-of-a-bitch, and His Honor is not pleased at all. In fact, he is highly displeased!" he roared out. "What were you going to say?"

Smith, a veteran of the Marine Corps at Belleau Woods and a quick thinker, retorted:

"Your Honor, I started to say that my partner here, Mr. Garvin, would like to speak a few words for the defendant," and punching the startled Garvin whispered, "Get up you sleepy bastard and say something! Anything!"

Garvin jumped to his feet and yelped out, "The defendant rests, your Honor."

"Well, I should think so," bawled Judge Anderson. "Sixty days in jail! Take him away and call the next case."

Another time a little Italian from Gary pleaded guilty to bootlegging.

"That will be a fine of $500.00 and costs! Take him away!" pronounced Judge Anderson.

"Thatsa all right, Judge. I gotta that $500.00 right here in my hip pocket," said the defendant brightly.

"Is that so?" snapped the Judge. "Just look in your other hip pocket and see if you can find six months!"

Once an attorney didn't show up, and the bootlegger-defendant pleaded for a continuance. Anderson was in one of his rare jovial moods.

"Now! Now! We can't delay justice. I'll be your lawyer and defend you and we will see if the District Attorney can make a case!" he said.

The trial started and concluded.

"Defendant found not guilty and discharged," announced the Judge, "I told you, Mr. Defendant, I didn't think they could beat us."

Incidentally, President Roosevelt lived to regret appointing Anderson, who ruled against him in a libel suit brought by Charles Fairbanks of the Indianapolis News, Vice-President under Taft, arising out of a political row. Someone introduced Roosevelt and the Judge at the Columbia Club, and the President refused to shake hands, turned his back and walked away. Not many people did that to Judge Anderson.

After the jury was sworn that Monday morning it was only 11:00 A.M., and there was time before lunch for the opening statements of counsel. District Attorney Elliott outlined the case for the prosecution. The United States would prove that defendant McCray had written at least $750,000 of worthless "paper," promissory notes, written on companies which did not exist, on companies with no assets, and companies owned by McCray himself; that he had also signed names of his farm managers to $200,000 of such worthless notes made payable to himself without their knowledge.

Elliott said he would show that the Governor then mailed his notes out to Indiana banks with letters stating they were payment for cattle sold to customers; that he claimed to have investigated them as having ample assets to meet the notes when due, and that the notes bore his endorsement and he was good for them, too.

Elliott said he would prove the Governor used influence and coercion on State depository banks to buy the notes and even had a bill passed by the legislature for a new Court in Bluffton to get a loan of $20,000 from a bank in the County. The Government also would show the defendant forged hundreds of such notes. Finally, he said, it was all a scheme to defraud by use of the mails.

James E. Noel, McCray's Chief attorney, made a brief opening statement and outlined the defense. Much of what Prosecutor Elliott said was true, he admitted, as to the physical facts of writing the notes and mailing them out. However, the Governor had no intent to defraud or commit a crime; that he was a victim of farm depression and merely was trying to tide himself over the crisis.

The first witness after lunch was W. E. Towers, of Kentland, former private secretary of McCray, who was asked to give McCray's farm assets. He listed ten farms in Indiana, Illinois, Minnesota, South Dakota, and Canada. He told of huge cattle sales prior to 1920.

Seven bankers testified and then the Judge adjourned Court for the day. All afternoon he urged the attorneys to speed up.

"I am anxious to bring this trial to as early a termination as possible," he said as the jury started to file out.

Twenty-one witnesses, all bankers, paraded to the stand on Tuesday, testifying to widespread mail negotiations with the defendant about the "cattle paper" and his own personal notes. One note for $7,000 signed by O. H. Herriman and Company of Kentland and endorsed by McCray to the Lincoln National Bank of Fort Wayne was put in evidence among others. The company was a small firm of which McCray owned one-quarter, and he had written it himself to himself.

The Government spun a web around the defendant strand by strand. The witnesses showed a pattern of negotiations usually opened by a letter from the defendant, often accompanied by a promissory note, stating he had a number of cattle notes received from sales well secured by ample property which he wished to discount. Upon request of a bank Governor McCray would supply financial state-

ments of his own and of the signer, but omitting to state that he had
signed other peoples' names without their knowledge, and further
that there had not been any such sales.

These notes were almost all alike—"I promise to pay to Warren
T. McCray on or before ninety days—." On maturity the Governor
would write asking extensions or substituting another note. Often
he wrote that the makers wanted more time.

One Evansville bank refused a $10,000 loan to the defendant.
The President testified that McCray then called long distance and
after a little talk said:

"By the way, have you got any State funds on deposit?"

The banker said they had none.

"Then the Governor says, 'If I get you about $10,000 in state
Funds could you discount my note for $10,000,' and I told him, 'Yes
we could,' and we did," the witness testified. "However, the State
funds came only after repeated requests," he added.

Not all of McCray's loans resulted from pressure or arm-twist-
ing. Lucius Harris, President of the Rising Sun, Indiana, Bank in
Ohio County, volunteered to buy a $2,500.00 cattle note, according to
John W. Johnson, cashier of Peoples Deposit Bank of Patriot,
Indiana, a small village near by.

"We had lunch together, and I was telling him about an offer
from the Governor to sell $2500 of his paper to me," he said on the
stand. "Mr. Johnson says 'If that is the way you put it, I want to
take $2500 of it, too,' so I wrote Governor McCray and told him
about it, and said, 'So you can furnish us each a note for $2500 to
show our kindly feeling toward our good Governor.' "

On Wednesday, forty-two other bankers testified to more letters
and more notes.

I learned after court adjourned that in the opening game of
baseball season Babe Ruth hit a home run, double and single, and
the Yankees beat the Boston Red Sox 13 to 4, that same day.

On Thursday, testimony was heard from O. S. Todd, President of the Studebaker Bank of Bluffton, Indiana, that his bank took
$15,000 in cattle notes and a $5,000 personal note from McCray. He
wrote a letter to the Governor thanking him for having State tax

178

money sent to his bank and for getting a bill passed by the Legislature creating a separate Circuit Court for the County.

All in all, 157 banks in Indiana were shown to have bought the notes. Many were located in hamlets such as Paris Crossing, Paragon, Dale, Patriot, Coal City, Rolling Prairie, and Klondike, places never otherwise heard of thirty miles from home unless their basketball team, by accident, won a sectional tournament.

Big city banks got in on it, too. The Harris Trust Company of Chicago held $100,000 in notes. Indianapolis banks were: The The National City Bank with $28,000; J. F. Wild Bank, $25,000; Meyer-Kiser, $10,000, among others. The First National Bank of South Bend, Indiana, bought $13,000 of the notes. Chicago banks held a total of $231,000 in alleged cattle paper.

All in all, the banks held a total of nearly $1,500,000 of such worthless assets.

Came Friday and the Government brought in W. J. Hendry, a young farmer from down in the hills of Morgan County with a southern Indiana drawl, who had managed a farm for McCray near Martinsville. Elliott showed him promissory notes totalling $160,000 signed with Hendry's name made payable to Warren T. McCray, which had been put in evidence.

"I never signed them, and didn't know about them at all until last fall," he testified, "I never gave Governor McCray permission to sign my name, neither," he told Elliott, "and I never owed him $160,000.00 nor any part of it."

He added, however, that he would have given such permission if McCray had asked him, and that it was all right with him that his name was thus used.

"Now what assets did you have to secure $160,000 loans your name was on?" asked Elliott.

"Didn't have none," was the surly rejoinder, "anyhow didn't owe $160,000.00!"

"No assets at all?" pressed Elliott.

"Well, I did own two heifers and a coon dog," replied the witness.

The manager of McCray's Allen County farm was next on the stand. His name had been signed by McCray to $50,000 of the

179

"cattle notes," payable to McCray. The witness said the signatures were not his, and that he had never owed the Governor anything.

Defendant McCray sat watching his two farm employees intently, nervously clasping and unclasping his hands. They both shook hands with him after court.

One of the last witnesses was Amos D. Lucas, the ex-cashier of the Discount and Deposit State Bank of Kentland, of which Governor McCray had been President until the August before. A life long friend and business associate of McCray, he testified in a whisper that on January 1, 1923, the Governor owed $209,000 to the bank on notes.

"What was the capital stock of that bank?" asked Judge Anderson, leaning forward.

"$90,000, your Honor," was the meek reply.

The witness said the Governor also owed the bank $44,000 more on "cash items."

"What were those cash items?" asked Elliott.

"Bad checks on Mr. McCray's own personal checking account," said the witness with downcast eyes, avoiding looking at defendant McCray.

They had been indicted together on charges of violating national bank laws, and Mr. Lucas had entered a guilty plea several weeks before. Elliott used him as a State witness in return for leniency.

All in all, 700 exhibits of letters, notes, etc., were placed in evidence, being only a part of those available.

McCray was the last witness, and the only one for the defense, on Monday, April 28, 1924.

He told the jury, yes he had done most of those things, but said he had no criminal intent. He evidently had a few set speeches he wanted to make to the jury exonerating himself and explaining his purity of heart and a sense of no wrong doing, one about the farm price recession. Elliott objected and Judge Anderson sustained each objection.

"Why, I—," said McCray at one juncture, appealing to the judge.

"I don't ask any conversation from you, sir," said the Judge curtly, "Indeed, I don't want any with you!"

A little later the defendant again volunteered some testimony. "I object again, Your Honor!" said Elliott. "All he wants to do is make self serving speeches to the jury."

"Won't you let me explain, Judge?" began McCray, his voice quivering and his lip trembling, after the objection was sustained.

Judge Anderson fixed him with a cold stare and said:

"I'd advise you to abide by the conduct of your case by your counsel. And if I were advising you, I'd advise you do a lot differently from what you're doing."

McCray wanted to explain to the jury that although he signed other peoples names to notes payable to himself, his endorsement on the back made them all right.

On cross-examination he told of how the note writing scheme started in a small way and pyramided, due to increasing financial losses and to the 8% discount or loss he had to take each time he cashed a note.

"I had to write more and more notes and more and more letters as time went on and get them ready for the next day mail," he testified. "At the last I was staying in my office at the State House until 1:00 or 2:00 A.M., the volume was so great."

The incoming mail was tremendous, too. I thought at the time that it must have been a huge task to keep track of all the notes in all the banks. No wonder the State's Chief Executive couldn't tell how much he owed or to whom.

"Oh what a tangled web we weave when first we practice to deceive," as the poet wrote. It surely applied to MCray.

Finally the trial ended, and the closing arguments were heard.

Elliott's closing statement to the jury was a stinging denunciation of McCray.

"Falsehood piled a mile high!" he shouted.

"$1,000,000 in fictitious paper."

"Two heifers and a coon dog as assets for $160,000 promissory notes," he screamed. "My God! Two heifers and a coon dog! Think of it."

"Floated a wheelbarrow load of bad notes over Indiana," he accused, slightly mixing his metaphors.

181

"Took a genius to do this thing. It was not the work of a country boy!" he declared.

"Forgeries occurred!" he stated.

"Absolute forgeries!" chimed in Anderson, like an old Methodist from the Amen corner carried away by a preacher's eloquence.

"Anarchy breeds of this kind of stuff," shouted Elliott.

"Government is threatened of this kind of stuff," he declared, while the Judge rocked in his chair and nodded his head approvingly. "This man is guilty as sin," Elliott charged the jury.

Defense Attorney Noel told the jury that his client had no intent to commit crime and only was a victim of hard times on the farm.

He was interrupted several times by the Judge.

Then Judge Anderson took over and read some legal instructions to the jury, the gist of it being that the Governor was a very, very guilty man, no matter what he said. The jury filed out at 6:15 P.M., and at 6:30 it returned after one ballot.

"Gentlemen of the jury, have you reached a verdict?" inquired the Judge.

"We have, Your Honor! We find the defendant guilty as charged on all counts."

McCray's face went white, and he gripped the edge of the defense table.

Judge Anderson addressed the jury after the verdict:

"As honest men you could come to no other verdict. There is a question in my mind as to whether I ought not to order this defendant into jail. Here is a man who devised a scheme to defraud and carried it on almost entirely by use of the mails. He himself has testified that he wrote 2,500 letters, and if so, he is guilty of violating the statute 2,500 times. He is guilty for forging hundreds of fraudulent notes. He is guilty of obtaining money under false pretenses.

"I think I'll have to order him to jail. The evidence has over and over again been of the most remarkable character. The circumstances show an utter, an absolute disregard of what is right. Taken in the field of conscience, what conscience did this man have?

"I myself think I have seen greater individual crimes, but I have never seen anything to approach this in the number of individual felonies which this man has committed. It is my duty to show this man that no matter if he is Governor of Indiana, no matter if he had broad acres, he can not escape the penalty that is customarily given to every criminal in this Court. There is no difference here between this man and the lowest criminal.

"The marshal will take this man into custody and put him in jail, to bring him here tomorrow at 10:00 o'clock in the morning for sentence."

However, sentencing was deferred until 10:00 o'clock on Wednesday, April 30.

The defendant was taken in custody by the United States Marshal, Linus P. Meredith. He had telephoned his wife that he would be late for supper, so he now telephoned home again from the marshal's office that he wouldn't make it at all. While there the Governor of Indiana, on his way to jail, pardoned a life termer at Michigan City, a southern Indiana half-wit who was in for murder. This was done on advice of the prison board and was his last official act as Governor.

"Good-bye, Bill, tell the folks to be brave," he said to his son-in-law, as he entered the Marion County Jail. "You'll have to be the head of the family now, Bill," he said and began to cry silently.

As he entered the "bull room" where he spent the night, a sleepless one, with 83 other prisoners, Joseph Stokes, a leading druggist of Indianapolis who was serving a term for "bootlegging," said, "Hello, Governor."

"Hello, Joe," he replied, shaking hands.

McCray could not go into Federal row because a case of smallpox was quarantined there.

Next day, by permission of Judge Anderson, McCray made a last visit to the Governor's office, accompanied by Meredith. There he and intimate friends and leading Republicans, who came in to say good-bye, had lunch. There he decided not to appeal. He sent a written resignation to the Secretary of State Ed Jackson, the man who had tried to bribe him with $10,000.00 four months before. It wasn't to be effective until 10:00 o'clock A.M. the next day, at the hour he was to be sentenced. He spent the afternoon with his family and returned to jail Tuesday night.

On Wednesday, April 30, he arose at 5:00 A.M., with all the other jail inmates, and had breakfast of rice, coffee, bread and molasses.

At 9:55 A.M. McCray entered the court room, jammed as usual, and at 10:00 A.M. Judge Anderson appeared, trailed by marshals, clerks, and pages.

"Hear Ye, Hear Ye! The District Court of the United States for the State of Indiana is now open pursuant to adjournment," the marshal intoned.

Judge Anderson made McCray wait until he sentenced Bobbie Lambert, age 23, a car thief from Kentucky, to two years in Atlanta Prison. He depicted Bobbie as a young man who never had much of a chance.

"You don't own any large farms, do you?" he inquired of Bobbie. The latter vigorously denied any such criminal association. He was an escapee of an Iowa Prison, had been convicted of violating liquor laws in Kentucky, and was under indictment in Indiana for breaking into a United States Postoffice in Preble, Indiana.

The Judge then called McCray before him, where he stood with head bowed and hands clasped for sentence. After excoriating him for five or ten minutes as one who had betrayed a public trust he pronounced the sentence:

"Ten years in Atlanta Prison and $10,000 fine."

The Times' presses were ready for the extra. I jumped out of my seat and hit the side door with a bang. It was locked!

"Who's making that racket down there?" snarled the Judge. "Sit down there and keep quiet or I'll give you sixty days in jail for contempt of Court," he declared, fixing me with his eye. "I'm not through here yet."

I sat right down on the lap of the nearest spectator, and the kindly Judge spent another five minutes working Mr. McCray over again just to show me—a newspaper reporter—that I had better watch out.

At the same hour, Emmet F. Branch of Martinsville, the Lieutenant Governor, was sworn in as Governor of Indiana.

Ex-Governor McCray and Bobbie Lambert left on the 2:30 Big Four train for Atlanta that afternoon.

"Good-bye, boys. Remember me," said McCray as he left. He also handed out a written statement to reporters:

"I still maintain with a clear conscience that I am absolutely innocent of any intent to do wrong. But I'll go down there and take my medicine like a man, and when it is all over I will come back and take my place among the people of Indiana.

"I believe in Courts and the enforcement of the law, and whatever the Court requires, I will do."

"Tell the people of Indiana I have tried to give them a good administration."

He appeared composed, calm, and collected as he went up the train steps.

As the train rolled through the Tennessee Mountains in the night, Bobbie Lambert, in handcuffs and leaving his coat, tie, shoes and socks behind, dived out a toilet window and escaped.

McCray spent three years and four months in Atlanta Prison. He was paroled on August 31, 1927, and President Hoover gave him a full pardon as a Christmas gift on December 23, 1930. While in prison, he taught a Sunday School class, edited "Good Words," the prison paper, and wrote his autobiography for the Breeders' Gazette.

In 1928, twenty friends raised $300,000 for him, and he regained control of his Orchard Lake farm. By diligence, he got it prospering again, though his famous herd had been scattered to the four winds. One breeder in Virginia sent him a grandson of Brummel Fairfax as a gift to help him start again.

In 1929 his portrait was restored to the Governor's office. He appeared before the House and Senate of the 1929 Legislature on the rostrum and was roundly cheered. I was present on this occasion, too, as a State Senator from Marion County, elected on the Republican ticket. It was the last time I ever saw McCray.

Alas! The panic of 1933 put the ex-Governor in bankruptcy again, and his Orchard Lake Farm was again sold for debt. However, the loyalty of his devoted friends was such that they again helped him buy it back once more. Like the Phoenix, he always rose from the ashes.

McCray died peacefully at his home on December 19, 1938, suffering a stroke while eating dinner, or supper as we called it then down on the farm.

The Ku Klux Klan in Indiana

Nearly fifty years have gone by since the Ku Klux Klan was introduced into Indiana. It was brought to this State by one David C. Stephenson and some others, who started the Klan in Evansville, Indiana, being Klavern No. 1.

Stephenson was an Oklahoma Democrat who showed up in 1920 in the Ohio River town of Evansville, down on the Mason-Dixon Line. There he went in business with a partner, one L. G. Julian, mining and selling coal under the name of the Enos Coal Company. He conceived the idea of making the Klan a political power by endorsing Klansmen in the Primary election of the Republican Party.

It is said he had the concession for selling the "Robes" at $10.00 per head, and that he made a profit of two to six dollars on each robe. He was reputed to have become rather wealthy with this procedure, although his business was very successful also. At one time he was quoted by Dun & Bradstreet with a net worth of $900,000, a tidy sum for that day, or even today.

I graduated from Indiana University at Bloomington with an A.B., in the spring of 1922, and I came to Indianapolis as a reporter on the Indianapolis Times in August of that year. It was here I first had my experience with the Klan. The Indianapolis Times was the only paper in town that was fighting the Klan. Apparently, the News and the Star were afraid to handle the subject as it was a pretty hot one. I have always thought that the Klan's greatest success, which was just after World War I, resulted from the "back wash" of that conflict, as about the time that the American public got all heated up and on fire against foreigners as the result of the war, all of a sudden it was over, and patriotism had no place to go. It was a revival of the old "Know Nothingism" against Catholics, Jews, Negroes, and the foreigners.

The second week I was here, the city editor put me on the

187

court house as a reporter to handle the court proceedings and other things that took place over there. I was there three and a half years as a reporter and then I served as Deputy to the elected Prosecuting Attorney of Marion County, Mr. William H. Remy, from January 1, 1926 to December 31, 1928, having graduated from night Law School in 1925. As reporter I covered Klan activities, politics, and Stephenson's trial for the rape-murder of a young woman; and as Deputy I assisted in all the Grand Jury investigations and trials caused by Stephenson's "squealing" on his former Klan and political allies when they would not come to his aid after his conviction.

In those six years I got a good education on political and Ku Klux Klan activities in the Hoosier State, and I believe there has never been another era in Indiana like that of the "Roaring Twenties" for political corruption and skull-duggery in all the 153 years of its Statehood.

The voting that fall resulted in the election of a Republican ticket in Marion County composed mainly of Klansmen, as that organization had infiltrated the Republican spring Primary and nominated a Secretary of State, many Legislators, and many County officials. All Klansmen, whether Democrats or Republicans, were ordered to, and did vote in the G.O.P. Primary elections in the early twenties. Two exceptions in the local election that year were William P. Evans, an anti-Klan Republican, who was elected Prosecutor; and Albert Losche, a promising young Democrat, who defeated Leonard Quill, a Catholic Republican, for County Clerk. Whether Losche, who later served as Democratic Mayor of Indianapolis, was a Klansman, or just plain made a deal with that body, I never knew, but most of his deputies were Republican Klansmen. Stephenson furnished the brains and much of the money for this wedding of the Klan and the Republican Party.

Right here may be a good place for a short review of the history of the Ku Klux Klan. There was an organization of that name founded in Pulaski, Tennessee, in May of 1866, and a famous Confederate General of the Civil War, Nathan Bedford Forrest, took charge as its Grand Wizard. Composed mainly of ex-soldiers of the Lost Cause, its motto was "The South will rise again." The newly freed slaves, enfranchised and sustained by Uncle Sam's federal bayonets in the hands of Northern Boys in Blue, elected Republican State Legislatures, Governors, and Congressmen. Eventually the whites in Dixie united under the Klan leadership in the Democratic Party, disenfranchised the Negroes, and regained control. The Klan finally died out and was disbanded in 1872 by an order of its Grand Wizard, General Forrest, leaving the Solid South.

In 1915, a resident of Atlanta, Georgia, one William Joseph Simmons saw the new movie "Birth of a Nation" wherein the Klan rode through the South on its midnight forays, and he founded Ku Klux Klan II, taking out a copyright on the name. Members were called Knights of the Invisible Empire, and its national head was the Imperial Wizard, Simmons, who ruled as absolute monarch. The new Wizard had been a failure as an itinerant Methodist preacher, as a salesman of ladies' garters and hosiery, and as a peddler of burial insurance. He was not much more successful with his new organization and until 1920 it only had a few thousand members.

The Klan's main idea was bigotry with emphasis on "White Supremacy." In 1920, an ex-newspaper man, Edward Young Clarke, took over the Klan under a contract with wizard Simmons, and rapidly made it a national power, mostly in the South and Middle West. Clarke had a flair for publicity and decided to make the Klan an instrument to reform the morals of a decadent nation. His response in the Bible Belt was tremendous.

Clarke had as his chief assistant in this moral crusade his lady paramour, one Mrs. Elizabeth Taylor, with whom he had previously been arrested and convicted of disorderly conduct and drunkenness. After about four years, Clarke was fined for bootlegging and transporting women across State lines for prostitution and went into oblivion, along with his lady friend. Colonel Simmons under his copyright resumed control of the Klan.

Stone Mountain in Atlanta, Georgia, was the "Mount Sinai" of the resurrected Klan. Colonel Simmons was fond of relating how on Thanksgiving Day of 1915, he and three Confederate Veterans, who had been members of the original Klan, climbed the mountain at midnight with some others and formed the new Klan as they burnt the first Fiery Cross.

189

Simmons, aided later by Clarke, invented a fearful and wonderful vocabulary for the organization, which grew to many hundreds of thousand members. The head of the "Invisible Empire of the Knights of the Ku Klux Klan," duly incorporated in Georgia, was the "Imperial Wizard and his fifteen Genii" all of whose titles began with "K". The "Kludd" did the praying; the "Kligrapp" was the secretary; the "Klarogo" was the inner-guard; the "Kleagle" was an organizer, the "Klabee" was the treasurer, etc.

The States were "Realms" and ruled by "The Grand Dragon and his nine Hydras." Parts of a State were Provinces headed by "The Great Titan and his seven Furies." Local Klans were presided over by "The Exalted Cyclops and his Twelve Terrors." These titles are from the Klan Constitution of 1922, a copy of which came before the Grand Jury in 1926.

In addition there were "Night Hawks" (messengers); "Klokanns" (auditors and investigators of errant brothers); and "Giants," the Imperial, Grand, Great, and Exalted "Giants" being ex-officers. There were also Kleepers, Goblins, and Tritons. The area of a local Klan was the "Klanton."

D. C. Stephenson at different times was Kleagle of eight states, Grand Dragon of Indiana, and an Imperial Genius. He helped Hiram W. Evans seize the office of Imperial Wizard in 1922, retiring Colonel Simmons as perpetual Emperor in charge of ritual with a gift of $146,000 of Klan treasure.

The Klan's Motto was "Non Silba Sed Anthar." ("Not for self, but for others." Some one evidently wrote "Silba" in error.)

Its emblem was two hooded and robed Klansmen holding flaming crosses astride two hooded and robed horses rampant.

The "Kardinal Kullors" of the Klan were White, Crimson, Gold, and Black. Colonel Simmons devised the white robe and the hooded mask with a red tassel, which the knights wore.

One day when I was at the Court House for the Times, D. C. Stephenson sued another Klansman, and the complaint embodied a Klan decree, which began: "To all Genii, Grand Dragons, Hydras, Great Titans, Furies, Kleagles, Grand Goblins, Cyclops, Imperial Night Hawks, Terrors, and citizens of the Invisible Empire of the Realm of Indiana of the Knights of the Ku Klux Klan," and ended thusly: "Done on the Deadly Day of the Frightful Friday of the Weeping Week of the Bloody Month of the Fearful Year of the Knights of the Ku Klux Klan LVIII."

The Klan had a calendar all its own, the first month of the year being May, and each day of the week, each week of the month and each month of the year having some such title as above.

In 1922, Imperial Wizard Simmons, who was somewhat of a trusting soul, was deposed by a palace guard clique headed by Hiram Wesley Evans and David C. Stephenson. Evans became Imperial Wizard and Stephenson became Grand Dragon of Indiana. Simmons became Wizard Emeritus on a pension with the empty title of Emperor. The allies soon fell out, and in 1924, Stephenson was deposed by Evans. Stephenson rebelled and called a Konvokation of the Indiana Klans, who elected him Grand Dragon of the Realm of Indiana of the Invisible Empire.

Evans appointed a Klansman from Liberty, Indiana, one Walter Bossert, as Grand Dragon, and from then on until D. C. went to the penitentiary in 1925, there was feuding between the two rival Klans. "Steve," or the "Old Man", as he was called, always went about with two hulking bodyguards, Earl Klinck and Earl Gentry. One evening the two Grand Dragons met in the lobby of the Lincoln Hotel, and the two Earls pinned Bossert's arms while Dragon Stephenson administered a sound thrashing to his reluctant dragon rival. It was not the only fight that the "Old Man" won with the aid of his gladiators, according to repute.

After Stephenson was convicted of murder, the Klan survived with ever dwindling ranks and exists today in scattered spots. One lasting result was the alienation of 90% of the Negro vote from the Republican Party. After 1865 in Indiana every Negro man could and did vote without any poll tax or literacy test to disenfranchise him, and each voted 100% Repbulican in memory of Lincoln the Great Emancipator. When Stephenson used the Republican Party to nominate and elect Klan Governors, Legislators, Judges, Mayors and other officials, the word got around. In 1924, when Ed Jackson, Stephenson's candidate for Governor, was elected, the 5th and 6th Wards in Indianapolis, Negro Wards along Indiana Avenue, went Democratic for the first time.

In 1928, when I was a candidate for State Senator on the Republican ticket, I saw an aged Negro at a voting place in a colored precinct on Boulevard Place wearing an Al Smith button. I said, "Uncle, how can you be a Democrat, after all these years?" Tears came in the good old man's eyes, and he thumped his cane on the ground and replied, "I ain't no Democrat. Don't you dare call me a Democrat! I was seventeen years old when Mr. Lincoln's boys in blue come down to Carolina and set me free, and I always been a Republican every since."

"But", he continued, "Let me tell you, young man, I'm going to vote for Mr. Al Smith. He's agin' that Klan. The Ku Klux Klan was the skunk what pissed on the Republican Party in this State, and it's going to be many a long year before the stink wears off!"

No truer words were ever spoken. That was the main legacy left Indiana by D. C. Stephenson and the Ku Klux Klan.

My first direct connection with the Klan was as follows: One day I was over at the Court House in the Clerk's Office, and a big Klansman Deputy Clerk, a Veteran of World War I, and a Republican, took me to one side and asked me, "How would you like to be naturalized tomorrow night?"

I said, "What do you mean 'naturalized'?"

"Well," he said, "You know, you pay $10.00 and you get naturalized. We are going to have a meeting out at Bridgeport in a grove."

I said, "Well, I don't have be be naturalized as I was born down by Vincennes, Indiana, and I am an American citizen and I have no reason for being naturalized, let alone paying $10.00. I suppose you are talking about the Ku Klux Klan?"

He said, "Yeah, that is about it, you ought to join, everybody else is joining."

I said, "Well, tell me, friend, what is it with you fellows in the Klan, what do you stand for?"

"We are against the Negroes, the Catholics, the Jews, and the foreigners," he said.

"Let me put it this way," I said, "Now there are about ten million Negroes, and there are about three million Jews in the United States, and God alone knows how many foreigners, and there are quite a few million Catholics, what are we going to do about this thing? We have three alternatives. We can run them all out of the country, or, second, we can kill them, or, third, we can live with them. You can see it is impossible to run all of them out of the country; it is going to be impossible to kill them all, and therefore, the only alternative we have is to live with them. Why don't we live in peace and quiet, that is what we are going to have to do. Let's have peace, quiet and harmony because there is nothing else we can do."

He said, "Niblack, you talk silly."

I said, "Maybe I am silly but I am not going to join because I don't believe in it. I think it is Un-American."

The consequence was that I didn't join, although I had many Protestant friends who did join. Quite a few politicans around the town and the State, major and minor, both Democrat and Republican, joined the Klan to obtain political preferment. Governor Jackson, who was elected in 1924, was one of them. I could name numerous others. The Mayor of Indianapolis, John L. Duvall, who was elected in 1925, was another.

There was a Catholic young man that worked in the Court House taking the news for the Indianapolis Commercial and he got into a fight one day with the same Klansman, a Deputy Clerk. I heard him say, "I'll tell you something, in about five years, you people around here—a lot of you— are going to be trying to get an affidavit to say you never belonged to the Ku Klux Klan." I will say this—Jimmy was right. It was less than five years when a lot of people wished they could get an affidavit to that effect.

The Klan got rather prominent around Indianapolis. They had a big parade which came down Indiana Avenue from one end to the other, down Capitol and along Washington Street, up Pennsylvania and around the Circle. They said they had 50,000 people. I stood on the corner of Capitol and Indiana Avenue counting the ones as they marched by in their hoods and robes and I estimated there were about 5,500 people. I remember that "Little Joe" Biggerstaff, a fellow Sigma Nu of mine at DePauw and a Phi Beta Kappa, who was State Kleagle of Kentucky, rode by on a white horse. He had a purple robe. The colored people stood along the sidewalk with me

193

on Indiana Avenue and watched the cavalcade and marchers go by. I remember some of them laughed and said, "Look at the little bitty Klansmen." There were included little children about six or eight years old with their little hoods and robes on.

There was no disturbance nor excitement that night. Colored people and many Jews and foreigners all watched them go. I made this count and wrote a story for the Indianapolis Times. In addition to the parade, they had various cross burnings on various hills and in some colored people's yards, but as far as I remember there was no violence recorded anywhere, by anybody, at anytime or anything, contrary to the impression people have nowadays, although there were floggings and beatings in Oklahoma and some other parts. I do think the colored population was somewhat terrified by the phenomenon of people marching around in these white robes and pointed hoods.

One of the favorite activities of the Klan was to march into some Protestant church in the suburbs during church services in their ghostly coverings of white and solemnly present the preacher with one hundred dollars in small bills, and then file out again, all in complete silence. They also held some Klan funerals at Crown Hill and other graveyards, complete with robes, hoods, and burning crosses.

On July 4, 1923, the three newspapers each sent a reporter to Mehalfa Park at Kokomo, which was a place owned by the Ku Klux Klan. There Mr. Stephenson was going to make quite a speech. We went over to the Century Building the day before, where Mr. Milton Elrod, editor of the Fiery Cross, the official Klan newspaper, had his office. We were Mr. Earl Bullock, for the Star; Mickey McCarty, for the News; and I, for the Times. Mr. Elrod arranged to take us up and gave us a press pass. He asked, "Are any of you boys card carrying members?"

Mr. Bullock said, "Yes, I have a card in the Klan," and he pulled it out and showed it to Mr. Elrod. I didn't have any and I told him so. Mr. McCarty said, "Well, I am a Roman Catholic, I don't have any, either."

The next morning we all got up at 5:00 o'clock and met Editor Elrod at 6:00 at his office. We put on our linen dusters and took off in an automobile over a gravel road to Kokomo, and went to the hotel headquarters there. It was later on that Mr. Stephenson arrived, as I shall tell you, but at the hotel, Mr. Bullock, the Star reporter, got hold of a quart of bootleg white mule whisky, and after sipping quite frequently on it, got into a shape where he couldn't go out to the grounds and see the proceedings. Mr. McCarty, being a Catholic, said he was afraid to go and he stayed at the hotel, and consequently, I was the only one of the three reporters to get out to Mehalfa Park to help welcome D. C., "the Old Man."

About 10:30 A.M., he came in a small airplane of those days, a yellow colored one, and circled around three or four times. It had underneath the wings the words, "Evansville KKK No. 1." He landed over in some field somewhere and came and got upon the platform before a multitude of some 10,000 cheering people, mostly dressed in their white robes and hoods, although later it was announced that there was 50,000 there. Fifty thousand seemed to be a favorite number given out by the Klan.

One report of the inauguration, or whatever it was, announced that 150,000 Klansmen were there, and that they showered Stephenson with money and jewelry when he mounted the stage. It was a clear, hot, July day, and my vision at that time was 20-20. I sat right behind D. C. at a little press table they brought on for me, and I can testify no money or jewelry was thrown at his feet or anywhere else.

I don't know if they took up a collection or not. I didn't see any being taken, and I didn't donate anything. As I said, it was pretty hot, and a lot of the yokels out in front got up a pretty good sweat under their robes. It was a rather weird sight at that—sort of like a mild nightmare, with 10,000 men in white sheets and masked pointed hoods staring up at me. Some of them may have been women, for all I know.

Mr. Stephenson mounted the stage whereon I sat, dressed in a business suit, and made a speech about the Little Red School House and the American Way of living, and this and that and the other, which didn't amount to two whoops, as far as I could see, but everybody cheered again.

Stephenson was born in Texas in 1891. He was not too tall, being about five feet eight and one-half inches in height, and was

195

plump. He weight some 160 or 170 pounds at the time of his conviction, though he went up to 200 in prison, he told the Grand Jury.

Like many a man before him, his downfall was liquor and women. He was married three times, being divorced by his first two wives.

After the speech, we went back to the hotel and I arranged an interview with Mister Stephenson. Passing quite a few guards, I was admitted to the august presence and I asked him some questions, such as: What did he intend to do with the Catholics, Negroes and Jews? Did he intend to kill them, run them out, or live with them? What is the ultimate objective of the Klan? And how much money did he make out of it? This last question almost brought rain, and when I got to that point, he said, "Just a minute, young man, just stop right there. You are a part of a national conspiracy to upset this Klan. I have been propounded this very same set of questions at least thirty different times in thirty different States."

I said, "Well, I don't know anything about that. I made the list up myself yesterday before I came up here."

He said, "I can see you are just a bigot, you are not for us, you are against us. So just get out of here."

I thereupon left and we returned to Indianapolis.

Stephenson had his office at Washington and Pennsylvania Streets on the southwest corner, on the third floor, in what was known as the Kresge Building. It bore the name of his coal company on the door and covered the entire floor.

I was going over to the Court House one day with our City Hall reporter, Mr. Walter Shead, who, incidentally, was a Catholic, and he said, "Let's stop and see 'the Old Man.'" He knew everybody in town it seemed. I said, "Who is that?", and he replied, "D. C. Stephenson." I said, "I have already met him, but I didn't know they called him 'the Old Man.'"

We went up to the Kresge Building and were admitted rather soon because Stephenson was publicity conscious. We went into his room and he was sitting at a big desk facing the old Indiana Trust Building. All of a sudden, he jumped up and came around the desk and said, "Get to one side! Don't stand there in front of that big window. There are people lying over there in the point of the Indiana Trust Building with high-powered rifles just trying to shoot me and they might shoot you by mistake." Needless to say, Shead and I both jumped to one side pretty quickly. That was about all there was to the interview, though we talked a little bit more, and then I went over to the Indiana Trust Building and walked up the six floors and made an investigation. This building was a triangle in shape, and in the front office on the point, facing Stephenson's office, on the sixth floor was the law firm of Senator Arthur R. Robinson and Frank Symmes, who were attorneys for the Klan; on the third floor was Robert Marsh, who was also attorney for the Klan, and there were other prominent law firms occupying the other three floors, while the bottom floor was occupied by the Indiana Trust Bank, now a part of the Merchants Bank. I went into each room of each office at the point, and saw no riflemen. I concluded that Stephenson must have been having hallucinations. In fact, after I knew him pretty well, I decided he was a slight mental case, which by no means dimmed his brilliance of thought or action. He certainly had a lot of the two main symptoms of dementia praecox, illusions of grandeur and delusions of persecution.

Mr. William H. Remy, Chief Deputy to Prosecutor Evans, and his successor, who was later Stephenson's nemesis and downfall, said he always thought that Stephenson believed he was a reincarnation of D'Artagnan, who went about with his two allies, Athos and Porthos. He had a way of snapping his fingers and saying, "Come on, boys, let's go", then wheeling around and marching briskly away with Klinck and Gentry at his heels, which reminded Remy of D'Artagnan, who had a similiar habit.

Mr. Remy, a graduate of Indiana University Law School, was elected in 1924, as Prosecuting Attorney on the Republican ticket. He was one of the few candidates in the spring Primary who broke through the Klan endorsement. He came from a long line of French Huguenot ancestors and was intensely devoted to the American way of life and liberty. I believe he was the most honest and fearless man I ever knew in all my life. He alone, being in charge of the Marion Count Grand Jury, was solely responsible for the downfall of the Ku Klux Klan in the State of Indiana.

I will add that Asa J. Smith, a Phi Delt fraternity brother of Remy's, was responsible for obtaining the written dying declaration of Miss Madge Oberholtzer which convicted Stephenson at his trial for her murder. Smith furnished the Prosecutor and the Grand Jury this tool, without which I doubt seriously that Stephenson or others would have been indicted and successfully prosecuted.

This said, it remains true that a lesser man than Remy could not or would not have brought the "Invisible Empire of the Knights of the Ku Klux Klan" to an end in Indiana.

Stephenson rapidly made friends and allies of the Republican leaders in Marion County and all over Indiana in 1922, 1923, and 1924. He lined up the Klan delegates to the County and State Conventions in 1924, and succeeded in electing George V. Coffin Republican County Chairman of our County. I was present in Criminal Courtroom in the old Court House in May, 1924, at the County Convention which put Coffin in.

There were one hundred armed city police in uniform in the halls to guard the outgoing Chairman, William Freeman, the City Hall leader under Mayor Lew Shank. There were also fifty uniformed and armed Deputy Sheriffs present to guard Stephenson's crowd.

Stephenson lurked in the background, darting in and out of the Chambers of Judge James A. Collins, a practical Republican politician who was not above drinking "Steve's" whisky now and then, and who knew votes when he saw them.

Fortunately there was no shooting. D.C.'s candidate prevailed.

Stephenson, the Klan, and his Republican Klan party officers, that spring nominated a Republican Klansman for Governor, Ed Jackson of New Castle, and another for Secretary of State, the Honorable Frederick Schortemeier. They also nominated a Klan ticket from Marion County for the Indiana Legislature, with two exceptions, and the Honorable Ralph Updike, a police court attorney, for Congress, as well as nearly all County Officials except Prosecutor Remy and the Judges, who were not up for election that year. All were swept into office in the Coolidge land-slide. Many of these people had been in politics for years before Stepehnson ever came to Indiana and merely joined up to get elected.

198

In 1925, Stephenson and his allies nominated and elected another Klan ticket headed by Mayor John L. Duvall, and including the City Council, City Clerk, and the Indianapolis School Board.

In March of that year, Stephenson had said, "I am the law in Indiana."

On November 4, 1925, David C. Stephenson stood on the peak of political power in Indiana. It was election day.

On the same date, the Indianapolis newspapers headlined, "The State of Indiana rests its case against D. C. Stephenson."

He was on trial at Noblesville, Hamilton County, Indiana, for his life, charged with the rape-murder of a young woman.

"Guilty of Murder"

The year 1925 was a fateful one for David C. Stephenson. On January 12th he was the center of attraction at the inauguration dinner and ball of the Republican Governor of Indiana, Ed Jackson of New Castle, whom he and his Klan forces had elected the year before at a cost to Stephenson of $227,000, according to his later sworn testimony before an Indianapolis Grand Jury.

The affair was a glittering event, held at the fashionable Indianapolis Athletic Club, and many a notable and his lady were there—as well as the pride and flower of the Republican Party and many Ku Klux Klan dukes and duchesses, all in tuxedoes and evening gowns for the occasion instead of their white robes and pointed-hood masks.

Steve, known as the "Old Man" to his Klan and political hench-gentlemen and hench-ladies, though he was only 34 years old, had also in the two years before engineered the election of a Klan delegation to the Indiana Legislature, a United States Congressman from Indianapolis, and a Secretary of State. He had laid the ground work for the later election in 1925 of the Mayor, City Council, and School Board of the State Capitol. All County officials except two had been chosen by Stephenson in 1924 and elected. Of the two County officials not in "the Old Man's" pocket, one was Prosecuting Attorney William H. Remy, born the same year as Stephenson. Remy was intensely Anti-Crime, Anti-Klan, and Anti-Stephenson.

Stephenson was at the peak of his power.

"I am the Law in Indiana," he said.

He was about 5' 8½" tall, and weighed about 170 pounds, being somewhat plump and well fed. He had a round face, blue eyes, a ruddy complexion, and his hair was thinning considerably on top. He was vigorous, lively, ready in speech, with the "gift of gab" as Hoosiers say, having a rapid and fluent way of speaking. He was quite intelligent and was a good organizer. He generally wore blue serge suits of fashionable cut. He had an imperious air of dominance and would brook no opposition. His lower lip was somewhat full and sensuous.

The Old Man's downfall started at the Governor's Inaugural Ball, when he was introduced to a comely young woman of 28 years, Madge Oberholtzer. She was a member of an old family in Irvington, an elite suburb on the far east side of Indianapolis. It was also the site of Butler University, where Madge had graduated, and there she had been a member of Pi Beta Phi sorority.

Stephenson, a man of violent lusts after women, especially when he had been drinking whiskey, which was often, liked the young woman's brunette looks and sprightly demeanor, and as his eyes roved over her shapely body, he mentally marked her for his own.

It was to cost her life.

Steve's method of dealing with the fair sex was not that of a seductive Don Juan. He had a touch of sadism in him that caused him much trouble. He had been married in Texas and fathered a daughter, but his wife soon obtained a divorce on the grounds of cruel and brutal treatment. Later his second wife, from Ohio, obtained a divorce on almost identical grounds.

Testimony before the Grand Jury described a case in 1923, in a hotel room in Columbus, Ohio, where Stephenson and two companions had a drunken brawl. He called room service to send a manicurist, and a young lady dutifully appeared with her tray ready for action, but not the kind Steve had in mind. He offered her money, and when she refused, he threw her on the bed and attempted rape, but her screams and the general rumpus attracted the two companions who had gone to an adjoining room, and they persuaded Stephenson to let the young lady go—which she did abruptly, summoning the police. He was arrested, but the case was hushed up.

The same week "Steve" was arrested in a "lover's lane" in Columbus in the act of intercourse in the back seat of an automobile. This case was dropped also.

A private secretary of Stephenson testified that he held her captive in his home one time, and forced her to drink some sort of sleeping potion and put her to bed, but whether he had relations with her while she was stupefied, she did not know.

A gentleman named Court Asher, at one time a messenger and body guard of "Steve's", and an unrepentant bootlegger from Muncie, Indiana, testified that "Steve" "was mighty impetuous and wild as to women when drunk." The urbane Asher further detailed how one of Steve's favorite orgies was when he played the Satyr to a bunch of naked wood nymphs. Asher said they would all strip naked and the Old Man would take a whip and lash the girls as they all whirled around the room to see who could stand pain the longest. The survivor would then be rewarded with a handsome gift of money, and get to grace the great man's bed the rest of the night.

Stephenson had three or four dates, in company, with Miss Oberholtzer, at some polite functions, one being a dinner at his house. He lived near the Oberholtzer family in Irvington, having bought the old sorority house of Kappa Kappa Gamma Sorority at Butler.

Then one Sunday afternoon, March 15, 1925, "Steve" and some companions got to drinking bootleg whiskey at his home. His passion rose, and he began to think of Miss Oberholtzer.

Let her describe the events that followed, that led her to a lonely grave in an Indianapolis cemetery and him to 31 years in the Michigan City State Prison of Indiana for murder.

SUBSTANCE OF THE DYING DECLARATION OF OBERHOLTZER TAKEN FROM VOLUME 205, OF THE REPORTS OF THE INDIANA SUPREME COURT, IN THE CASE OF STEPHENSON V. STATE OF INDIANA

The victim of this homicide is Madge Oberholtzer, who was a resident of the City of Indianapolis and lived with her father and mother at 5802 University Avenue, Irvington. She was twenty-eight years of age; weighed about 140 pounds, and had always been in good health; was educated in the public primary and high school and Butler College. Just prior to the time of the commission of the alleged acts in the indictment of appellant upon her, she was employed by the State Superintendent of Public Instruction as manager of the Young Peoples' Reading Circle.

Miss Oberholzer was introduced to appellant by her escort at a banquet in the City of Indianapolis, January 12, 1925. This introduction was their first meeting.

Appellant resided at ——— ——————— Street, Irvington, City of Indianapolis, at the time of the beginning of the actions disclosed by the evidence. His home was but a short distance, some two or three city blocks, from the home of the Oberholtzers. After the meeting of appellant and Miss Oberholtzer at the banquet, he invited her several times for a "date." She gave him no definite answer. She later consented to his insistent invitation to take dinner with him at a hotel in Indianapolis, Indiana, and upon the occasion, he came to her home for her with his automobile and they dined together.

Thereafter, appellant called her several times by telephone, and once again she had dinner with him at the same hotel, at which another person was a third member of the party. Subsequent to the second dinner, Miss Oberholtzer was at Stephenson's home at a party with several prominent people, where both ladies and gentlemen were guests. The two principal actors to this tragedy did not see each other again until late Sunday evening, March 15, 1925. The afternoon of that Sunday, she had been away from home and returned between nine and ten o'clock in the evening. Upon her return, her mother, Mrs. Matilda Oberholtzer, informed her that a telephone message came for her, which the mother delivered to her daughter, which was a piece of paper upon which there was the telephone number Irvington 0492. Miss Oberholtzer called the number and Stephenson answered the call. He asked her to come to his home for he wished to see her about something very important to herself and that he was leaving for Chicago and it was necessary that he see her before he departed. In the telephone conversation, Stephenson said to Miss Oberholtzer that he could not leave, but that he would send someone for her. Very soon thereafter, a Mr. Gentry, whom Miss Oberholtzer had never seen, came for her and said he was from Stephenson. She walked with Gentry to Stephenson's home. When they arrived, they went inside the home and there saw Stephenson. He had been drinking. Stephenson's chauffeur, whom he called "Shorty," was there also. As soon as she got inside the house, she grew very much afraid when she learned that there was no other woman about, that Stephenson's housekeeper was away, or at least not to be seen. Immediately upon her arrival at Stephenson's home, he, with the other men, took her into the kitchen and some drinks were produced. At this time another man by the name of Klinck came in by the back door. She said she did not want to drink, but Stephenson and the other men forced her to drink, and she submitted because she was afraid to refuse, and drank three small glasses of the liquor produced. The drinks made her very ill and dazed and the effects of them caused her to vomit. Stephenson then said to her, "I want you to go to Chicago with me." She said she couldn't and would not; and that she was much terrified and did not know what to do and said that she wanted to go home. Stephenson replied to her, "No, you can not go home. Oh! yes! you are going with me to Chicago. I love you more than any woman I have ever known." She then tried to call her home by telephone, but could get no answer. Later, when she again tried to get to the telephone, they prevented her from so doing.

The men then took her up to Stephenson's room and Stephenson opened a dresser drawer, which was filled with revolvers. He told each of the men to take one and he selected a pearl-handled revolver and had "Shorty" load it. Stpehenson then said first to her that they were going to drive through to Chicago. She told him that she would not go. Then Gentry called a hotel in Indianapolis, at Stephenson's order, and secured reservations in a drawing room for two persons. Then all of the men took her to the automobile at the rear of Stephenson's yard and they started the trip. She thought they were bound for Chicago, but did not know. She begged them to drive past home so that she might get her hat on a ruse that if she did get inside her home she would be safe from them. Before they left Stephenson's house, Stephenson said to Klinck, "You get in touch with," (an officer) "right away and tell him we are going to Chicago on a business deal to make money for all of us." Then they started. Klinck was not one of the party in the automobile. Stephenson and Gentry sat in the car all of the time with her until they got to the train. On the trip from Stephenson's home to the railway station in Indianapolis, the automobile was stopped at the hotel and there "Shorty" went into the hotel and came back. While at this stop, Stephenson and Gentry refused to let her out of the automobile. At this time she was in a dazed and terrified condition and feared that her life would be taken by Stephenson. He told her that he was the law in Indiana and said to Gentry, "I think I am pretty smart to have gotten her."

Stephenson, Gentry, and she boarded the train, where all three went at once into the compartment or drawing room. She was in such condition that she could not remember all that happened after that, but she did remember that Gentry got into the top berth of the compartment. Stephenson then took hold of the bottom of her dress and pulled it over her head, against her wishes, and she tried to fight him away, but was weak and unsteady. Then Stephenson took hold of her two hands and held her, but she did not have strength to get away, because what she had drunk was affecting her. Then Stephenson took off all her clothes and pushed her into the lower berth. After the train started, Stephenson got into the berth with her and attacked her, and, in so doing, he held her so she couldn't move and did not know and did not remember all that happened. She did remember that he chewed her all over her body; bit her neck and face; chewed her tongue, chewed her breasts until they bled and chewed her back, her legs and her ankles and mutilated her all over her body. She remembered of hearing a buzz early in the morning and the porter calling them to get up for Hammond. Then Gentry shook her and said it was time to get up and that they were to leave the train at Hammond, Indiana. At this time, she became more conscious, and, before they left the train, Stephenson was flourishing his revolver. Then she asked him to shoot her. He held the revolver against her side and she said to him again to kill her, but he put the gun away in his grip. During the night on the train, she heard no sound from Gentry. After the car porter called them, Stephenson and Gentry helped her to dress; then the two men dressed and took her off the train at Hammond. After leaving the train, she was able to walk with the two men to the Indiana Hotel. During the night she begged Stephenson to send a telegram to her mother. At the Indiana Hotel, Stephenson registered for himself and wife under the name of Mr. and Mrs. W. B. Morgan, address, Franklin, and were assigned to room 416. Gentry then registered under the name of Earl Gentry, address, Indianapolis, Indiana, and was assigned to room number 417. The time they reached the hotel was about 6:30 o'clock in the morning. In the hotel lobby, when they entered, were two colored bell boys and two colored girls. The three, as guests of the hotel, were taken up the elevator and shown to their rooms. During this time Miss Oberholtzer continued begging Stephenson to send a telegram to her mother. Stephenson then made her write a telegram and told her what to say in it. After the telegram was written, Gentry took it and said he would send it immediately. Stephenson then laid down on the bed and slept, while Gentry put hot towels and witch hazel on her head and bathed her body to relieve her suffering.

Breakfast was served in their room. Stephenson ate grapefruit, coffee, sausage and buttered toast. She drank some coffee, but ate nothing. At this time, "Shorty" came in the room. He said to Stephenson that he had been delayed getting there because he could not find the hotel where they were guests in Hammond. Then she asked Stephenson to give her some money, for she had none, so that she might purchase herself a hat. Stephenson told "Shorty" to give her money and he gave her $15.00 and took her out in the automobile. "Shorty" waited for her while she went into a store and purchased a hat, for which she paid $12.50. When she returned to the car, she asked "Shorty" to drive her to a drug store so that she might purchase some rouge. He then drove the car to the drug store, where she purchased a box of bichloride of mercury tablets, put them in her coat pocket and returned with "Shorty" in the automobile to the hotel. During the morning at the hotel, the men got more liquor at Stephenson's direction. Stephenson said they were all going to drive on to Chicago and made her write the telegram to her mother saying that they were going to Chicago. This was the telegram that Gentry took.

After she and "Shorty" returned to the hotel, she asked Stephenson to let her go into room 417, which was the room assigned to Gentry, so that she might lie down and rest. And Stephenson replied, "Oh, no, you are not going there, you are going to lie right down here by me." She then waited awhile and until she thought Stephenson was asleep and then went into room 417 and Gentry remained in room 416 with Stephenson. There was no glass in room 417, so she procured a glass from room 416, laid out eighteen of the bichloride of mercury tablets and at once took six of them, which was about ten o'clock in the morning of Monday, March 16, 1925. She only took six of the tablets because they burnt her so. Earlier in the morning she had taken Stephenson's revolver and thought to kill herself in Stephenson's presence while he was asleep. It was then she decided to try and get poison and take it in order to save her mother from disgrace. She knew it would take longer for the mercury tablets to kill her. After she had taken the tablets, she lay down on the bed and became very ill. It was nearly four o'clock in the afternoon of Monday that "Shorty" came into the room and sat down to talk to her. He said to her that she looked ill and asked her what was wrong, and she replied, "Nothing." He asked her where she had pain and she replied that pain was all over her. He then said to her that she could not have pain without cause. When she asked him, "Can you keep a secret?" He answered, "Yes." She said, "I believe you can." Then she told him she had taken poison, but that he should not tell Stephenson. She had been vomiting blood all day. When she said to him that she had taken poison, "Shorty" turned pale and said that he wanted to take a walk. He left the room and, in a few minutes, Stephenson, Gentry, and "Shorty" came into the room very much excited. Stephenson then said, "What have you done?" She answered, "I asked 'Shorty' not to tell." Stephenson then ordered a quart of milk and made her drink it and then she said to him and to others that she had taken six bichloride of mercury tablets, and said, "If you don't believe it, there is evidence on the floor and in the cuspidor." Stephenson then emptied the cuspidor, which was half full of clotted blood, into the bathtub and saw some of the tablets. She then asked Stephenson what he intended to do, to which he replied, "We will take you to a hospital and you can register as my wife. Your stomach will have to be pumped out." He said that she could tell them at the hospital that she had gotten mercury tablets through a mistake instead of aspirin. To Stephenson's suggestion, she refused to comply as his wife. Then it was that Stephenson said that they would take her home. She then said to Stephenson that she would not go home, but would stay at the hotel, and asked them to leave her and go about their own business or to permit her to register at another hotel under her own name. Stephenson then said, "We will do nothing of the kind. We will take you home," and that the best way out of it was for them to go to Crown Point and there she marry him, to which suggestion, Gentry said he agreed it was the thing to do. She refused. Stephenson then snapped his fingers and instructed "Shorty" to pack the grips. Then they departed from the hotel. Stephenson assisted her down the stairs. Before leaving she asked "Shorty" to telephone her mother. Stephenson said that he had already called her. She asked what her mother said and Stephenson answered, that, she said it would be all right if her daughter did not come home that night.

"Shorty" checked out of the hotel for the three and they then put her in the back seat of the automobile with Stephenson and the luggage and started for home. Her mind was in a daze and she was in terrible agony. After they had proceeded in the automobile for a short distance, Stephenson ordered "Shorty" to take the auto license plates off the car, which "Shorty" did, and Stephenson then directed him to say, if questioned, that they had parked in the last town where the auto plates had been stolen. On the journey back to Indianapolis she screamed for a doctor, and said she wanted a hypodermic to relieve the pain, but the men refused to stop. She begged Stephenson to leave her along the road some place, that someone would stop and take care of her, and said to Stpehenson, that he was even then more cruel to her than he had been the night before. He promised to stop at the next town, but did not. Just before reaching a town he would say to "Shorty," "Drive fast, but don't get pinched." She vomited in the car all over the back seat and the luggage. Stephenson did nothing to make her comfortable upon the trip. He said to Gentry, "This takes guts to do this, Gentry, she is dying," and that he said to Gentry he had been in a worse mess than this before and got out of it. Stephenson and Gentry drank liquor during the entire trip. Stephenson said also that he had power and that he had made a quarter of a million dollars and, that "his word was law."

Miss Madge Oberholtzer died on April 14, 1925, from infected teeth bites and bicholoride of mercury poisoning.

Some days prior, William Lowell Toms, who was the Times

reporter at the State House where she was employed in the office of the Superintendent of Public Instruction, got wind that the "Old Man" was in serious trouble about some woman. "Tubby", as he was called, and I were jointly assigned to the case, and we continued on it until the final verdict in the Circuit Court of Hamilton County, Noblesville, Indiana, on November 14, 1925. Tubby was one of the finest reporters in my time, ending up writing a column entitled the "Great Outdoors," which ran for many years in the Indianapolis News.

On April 2nd, George Oberholtzer, the father of the dying girl, obtained an arrest warrant from Prosecutor Remy charging Stephenson with rape. D. C. came down the next afternoon to surrender in Criminal Court.

Several of us reporters were waiting at the Court House and finally cornered him in the office of the County Commissioners, where he was waiting to meet his attorney. We asked him if he had any statement.

"I refuse to discuss such trivial matters," he said airily. "How would you boys like to be fishing right now and watch a red darter spinning in front of a bass?"

"Yeah, it would be nice," I said, "but what about this charge, Mr. Stephenson?"

"Nothing to it! Nothing to it! I'll never be indicted," he replied.

He was indicted shortly thereafter, along with his aides, Earl Klinch and Earl Gentry, on four counts, charging first degree murder.

"I'll never be tried," he told us reporters then. He was tried.

"I'll never be convicted," he told us as the trial began. He was convicted.

"I'll never serve," he told us after the verdict. He served 31 years.

The murder indictment was in four counts. The first count charged the three defendants with kidnap-assault and refusal to get Miss Oberholtzer an antidote for a deadly poison, to-wit: bichloride of mercury she had taken while keeping her in forcible custody, whereby she died.

Count No. 2 charged that they caused her to take the poison by her own hand, being under duress, fear, and compulsion of the defendants.

Count No. 3 charged that the defendants did feloniously assault her by striking, beating, biting and wounding the body of the decedent with intent to forcibly ravish and rape her, causing her to sicken, languish, and die as the result of such actions.

Count No. 4 charged that the defendants kidnaped Miss Oberholtzer, put her in their custody and control, beat, assaulted and bit her, and that while in the throes of bodily pain and anguish, mental pain and distraction she swallowed the poison, and that defendants refused her a physician or an antidote, though able to provide the same, and continued to restrain her from her liberty until too late, whereby she died.

Counts one, two and four proceeded upon a rarely used but well-known theory of murder wherein a person under control, duress, and custody of another, takes his own life because of duress, fear, shame, etc.

The third count directly charged that Miss Oberholtzer died as a result of beating, rape, bites and other wounds.

I have always thought the jury probably believed the third count had been proved, as a doctor testified at the trial that she died of an acute pus infection caused by teeth bites.

The other three counts had direct testimony to support them, as the written dying declaration of the girl was introduced into evidence, under an established exception to the rule against hearsay evidence. If given by a person mortally wounded, who knows he or she is about to die, it is admissible, either oral or written, as though the deceased was on the witness stand, under the theory that a person about to meet her Maker will not lie. I have wondered what would happen in such case if a defendant could show the decedent as an atheist.

Grand Dragon Stephenson at the time of his arrest and for a long time thereafter was confident he could handle the situation. After all, he had been in pretty tight spots before and had always wriggled out. He had plenty of money with which to bribe public officials, jurors, and witnesses, and he had done it before.

However, he had not counted on William H. Remy, the Prosecuting Attorney of the 19th Judicial Circuit. Once he had taken hold of a case, he pursued it relentlessly through thick and thin, like a bloodhound on a warm trail. He had a keen, logical mind, a world of determination, and he was an ideal Prosecutor to represent the public. He hated organized or premeditated crime like the Devil hates Holy water. He had high ideals for public office, and for crooked politicians and cheating public officials he had only the highest disdain. He was a masterful trial lawyer before a jury. There was none better in the State of Indiana.

Mr. Remy obtained a Grand Jury which would and did indict the three men. Then Stephenson took a change of venue out of Marion County to Hamilton County, with its Civil War vintage red brick Court House and jail on the town square in the heart of Noblesville, Indiana, a city of some 5,000 persons.

Mr. Remy went along with the transcript in the case, as under Indiana law he retained full jurisdiction to prosecute. Next, Stephenson wanted a change of Judge, and the Honorable Will Sparks, of Rushville, Indiana, from a distant Circuit, was chosen. He was a jurist above reproach, and an able lawyer.

So the trial began, on October 25, 1925. Stephenson's battery of lawyers was led by the Honorable Ephraim Inman of Indianapolis, a silvery haired orator who had acquired fame back in the Gay Nineties as a young man with his ability to sway juries. Also, there were Floyd Christian of Noblesville, a like celebrity in his own bailiwick, and Ira Holmes, a leading criminal lawyer of the old school in the city of Indianapolis, with a fine mane of black hair.

Prosecutor Remy was assisted by Prosecutor Justin Roberts, of Hamilton County, and some special deputy prosecutors, including Ralph Kane, formerly of Noblesville, and a formidable figure in the Court room. Kane had deep roots in Hamilton County, and was successful in getting an unbiased jury, though it was common knowledge that Stephenson's agents made frantic efforts to get to the talesmen and later to the chosen jury.

The trial lasted from October 25, to November 14, 1925, the State resting its case on November 4, Election Day in Indiana, and the same day when Stephenson's Klan Republican ticket swept the

211

board in Indianapolis. Stephenson and his two co-defendants refused to take the stand, insisting through their attorneys that the young lady decedent had voluntarily committed suicide. About the only thing that both sides agreed on completely was that she was dead.

I had a 1919 Model T Ford coupe with a hand crank starter and no windshield wiper, which I kept parked in the alley beside my rooming house at 16th and Illinois. Each morning Tubby Toms and I would ride up to Noblesville in the old crate and return that evening. The Times never even bought my gasoline, as Scripps-Howard was frugal. We would dictate, via telephone, from two to fourteen columns a day from the press room behind the Court room. It was a converted public toilet about ten by twenty feet in size.

The trial was a field day for reporters. All three Indianapolis papers were there. The Chicago Tribune was represented by a man named Hunt, and the two Chicago Hearst papers by reporters Quizno and Bensinger. The latter's life was later portrayed in a successful stage play, "The Front Page." Many other news men were there.

Stephenson and his buddies lived in style in the old jail, guests of a kindly old sheriff who became so attached to Stephenson he shed tears when he was taken to prison. He was firmly convinced Stephenson was innocent, believing wholeheartedly in D. C.'s vociferous charges, long and loudly repeated, that the whole thing was a gigantic frameup invented by Klan Imperial Wizard Hiram W. Evans and Stephenson's successor Grand Dragon, Walter Bossert of Liberty, Indiana.

Stephenson had company at the jail almost every evening, sometimes a lovely lady whom he entertained in private. According to testimony before a subsequent Grand Jury, a United States Senator, some County and State officials and some Klan friends sent him much money, books, food, and liquor. The latter was said to have come from a huge cache of fine whiskey, confiscated from a Squibbs Company by U. S. Prohibition Agents as bootleg and stored in the Indianapolis Federal Building basement. It was under control of United States employees who were deep in politics with the "Old Man." Much of the whiskey disappeared during those corrupt days of the national "Noble Experiment."

The three defendants were never in irons or hand-cuffs. They

212

would amble over every morning for trial, half of the time unaccompanied by any deputy and sit all day at the defense table unguarded. On adjournment, they would fool around a while and finally go back to jail for supper and the night.

"Steve" enjoyed a good relationship with a lot of the press, as he was liberal with presents of good whiskey and money to those of the boys who would deal with him and some did, though they were the minority. Some of the out-of-town reporters from far off, who roomed in Noblesville, would visit him now and then at night in the jail.

It got rumored around about this business, and Tubby and I discussed what we would do if offered money to touch-up the news or slant it. Tubby had an inspiration, "We'll take the dough, and expose the attempted bribe and give the money to charity," he suggested. Accordingly, the next morning before we left for Noblesville we conferred with our City Editor, Volney Fowler. "A swell idea," Volney agreed.

About two days later we had a headline, "Defense Scores Important Point." The next morning I was in the little press room and one of the Chicago reporters approached me with a $100 bill, which he put in my hand with the statement, "Here's a little present from Steve for you, and I have one for Tubby, too."

"What's this for? What's this all about?" I asked, though I thought I knew.

"It's for that good story you had in the Times yesterday. Keep it up! Get Tubby here, will you"?

I was excited, realizing our trap had sprung. I raced out and plucked Tubby by the arm as he was interviewing the Prosecutor just before Court convened.

"Come here, Tubby, at once. Come with me," I said.

"In a minute. Leave me alone now. I'm getting a story," said Tubby, who sometimes had a short temper. I dragged him away anyhow, which was a mistake, as he got hot under the collar. "Steve's" reporter friend shoved the $100 bill into Tubby's hand. "What's that for"? he inquired, with a blank look.

"Why that's from Steve for you for that good story."

"Well, for God's sake!" he exclaimed in rage. "I don't want

213

his dirty money. Just tell him to stick it up his backbone," and with that he threw the money on the floor and stomped back to the Court room.

Well, there stood Ole Honest John, red faced and foolish. The reporter picked up the bill. I pulled out my pocketbook and handed him back my $100 bill. "I guess I don't want mine either," I told him, looking silly.

I never said anything all day about it to Tubby until we were on our way home.

"Tubby, don't you remember you and Fowler and I made it up if Steve gave us money we would take it and expose him?"

"Well, for goodness sakes! I sure do. I forgot all about it, I was so mad, I forgot. Excuse me, Nibby," he said, and more.

"Well, you sure made me look like and feel like an ass," I replied.

One of my chief memories of Toms concerns a hot July day when several of us reporters went out to his house on North Illinois Street and ate copiously of watermelon which we washed down with a lot of near beer spiked with medical alcohol, and I wound up somewhat indisposed, to say the least. I never tried that combination again.

Later on during the trial, just after the Court adjourned one day, I was still at the press table while Judge Sparks was gathering up his papers on the bench, and the Court room was clearing. Stephenson came up to me and said, "Niblack, I think I'm going to punch your nose!"

Taken back a little, I asked, "What for?" He never said a word, just glared, and I said, "Go ahead, try it. You're too yellow!" Whereupon, Klinck stepped up doubling up a fist as big as a ham. "Let me hit him, boss! I'll knock him out that window," he said.

"Hold on, that's a little different," I exclaimed, as I rapidly scuttled behind the table, ending the incident.

I found out later Steve was indignant at a description I had written of him the day before as "a somewhat plump, balding man of 38 years." We didn't know at the time that he was only 34 years old. The rest of the description was true, however.

Under the masterful tutelage of Prosecutor Remy, a long parade

214

of hotel clerks, bell boys, Pullman porters, trainmen, nurses, doctors and other witnesses passed in review on the witness stand tracing each step and each member of the ill-fated trip to Hammond and back. Dignified matrons and college chums from Irvington testified to the good character of the deceased young woman.

Came the last day of the trial, a gray November day. Walter Watson, the famed City Hall reporter of the Indianapolis News, who loved booze as much as anyone I ever knew, showed up ready to help us reporters while away the tedious hours while the jury would be out, and incidentally to turn a little profit for himself. He brought along 13 half pints of white mule whiskey, each wrapped very carefully in a piece of newspaper, and all in a tote bag. Watty generously offered his liquid to us at $1.00 per bottle and found ready sale for all but three or four of his wares. After a lot of impassioned oratory about Murder vs. Suicide and vice-versa, the jury filed out, and after a while returned with its verdicts, late in the afternoon.

"We, the Jury, find the defendant David C. Stephenson guilty of murder in the second degree, and that he be imprisoned in the State Prison for his natural life."

Klinck and Gentry were found not guilty.

Tubby and I rushed the verdict by telephone, and soon the news boys were hawking Times extras on the Streets of Indianapolis shouting, "Stephenson Guilty of Murder."

Alas for the Indianapolis News! Watty was under a table in the press room, having imbibed too much of his surplus stock, and all he could do was moan, "Whash goin' on, boys? Wherrish jury?" The News telephone rang and I answered. Micky McCarty, their Assistant City Editor, was on the other end and asked if the jury was in. I told him it was, and he asked for Watty. I said, "He's under the table," and Micky groaned, as this had happened before to their star reporter.

"What was the verdict, Nibby?" Micky asked forlornly.

"I'll tell you, Micky, just as soon as we get on the street with our extra," I replied.

In about ten minutes he insisted on knowing, so we told 'im Stephenson had been found guilty, and we propped Watty up to the phone. By this time he could talk some.

"What did 'Steve' say, Watty?" asked Mr. McCarty.

"Ole 'Steve' shez, 'Fight Hell, I jush begun to Shurrender!' " was the answer.

However, Stephenson never did surrender during the 31 years he was in Michigan City Prison.

He went to prison all right, but he didn't go quietly, and a lot of high placed moguls in public office were shivering in their boots as the ex-Dragon loudly vowed revenge on ungrateful folks who had let him down.

The "Old Man" Squeals

The "Old Man," David C. Stephenson, head of the Invisible Empire of the Knights of the Ku Klux Klan of Indiana, after his conviction of murder in 1925, was duly conveyed in handcuffs to his new home in the Indiana State Penitentiary. This was located in the exteme north of the State on the shores of Lake Michigan, the "Shining Big Sea Water" of the Hurons. There he was to stay for 31 years, with brief interludes on the outside at court hearings or on violated paroles.

The Grand Dragon was mighty unhappy in his predicament. From deep within the confines of his prison walls could be heard his bellowings and roarings—dire threats against former friends and enemies to "reveal all" about political corruption unless he was paroled or pardoned by the Klan Republican Governor he had helped elect, the Honorable Ed Jackson, of New Castle, Indiana.

Politicians and office holders of the Hoosier State heard the rumblings clear down to where Indiana joins Dixie at the Ohio River, 350 miles away, and quite a few didn't feel so good.

"David C. Stephenson is guilty of murder of a young girl, and I will not be blackmailed into giving him a pardon," primly declared the Governor from his office in the State House at Indianapolis. In fact, Jackson almost convinced himself that he and D.C. were strangers, although later testimony at Jackson's trial showed he had accepted the "Old Man's" money in large but disputed amounts, was a frequent visitor at his Irvington home, where he had drunk D.C.'s good whiskey, and had the "Old Man" manage his campaign for Governor in 1924, both in the Primary and the Fall elections.

Stephenson appealed his conviction to the Indiana Supreme Court, where it was upheld by a vote of 3 to 2 in January, 1932. He had kept the upper court so busy with writs of habeas corpus, certificates of error Coram Nobis, petitions to be let to bail and other legal moves his lawyers thought up that it had no time to consider his regular appeal and attend to other business for seven years. All in all, the "Old Man" filed close to forty legal action in State or Federal courts, including the Supreme Court of the United States, attempting to void his sentence.

Someone later asked Prosecutor William H. Remy, who put Stephenson away, if he thought the man was guilty. "Well, a jury and seventeen courts, both Federal and State, have said he was guilty. That's good enough for me," was Remy's answer.

At one time he retained Clarence Darrow, famous criminal lawyer of Chicago, who appeared for "Steve" in some of the appeals, to no avail. The irony of it was that he would have been paroled after fifteen years, under Indiana Law if he had chosen to keep silent and be a model prisoner. His battery of ever changing lawyers and his press agents kept his case hot on the front pages for many a year.

During the three years beginning January 1, 1926, I was a Deputy Prosecutor under Mr. Remy, and assisted in the three Grand Jury investigations which considered "Steve's" charges of political corruption and in the trials of Governor Jackson and others who were indicted as a result. My salary was $200 a month, about $1,000 a year less than I had been making on the Times. However, I was tired of working for a large corporation and wanted to get into law, where I could be my own boss, and go fishing or golfing whenever I desired. Such habits and the Great Depression under F.D.R. kept me from getting very rich as an attorney.

The "Old Man" claimed he was not allowed visitors without supervision, that he was kept in the "Hole" on bread and water until he lost thirty pounds, and he charged that various wardens had orders to do him in. Yet, when two reputable attorneys from Indianapolis, at the prison on other business, asked if they could see the famous prisoner, the warden said he would find out, if they would send their cards to D. C., which they did.

In a few minutes they were ushered into the presence of the great man by D. C.'s Japanese servant in his private quarters as head of the prison laundry, in a remote corner of the prison complex. They told me later that "Steve" was not dressed in prison stripes but wore a natty business suit, white shirt and pearly gray tie, and that he chatted pleasantly with them, asking what was new in Indianapolis.

218

In the spring of 1926, rumors started that the prisoner was bringing pressure on Governor Jackson to pardon him, and that he was being kept in isolation to keep him from talking. That summer an ex-bootlegger named Court Asher, of Muncie, a former guard or messenger of the "Old Man," smuggled a long letter out of the prison to the newspapers offering to "tell all" about corruption in high places, if he were only permitted to do so.

Asher tried to sell his services to Hearst's Chicago American, which at first took him on, but soon backed out. Asher then made a deal with Boyd Gurley, the new editor of the Indianapolis Times, and gave him a facsimile copy of an alleged contract between John L. Duvall, Mayor of Indianapolis, and Stephenson by which "Steve" was to support Duvall in his 1925 campaign and in turn receive the privilege of naming the Board of Works, Park Board, and the Safety Board. The Times said Stephenson would reveal official corruption on a gigantic scale about bribed Governors, venal Legislatures, fixed Judges, and you name it, he had it.

These stories caused an uproar. Elderly Tom Adams, my first employer on the Vincennes Commercial, arose in wrath to purify and save the State. Adams was independently wealthy from a patent medicine he invented, and in the next year he spent a lot of time and money, much of the latter winding up in Asher's pocket, alternately trying to get Stephenson to talk as promised, or in explaining to the Grand Jury there was a huge evil conspiracy in charge of the State, but he couldn't put his finger on it. He organized a committee of fifteen prominent editors, and invited Governor Jackson to meet with it and defend himself. The Governor promised to do so, but failed to show up.

Stephenson was brought to the Grand Jury rooms in Indianapolis on October 13, 1926, and Mr. Remy asked him about his smuggled letter which had appeared in the Times. The article was entitled "What Stephenson Could Tell." I will give the substance only, as it was long.

"He could tell:

"(1) Taxpayers about graft in public office which would fill a large library with interesting data, but his lips are sealed now. Two powerful influences keep him silent. One is a threat never to let him see the light of day again.

"(2) Who furnished $120,000 in the campaign of 1924.

"(3) Why the Republican State Committee never received a fat purse sent it from Chicago, but which landed in the pocket of an individual. (The next year, before the Jury, he said that was $15,000 sent by the Insull Public Utility interests through Jackson and retained by him.)

"(4) How favorable decisions were induced from certain courts.

"(5) How $200,000 was spent in the 1924 campaign to buy votes and stuff ballot boxes with spurious votes.

"(6) How certain large liquor dealers could operate under protection of law officers, and the money paid for protection.

"(7) How four bills passed by the last Legislature were stolen and never became law.

"(8) And much more.

"(9) If D. C. Stephenson could and would talk, his knowledge of dishonesty in pubic affairs would create a State scandal. If no one is afraid, why not let him talk?"

After reading this long letter to Stephenson, Mr. Remy asked, "Did you write such a letter, Mr. Stephenson?"

Stephenson replied, "Mr. Remy, I desire to stand on my constitutional rights and decline to answer any questions asked me."

The witness was then asked about two black metal boxes about eighteen inches long, eight inches wide and eight inches deep belonging to him which Adams and Asher had previously told the Grand Jury contained many contracts, letters and other matters indicating political corruption, and which were said to be buried in the ground somewhere in Indiana, Pennsylvania, or Illinois. Stephenson, however, clammed up and would say nothing, and he was hustled back to prison.

His bluff, if that was what it was, didn't work, as the Governor and the other former allies of the jailed Dragon kept silent.

In May, 1927, Stephenson implored Jackson to give him at least a ninety day parole. It was denied. In June, Steve decided to "sing" and sent for Mr. Remy to come to his cell at Michigan City.

There on July 1, they had a long conference in which Stephenson "told all" he knew, or a large part at least. He also made arrangements with Remy to deliver the now famous black boxes to the Grand Jury and to appear before that body as to alleged political corruption. On July 13, Stephenson, through an attorney, made public facsimile copies of thirty-one checks drawn in 1924, which he said were for Jackson's campaign. The largest was one for $2,500.00 payable personally to Jackson himself. The Governor had previously denied he had gotten any money at all from Stephenson but confronted with the check, he was now able to recall that he had sold Steve a horse for $2,500.00, named "Senator." Reporters never could find "Senator," although they were told that the unfortunate nag had choked to death on a corn cob somewhere.

The Grand Jury got the black boxes under an aura of mystery. Mr. Remy delegated me and Emsley W. Johnson, Sr., a prominent attorney retained as Special Deputy, to get the boxes. Accordingly, on a warm sunny Thursday, July 24, 1927, Mr. Johnson and I and his fourteen year old son, in knickerbocker, Emsley, Jr., later a Superior Court Judge here, motored down to Lick Skillet, Indiana, a little town just south of Washington, and amidst great secrecy, "Steve's" partner in the Coal Company met us in a round barn on a farm belonging to Johnson's wife's cousin. After a few wig-wags, yoo-hoos and other preliminary signals, previously agreed upon, he gave us the two black boxes and their keys. His name was L. G. Julian, and he had driven up from Evansville in an ancient jalopy to meet us.

Mr. Johnson and his son stayed over for a little visit and well earned vacation, and they exhibited the famous boxes at a dinner and family reunion given in their honor the next Sunday, where they showed them to wondering relatives, though refusing to let them see the contents. I went on over to Wheatland, in the next township, where I was born, and did a little feasting at my father's home in my own right.

Stephenson was brought down from prison again and appeared on July 31, before a new Grand Jury. The old one had been discharged because James Armitage, a local politician, had tried to bribe two members to "lay off," though he did not belong to Stephenson's crowd, but was a brother of William H. Armitage, the slot machine king of the County, who also had donated an unreported $10,000 to the Mayoralty campaign of John L. Duvall. The new Jury was a blue ribbon one, headed by William J. Mooney, Jr., president of a large drug firm.

Stephenson was a willing witness this time. He testified freely as to the contents of the black boxes, and other papers, and answered nearly all questions, though he balked at a couple of names. He devoted a large part of his testimony to Governor Jackson, Mayor Duvall, and Republican County Chairman George V. Coffin.

I had been present when the black boxes were opened, and instead of a rich cache of contracts with politicians, there were only two, a written promise by Ralph E. Updike, United States Representative from Indianapolis, elected in 1924, to allow "D.C." to name his patronage; and a like one by Congressman Harry Rowbottom of the 1st Congressional District. There were other papers and photostats of the thirty-one checks signed by Stephenson. There was also a large ring that belonged to "Steve" which had a vacancy where a diamond about the size of a hazelnut had once nestled. I was afraid "Steve" would accuse me or Mr. Johnson of having made off with it, as he demanded to know where it was, but he didn't do so.

Each of the thirty-one checks had a piece of paper attached with a notation in Steve's handwriting explaining its purpose. The note attached to the largest check of $2,500.00 to Jackson, then Secretary of State, dated September 12, 1923, stated, "This check is the first one-fourth of $10,000 given Jackson personally for primary expenses."

"It was given to Jackson sitting on my back porch at 5432 University Avenue," "Steve" told the Grand Jury. "The later payments were made, $5,000 in cash, no check, delivered to Mr. Jackson on December 24, 1923, at his home in Irvington in the presence of Mr. Fred Butler, my secretary. I took the money out of my safe in the library, counted it, and we drove over to Ed Jackson's home. There I gave Mr. Jackson an envelope containing $5,000 in currency. Jackson gave me a second-hand Marlin shotgun that night for a Christmas present. I don't know whether he considers I bought a second-hand shotgun from him for $5,000 or not." (This remark was a sarcasm delivered by the "Old Man" in reference to Jackson's recent statement about the horse "Senator.")

"The remaining $2,500 was delivered in a sealed envelope at his office in the State House, as he then was Secretary of State. He telephoned and said he had just received it, and thanked me."

"Was this campaign contribution reported?" Remy asked.

"No! I knew he was not going to report it, and I joked him about it. He laughed and said a man was justified in perjuring himself on his own behalf and he asked me if I didn't think so. I evaded him," "Steve" testified, and added piously: "Anything I hate is a liar and a perjurer."

The ex-Dragon also testified he took up a pot of $23,000 from public utilities for Jackson, including $15,000 from the Insull interests in Chicago, the firm that built Lakes Freeman and Shaffer on the Tippecanoe River, and some from the Water Company and Telephone Company of Indianapolis, which was given to the candidate to turn over to the Republican State Committee.

"He never delivered a dime of it to the Committee. He bought a farm over in Hancock County with part, paid off a note, and stuck the rest in his sock," Stephenson told the Jurors, "It never was used in the campaign."

Other checks in the list were made out to W. H. Jackson, "Big Jack," an old time Negro Republican political leader on Indiana Avenue, and to the Reverend C. T. Sanders, a Negro preacher, for helping in the Governor's campaign. Others were for an auto, chauffeur, and hotel expenses furnished Jackson in his speaking tours over the State, and for workers in all the big cities.

Stephenson told the jury he had spent $227,000 on the Governor's campaign.

"I had a written contract with him that I was to get it back by getting the coal contract from the State, by control of the Highway Commission, and of the State Purchasing Department," he said.

Stephenson's testimony, this time before the Grand Jury filled 101 closely written typewritten pages. He testified he had a written contract with Mayor John L Duvall of Indianapolis whereby he was to have the appointment of the Board of Works, the Park

Board, and the Safety Board, if Duvall was elected, in return for his powerful support.

All "Steve" wanted was the control of the Police Force and the letting of lucrative contracts for the other Boards, he said. He didn't know what had become of both contracts while he was in prison. They should have been in the boxes, he thought.

The witness then told how he, Coffin, Jackson, and Robert I. Marsh, a Klan attorney, conspired to bribe Governor Warren T. McCray on December 8, 1923, with $10,000 of Stephenson's cash to appoint a Prosecuting Attorney of their choice for Marion County to fill a vacancy caused by the resignation of Prosecutor William P. Evans. Their man was James E. McDonald, a prominent Klan attorney of this city. McCray had been indicted by the Marion County Grand Jury on charges of embezzling $55,000 of State Agriculture funds—(It was a great era—the early days of the Roaring Twenties) and, Evans was his son-in-law. The bribe was refused, Stephenson said, although he tried once and Secretary of State Jackson tried twice.

This testimony resulted in Governor Jackson's indictment on a charge of conspiracy, and his co-defendants were Marsh and Coffin. Remy chose not to include Stephenson in return for turning State's evidence, both before the Grand Jury and at the subsequent trial of Jackson and his cohorts.

This investigation by the Prosecutor and Grand Jury also resulted in charges against the Mayor, six Republican Klan members of the City Council, the City Controller, Charles "Chick" Buser, (Mayor Duvall's brother-in-law), John J. Collins, the City Purchasing Agent, and even Earl Garrett, the Klan City Market Master, who was charged with seeking a bribe of $5.00 from an applicant for a stall. No sum was too small, it seemed, if it could be had, as illustrated by the following account, gathered from Grand Jury testimony:

The four leaders of the Klan dominated City Council called themselves the "Four Horsemen." One was a barber. The president of the outgoing Council, John King, testified that shortly after their victorious election in November, 1925, the Horsemen came to see him, and asked, "Mr. King, how do you do that graft?"

"What do you mean, how do I do what graft?," King replied. "Come on now, King, don't act so damn dumb. You know what we're talking about! You've been in four years, and got yours and now we've been elected, and we're going to get ours! What we want to know is, how to do it!", they retorted.

A Northside citizen wanted to get a small zoning variance, and went down to the City Hall an Alabama Street to see about it, he testified. He was refused, but a hanger-on whispered, "See Mr. Boynton Moore, president of the City Council, he will fix you up." The Council could grant variances by City ordinance.

"I was introduced to Mr. Moore," the witness said, "and he told me: 'Sure we can do it for you. You citizens deserve a break.' I thanked him and started to walk away, and he says, 'Now just a minute, there will be a little expense to this thing, and you'll have to put up $100.00 to take care of the boys' expenses.' I told him I wasn't interested. Moore then offered to have it done for $50.00, then for $25.00, and finally for $10.00."

"I never had had the honor of having a special ordinance introduced in my favor, so I gave him a $10.00 bill, and my variance went through," the witness said.

Moore was subsequently indicted and tried on a charge to taking a $100.00 bribe to not vote for impeachment of Mayor John L. Duvall. He was tried by a jury, found guilty, and pardoned by Governor Ed Jackson before his appeal could get out of Criminal Court.

All these folks had been part of the Grand Dragon's "Invisible Empire."

The Indiana General Assembly in the Roaring Twenties

The Forty-Third session of the noble institution known as the Indiana General Assembly convened on Thursday, January 8, 1925, at 10:00 o'clock, A.M. to hear outgoing Governor Emmett F. Branch of Martinsville give his state of the State address. Emmett had been Lieutenant Governor until the April before when he succeeded Govenor Warren T. McCray, who resigned to go to Atlanta Prison on a Federal charge.

The Indiana Ku Klux Klan had elected many members, mostly Republican, along with the incoming Governor, the Honorable Ed Jackson of New Castle. Behind the scene lurked the two rival State Klan Grand Dragons, David C. Stephenson, elected by most of the Indiana Klaverns, and Walter Bosset, of Liberty, Indiana, appointed by Grand Wizard Hiram Wesley Evans of Atlanta, Georgia, Imperial Potentate of the Invisible Empire of the Knights of the Ku Klux Klan.

I was present as a gentleman of the press with a front row seat reporting for the now defunct Scripps Howard Daily Times, assigned to cover the Senate. The Times was anti-Klan and so was I.

To help orient your mind, the 1925 fiscal year budget for the entire state of Indiana was $49,560,000, and the population was 3,200,000. For the fiscal year 1971, the State budget was $1,455,678,560, thirty times as much, while the population had increased to 5,200,000, being sixty-two percent.

The problems before the 1925 Legislature were the same to a startling extent as those of today. Governor Branch outlined several in substance, as follows:

"There are hundreds of mental defectives in the state for which no provision is made. Inflation is upon us as in the last four years the purchasing power of the dollar has sunk to sixty-five cents. The people are demanding better education and facilities, and the state colleges are overcrowded and need expansion. More roads are needed and they cost $16,000.00 a mile (!) but the trucks and buses are not paying their just shares. Penal institutions are sadly overcrowded, though the new Pendleton Reformatory has just been opened. The primary law whereby the State officials and United States Senators are nominated in direct primaries should be repealed and State conventions of delegates put in, as direct primaries are controlled by a few individuals (meaning leaders of the Anti-Saloon League, Klan, and Labor Unions) and they are too expensive for an ordinary man. The marriage license laws should be tightened, as hasty marriage often brings poverty and grief. The Governor's Mansion on Fall Creek is big and old, and the furnance and plumbing are shot. There are 30,000 cases of active T.B. in the State and only 300 beds."

There was one exception. Branch said Indiana had an ideal tax structure—"the best in the nation," being real and personal property tax, plus a one-cent gasoline tax. "Don't tinker it," he said.

The next Monday, incoming Governor Jackson gave his address. He said, "There will be those who offer counsel from a class viewpoint, and those prompted by selfish motives and those who will try to dictate. Against all these one must be fortified by manly courage to do right undeterred. We must allow nothing to insinuate into our government that will weaken it or be detrimental. Holding public office cannot clothe the holder with honor unless the office be honored by conscientious discharge of duty."

Slightly more than a year before, Jackson, then the Secretary of State, had offered Governor Warren T. McCray $10,000 of Klan money as a bribe, which was refused. He was indicted for it later, but was excused by the statute of limitations.

The new incoming Lieutenant Governor, Harold Van Orman, next was introduced. Van had the "gift of gab" and a florid style of oratory. He said he was "particularly fortunate in serving under such a splended man as Governor Ed Jackson, a man of highest ideals and morals, a man marked by an inherent sense of honor and responsibility." He closed by reciting a little poem he thought befitted such a high occasion, an eulogy to the new Governor:

"Statesman, yet friend of Truth! Of Soul sincere!
In action faithful, and in honor clear.

Who broke no promise, served no private end,
Who gained no title, and who lost no friend."

Thus safely launched, the 1925 Legislature got underway. The fifty Senators and I trooped back to the Senate Chamber while Statesman Jackson went down to the Executive office and seated himself at the Governor's desk whereon he had piled the Ten Thousand Dollars in currency once upon a time.

There were 82 Republican members in the House of Representatives to 18 Democrats. In the Marion County delegation from Indianapolis twelve men were Republicans and all but two belonged to the Klan. D. C. Stephenson, the "Old Man" of the Klan, age 34, conferred frequently with the "boys." A few days after the session ended he was arrested on a charge of the rape-murder of Miss Madge Oberholtzer, a shapely State House employee in the school lunch division, to whom he was introduced at Governor Jackson's inaugural ball.

Over in the Senate where I toiled there were 32 Republicans including six from Marion County. They were Thomas A. Dailey, an attorney; Robert L. Moorehead, Sr., publisher; William Quillen, attorney; Colonel Russell B. Harrison, attorney and son of President Benjamin Harrison; Fred M. Dickerman, a farmer; and William E. English, hotel owner. Moorehead and Dailey were anti-Klan and anti-George Coffin, the Republic County Chairman, who was allied with D. C. Stephenson and the Klan. The other four were in Coffin's camp. There were 18 Democratic Senators, and as 34 members were needed for a quorum, they had more influence than their House colleagues.

Lieut. Govenor Van Orman presided over the Senate. He was from Evansville where he owned the McCurdy Hotel. Harold was a six-foot dapper lady's man who combed his long silvery gray hair straight back from his slightly bulging blue eyes. He was a fashion plate dresser and had a lithe and curvesome lady secretary, a honey colored blonde, well rounded in the right places, who attended to his business at all hours of day or night. Van also enjoyed other feminine companionship. In his long career he had several wives between divorces, one being a lady bare-back circus rider. At one time he had three ladies stashed on three different floors of the Mc-

Curdy: the immediate past spouse, the current one, and the next in line. One day the three ladies coincided in the lobby and a lively free-for-all took place with shreds of lace, high heel shoes, and wisps of hair flying amid shrieks and curses.

Endowed with a quick wit and a flair for the quip, Van Orman had a lot of fun prancing around on the rostrum. One time he looked out over his flock and announced, "I preside over the best group of men that money can buy." The State of Indiana paid a different preacher $10.00 to pray each morning. One day Van introduced a Presbyterian divine and told him, "Parson, give this crowd a good look and then pray long and loud for the State of Indiana!"

The Senate met in the old Senate Chamber in the big center wing on the second floor, just west of the rotunda which is under the State House dome. It had a high ceiling, the room occupying all the space now taken up by the present Senate Chamber and two floors of offices above. There were outside windows and in winter the Chamber was drafty, cold, and dirty. In summer we sweltered. There was no air-conditioning and the janitors in my time were Republican Precinct committeemen, more honored for toiling at the polls than with the broom.

While our rival, the Indianaplis News, had five reporters, plus a couple of journalists and a cartoonist covering the Legislature, the frugal Times made do with three. In addition to me, William Lowell "Tubby" Toms covered the House and Walter Shead a genial Irishman, was our liaison and third member. Walter was a Roman Catholic and had about as much tolerance for the Klan as it had for him, but he got along well with a lot of its members in the assembly, as many of them had paid their $10.00 "naturalization" fee merely to help get elected. Shead drank a lot of good Klan contraband whiskey—a lot of it fine pre-prohibition bourbon which had been confiscated by Uncle Sam from the Squibbs Company, and which was supposedly under lock and key over at the Federal Building. However, the Klan political connections ran deep. For instance, our two Senators from Indiana were Republicans, the Honorable James E. Watson and the Honorable Arthur R. Robinson, and Arthur and his partner, Frank A. Symmes, were attorneys for the Klan, while the venerable Watson was not unsympathetic to it. In addition, the Honorable Ralph Updike, our Congressman, belonged

229

to "Steve" body and soul under a written contract. Local United States political employees, including prohition agents, had to be cleared with Steve, and they had the key to the liquor vaults.

Tubby and I even got a nip or two now and then over at the Claypool Hotel, the night headquarters of the Legislators. There most lobbyists maintained Hospitality Rooms wherein was decided the fate of many an important bill. Good looking damsels of seductive habits frequented the rooms, too, many of them in the employment of the lobbyists. In my time I knew one such gal to sit on the steps of the rostrum of the Speaker of the House with a written list of bills he should hand down or keep bottled up.

"She was the best piece I ever had," he declared later in fond retrospection. Thus were laws made now and then.

The 1925 Legislature was marked by some "Ripper Bills" introduced at Stephenson's behest, one of which was designed to give him control of the Highway Commission. "Steve" later testified before the Marion County Grand Jury that he had spent $227,000 on Governor Jackson's primary and campaign and that he had been promised repayment by control of the Commission and the State Purchasing Agency. He did spend a lot of money on Jackson's successful cause, including proselyting a lot of Negro preachers, editors, and politicans, but it was much less than he claimed.

A House Bill was the vehicle which was to reorganize the Highway Commission for Steve's control through appointments of the Dragon's henchman as Director by Governor Jackson. It passed the House but died in the Senate. Stephenson, who that winter stated "I am the Law in Indiana," also planned to have Governor Jackson appoint his man as State Purchasing Agent after the session. He owned the Enos Coal Company in Pike County, and planned to furnish all the coal for the State institutions at his own price. This scheme failed also as D. C. wasn't around after the session. He was in jail without bond.

In February, the eighteen Senate Democrats gave the newspapers great joy. They broke a quorum and fled to Ohio in opposition to some Republican bills they opposed, one in particular being Senate Bill No. 300, introduced by Republican Senator Will K. Penrod of Bedford, to move staunchly Republican Orange County of the overwhelmingly Democratic 3rd Congressional District into the 2nd District where U. S. Representative Democrat Arthur Greenwood had been elected by a slight margin. The Democratic leader, Senator Joe Cravens of Madison, screamed "Foul" and "Gerrymander," and had his colleagues hide out to prevent a quorum.

On Tuesday, February 24th, at 2:00 P.M., thirty-three Senators were present, not being two-thirds of the membership which under the rules were necessary to transact business. Senator Cravens was present as a lookout.

Cravens explained that his fellow Democrats had gone to a fish fry at noon and were "detained longer than expected." Came 10:00 A.M. on Wednesday, February 25th, and there was no quorum again. This time Senator Cravens blandly attributed his fellow partisan's absence to bad ecology of Indiana streams—maybe the first such accusation ever made against Indiana.

"They are absent due to illness resulting from eating fish taken from the polluted streams of this State!" he exclaimed.

This was a little too much for the grumpy Senate Republicans. The Chief Door-keeper, Mr. Jerome Brown, was instructed to find the absentees and bring them in. Senator Thomas A. Dailey, of Indianapolis, read from the Indiana Constitution about wilfully breaking a quorum and the pains and penalities thereof. Doorkeeper Brown returned and reported he had found a number of the absentees in State Democrat Headquarters, but they defied him and refused to come along.

The 1925 Senate Journal continues the debate: Senator Murray Barker of Thorntown moved: "That as certain minority members have unlawfully absented themselves, the doorkeeper be instructed to secure necessary assistance and bring them in so business can be done." Motion adopted.

This smoked Senator Cravens out. "There's a reason they are absent. A measure pending before this house, S.B. 300, is politically unfair, injurious and unreasonable, and until it is withdrawn, our Democratic Senators will continue to be absent. We are trying to protect our interest," he said.

Reminded by Senator Penrod that in a prior session Senator Cravens himself caused a Democratic Legislature to remove Orange County from the same 2nd District into the same 3rd District where

231

its Republican majority was snowed under, Senator Cravens loftily replied that such was required by the 1910 census.

Came 4:45 P.M., and Doorkeeper Brown reported he "has no help as yet."

Senator Oliver Holmes of Gary begged to inquire "if he had tried to get help?"

Senator Moorehead was recognized to state that the Marion County Sheriff, the Honorable George Snyder (a fat Republican Klansman) was on the way with two deputies.

Senator Waldron Lambert of Columbus thought that the doorkeeper had the right to wire any sheriff in Indiana for help.

Senator Homes stated that the Governor had offered help, presumably including the National Guard.

Senator Quillin of Indianapolis spoke in favor of the Chief Doorkeeper.

Senator Edward J. O'Rourke of Fort Wayne, a Beau Brummel who always wore a flower in his lapel, said that men of authority were here and advised action.

The Senate took action.

It adjourned.

On Thursday, February 26, thirty Republican Senators met only to find that during the night their Democratic colleague had flown the coop. They were in Dayton, Ohio, at the Gibbons Hotel, where the faithful Jerome, fully earning his $6.00 a day salary, found them and read his arrest warrants, only to be laughed at as he plaintively informed the Senate by telephone. He was told to bring his three assistants and come home.

The Lieut. Governor of Ohio telegraphed he would exchange five Ohio Senate Republicans for the sixteen Indiana fugitives, a fair swap, he thought.

The Democrats wired Representative Greenwood in Washington, D. C., that they were doing all in their power to make the 2nd District safe for Democracy.

The Marion County Grand Jury, under Prosecutor William H. Remy, swung into action and heard testimony from Republican Senators.

Lieut. Governor Van Orman, anxious to get in on the juicy

1931 Cartoon by
Kin Hubbard,
Indianapolis *News*

Newspaper Reporter
Indianapolis *Times*, 1925

ED JACKSON
Governor, Indiana, 1925-1928

WARREN T. McCRAY
Governor, Indiana, 1921-1924

JOHN L. DUVALL
Mayor of Indianapolis
1926-1928

DR. E. S. SHUMAKER
Executive Secretary
Indiana Anti-Saloon League

WILLIAM H. REMY
Prosecutor, Marion County
1924-1928

DAVID C. STEPHENSON
Grand Dragon
Indiana Ku Klux Klan

HAROLD VAN ORMAN
Lieutenant-Governor, Indiana
1925-1928

WILLIAM P. EVANS
McCray's Son-in-Law

SUNDAY AFTERNOON ON THE
FARM—1914

U. S. NAVAL AVIATION
1918

SUPERIOR COURT
1950

"PLAYER OF THE MONTH"
Blackwood Bridge Center
February, 1967

publicity, phoned the fleeing Democrats an offer to be his guests at his hotel in Mansfield, Ohio.

Republican Senate leaders refused to negotiate, though the end of the session was drawing near, and no budget bill had been adopted. However, the papers reported that both Klan Dragons, Stephenson and Bossert, went over and conferred with the absentees and assured them that enough Republicans would default on the bill to prevent its passage. Whatever the deal, and some thought that Van Orman had promised to squelch some other bills obnoxious to the Democrats and that S.B. 300 was only a smoke screen, on Friday, February 26, at 10:00 A.M., everyone was in his seat. They had rolled back to the Claypool Hotel at 1:00 A.M., singing "Back Home Again in Indiana" and "Home Sweet Home" as their bus crossed the State line, according to the News and Star Reporters who were along. I didn't get to go as I stayed behind to cover the home front.

Lieut. Governor Van Orman banged his gavel and announced: "My cup of joy is filled to overflowing and runneth over on this bright and beautiful morning. Pray, Parson! And earn your $10.00."

Over in the House the eighteen Democrats had made a virtue of necessity—it wouldn't avail to run away as a House quorum was sixty-seven. Speaker Leslie commended them for staying home and they purred under such unusual praise. All joined in singing "Blest be the Tie That Binds."

Senate Bill 300 passed the Senate on March 9, 1925, by a vote of 27-0, one more vote than necessary, and became law.

The Klan members in the 1925 Legislature felt a need to reform the morals of a decadent era, to inculcate patriotism, and to rescue Indiana from the clutches of the Pope and his Catholic legions. Most of their bills dealt with what other members deemed trivia. Reading the Bible in public schools, flying the American flag over all schools, teaching the American Constitution, prohibiting teachers in public schools from wearing religious garb, requiring parochial and public schools to have identical text books, and those non-sectarian; and to release public school children from school for religious instruction were some of their bills. Nearly all failed, though Senator George Sims of Terre Haute, a Republican, finally got a law requiring flags on school houses and making June 14 Flag Day. Senator Dickerman of Indianapolis thought students at State supported colleges ought to have religious instruction, but his bill failed.

Other Klan bills which failed to impress the majority in one House or the other, or the Governor, were:

(1) Stepping up penalties for adultery and fornication.
(2) Regulating the sale of smutty or salacious magzines.
(3) Creating a censorship board for movies.
(4) Prohibiting baseball or any athletic event on Sunday.
(5) To prohibit cutting off a dog's tail or ears.

Senator Oliver Holmes of Gary, a non-Klan Republican, batted 50-50 on two bills, one to prohibit sales of snuff to children and the other to create the present State Library and Historical Department. The snuff bill failed.

Senator Robert Moorhead, Sr., also non-Klan, of Indianapolis, introduced a bill to establish a whipping post to punish people who carried concealed weapons, but it fell on thorny ground.

The 1925 Legislature in addition to the Library law passed other good measures. It prohibited the sale of unpasteurized milk; authorized purchase of the Indiana Dental College by Indiana University; ordered free fishing and hunting licenses for Veterans of the Wars; and ordered the State House to go on half days on Saturday. It also created the Marion County Municipal Court as a reform measure of the Indianapolis Bar Association.

For their labors of sixty-one days, each member received $6.00 a day, plus a small travel allowance, I believe, ten cents a mile. The '25 session cost $51,170.71 for the House and somewhat less for the Senate, all totalling under $100,000. Doorkeepers got $6.00 a day, too, while pages and janitors drew $3.00 and stenographers, $5.00.

Among other bills which failed was one to classify the Bob White as a song bird (which would have ended hunting it); prohibit polluting streams; establish training homes for colored women by Senator William E. English, of Indianapolis (this was referred to the Committee on Banks and Banking where it died); prohibit live stock from running at large on public roads; Senator Moorehead's bill to allow Central Insane Asylum to sell its garbage; a bill by farmer Senator Lonzo Lindley of Kingman to license stallions, and another to license barbers and lady hairdressers; the Highway Commission bill sponsored by Grand Dragon Stephenson; one by Representative William Ebaugh of Indianapolis to require manufacturing plants giving off noxious odors to get out of cities and locate in the countryside (the farmers knocked this one off); a bill to create a naval militia on Lake Michigan, the Wabash River, and the Ohio River; one empowering Indianapolis to hire women as City firemen; and one by Representative Frank Borns of Indianapolis to require "hidden demonstrators to wear badges or display notices," evidently aimed at the Klan.

As the sixty-first day dragged into its second night, with the clock stopped as usual at 11:30 P.M., the Senate enlivened the time by whooping it up. The flowing punch bowl, or its equivalent in White Mule, passed freely among the Senators, lobbyists and the Fourth Estate. Jep Cadou, Sr., of the Hearst papers, always the bon vivant par excellence, took the Senate rostrum, as was his wont for many a year on last night, and presided over a lot of tomfoolery and comic motions and resolutions which only John Barleycorn could inspire. Everyone had to do something while we waited on the printing of the bulky budget act—always passed at the last possible moment.

At 3:00 A.M., Shead, Toms, and I made our last call into Volney Fowler, our City Editor, who had stayed down. The News and Star boys were going to get a week's vacation.

"Be down at 6:30 A.M., half an hour early today," Volney told us in best Scripps Howard fashion.

"What the Hell! We won't be there!" we assured him stoutly.

"Oh, yes, you will, or get fired," Volney retorted.

Shead and Tubby both resigned right then and there via phone, and took a week's vacation. Fowler took them back later on without pay for the vacation, and Tubby and I together during the rest of 1925 spent most of our time jointly reporting the Stephenson story, one of the biggest ever to hit the State of Indiana because it had so many elements of a good story; a prominent politician millionaire involved with rape and murder of a beautiful young society girl.

Me? Niblack dutifully reported into the City Room at 6:30

235

A.M., like a good little man and got a salary increase and promotion to head reporter.

I had considerable contact with the Indiana Legislature after 1925, serving as an elected Republican Senator from Marion County in the regular sessions of 1929 and 1931 and the special session of 1932. On quitting the Times on December 31, 1925, I joined the staff of Prosecutor William H. Remy for three years and helped him investigate and prosecute various Klan public officials from Governor Ed Jackson down to City Market Marketmaster, Earl Garrett, all accused of bribery and malfeasance, or corrupt practices. In 1928, I ran for the Senate, and was nominated with the help of the Indianapolis City Manager League of 51,000 members who were sick of political bossism, Klanism, and corruption in public office. They wanted a legislative delegation from Indianapolis which would get a city manager law.

It was a coincidence that Mr. Walter Esterline, a prominent business man and president of Esterline-Angus Manufacturing Company, was General Chairman and also a Sigma Nu brother of mine. He and I met each Thursday noon at our weekly luncheon and bowled on our association team. Walter readily agreed I should be endorsed, and so it was done. Thus it can be seen that superior talent prevails every time. Our ticket was swept in with Hoover that fall. Marion County going Republican 100,000 votes to 78,000 Democratic. Our other City Manager Senators were publisher Senator Robert Moorhead, Sr., a second termer; Senator Thomas A. Dailey, an attorney and also on a second term; J. Clyde Hoffman, attorney; Winfield T. Miller, age 81, a retired businessman and a wonderful old gentleman; Joe Rand Beckett, an attorney, a rich man's son and a good man, and myself. Our sixth Senator was a holdover, the Honorable Sumner Clancy, an attorney who belonged in the political stable of the County Republican boss, George V. Coffin, known as "Cap" Coffin. Sumner was one of my instructors in the old Benjamin Harrison night Law School and a fairly nice fellow. I never knew him to cause anyone harm.

We City Manager endorsed folks swamped Cap's ticket in the spring primary. All three newspapers supported the City Manager plan and denounced Coffinism, Stephensonism, and Klanism, as one and the same thing, so our side wore the White Hats and were full of civic virtue, we thought. As an ex-newspaper reporter filled with the cynicism of such folk and sure that I now at last could catch the thieves from the inside, I am afraid I didn't make a very good legislator. For one thing, I was a bumptious young ass just out of law school and I thought I knew it all, something like our young college graduates of today. I made it a point to read every bill, and generally spoke on each one much to the disgust of older members. I never got many bills through as law mainly because I opposed so many local bills from other counties which were none of my business, under Ancient Senate custom. Also, I never "log-rolled," or swapped votes, whereby a Senator promises to support other people's bills in return for a like favor. It works real good.

The 1929 Senate had thirty-three Republicans and seventeen Democrats.

Not so long ago I went over to the State House to visit the Legislature and stopped to chat a moment with the boys in the Third House—the paid lobbyists who congregate on the second floor between the two houses in their idle moments while the solons are in session. They have a pretty good time swapping yarns and lies, and sometimes glean a little information from each other. I saluted one genial fellow, a plump man smoking a cigar.

"Say, didn't we serve in the Legislature together?" I asked.

"Hell, no!, Judge. You tried me for drunk driving," he responded with a grin.

After I was elected in 1928, I immediately went over to Straus' men's store and bought a pair of pin striped trousers and a beautiful gray vest and coat to top it off. I also ordered a Model A, Robin egg blue, Ford roadster, a one seater with a collapsible top and a rumble seat. I also quit the job as Deputy Prosecutor under Mr. William H. Remy, and went to practicing law on my own, earning about $1700.00 my first year. The Senate job paid $10.00 a day which was $4.00 more than the 1925 law makers received. I got by real good, as I was a bachelor.

Five of our Marion County Senate delegation and eleven or twelve in the House were City Manager men. Among us we got a bill through to have a City Manager plan Government for Indianapolis, though our Indiana Supreme Court threw the law out that

237

same year. "Cap" Coffin might not control the 1929 Legislature, but he had ties on the Court.

The Legislature of 150 members in which I served included two Phi Beta Kappa scholars; several assorted drunks; a few lechers, who spent a great deal of their time in the Claypool cavorting in the bar and bedrooms; one moron, and a lot of fine men and women from all walks of life—the farmer, merchant, doctor, attorney, labor leader, businessman, you name it, he was there. There was even a solemn visaged undertaker, not to mention the Honorable Lee Evans of New Castle, State President of the Indiana Fox Hunter's Association, who, after a few drinks on festive occasions, could and did give out with the mournful cadence of a trailing hound.

I remember one time Senator Glenn Slenker, of Monticello, and Senator "Shorty" Beeson and I were walking down the hall on the 7th floor of the Claypool Hotel, when we saw Representative Curt Bennett, of southern Indiana, coming down the hall toward us about fifty feet away with a lady on his arm. He waved and shouted a loud greeting:

"Hi Fellows, Hi! I want you to meet my wife! This is my wife!" He screamed to put us on guard.

Slenker stayed in the Legislature for forty years, and was one of the most respected men ever to serve there. He went over to the House after his one term in the Senate.

I introduced one real good bill which would have created a State Police Force. Indiana had none. I put a lot of work on it before the session, studying the Pennsylvania State Trooper statute, and the acts establishing the Royal Canadian Mounted Force and the Texas Rangers. Alas, it failed 20-23, due to Otto Fifield, Republican Secretary of State, who had a force of twenty excise men he called "state police," and he did not want to lose the patronage.

I was co-author of a law to buy the First Baptist and the Second Presbyterian churches which sat where the World War One monument is now. Also, I was author of the law creating the present Citizens Gas and Coke Utility, a public owned corporation which bought the old Gas Company.

In 1923, Stephenson had seized an old law authorizing Horse Thief Detective Associations and revived them as the armed branch or enforcement arm of the Klan. I introduced a repealer, but it failed, and not until 1933 did McNutt's Legislature end the law. I got in Dutch with organized labor over their bill to put in a State Barber Board three sessions in a row. The bill provided for a Board to consist of union barbers appointed by the Governor which would license barber colleges, barber shops, and barbers. It was proposed as a health measure, and was so worded that the union would operate the only barber school. A person had to have 1000 hours training to learn to cut hair which he could learn in two weeks under any barber.

Each time the bill passed the House, and each time I tacked on an amendment that the State Board of Health would inspect the shops, and would also issue for $1.00 a Certificate of Health to any barber who brought in a doctor's clearance. This killed the bill each time. The President of the Barbers Union, one Chamberlin from Terre Haute, gave me a loud, red-faced bawling out each time, and had me black listed as a foe of Labor. I didn't care, as I knew all the Labor leaders were Democrats. Sure enough when I ran for renomination as Senator in 1932, I led the ticket in the Primary.

In 1933, McNutt's Democratic Assembly passed the Barber Bill.

The 1931 Session was about the same. The only real excitement I had was when the Indiana Farm Bureau had twenty-five votes lined up to pass a Gross Income tax for property tax relief, and came down hard on me to give the needed twenty-sixth vote. Poor Devils, they almost assured me I could have a good job as one of their attorneys, but I was sure it was unconstitutional and refused. I felt like a heel, as lots of my folks were farmers, and the farmer Senators, especially Lon Lindley from Kingman, were real nice men.

The 1932 Special Session was called by Governor Harry G. Leslie for July and August to deal with the financial crisis in the State and nation. It also was a financial crisis in my life, too. I opened my law office in 1928; the stock market crashed in 1929; Marion County elected a Courthouse full of Democratic Judges in 1930 who wouldn't allow a Republican attorney in the Court room unless he had a Democrat co-counsel; I got married in 1931, and my new wife quit her job; and men sold apples in the streets. I was glad to get the $400.00 salary for the forty-day session.

We met and sweltered for forty days and nights, just the same length of time that the rain fell on the Ark. Unlike Noah, we didn't

239

accomplish much. All we could come up with was an idea to reduce expenses. We made a law that cut everybody's salary ten percent, from Governor to Justice of Peace and Dog Catcher, and also their budgets.

A grateful electorate that fall turned us out and President Hoover, too, and elected people who knew how to spend public money, headed by President F. D. Roosevelt and Governor Paul V. McNutt. Whereas Marion County had gone Republican in 1928 by a vote of 100,000 to 78,000, in 1932 it went Democratic by 105,000 to 100,000. We Republicans didn't lose any votes but we didn't gain any either.

An ex-butcher's boy from Brooklyn, New York, one Honorable Jake Weiss, who had been in Indianapolis about two and a half years, took my place in the Senate. He helped repeal the bone dry prohibition law; was the author of McNutt's liquor license and beer and whiskey distributorship law, and was duly rewarded with one such distributionship, a financial El Dorado, returning back East in a few years a wealthy man after serving a stretch in the penitentiary for income tax evasion.

Trial of John L. Duvall, Mayor of Indianapolis

On Monday, September 12, 1927, John L. Duvall, Mayor of Indianapolis, went on trial in the old Marion County Courthouse on charges of violating the corrupt practices Act in his election in 1925. He was tried by a jury and Special Judge Cassius C. Shirley, an Indianapolis attorney.

Mr. Duvall, President of the Marion County State Bank, incumbent Marion County Treasurer, and a Republican politician, had been elected Mayor of Indianapolis on November 4, 1925, by a vote of 52,849 to 43,858 over his Democratic opponent, attorney Walter Myers. The Negro voters of the 5th and 6th Wards along Indiana Avenue stayed home as the Indianapolis newspapers had published reports that Duvall was backed by the Ku Klux Klan and D. C. Stephenson.

With him were elected six Republicans who were Klan members as City Councilmen: Otis E. Bartholomew; Boynton J. Moore; Claude E. Negley; O. Ray Albertson; Dr. Austin H. Todd; and Walter R. Dorsett.

The Marion County Grand Jury and Prosecutor William H. Remy got busy in the summer and fall of 1926, investigating charges of political corruption in the election, which charges were being leaked out of Michigan City Prison by Dragon Stephenson.

Early in 1927, a Grand Jury was discharged after one of the jurors, one Claude Achey, made affidavit that James Armitage, a minor Republican politician, had offered him a bribe of $2500.00 cash and a city job if he and one other juror would block the indictment of Duvall. Remy then caused a charge of contempt of court to be filed against Armitage for jury tampering, and he was tried, found guilty and sentenced to ninety days in jail and fined $300.00 — the maximum. James was the brother of Will H. "Big Bill" Armitage, widely known as the Marion County slot machine king. Bill was a member of the rival City Hall Republican faction and had a key to the office of the preceding Mayor, the Honorable Lew Shank, but this had not prevented him from making a deal with Mr. Duvall to aid his election. The latter belonged to the courthouse faction dominated by Stephenson, "Cap" Coffin, and the Klan.

Mayor Shank became famous for his deliberate use of bad grammar. The Indianapolis News once quoted him saying: "If I'd aknowed I coulda rode I would've went, but if I hadda went I wouldn't of et nuthin."

Jimmy's contempt conviction brought the "house of cards" tumbling down around the unfortunate Mayor, the City Council, and numerous city officials who had been appointed by Mayor Duvall. "Big Bill" previously had refused to testify before the Grand Jury but he now rushed to the defense of brother James, and testified against Duvall in return for a suspended sentence for Jimmy.

"I will not see my brother go to jail just to protect another man who caused it all," William stated — a remark somewhat beside the point, as it takes two to tango, according to an old song.

On May 16, 1927, following the testimony of Armitage and some others, including George S. Elliott, an Indianapolis attorney who had been Grand Exalted Cyclops of the Indianaplis Klavern No. 3 of the Invisible Empire of the Knights of the Ku Klux Klan, Mayor Duvall was arrested on seven charges of political corruption.

Four of the charges were as follows:

(1) That he had received a $14,500 cash campaign contribution from Armitage in return for a promise to let "Big Bill" name the Board of Works and the City Engineer, and that he failed to report the same as required by the Indiana Corrupt Practices Act.

(2) Promised to appoint Elliott as City Purchasing Agent.

(3) Promised Reverend George Henninger, Pastor of the East Tenth Street Methodist Church, and head of the Political Action Committee of the Ku Kiux Klan, that he would accept the political policy of the Klan and would make eighty-five percent of all his appointments from persons named by the Klan, and that no Catholics at all would be appointed. (It was interesting to note that Mr. Duvall was defended at his trial by the prominent legal firm of John Ruckelshaus and Mike Ryan, both Roman Catholics).

(4) Promised Elliott and the Reverend Henninger he would stand by them in all disputes with George V. Coffin, Stephenson's ally and County Republican Chairman.

242

All these and more were concealed and not reported, it was charged.

It turned out at the trial that Duvall, who was a good banker, and who among other things invented the Christmas Savings Clubs, was 1) a rather poor politician in that he got carried away by his enthusiasm and promised his appointments to three different groups for their aid in his primary; and 2) he got caught. I don't suppose Mr. Duvall was too much different from the mine-run of politicians of both parties in the last half of the 19th century and the first part of the present one, but the murder conviction of that strange character, David C. Stephenson, lanced a monstrous political boil that spattered blood and corruption all over Indianapolis and the State of Indiana when it popped.

Evidence at the trial showed that Duvall had promised 1) the Klan; 2) Stephenson and Coffin; and 3) Armitage and his crowd his patronage appointments, and his troubles began with his congratulations on November 5, 1925.

Stephenson claimed and produced a written contract signed by Duvall, which the latter said was a forgery, that "Steve" could name the Park Board, the Board of Works, and the Board of Public Safety, which latter controlled the police. All three groups claimed the Chief of Police.

Soon after the election Duvall appointed Charles J. Orbison, ex-Judge of Superior Court, Room 1, a Democrat and a high Klan official, as City Corporation counsel. This didn't suit Coffin, so Duvall rescinded the appointment and named Alvah J. Rucker, who was more to "Cap's" liking. He also rescinded his appointment of Klansman Arthur McGee as inspector of police, and put in an experienced police officer, Walter White, following a storm of protest by Negroes and others. The Park Board was supposed to consist of two Republicans and two Democrats, but Duvall appointed three Republicans and let it go at that, stating he would appoint a Democrat later. This put the Democrats on his neck. The Klan was already there, because the Mayor didn't honor his alleged promises to it. They held mass meetings in their headquarters at Buschman's Hall at 11th and College Avenue, and made marches, led by the Exalted Cyclops, on the Mayor-Elect at his Treasurer's office in the Court House.

Mr. Duvall wasn't there, however, to be marched on. He and

his brother-in-law, Charles "Chick" Buser, who had been his campaign manager and chauffeur in the primary, when I, Horace Coats of the Star, and other reporters rode with the candidate from Klan meetings in Brightwood (where we didn't go in) to Negro meetings on Indiana Avenue (where we did go in) had gone to the "Kingdom of Seclusion" in Illinois early in November. Poor Duvall was hounded, distracted, and pulled this way and that by the different groups until he fled and never returned until he took his oath of office in January, 1926.

Incidentally, during the fall campaign Democrat candidate Myers made speeches accusing Duvall of being a Klansman and having support of the Klan and also of D. C. Stephenson, who was under indictment for murder-rape. The Indianapolis Star, on October 30, 1925, carried Duvall's denial:

"Statements that D. C. Stephenson, ex-Ku Klux Klan leader now on trial at Noblesville on a charge of murder, is connected in any way with the Republican City ticket is characterized as absolutely false by Mr. Duvall. He also denied any connection with William H. Armitage, the "City Slot Machine King," who has a key to Mayor Lew Shank's city hall office."

"It's mud slinging and besmirching," Duvall said, referring to such charges by Walter Myers, his Democrat opponent.

The Mayor testified at the trial in his own defense. He said, "Yes, I did get some money from Armitage. I met Big Bill one evening after dark," he said, and the latter slipped $5,000.00 in cash wrapped in newspaper into his pocket and that he didn't report it, but that he promised Armitage nothing. He stated he got $10,000.00 in all from Big Bill, but "I gave it all back." The defendant also said he "made agreements" with the Women's Christian Temperance Union. He added all the state's witnesses were an "Ananias Club."

One of the said witnesses was a Mr. Frank Sipe, an officer of the Horse Thief Detective Association, which D. C. had made into the armed branch of the Klan. He testified that Duvall fixed $3,000.00 as his price for appointing Sipe as City Market Master, but he couldn't pay it so he didn't get the job. The Mayor appointed one Earl Garrett, a Klansman, who was arrested also that summer on seven separate charges of taking money for letting stand concessions. He pleaded guilty on one charge of getting $5.00 and was fined later. No piece of change was too small, it seemed, for political favoritism in the Roaring Twenties.

The Jury heard the evidence, and found a verdict of guilty of violating the Corrupt Practices Act, and decreed a fine of $1,000.00 and a thirty-day jail sentence, and also that Duvall be barred from holding any public office from January 1, 1926. He resigned his office the next month, and L. Ert Slack, a Democrat attorney was elected Mayor by the City Council. Duvall appealed his conviction but it was affirmed in 1931, and he served out his sentence.

The six Republicans on the City Council, all Klansmen and known as the "Six Horsemen," also were arrested and tried on various charges as a result of the 1925 political scandal. Boynton Moore, President of the Council, was found guilty by a jury of taking a $100.00 bribe not to vote for impeachment of the Mayor in August 1927 before the City Council. Governor Jackson, who had been elected by the Klan, pardoned him within a matter of weeks. I have often wondered if Governor Jackson would have pardoned himself if he had been found guilty of bribery on his own trial in the same court five months later in February of 1928. It surely is an interesting point of law.

Other members of the Council pleaded guilty to minor charges and paid fines and resigned. John J. Collins, a Republican of Coffin's crowd whom Duvall had appointed City Purchasing agent instead of Cyclops Elliott, was indicted on charges of soliciting a $500.00 bribe from the Armstrong Medical Supplies Company in re purchase of surgical supplies and equipment. He never served any time on it, as I remember.

I was present as Deputy Prosecutor at all the proceedings and the trial in Criminal Court during 1926, 1927, and 1928.

Although not directly connected with the political trials and tribulations of the 1920's, but yet part of the warp and woof of the period was the case in 1927 of the Reverend Dr. E. S. Shumaker, head of the Indiana Anti-Saloon League. Doctor (not an M.D. or a Dentist) was a Methodist preacher and headed one of the most potent political machines ever devised in the U.S.A. The League's foundation stones were the pious, the hard working, the simple, God-fearing folk of the hamlets and farms of the Hoosier State, although it had considerable influence in Indianapolis and the other cities, too.

Reverend Shumaker finally got "too big for his britches" as the Hoosiers say, and wound up in the "pokey" at the Indiana State farm for contempt of the Indiana Supreme Court.

The Anti-Saloon League head led his fellow Methodists, and all other Protestant churchmen and ladies in their stirring battles against the Demon Rum and John Barleycorn. The Temperance forces of the United States turned the country "dry" in 1919 when the 18th Amendment was adopted forbidding all traffic in the fermented or distilled juices of alcohol. Soon bath tub gin and contraband "White Mule" flooded the land, resulting in many trials of "bootleggers," as the purveyors were known.

Old Doc was a well cushioned fellow who generally traipsed about town armed with a sheathed black umbrella and his ever attendant Anti-Saloon League attorney, the Honorable Jesse Miles, a good Sigma Nu Methodist, who walked one pace to the right, and one pace behind his boss.

Before each primary and general election, Doctor sifted and weighed the candidates of both parties as to their being "Wet" or "Dry," and in due time separated the sheep from the goats, notifying all church members and members of the temperance unions as to who was which. Like Annie Laurie before her lover, the politically ambitious candidate "swooned with delight at his smile and trembled with fear at his frown."

The Anti-Saloon League was well-heeled financially by collections from the good folks, whose meetings in churches favored such songs as "Father, Dear Father, come home with me now"—the plea of a ragged little girl tugging at her drunken father's sleeve in a saloon at midnight, and such slogans as "Lips that touch liquor shall never touch mine." The League had its own newspaper, too.

Shumaker took exception to the Indiana Supreme Court throwing out bootlegging convictions because of no search warrants. Prohibition agents would take crowbars and pry open a "joint" at their own whim without a writ, or would arrest some hapless wight standing on a street corner minding his own business, on suspicion, only to find a half-pint of booze on his hip. The High Court took a dim view of such antics on appeal.

Reverend Shumaker gave the court several dirty write-ups in his paper. "The Court is shielding bootleggers and operators of 'Blind Tigers' (clandestine saloons) and is not following the law," he wrote.

This was too much for the Five Fearless Legal Fathers over in their sanctuary at the State House. Led by Judge David A. Myers of Greensburg, one of the founders of the Indiana State Bar Association, they had Attorney General Arthur Gilliom of South Bend—by no means a "Dry"—cite the Reverend to appear and show cause why he should not be held in contempt of Court.

He was given short shrift at the trial held on August 5, 1927, and the next day on August 6th, he was sentenced to sixty days on the Indiana State Farm.

Governor Jackson, who had a keen sympathy for any man who felt the halter draw, issued a pardon to the venerable convict, but it was in vain. The Supreme Court ruled that the Governor's pardoning power, under the Indiana Constitution, did not extend to convictions for contempt of Court in general, and to the Doctor's case in particular.

It must be noted for posterity that the good Doctor did not go quietly. In his distress, he called upon our United States Senators, Arthur R. Robinson and James Eli Watson, two good stalwart Indiana Republicans, and two stout lookers upon the cup that cheers, who had received the Anti-Saloon League's blessings in their campaigns because they said they were "Dry" and would vote for the League's measures.

Attorney General Gilliom gave both Senators a good trouncing in the press. He accused them of telephoning the Supreme Court Justices to ask mercy, leniency and/or a suspended sentence for their political chum. According to Gilliom, Dr. Shumaker declared Senator Watson told him over the phone that he had conferred with three Supreme Court Justices who were unfriendly to the defendant, and they assured him that there would be no decision until after election, and no jail sentence then.

Senator Watson unloaded in a hurry from this horse, denying all, and in February, 1928, the Sheriff delivered the good Doctor to the Indiana State Farm where his corpulent figure shed a few pounds

247

as he labored at tending the milch cows until his release in April. He was rather careful in his remarks thereafter.

The Anti-Saloon League, of which my father was a sincere member, also went into a decline after F.D.R. was elected, but it is still around and does harm to nobody.

Ed Jackson's Trial

On September 9, 1927, at 4:00 P.M., the Marion County Grand Jury at Indianapolis, presented an indictment to Criminal Court charging the 32nd Governor of Indiana, the Honorable Ed Jackson, of Newcastle, and two associates with bribery, a felony. The startled Presiding Judge, the Honorable James A. Collins, an ex-Y.M.C.A. secretary from Lyons, New York, opened the paper and noted its contents:

"The Grand Jurors for the County of Marion, State of Indiana, upon their oaths present that on or about December 8, 1923, in said County and State, one Ed Jackson, then Secretary of State, and one Robert I. Marsh and one George V. Coffin did then and there feloniously and unlawfully unite, conspire, confederate and agree with each other and with one David C. Stephenson to feloniously bribe and offer to bribe one Warren T. McCray, then Governor of Indiana, by offering him $10,000.00 in lawful United States currency to appoint one James E. McDonald as Prosecuting Attorney of Marion County to fill a vacancy, said appointment being the official duty of such Governor, —all contrary to the statute in such case made and provided, and against the peace and dignity of the State of Indiana. And your jurors further allege that the defendants concealed said crime."

The indictment bore the written approval of William H. Remy, Republican, Prosecutor of Marion County, the relentless scourge of the Indiana Ku Klux Klan and all its political associates, and they were many. The concealment allegation was to get around a two year statute of limitations. I am quoting the indictment from memory after forty-five years, but it is reasonably accurate, as I helped prepare it as Deputy under Mr. Remy. I was in his office for the three years of 1926-27-28, and I accompanied him and the Grand Jury into the court room that day and also assisted at the trial which began before a jury on February 7, 1928.

Judge Collins fixed a bond of $2,500.00 each for the three defendants. The Sheriff telephoned them and at 5:00 P.M., they surrendered at his office in the Court House, where bondsmen awaited.

"I want to be arrested," said Governor Jackson, a slender man about five feet nine inches tall.

His co-defendant, George V. "Cap" Coffin, Republican party boss of Marion County, was not quite so happy. A well cushioned, red faced ex-Indianapolis police captain with a cigar perpetually protruding from his pink complexioned face, George merely grunted when the news reporters asked his opinion about the charge. The third defendant, attorney Robert I. Marsh, a Klan lawyer with a flowing senatorial hair cut who always wore a semi-frock coat, kept silent, too.

The indictment resulted from testimony given by Stephenson, Grand Dragon of the Realm of Indiana of the Invisible Empire of the Knights of the Ku Klux Klan, before the Grand Jury in July, 1927. "Steve" was in the Michigan City State Prison, convicted of murder. He had been Jackson's campaign manager and principal financier in the Governor's successful primary and fall elections in 1924 . Following 18 months of trying to get his erstwhile friend and candidate to pardon him, Steve gave up after a final desperate appeal to Jackson in May of 1927, for a ninety-day parole, which was ignored. "Steve" sent for Remy to come to the prison, and there he "sang" a plenty. He appeared before the Grand Jury and testified freely. He accused the Governor; the Mayor of Indianapolis, the Honorable John L. Duvall; the City Council and about everyone else he could remember, of political corruption, or worse, including two Congressmen, the Honorable Ralph Updike of Indianapolis and the Honorable Harry Rowbottom of Gary, both Republicans. He testified he had spent $227,000 on Jackson's campaign, and showed a cancelled check for $2500.00, dated September of 1923, made out to Jackson as some evidence. Until then the Governor had denied ever getting any money from "Steve" at any time.

"D. C. Stephenson is in prison for the murder of a young girl and I will not be blackmailed into giving him a pardon," he said. However, the Governor was now able to recall the check: It was for a riding horse named "Senator" who had since choked to death on a corn cob and was buried he didn't know where.

Judge Collins privately asked the defendant's attorney to take a change of Judge. The case was too hot for Uncle Jim to handle, as he was up for re-election in a year or so. Circuit Court Judge Charles M. McCabe of Crawfordsville was selected. He mounted the bench promptly at 9:00 A. M., on Monday, February 7, 1928, and the trial began.

A battery of high priced attorneys represented the defendants. They were Silas C. Kivett of Martinsville, Indiana; ex-Supreme Court Judge Lewis B. Ewbanks, and Clyde H. Jones.

Prosecutor Remy was Chief of Staff for the State, assisted by deputies Judson L. Stark and myself, and a Special Deputy, Emsley W. Johnson, Sr.

A large venire of scores of citizens were present for jury duty, and after several days of questioning, a jury of twelve good men and true were selected, and testimony began. The Jury consisted of two machinists; two farmers; two business executives; two salesmen; one preacher; one carpenter; one secretary of the Indianapolis Board of Trade, and one laborer. The latter was Sam Colbert, a colored man from my home town of Wheatland, Indiana.

The star witness was expected to be Stephenson, backed up by Governor McCray; his chief counsel, James A. Noel, a prominent attorney of the city and a graduate of Purdue University, and Fred Robinson, an attorney and Republican politician who had been McCray's campaign manager in the 1920 election.

Remy had trouble with his first witness, ex-Dragon Stephenson, who had been brought down under guard from Michigan City Prison to testify. The rotund Klansman testified somewhat freely at first, stating that he had been ordained or installed as Head of the Indiana Klan on July 4, 1923, at Mehalfa Park at Kokomo, Indiana, a farm owned by the Klan. When he got down to the meat of the case, the defense battery of attorneys spent most of the afternoon in loud and repeated objections to his further testimony, and finally Judge McCabe recessed the case until the next day so he could mull over the objections and ponder his decision, among other things an objection that Steve was a convict and not a competent witness.

On the witness being recalled to the stand the next morning, the Judge ruled he could testify.

Much to everyone's surprise Steve announced, "Your Honor, I refuse to answer the question on the grounds it might incriminate me."

It developed that during the night one Clarence Benadum, a Muncie attorney allied with the Klan, had been summoned by someone and he had advised Stephenson not to testify any further. "Steve" was called into private conference by the Prosecutor and by his attorneys, and back onto the stand three or four times, but was adamant.

"It is a matter of life and death with me," he told the Judge in the absence of the jury. "I fear the consequences if I tell the story of the alleged bribe."

Judge McCabe finally lost patience.

"Remove him from the courtroom, and call another witness, if you have any. Let's get on with this case," he said.

Prosecutor Remy ordered the sheriff to take Stephenson back to jail and hold him there pending further orders, and not to return him to the prison.

The next witness was Fred B. Robinson, above mentioned, whom McCray had appointed as State Purchasing Agent as a reward for toiling at the hustings. Fred was a good natured, placid sort of fellow, and he readily told his story about as follows:

On Saturday, December 8, 1923, that he was in his office at the State House when about 10:00 o'clock, A.M. he received a telephone call from Secretary of State Ed Jackson, summoning him to come to Jackson's office on "a matter of importance." On arriving, he met Secretary Jackson, defendant Coffin, and one Robert W. Lyons, an attorney from eastern Indiana and a high official of the Klan, according to the witness. After some talk, Robinson was handed a satchel containing the $10,000.00 in currency and told to take it into the Governor's office next door and give it to McCray, if he would promise to appoint Klan attorney James E. McDonald as Prosecutor of Marion County.

McCray had just been indicted that week by the Marion County

252

Grand Jury on a charge of embezzling $155,000 of state funds, and his new son-in-law, Mr. William P. Evans, who happened to be Prosecuting Attorney of the County, resigned on the spot. Robinson was to tell the Governor he would be guaranteed immunity from prosecution and conviction on the charge.

Robinson testified he picked up the satchel and dutifully carried it into the private office of Governor McCray, who was sitting there conversing with son-in-law Evans.

"I put the matter to the Governor and he refused the money. I told him Jackson and Coffin sent me!" he said. "Governor Mc-Cray turned in his chair to face me and said, 'Under no circumstances will I entertain such a proposition, Fred. I have already decided to appoint William H. Remy, the Chief Deputy.' "

Robinson toted the satchel, which contained D. C. Stephenson's money, back to the three men. Jackson berated him and said he would take the money himself to McCray.

"You didn't put it to him like you should, or like I would. I will take it myself," Robinson testified the defendant Jackson said, and added that he walked out the door with Jackson who had the satchel in his hand, and he saw him enter the Governor's office, but left him then. Robinson had not been indicted for his share in the bribe, as he had testified freely before the Grand Jury and the State used him as a witness.

At this juncture for some reason known only to himself, Stephenson, certainly the most extraordinary man ever to enter our State of Indiana, decided to testify, and he took the stand and did so. He freely admitted he had been part of the conspiracy, spending his money freely in an effort to gain control of the prosecution forces of Marion County. Prominent people were in on it, he said, but he refused to name them. He did say he had talked to Jackson four or five times regarding the appointment and to Marsh and Coffin, too.

"I was designated to see Mr. Noel (James), McCray's attorney about it," he said.

"When was that? What was the date?" Remy asked.

"It was in December, 1923, I don't remember exactly. It's been five years (really only four) and I've had a little trouble of my own since then, as you may remember, Mr. Remy," he said.

253

D. C. then stated, "I gave $10,000.00 of my own money to Mr. Marsh there to give to Jackson for Governor McCray. I took it out of my strong box. I had $65,000.00 in my strong box, and I got the money there."

Marsh and D. C. first went to attorney Noel, carrying the cash with them. They went to Noel's office.

"I told Mr. Noel here was $10,000 for Governor McCray for his attorney fees if he would appoint McDonald to succeed Evans. He turned it down," Steve said.

Attorney Noel, a suave well-groomed man and able lawyer, took the stand and corroborated Stephenson's story.

"Mr. Stephenson came in to my private office. Marsh was with him. He said 'We want Governor McCray to appoint James E. McDonald as successor to Evans.' I said the Indianapolis News has already said William H. Remy would be appointed, and Mr. Stephenson replied, 'The commission has not been issued. The matter is still open. We want to nominate Ed Jackson for Governor and we have got to have Marion County to put him over, and we've got to have that office.' "

The witness stated that "Steve" offered to back Mr. Remy in the coming 1924 Primary for Prosecutor. Noel said he told Stephenson he didn't know why "they" needed the office of Prosecuting Attorney; and that McCray would not recall the appointment.

"We have $10,000 right here and will turn it over to McCray if he will make this appointment, and further, we will guarantee McCray he will not be convicted in this or any other County of any crime by any Jury."

"I said that is a pretty large undertaking, Mr. Stephenson, and he replied, 'I know what I am talking about. I have an organization in this State so complete that if you want to know I can tell you tomorrow what any man you can name does today' and I then said 'I know Governor McCray, and he will not take your money. Save yourself the humiliation and trouble of a refusal. He will not have any part of it.' "

The witness then added: " 'Steve' slapped his leg and said in a loud rasping voice, 'I want McCray to declare himself! He's the one who has got to decide. Furthermore, Remy is a good friend of Mc-

Cray and he will be glad to step aside for awhile rather than see him convicted and sent to prison!' "

"He then asked me to convey this message to the Governor himself, that he would give him $10,000, saying it was for his attorney fees—perhaps for my benefit."

Stephenson and Marsh then left, Noel said, but came back the next day for McCray's answer. Noel testified he had indeed relayed the proposal to Governor McCray, but it was refused, and that the Governor had refused to discuss it.

Stephenson, in the five short years that had elapsed since he first came to Evansville as a Dixie Democrat and evil bird of omen of the Ku Klux Klan, was not accustomed to being brooked or thwarted in any such high matter of state. He had built a political and financial empire in an incredible short time, and public officials from United States Senator down to Indianapolis Market Master obeyed his every behest.

He now called up his reserves, the big guns. He sent Marsh over to the State House with the money with orders to have Jackson get McCray's campaign manager Robinson to clench the deal.

The next witness was ex-Governor McCray himself. It was his first public appearance since being paroled from Atlanta Prison in the sumer of 1927. McCray took the witness stand where he had sat and testified in his own defense in March of 1924 on the embezzlement charge. That trial resulted in a hung jury, and the charge was dropped after Judge Anderson and a jury in Federal Court had found him guilty of mail fraud.

McCray's presence recalled vividly when as Governor his three million dollar cattle empire blew away, and his other troubles accumulated. Prosecutor Remy, whom he had appointed instead of McDonald, and who had been renominated and elected over the furious opposition of Stephenson and the Klan, and his other political allies, including Coffin, asked McCray to continue where Robinson had left off.

The ex-Governor said that Robinson, his political ally, had come into his office that morning, and made the proposition.

"I said, 'Why, Fred, you know I couldn't think of doing a thing like that. You will have to carry that word back to those who sent

255

you here,' and he left," the witness testified.

Robinson's part in the bribe resulted from his loyalty to his boss, Governor McCray. The latter was in a jam, broke and under indictment, and the defendants had convinced him he was helping Mr. McCray out of a deep hole.

"Mr. Jackson came next," McCray said. "He repeated the same proposition, and I give him the same answer. My son-in-law was present and heard it all. Secretary Jackson talked about Mr. George V. Coffin as the greatest political genius in the Midwest and that Coffin felt I was making a great mistake in not taking the money and the offer."

The ex-Governor then stated that Jackson urged him to go in a taxi and see a man about five or six miles east of the State House about it, (Stephenson lived in Irvington, a suburb of the city five miles east).

"I refused, and told him I was not in the habit of leaving my office to see men," he said.

Jackson and his colleagues were not easily put off. McCray testified that in about an hour and a half the Secretary of State returned to the Governor's office, and a fourth attempt was made to make him accept the bribe, which he had with him again.

"He pressed me some more, about my desperate situation, and so forth, and he said, 'Now, Governor, you just go out into your secretary's room a little while, and when you return, I will be gone, and there will be $10,000.00 in your desk drawer here, and you can tell Remy you have changed your mind.' That is what he said."

"I said, 'Ed, I am amazed. It looks like I have lost my fortune I strived for twenty years to make, and my office is threatened, and my liberty, but I am not going to surrender my self-respect.' And Mr. Jackson left for good then."

As the ex-Governor recalled his ancient wrongs and tribulations, his voice choked a little, and he bowed his head and put his hands over his eyes. He then left the stand.

William P. Evans, the son-in-law, was a witness. He was a Phi Beta Kappa graduate of DePauw University. After his resignation as Prosecutor, he entered the practice of law in Indianapolis, where he was very successful, and late in life he served as a Republican State Senator from Marion County with distinction.

Evans corroborated McCray on the visit of Robinson, and the first visit of Jackson. He had left by the time the Secretary of State had made his second futile trip.

"Robinson said he had been called into a conference in the Secretary of State's office and asked to deliver a message to the Governor, and there were some representatives of powerful organizations there, and he made the offer," Evans testified. "Mr. McCray said he could not do that. Pretty soon Mr. Jackson came in and said he wanted to help Mr. McCray and this would be a big help to him if he would appoint McDonald. Mr. McCray told Jackson he couldn't do it and keep his self-respect."

Prosecutor Remy vainly tried to elicit from all the witnesses that the defendants had concealed the crime, but Judge McCabe held that too many other people knew about it.

On motion of the defense at the end of the State's case, the Judge made a decision which was a variation of the old Scotch verdict of "Guilty but not proved." He directed the Jury to return a verdict of "Proved but not Guilty."

Judge McCabe said, "Although the State has proven a conspiracy by all the defendants that the bribe took place, it has not proved a positive act of concealment. Under Indiana Law if a felony charge is not filed within two years of the act, homicide excepted, the defendant cannot be convicted unless he has been out of the State or concealed the crime. Therefore, I instruct you to return a verdict in this case of "Not Guilty" as to all defendants."

Governor Jackson broke into a delighted smile, something which rarely crossed his face as he was somewhat taciturn by nature, and he and the other two defendants shook their attorneys' hands.

Because of Judge McCabe's finding that the State had proved a conspiracy to bribe had taken place, many civic and church groups pressed Governor Jackson to resign. He refused to do so, and finished his term in office as though nothing untoward had happened, and he gave a State of the State address to the incoming Legislature at the end of his term.

The Republican Party, however, cast Jackson off. He was not

permitted to address the 1928 State Convention at the State Fairgrounds the following summer, which nominated Harry G. "Skillet" Leslie for Governor. The Convention also refused to elect him as a delegate to the G.O.P. National Convention that nominated Herbert Hoover, an action unheard of.

As to defendant Marsh, he returned to the practice of law, and "Cap" Coffin resumed his mastery of the local Republican political machine, keeping a firm control as long as he lived, which was about ten years after the trial.

Split Second Justice

Governor Henry F. Schricker, a Democrat, started me on my judicial career in 1941, by appointing me Judge of Municipal Court, Room 4, commonly known as Police Court, which handled one thousand cases of small crimes and traffic charges a month.

One Sunday afternoon in November 1941, I was raking leaves in my yard when my elder daughter Nancy, age 7, came out and announced, "A man who says he's Governor Schricker wants you on the telephone." I had some doubts, as even at that age, she liked to kid me. However, it was the Governor, and he said, "Mr. Niblack, there is a vacancy in Police Court, Municipal Court, Room 4, and I would like to know if you would be interested in being appointed to it."

"I'll take it, Governor," I said without batting an eye, and he told me to come down to his office in the State House. I got in my 1932 Plymouth sedan and went down.

Times had been a little hard with me lately. I opened my law office in 1928, with no clients; the stock market crashed in 1929; the Democrats elected a Court House full of Judges in 1930; I got married in 1931; I was defeated for relection to the State Senate in 1932 by a Democrat, and ex-butcher boy from Brooklyn who had been in town about three years; and Franklin Delano Roosevelt closed the banks in 1933. Two daughters appeared in 1934 and 1936. All in all, the new Plymouth I bought in 1932 was still in use.

Governor Schricker, he of the famous white hat, was a Democrat and a good honest Governor. By law this appointment had to be a Republican attorney.

"You know, Judge Karabell (Charles) just died after an incapacity of eighteen months and that Court is in one heck of a mess," he said. "The professional bondsmen and police court attorneys have been running it, and I want it cleaned up. I have had fifty applications and recomendations from both political parties, labor leaders, church people, and about everyone else. I finally asked Judge Nate Swaim of the Supreme Court to recomend to me a Republican attorney who had not applied, and he gave me your name."

Judge Nathan Swaim was from Indianapolis and a good Sigma Nu college fraternity brother of mine. Some time before I had helped get him elected to the Indianapolis School Board, a spring-board to the high Court, and also we were members of our local Sigma Nu Alumni Association and its bowling team. Thus, you can see, Judges are sometimes appointed solely on merit, as in my case.

I had never met Governor Schricker before, but I was glad to meet him now, and I promised I would be a reform Judge and wear no man's collar—as Andy Gump used to say in the comics—so he gave me a commission. I went to work on November 17, 1941, and have been Judge ever since in one Court or another, with my present term as Circuit Judge scheduled to end on December 31, 1974.

I found my salary was $5,000 a year, which was $800.00 less than I took in at my law office in the first ten months of 1941, my best year. There were no income taxes, either Federal or State, on a judge's salary then, though that omission long since has been handsomely corrected.

We had a swearing in ceremony with bouquets of roses, and Mr. William H. Remy, my former boss and then present law associate, was Master of Ceremonies. My wife, the former Margaret Wood, and her parents, Circuit Judge and Mrs. Walter Wood, of Sullivan, Indiana, and our two daughters, Nancy and Susan; my father and brother, Grif Niblack, a reporter on the News, and his wife; and some other relatives and friends came down to the ratty and smelly old Police Station for the event. The room was also packed with politicians, police court bondsmen and their runners and the attorneys who practiced there.

Police Court was then and is now the most important Court in town, as ninety-nine percent of the people who are ever in a Court of justice, go there—the only one they ever see. It is the poor man's Court, as the great majority never have a lawyer and appear before the Judge abashed and frightened, and most plead guilty even when they are not, especially in traffic cases. Police Court also holds preliminary hearings on major crimes, such as rape or murder, with power to hold for Grand Jury, and fix bond or deny it, as the case may be.

As an ex-newspaper reporter and a politician who was always on the outs with our County Republican organization, largely a hang-over from the Stephenson-Coffin crowd, and being naturally a little bossy (if that is the word) and being independent, I felt entirely free to be Judge and make my own decisions—a platform I have followed ever since. I have always liked the 1851 State Constitution, and particularly the part written by the great man from Southern Indiana, Robert Dale Owen, which reads: "Justice shall be administered freely and without purchase; speedily and without delay; completely and without denial."

My inaugural address was short, but it followed Governor Schricker's admonition. The new Judge knew several thousand friends, relatives and acquaintances in town, he said, and all cases would be tried from the bench in the Court Room, as he would be too busy to try them once on the phone, once in the back office, and once in Court. This would apply to the police, also.

This made a powerful impression on everyone, which lasted about eighteen hours. The next morning when I went down the side hall to my chambers, there was a group of some twelve or fifteen men and women waiting for me. I said, "What do you folks want?"

Otto Fritz, an elderly, kindly labor leader, spoke up, "Judge, one of my boys is coming up this morning, and I want to talk to you about him. He's a good fellow."

I said, "Otto, for God's Sake! You were at the ceremony yesterday and heard me, now what is there you can't say in Court for your man that you want to say here?"

Nothing, he thought, so I told him to get out in the Court room and when the name was called, he could come up and testify for his man. The others in the group included a couple of precinct comitteemen, a Ward Chairman, some mothers and wives, some employers, a newspaper reporter, and a policeman. They all got the same advice, and all complied.

I was always glad to have such folks come forward for a defendant, as it really helped out the Judge as to the background and so on. Quite frequently I made an employer, or labor leader, or Ward Chairman, the parole agent or probation officer of his man. This practice completely cured some of them from ever coming up again on a case.

Trying all cases on the bench in the Court Room saved me a lot of time, and the people got about the same results they would have gotten in the back room, as a Police Court Judge who is worth his salt does not like to put people in jail. His motto should be that all people stand equal before the bar of justice. I found early that it was difficult to give a rich man a fair shake when involved with a poor man, or a white man a fair trial if the accuser was a Negro, without being accused of prejudice. Generally, I tried to listen to all the evidence on both sides, consider the law and then give the guilty man about one-third of what he had coming and let him worry about it. I had another comforting guideline. If there was going to be any heat about a criminal case, I would let the fellow who started it sit in the hot seat.

The Court met every day in the year except Sunday, Christmas included. The two Police Courts held forth in the Police Station, an old brick building erected about 1885, as a pest house and city dispensary. The Police bullpen or overnight accommodations were there, as also was the Police Headquarters. It was on South Alabama Street, one-half block south of Washington Street, on the edge of the railroad yards. The bondsmen, eight or ten of them, had small offices up and down the street in which they lurked.

When I mounted the bench at 9:00 A.M., I usually was confronted by a Prosecutor without any preparation, a policeman without a warrant, and a defendant without any defense, except maybe some fellow had hired a lawyer who he hoped was an intimate friend of the Judge, or better yet, had something on the Judge. Many of the attorneys who practiced there were not at all bashful in assuring their prospective clients that such indeed was the case.

The Christmas morning crowd was generally a pretty sad looking bunch, what with office parties the afternoon before that hung over. One Christmas day I was confronted with twenty-three cases of drunken driving. One of them was old Santa Claus himself, who had spent the night in the "pokey" in his red suit. He had officiated at some Christmas party and had partaken of too much Cherry Bounce, something like hard cider, I guess.

Another case was a well-to-do, nice looking business man who had imbibed too heartily at the office Christmas Party and had ended up with his car on Indiana Avenue about 11:00 P.M. where some folks saw he was a stranger and took him in, incidentally relieving him of $200.00 in cash, a ring, and a gold watch. He had a dandy hangover in Court and said his wife and three children had been going to help him trim the Christmas tree when he got home. I let him and Santa go home without requiring bond, as they were householders, thus cheating the professional bondsmen out of some prey.

A bond cost $10.00 a hundred—thus if you had a $500.00 bond, the bondsman would fine you $50.00 before the Judge got to you, and would then turn you over to his partner, a police court lawyer, who would also fine you any fee he could get, up to $250.00 for a drunken driving charge. The Judge would take his pen and commit a person to jail, and within five minutes a professional bondsman, not a graduate of a law school, nor admitted to the bar, nor elected or commissioned by anyone, and most generally a crook of the first water, could take his pen and set the man free.

For the five years, one month and thirteen days I served down there I fought a vigorous, continuous, and often losing action with the professional bondsmen. There were a couple of them who were pretty decent fellows, but two-thirds of them had criminal records. One had been in the penitentiary for robbery, and he also was the husband of a notorious madam of a house of ill fame. Another, a precinct comitteeman, had been arrested for oral sodomy on an eighteen months old baby girl, which case had been quashed by one of our Prosecuting Attorneys in return for the defendant "getting right" in the County convention and joining the Prosecutor's political faction. (Politics sometimes got a little dirty in those days!) This same bird had been in for hog stealing, had done time for auto banditry reduced to larceny, and he later did six months for using obscene language over the telephone. A third bondsman had been in the penitentiary for embezzling public funds and for using slugs in a pay phone, a Federal offense. There were others of like ilk.

In this connection, two of the bondsmen got into a private war.

One of them, Ralph, hired a tree surgeon to go to the home of his rival, named Bill, with orders to top some fine maple trees there.

"I own the place, but my tenant is peculiar, and he doesn't want it done," he told the unlucky tradesman, "You just go ahead anyhow."

The fellow climbed up in a tree and pretty soon a limb crashed down. Out ran the outraged bondsman owner, who happened to be home, and roared, "What in the Hell are you doing to my tree? Get down out of there!"

"Now, I've been warned about you. Just go back in the house. It's all right," the tree surgeon replied soothingly.

William ran in the house, came out with a shotgun and pointed it at the man and said, "I'm going to blow your God damn brains out if you're not out of that tree in twenty seconds!" The fellow let go all holds and fled, glad to escape with his life.

Bondsman Bill, in revenge, sent an undertaker to Ralph's home to get the alleged corpse of the rival's mother-in-law, who was cooking supper when the ambulance came for her. He also sent ten dozen roses for a non-existent wedding, and had five tons of soft coal delivered, which he ordered dumped in the driveway.

"My yard man will wheel it in," he told the coal company. Ralph was sued for the bill.

Another bondsman, a lady, hit a rival bondsman over the head with a two-by-four beam, out in Alabama Street one day in a quarrel over a prospective client, and laid him out cold. He was her brother, so he didn't have her arrested.

I barred the bondsman who owned the trees for victimizing a poor drunk, a married man with a job, a wife, and a child. The man would go on a spree, get down, and wind up in jail. I suppose I tried him six or eight times. I used threats, probation, suspended sentences and lectures, to no avail. The next to the last time he was in, I gave him six months on the State Farm and suspended it on probation, and I said, "This is it! The next time you get drunk, this probation will be revoked and out you go to Putnamville! Out to the brick yard there!" That didn't work either. About a month later Hoyt was back. Same old charge. This time he had a lawyer, a henchman of bondsman Bill.

"Probation revoked! Take him away," I said, "I'm sick of looking at you."

That afternoon his wife and sister came to see me after Court. "That bondsman took the title to our car, and had Hoyt write a check for $300.00, and he only has $21.00 in the bank. And the lawyer guaranteed him he would get off!" they told me.

It developed the bondsman took Hoyt out on bond on Saturday night, kept him at his home over Sunday (incidentally making him paint his garage) and told him he would fix the case with me by phone. He called the lawyer, who pretended to be me, according to Hoyt's affidavit. I made the bondsman give the title and the check back, suspended the sentence, and barred Bill from bonding in Room 4. He merely hired the Honorable Ira M. Holmes, a very fine criminal lawyer, who appealed the case to the Supreme Court of Indiana.

"Tut! Tut! Niblack!" said in substance the five fearless legal fathers over at the State House, "You can't do that. The man has a right to make an honest living and you can't make such arbitrary rules." The case is in the Supreme Court Reports.

I have always tried to follow the law as a Judge, even if lack of a search warrant freed some guilty rascal. If a Judge doesn't follow the law, I don't know who should. But I have had, and do have, reservations about Supreme Courts. The trial Judge never knows what the High Court will say, as it has the last word. Quite a few Supreme Court Justices are dedicated men, but to what is sometimes a mystery.

I had been Judge there about three weeks when one Saturday morning we had some two-hundred people jammed in the room. The Prosecutor called the next case: "Mr. Deb Farr!" I saw my old college acquaintance from Bloomington, the slightly loony town fellow who used to play cards with us, come creeping out of the bullpen with a black eye.

"Mr. Farr, you are charged with drunk, disorderly conduct, profanity, public indecency, and resisting arrest! What is your plea?"

Deb paid him no attention, but looked up at me—the new reform Judge—on that old high bench in Room 4.

"Now, Johnnie, you remember me! You remember old Deb

who used to come down to the Sigma Nu house and riffle them little cards and play a little poker with you, and drink a little whiskey now and then with you," Deb bellowed. "Just tell all these people old Deb ain't so bad, Johnnie!"

The horrified reform Judge just had enough mind left to lean over to the Court clerk and whisper, "Let the record show a Plea of Guilty, sentence suspended and get the —— out of here in a hurry," to a lot of snickers.

Deb was slated once more into my Court about a year later. One morning before Court the bailiff informed me he was in again. He liked the women and it developed that while servicing a second-rate prostitute in a third class hotel, behind locked doors, poor Deb had a fit and began to foam at the mouth and yell, whereupon the poor girl, unable to move, likewise began screaming bloody murder, and the hotel manager and others had to break in the door and rescue her, almost dead from fright.

"Transfer this case to Municipal Court, Room 3, and let Judge McNelis try him. It's a little racy for me," I commanded. I had never been out with Deb on any wild parties, but I wasn't taking any chances.

One of the heaviest burdens in a Judge's life is that of mental cases. It never lets up. In 1941, insane persons were kept in jail until inquest, held on a Police Court charge of "Mental Vagrancy." There was no such charge. I didn't like them to be in jail, so I would order transfer to the General Hospital pending inquest. Twice I was cited to appear in Superior Court on a Writ of Habeas Corpus for illegal detention. Judge Hezzie Pike and Judge Walter Pritchard, the latter a former Police Judge himself, both fine Judges, released the prisoners, crazy or not, amid fanfare on the front page that Judge Niblack was doing wrong.

"There is no such law as Mental Vagrancy," they both decreed, and they were right. However, it was a condition, and not a theory that confronted us Police Court Justices.

One winter morning the Prosecutor handed up another "Mental Vagrancy," that of a Southside man who would go mad, strip off his clothes and run up and down the streets. The police had picked him up the night before, naked as a jay bird.

There the poor fellow stood, eyes staring, a bailiff on each arm, and his wife and mother along side. They had brought down his clothes, and the police had dressed him, with his hat jammed on crossways.

"Now, Mr. Prosecutor, you know and I know there is no such charge as "Mental Vagrancy. Why are you bringing such a silly charge again? Haven't you read the papers lately?"

The Prosecutor was aghast, "Why, Judge, this man is out of his mind. His folks here called the law, and we have to hold him for his own safety or he'll freeze to death."

"Mr. Bailiff, you take this poor fellow up to Superior Court, Room 4, to Judge Pritchard. Just march right in the Court room and up to the bench, turn him loose, and say, "Judge Pritchard, this man is crazy and Judge Niblack wants to know what to do with him," I ordered.

Away they all went, the women trailing.

In about ten or fifteen minutes, I got a telephone call from my good friend Judge Pritchard, who sometimes got a little excited.

"Johnnie, Johnnie! What in the World! You sent two police up here and a crazy man who started taking off his clothes right in the middle of a divorce case! What do you mean?"

"Well, Judge Pritchard," I explained, "It's another "Mental Vagrancy," and you outlawed that last week. So *you* tell *me* what to do before another habeas corpus case comes up."

"Just send him to the General Hospital. I did it myself hundreds of times when I was Police Judge," he said.

"O.K., Judge, if you order me to do it, I will," I told him.

"Sure! Sure! I order you to send him there! Only just get him out of here!" the good Judge said. There never was a nicer fellow than Pritchard.

So that is how the Order read: "Municipal Court Commitment by Special Order of Superior Court, Room Four."

I sat down then and wrote out in longhand a bill for the next Legislature authorizing temporary lawful detention in the Psychopathic Ward of General Hospital of persons found insane on the streets, or suspected of being insane at home. In the latter case, the family had to apply to the Superintendent of the Ward, a Medical

Doctor, who could issue a warrant, instead of applying to the Prosecutor.

This Bill passed the Legislature in 1945, and is known as "The Preliminary Mental Statute for Cities of the First Class." I also devised all the writs and forms, and they are still in use.

I was Police Judge during the World War II years, and the police and Military authorities waged a mighty skirmish with the Legions of the Ladies of the Evening—not so much to protect the morals of the G.I.'s as their health. The authorities were always afraid their charges would get a veneral disease, and many of them did in spite of everything, including argerol. The City kept a sort of pest house, or isolation ward, out at 1140 East Market Street, where the girls were confined ten days without bail to see if they were pure—due process, civil rights and all that fol-de-rol blithely ignored in an all out effort to whip the Hun. The place had once been a private sanitarium. If a lady was found to be infected, she was retained until cured. The girls were held under commitment from Municipal Court.

Week ends yielded the richest hauls as the minions of the law and the Military Police seined blondes, brunettes and red heads from the depths of the Palm Gardens Tavern, the Claypool Bar, and other watering places favored by the service men. Each Monday morning we would face the "Chorus Line," as the Bailiff called it, of pretty, high-heeled, silk-stockinged dames and flat-heeled, bow-legged slatterns, all held on charges of disorderly conduct, entering the room of the opposite sex, obscene conduct, or just plain old prostitution. After a short ceremony of taking names, ages, and places of origin, the Paddy Wagon would take them out to East Market Street.

Two young girls from Tompkinsville, Monroe County, Kentucky, and a taxi driver appeared in Room 4 one Monday, after a week end in jail. It developed the girls arrived on a bus about 11:00 P.M., on Saturday night, and retained the taxi man to take them out to see a cousin Ethel.

"We only got thirty-seven cents, but Ethel will pay you," they told the man, "she is in a big private sanitarium taking the rest cure," and they gave him the address, 1140 East Market Street. The

268

taxi driver was new on the job, though not so new but what he recognized the Isolation Ward when he got there.

"Ladies, this ain't no private sanitarium. It's the Clap Trap," he told them on arrival. Needless to say, Ethel couldn't get out to pay the fare, a big brawl ensued, and the night watch ran out and arrested all three, and here they were in Court.

"Well, you want to visit your cousin Ethel so badly, you just go on out there and see her," I told the girls, and let the hapless taxi driver go on home to his wife and children. The sequel was that the nineteen-year old was found to have gonorrhea, (she said she had been on a little vacation with some soldiers up to Cincinnati some time before), and had to stay a while.

The eighteen year old girl turned out free of disease, and I had the Probation Department write her mother to come get her. In a few days the bailiff said there was an elderly lady out in the hall in a sun-bonnet and smoking a clay pipe who wanted to see me, and after Court I talked to her.

"I've come after my baby dotter," she said, after identifiying herself.

"Say, do you know Clarence Harbin down here?" I asked, "He was on probation here for a year about whiskey and finally went back down there."

"I shore do know Clarence. He married my oldest dotter," she replied.

"How is he getting along?"

"Well, jist fine. No trouble as I know of. He lives right over by the big road where the law could get him easy if he was needed," she said. She got her "baby dotter" and they left.

Clarence had been a roofer here working for Ralph Reeder Roofing Company. He was arrested for chasing another sister-in-law up in a yard with his new red Overland Whippet one Saturday afternoon while drunk. He made $55.00 a week when he worked, but his wife had to work part time at Armour's for $18.00 a week to feed their five children as Clarence spent his time and money after work and on week ends on whiskey, women, and red automobiles.

At his trial, his sister-in-law said he was a "sweet-singer" as well as a roofer, which it developed, was a term used in the foothills of the Appalachians for a ballad singer.

"Judge, it means a feller who plays a guitar and sings them old time songs," she explained.

I asked Clarence how old he was when he first drank whiskey.

"Lord God, Judge, I can't rightly tell you. Must've been 'round eight year old, I reckon. Pappy kept a jug of hit on the kitchen table, and airy one who wanted to jist taken a drink," he said.

I had an investigation made by Mrs. Sarah Rodocker, head of the Probation Department. She told me "Judge, that is the dirtiest house I ever saw, and I've seen some daisies. They have an outside toilet but evidently don't use it too much as every pot and chamber in the house, and even a couple of skillets and a bucket were full of human excrement of various ages."

The Court found Clarence guilty and pronounced sentence of six months on the State Farm, with an alternative of being on probation and turning over a new leaf: Have the probation department sell his car and put the money on the five children; clean up his house, get on the water wagon, and work steady.

"Judge, I won't do'er! I ain't goin' to sell that there Whippet. That's my pride and joy," Clarence announced firmly on hearing his probation terms.

"O.K., go on out to the farm and do your six months, then. You won't get any whiskey there," the Court assured him. I privately ordered the Sheriff to keep him ten days in the jail before taking him away.

At the end of six days, Clarence sent word he was ready to go along with the Court, and he served his year's probation in a more or less satisfactory manner. At the end, he had his brother move them back to Kentucky, and like St. Paul, he stamped the dust of the City off of his feet and left, telling the probation woman:

"This here is the God damnest town a man ever saw. They won't let a man take nairy a drink of whiskey in the God damn town!"

An eighteen year old colored boy from Woodlawn, Tennessee, came to town after he graduated from high school down there and got a job as dishwasher in the Claypool Hotel. One afternoon a policeman found him sitting in Virginia Avenue, blocking a street car, with a quart bottle half full of Old Rocking Chair whiskey in his hand, and the other half in his belly, and he was brought in. He said his father was a substantial landowner down home who didn't want him to come north, but wanted him to either stay home and farm or go to college. I didn't see much future for the lad up here, so I exiled him back to Tennessee, ordering either that or one year on the State Farm. He chose to go home.

"Don't ever come back here. You do what you father says," I told him. "If you ever cross that Ohio River again, the F.B.I. will let me know, and it's out to the Farm for you. You write me a letter when you get home!"

In due time I received a letter from the boy, who said he was glad to be home, and that his folks were overjoyed to see him.

A lady in the Probation Department reported me to some fellow bleeding hearts in an association about this incident and I was reprimanded by a committee who assured the Court it had no lawful right to deport anyone out of the State. I told them that was true, but that the boy had made a voluntary choice, and that if they would mind their own business, I would mind mine, and to please get out of my life.

A Police Judge sees the seamy side of life. There was one man here, an engineer for a foundry who had seven daughters and three sons. As each girl child arrived at the age of puberty, papa would take her into the bedroom and complete her sex education. This went on for years, but he never was sent up for incest because the wife or family would not testify against him. He was the head of a harem of eight females. The sordid details became known through probation of some of his daughters, most of whom turned out to be prostitutes.

There were twin brothers living here named Spivis. One was unmarried and was an alcoholic bum. I kept him on the State Farm six months at a time, although he was allowed two sprees between each term. He was perfectly sober out there and enjoyed good health, but he didn't like it.

"Judge, you're having me serve a life sentence out there on the installment plan," he told me once, but I assured him it was his own

271

choice, not mine.

"While you're there you are not lying drunk on the Courthouse yard in the rain," I reminded him, "And further you are helping raise vegetables for the State Insane Asylums and Prisons and thus pulling an oar in the ship of state."

In re this practice, which was condemned by a lot of bleeding hearts who really had no better ideas, my Democratic colleague, a genial Irishman, the late John L. McNelis, was too kind-hearted to help me out. We alternated months on traffic and misdemeanors.

One day I said to him, "Come on now, Judge, and send those chronic drunks out to the Farm for six months. Bill Spivis just came in before me today, and the finger print record shows he was in front of you three times last month, and you gave him $1.00 and costs, suspended. Each case means a new trip for the paddy wagon, a new affidavit, a new sheet in the docket book, another trial for a policeman on his own time, and so on."

John just laughed and patted my arm, "Johnny, I know you'll take care of them when it's your month."

The other Spivis twin, unfortunately, had gotten married, and fathered five sons and two daughters. He worked steady at a plant, but was a week end drunk. One time he was arrested for chasing everyone out of the house with a ball bat, red-eyed and roaring. The boys became prime juvenile delinquents, one of them winding up by murdering in cold blood a policeman, who stopped the youth's car about a traffic violation.

One north side man with a good job and a nice family had a bad habit of going in home two or three times a month at midnight roaring drunk, and raising hell. His nine year old daughter became so nervous she developed St. Vitus dance, poor little thing.

A Police Judge learns that there is a great lot of hereditary feeble-mindedness, drunkenness, gambling, drug using, and general cussedness that causes poverty, distress, and hard core unemployment. "What will maintain one vice will bring up two children," Benjamin Franklin said.

Speaking of the "Chorus Line," I had the duty of trying the last wild Indian ever captured alive in Marion County, a 23 year old lady who was one-quarter Cherokee, one quarter Negro and one-half white. She came up from North Carolina and lived on North New Jersey Street with her husband and two papooses.

One Saturday morning she went to the grocery and met a taxi driver who had a quart of fire water, and they took off. About 1 :00 A.M the next Monday morning, or just after midnight Sunday, the farmers down in Franklin Township heard screaming and laughing out in a cornfield and summoned help. The Sheriff found the taxi mired down in the mud there, with the worthy duo wallowing around in it in their cups. Claudia (that was her name) was a real beauty with olive skin, black eyes, and exquisite figure. She was sent to the isolation Ward and turned out pure.

This entire episode was of great interest to the Indianapolis News reporter who covered the police station, as he had heard the trial. He was a mighty Don Juan, a lover of woman flesh.

"Judge, let me know if that girl comes out clean," he begged.

The day she appeared with the "line" for discharge, right in the middle of the hearing the unfortunate fellow was called to the phone by his City Editor. After Claudia had gone here he came, and finding out she was gone, went running out through the halls in vain search.

"Damn the luck!" he told me later, "That was the only chance I've ever had of going to bed with three nations at once."

Not realizing at first that I was but one cog in the administation of Justice, I sort of got carried away by the idea of cracking down on drunken drivers. I would stop that in this town, I resolved. So, the first few weeks, anyone found guilty of such charge drew a minimum of thirty days in jail. All of a sudden, I wasn't trying drunken drivers any more, as one-hundred percent of such defendants took a change of venue from me.

I found out the American public doesn't enjoy jail at all, whether it drives while drinking or not. I finally decided to go along with what the public and the Bar demanded, and what the law allowed, and reserve jail for real serious cases, like where some old lady was run over and injured, so I was allowed to try such cases again.

In this connection I also discovered that the Great American public, the tax payer, is hell-bent on sending all drunken driver to jail, except for "me and mine."

"Give them the limit in jail, Judge. Break it up," a man would tell me after I had addressed a noon luncheon club on law and order. The next morning if his son was arrested for driving while under the influence of intoxicating liquor the same fellow would beat the bushes frantically to find an attorney who was a friend of the court, or who could fix a jury, or was a partner of the Prosecuting Attorney—just anything to beat the rap on his beloved offspring.

Oh! Well! "Blood is thicker than water" is an old saying, and I can't say that I blame people for coming to the aid of relatives. It's human nature.

There was a colored gentleman named Fruster Jones, who had a record of about forty arrests and convictions in re women, gambling, bootlegging, dope—you name it. One time the police took a crow bar and broke in his house of joy at 25th and Martindale without a search warrant and arrested poor Fruster once more for keeping a dive. When the case came up, his attorney made the usual motion to supress the evidence because of no warrant and thus beat the case. Many a police court attorney amassed a fortune with only two legal weapons in his arsenal: 1) a partnership with a professional bondsman; and 2) enough legal knowledge to say "I move to dismiss the case, Your Honor, because of no search warrant."

"Now, Judge," said my Deputy Prosecutor, Mr. Virgil Norris, a young attorney who later was Judge on the same bench in Room 4, "You ought not sustain this motion. Everyone knows Fruster Jones is no good and has a long record."

I called for a copy of the Indiana Constitution and read from the Bill of Rights to the contestants, as follows:

"Every person shall be secure in his house, his property, his person and his effects except Fruster Jones, whom Deputy Prosecutor Norris says is no good".

"Judge, that doesn't say that!" protested Norris.

"Well, that's what you want it to read," I retorted. "The mantle of the law protects everyone alike—good or bad."

The case was dismissed. Norris told that story on himself many times.

Speaking of Deputy Prosecutors, there was one I will call Jimmy (that was not his name) who served in Juvenile Court. He had a bad habit of parking his car anywhere he wished, by fire plugs, bus stops, walk ways, and other prohibited areas. They didn't tow cars away in those days, and Jimmy accumulated at least one hundred tickets without paying any. Finally, despite his office and the fact he was a Republican Precinct Committeeman, the City Prosecutor filed twenty-eight traffice charges in my Court, and Jimmy finally was forced to trial. He was found guilty, and fined $1.00 and cost of $5.00 on each charge, totalling $168.00.

"I will suspend the costs and you can pay the Clerk $28.00, if you will cut out your unlawful parking," I told the defendant.

"Judge, that's an awful lot of money," he replied.

"Well, that's an awful lot of tickets, too, Jimmy," I replied.

He went out in the Clerk's office to pay his money and the bailiff said Jimmy threw his hat on the floor and jumped up and down on it, and screamed "The Son-of-a-Bitch! I thought he was a friend of mine. I'm going to tell Governor Schricker not to reappoint such a narrow minded bastard!"

However, Governor Schricker reappointed me for a full four year term.

I had another run in with a Republican politician, this time the County Chairman, Jimmy Bradford, a nice young fellow who had served with me in an anti-political machine faction, and then sold us out to our enemies the night before the Primary. Jimmy called me at home one day and said, "Judge, I got a ticket to be in your Court next Wednesday for speeding. What'll I do about it?"

"Well, you come down Wednesday and you can make up your mind by then whether to plead guilty or not guilty," I told him.

"Thanks, Judge," he replied drily.

On Wednesday, Jimmy came down and as his defense attorney, he had my good friend Joseph J. Daniels, the Republican district chairman and head of a leading law firm, Baker and Daniels.

Despite Jimmy's testimony and Mr. Daniel's eloquence he was found guilty of going 45 miles an hour in a 30-mile zone and was fined $1.00 and costs—a total of $6.00. Brother Daniels promptly appealed the case to Criminal Court, presided over by the Honorable

Duke Bain, Washington Township Republican Chairman, who gave poor Jimmy a fair trial and promptly found him not guilty, reversing the lower Court.

This little business with the Deputy Prosecutor and the County and District Chairman, and my general attitude, cost me my job, as Joe Daniels had the say so as to who would be appointed in my place by the new Republican Governor, the Honorable Ralph Gates.

I had one case of an ex-school mate, named James, from Wheatland, Indiana, my old home town. He was enamored of a widow on the Southside, and one evening while under the joint influence of beer and the pangs of unrequited love, he made forcible entry by kicking the door down. My old chum received probation, an order to pay for the door, and another to stay away from the widow. We had a repeat in about two weeks, whereupon James was sentenced to six months on the State Farm.

"Six months on the State Farm or six months in Wheatland, take your choice, Jimmy."

"Oh, No! Not six months in Wheatland!" and the sweat broke out on his face. However, he finally decided to do his time in Wheatland.

"Say, what did you do to Jimmy up there in Court?" someone asked me when I went down home later. "He came back here and stayed six months with his brother, and I believe he gave you a cussing every day he was here!" I gathered my old chum wasn't so fond of the old home town.

My Court had traffic every other month, and I became an advocate of "no fix" on such charges. I didn't like to fine young people or put them in jail, so we adopted a policy of sending them to traffic school on first offense, or taking a kid's license and holding it in my desk thirty days, plus a lecture, or some similar tactic, which were more impressive than a fine. People who "fix" their children's traffic tickets or go in and pay a fine in the child's absence are asking for trouble later on.

The essence of speeding charges in those days was reckless driving, with more than 30 miles an hour in a residential district a prima facie case of recklessness. This could be rebutted by showing of facts, such as driving on West 16th Street by the ball park, at that time the only building there. The police loved the place as there was no danger of accidents in chasing speeders. Motorists, recognizing what the National Safety Council called the "common law of safe driving," would drive forty miles an hour there where there were no residences, no cross streets, and in broad daylight and on dry streets. I warned the traffic chief about it several times, as people did not know their rights and couldn't afford to hire a lawyer. The affidavit was the usual pink colored form the prosecutor used charging "in a residential district."

One afternoon there were 51 such motorists in Court from West 16th Street again. I tried two cases, and no recklessness was involved nor could the State prove it was a residential area. I sent for the Traffic Chief and in his presence gave a mass discharge of all 51 cases. I tried to explain it to the crowd, but at least five or six stayed to argue with me, wanting to plead guilty.

A Judge has to have some knowledge of human nature. We had a business man in one day charged with going 35 miles an hour in a 30-mile residential zone, who protested long and loud as to his innocence. The policeman was equally positive. I finally made a finding of guilty and the fine was $6.00. The defendant shook his head pretty mournfully, "It's a mighty sad thing, Judge, for me to have to pay it," he said.

"Well, friend, just go on out there and pay your fine, and as you go, think of some time when you were going 50 miles an hour in that zone and didn't get caught and put it on that," I told him.

He broke out in a happy smile, and said, "You've got me there, Judge, I'll just do it."

I could write about a thousand other interesting cases down there, but one more will have to do. There was a man, age 70, and his wife who lived at 40th Street. He had an ex-State Policeman with a eleven year old son who lived across the street. The boy was a smart-aleck, and he persecuted the old couple no end, despite their complaints to his doting parents. He stuck a railroad spike in the grass, and broke the old man's lawnmower. He tore down a fine stand of morning glories from a telephone pole, and climbed up on the back porch roof and made moaning sounds outside the old lady's bedroom window one evening, scaring her half to death. The old man, in frustration finally took a stout switch and gave Junior a good lamming. Whereupon, he went bawling tearfully home. The ex-policeman came over and gave Grandpa an ultimatum.

"Egbert will be waiting at his home this evening at 7:00 o'clock to receive your apology. If you don't come, you will be arrested for assault and battery on a child."

The old man refused to go apologize, so here they all were, facing me. I heard the story in full. Egbert and his papa stood triumphantly eyeing the aged citizen as the Prosecutor presented his case. At the end the Court pronounced judgment:

"I can see there has been a mistake here, and the wrong man has been arrested. Mr. Bailiff, take this father and arrest him on a charge of contributing to the delinquency of his minor child. Slate him in Juvenile Court, and the bond is fixed at $1,000.00," I said, and I also admonished the daddy, "And in the future, try to exercise some control over this child of yours."

The old man was found not guilty and lived in peace afterward.

At the beginning of my last year, I found I was not going to be reappointed by the new Republican Governor, the Honorable Ralph Gates, as the County and District Chairmen definitely were not on my side, so I beat the rap by filing for Superior Court, Room 1, which paid $10,000 a year, anyhow. All the drunks, bondsmen, and a whole lot of politicians helped kick me upstairs to the Court House.

I was nominated and elected. My last day as Judge in Police Court was December 31, 1946.

Hog Calling Contest Helps My Judicial Career

Like an ex-G.I., I know exactly how long I served in police court. It was five years, one month and thirteen days. My antics on the bench, such as fining the Republican County Chairman Jimmie Bradford $1.00 and costs for speeding fifty miles an hour in a thirty-mile zone didn't please James. Neither did it please his attorney, the Honorable Joseph J. Daniels, a very respectable member of the old and respected law firm of Baker & Daniels, which had been founded by ex-Governor Conrad O. Baker. Joe was also Republican District Chairman. They took an appeal to Criminal Court where presided the Honorable William "Duke" Bain, Republican Party Chairman of Washington township. Duke was an occasional fishing companion of mine, but he didn't let friendship, facts, testimony, or anything else obstruct the due administration of justice, and Mr. Bradford was given his constitutional right of a speedy trial and found not guilty. Duke knew an emergency when he saw one.

There is an old saying that politics make strange bedfellows. Fishing does, too. That same summer of 1946, Judge Bain, Judge Mark Rhoads of Juvenile Court, Eddie McClure, County Republican Election Comissioner, and I all went to Kentucky Lake on a fishing expedition. Bain and Eddie were stalwarts of the Republican machine, I was strong anti, and Judge Rhoads was in neither faction. We didn't take any alchoholic libations, except for Bain who took some gin and lemons, and drank what he called a "switch itch." He would put some salt on the back of one hand, hold a half lemon in the fingers and take a jigger of gin in the other hand, lick the salt, swallow the gin and suck the lemon almost simultaneously. Unfortunately, this particular Kentucky County was dry, and we had to drive fifty miles into Paducah to get relief: three quarts of Old Crow, and two quarts of milk as I had an ulcer. I was carrying all five into our cabin when I tripped, and two of the Old Crows were broken, but I saved all the milk, much to McClure's disgust. His guide, a local swamp angel came in, and we invited him to have a drink. He poured out a large tumbler of whiskey and swallowed it in one breath. A little later the guide said, "Mind if I have another?" Eddie grabbed the bottle and replied, "I'll pour." Eddie's idea of fishing was to gun his seventy-five horse power outboard motor along at fifty miles an hour with the bow sticking up at a forty-five degree angle. One ride with him sufficed.

As for me and my theory that all men were equal before the bench, my political goose was cooked by this Bradford episode and a few similar ones. Under the system then prevailing, the Governor of Indiana appointed our Marion County Municipal Judges, usually upon the advice of the county political hierarchy. My term expired on December 31, 1946, and the Honorable Ralph Gates of Columbia City, a Republican, was elected in 1944 to succeed Governor Schricker.

Not having been born yesterday, early in March of 1946, I went over to see Mr. Daniels, with whom I had worked closely in the Citizens School Committee for years, and asked him if I would be re-appointed. Always a diplomat, Joe didn't mention his futile defense before me of his County boss, Mr. Bradford, or the fact that I refused to dismiss ("fix") traffic tickets for the Republican Party machine, its precinct committeemen, and their friends. Instead he merely said, "Johnny, there are a lot of fellows who would like to have your job and I wouldn't be surprised if someone got it."

There was one other episode Mr. Daniels didn't like. Norman Perry, President of the Indianapolis Power and Light Company and Republican district treasurer, had seven martinis one social evening at the Columbia Club, according to his admission on the witness stand, and ran into the back of a police car parked on West Michigan Street, giving a policeman a severe whip lash and wrecking the automobile. Someone in the office of Mayor Robert Tyndall had Norman released without bond and told him he needn't show up in court at 9:00 A.M., as Norman wasn't feeling so good. When his case was called he was in a Turkish bath getting boiled out. As my court had been pretty sharp with defendants who didn't show up for trial there were half a dozen newspaper reporters present, pencils poised, when court opened, waiting to see if Perry would get preferential treatment. On the bench, I had one comforting theory that guided me through the quicksands and pitfalls of running a police court in Indianapolis—if there was a hot seat which would have to be occupied by someone in the morning paper, as between me and the one who brought it about, the latter could take the heat. Therefore, I ordered a re-arrest warrant for defendant Perry, and in half an hour he showed up, and was granted a continuance, the same as anyone else.

In due time Norman went to trial defended by another fishing companion friend of mine, attorney Harry Gause, selected solely for that fact. The drunkometer test showed the defendant had a blood content of .14 percent alcohol. At that time .15 percent was considered enough to make a man drunk, though it has since been lowered to .10 percent. Plus all the other evidence and the defendant's admission of seven martinis, I found him guilty and rendered a verdict of a fine and driver's license suspension.

"It seems like a person might as well not be a friend of Judge Niblack," Gause told someone. The case had a happy ending, however, for the Party treasurer. An appeal was taken to Criminal court, and being closely hounded by the press, Judge Bain disqualified himself and appointed as Special Judge a former Democratic Prosecuting Attorney, George Dailey. Mr. Perry was acquitted on the ground that the drunkometer test lacked one-hundreth of showing complete drunkenness. The Special Judge later resigned from the bar and left town after some difficulty with Uncle Sam about monies collected in the "red-light" district during his term of office —a Federal case settled and compromised to the satisfaction of all parties.

Such performances were not unusual in the old days, as the professional bondsmen, some Judges, Prosecutors and Deputies, and a lot of Criminal Court attaches were ward chairmen or precinct committeemen of one political party or another, and were willing to cooperate, or were subject to pressure to hold their jobs. In fact, one Criminal Court Judge and his help didn't bother to keep books on who was tried or who was sentenced for how long or what for.

Of course, many Judges, Prosecutors and others were good honest men and never took a dollar from anyone to influence justice, even though some of these would let political consideration temper a sentence with mercy.

Well, to get back to my interview with our Marion County District Republican boss and my request, I said, "Well, Joe, if I am not going to be reappointed by Governor Gates, how about endorsing me for one of those $10,000.00 a year jobs at the Court House, say, for Superior or Probate Court?"

"That's a pretty serious matter. I'll have to let you know, John," he said. "I'll study about it."

Endorsement in the May Primary by the Party machine generally was tantamount to nomination in ninety-five percent or more of cases. As expiration time to file approached, I kept calling Mr. Daniels, but he was always out, or "would return my call" which he never did. Not having seen in Father Adam's will that Joe Daniels had been devised the fee simple title to the Marion County Courts, on the last day I went over to the State House and filed for Judge of Superior Court, Room One, whose incumbent Judge, the Honorable Judson L. Stark, had decided to run for Prosecuting Attorney. He and I had been fellow deputies under William H. Remy, the nemesis of D. C. Stephenson and the Ku Klux Klan and its victim the Marion County Republican political machine, which it infiltrated and dominated under George V. Coffin and his successors clear down to Jimmy Bradford.

Therefore, Stark and I were not on the favored list. We were both veterans of World War I and we got up a Republican ticket largely of veterans of that war plus some other prominent Republicans who were anti-organization.

We were backed by a large part of Mayor Tyndall's city crowd, as Mr. Remy was chairman of his Board of Safety. The organization chose largely a group of returning World War II veterans. The Indianapolis Star and News, at that time owned by different parties, backed our insurgent ticket, and we were all nominated and subsequently elected that fall.

I was opposed by four other candidates, including the organization-backed young Lawrence Hinds, a personable and able attorney who had weathered the war in the combat zone in the Pacific as a lieutenant in the Navy in its major battles, especially at Okinawa. The County machine's publicity agent, much to Hinds, discomfiture, played up his part at Okinawa, and introduced him as "the hero of Okinawa" at the politicol meetings.

The County Republican machine by this time was headed by Mr. Henry Ostrom, a good old soul and a prominent building contractor and politician, and it controlled most of the campaign meetings in the wards and precincts during the primary. Stark and I and other anti-candidates were not too welcome, and in fact, we were not notified about times and places of such. However, we attended anyway.

The usual proceedings at the meetings went about as follows: There would be anywhere from ten to fifty voters present, largely being precinct committeemen and women, vice-chairmen, poll takers, election board members and other hench gentlemen and hench ladies of the boss. Then there were the organization candidates and our own anti slate. As there were nine courts and many county offices with two or more candidates for each position, and seventy candidates for the Legislature, we would have quite a long evening. The candidates would string in and out and, needless to say, our boys were introduced last. I would hear young Hinds praised and recommended highly, then along toward ten or eleven o'clock the chairman would say "and here is Judge Niblack who will speak a few words. Judge, you have one minute."

After a few such episodes, I evolved a short speech which started out with a joke or two about some Southern Indiana character; gave a little of my background and my war record, and closed by saying:

"Ladies and gentlemen, you have heard my worthy young opponent praised as a commissioned officer of the Navy. I also was in the U.S. Navy in World War I, in the Naval Aviation, but I never saw the ocean or got in the air—just fought the battle of "pork and beans" at Great Lakes a while, where I got up to second class gunner's mate, couldn't even make first class. Now all of you people who were officers in the Wars, any of them, vote for Mr. Hinds, and all you ex-buck privates vote for poor old Niblack." I was nominated. The Republican ticket went over that fall 88,717 to 65,247.

In addition to the above mentioned support, I received active backing in the spring primary from a large police court alumni association composed of bondsmen and other characters, both Republican and Democratic, who haunted Municipal Court halls. One Irishman whom I had favored with many repeat trips to the penal farm for public drunkenness—albeit a fine gentleman when sober

283

—stopped me on Washington Street after my primary victory.

"I congratulate ye, yer Honor," he said beaming, "I voted for yez eleven times in the fifthteenth ward!"

"For God's sake, Jimmy! Not so loud! Why did you do that?" I inquired. "I thought you were a Democrat."

"Well, Judge," he said "me and the boys thought you would make a lot better divorce judge than trying us people down here."

I found out early in my political campaigns, and I ran in eighteen of them come spring and fall from 1928 to 1968, not counting campaigns for delegate to the Republic State convention, that I was no spellbinder at the hustings, but could make a pretty good informal talk to the crowds. Many candidates were good conscientious men who would make serious speeches and pound the lectern in earnest fervor outlining their platforms and experiences. After a dozen or score of these the crowd began to yawn. I would start off with a couple of corny jokes, maybe quoting Abraham Lincoln or Grandpa McClure.

I remember one hostile presiding officer introduced me by asking why I was running for Superior Court, Room One, and I told the crowd that the salary was much better, and the work a lot lighter than in police court. Another time I told a crowd down in Acton that I had the duty of trying the last Indian captured alive in Marion County—a twenty-three year old gal from North New Jersey Street named Claudia who was one-quarter Cherokee, one-quarter Negro and one-half white, whose career I have described in another chapter.

I early learned why precinct committeemen (precinct captains) are important and why politicians treat them with respect. Mr. Isadore Wulfson, a good Republican and a father in Israel, was one of the seven justices of peace in Center Township, Indianapolis in 1926. He also was a precinct committeeman. The 1925 Legislature abolished all but one of the J.P. Courts in Center, and all seven incumbents ran for re-nomination as Justice of Peace. Unfortunately, Isadore lost, but he kept on serving anyhow, marrying couples and what not.

"I was elected to serve until my successor was elected and qualified, and I have no succesor," he declared firmly.

Complaints began to come into the Prosecutor's office about the case, and Prosecutor Remy assigned me as deputy to clear it up. I

284

pleaded with Isadore to quit, to no avail, and he finally was arrested on a charge of Usurpation of Office, whereupon he resigned and the charge was dropped.

In the spring of 1928, I ran for the State Senate in the primary and one cold March day I got into a large meeting down on Union Street and Lo and Behold! Brother Wulfson was presiding. My seat was near a hot stove, and I sweat through two hours waiting. Finally Isadore announced:

"I have saved the best for the last. Mr. Nigh Black, please come up!"

While I stood beside the Chairman, uncomfortable and red faced, he introduced me:

"Mine friends, relatives and neighbors, here is a fine young feller which wants to be state senator. Let me tell you about him! This young feller filed a criminal charge against poor old Isadore and took away mine living as Justice of Peace. And not only that, he sent a big Irish cop down to mine home at one o'clock in the morning ven I vas asleep in my family, and arrested poor old Isadore and took him down to jail.

"Now look at him! He vants you and me to vote for him- Proceed, mine friend!"

Amid dirty looks my speech was very brief. I was nominated, and elected in the fall, but not by the voters of Mr. Wulfson's precinct. It was true I did file the charge, but the midnight arrest was the Irish cop's own idea. He was a brother of the Democratic precinct committeeman there.

Precinct politics was where the real in-fighting went on. One time a fellow member of the Synagogue, one Elias Dulberger, ran against Mr. Wulfson for precinct committeeman, and of course they both lived in the same precinct. Elias received no votes. In a rage he declared:

"Well, my wife might have double crossed me, and maybe so did my brother and sister-in-law, but I sure as Hell voted for myself."

The precinct committeeman in those days appointed the election board, and sometimes the inspector had a nasty habit after the polls were closed of using the official blue pencil to mutilate ballots he didn't like.

285

Another time, being 1956, the organization took a dislike to Circuit court Judge Lloyd D. Claycombe, the incumbent, and he and I and Judge Norman E. Brennan of Superior Court Room Three competed for the nomination, and we learned each others speeches by heart as we made the tour. Judge Claycombe, my senior in age, would lead off by detailing his experience of twelve years as Circuit Judge, his maturity and legal wisdom, all of which was true; and young Brennan, my junior, and a lusty young fellow, would outline his youth and virility—he had four and a half children at the time —then I was called.

"My two worthy opponents seem to have a corner on the age and experience and wisdom and youth and virility," I said. "About the only thing I can think of right now that would qualify me to be Circuit Court Judge is that I won a hog calling contest in Michigan one time."

I was nominated by a vote of 25,000 to Judge Claycombe's 15,000, and Judge Brennan's 9,000, and was elected that fall by a vote of 154,710 to 106,945.

This was in 1956, when I still had two years left on my third term in Superior Court, Room One. In 1958, when I would have been up again, there was a Democratic landslide and for four years I served with five Democratic Superior Court Judges, Circuit Court being a six-year term, and Superior Court a four-year term. Boy! Was I lucky!

I was re-elected Circuit Court Judge without much opposition in the primaries in 1962 and 1968, again missing another Democratic landslide in 1964. It was the first time in the history of the Nineteenth Judicial Circuit that one Judge was elected for three full six-year consecutive terms.

Trip to Hawaii

In July of 1960 as an official of the United States Golf Association, I took the Indiana team to the finals of the 35th Amateur Public Links Championship of the U.S.G.A., which was held at Ala Wai Public Golf Course, Honolulu, Hawaii, a stone's throw from the Waikiki Beach. We had a team of five, headed by Don Essig III, a former member of the Shortridge High School and Louisiana State University golf teams. Other players were Charles Farrington of Kokomo; Ronnie Atwell, Robert Ludlow, and Warren Strout of Indianapolis. Don had won the national title in 1957 at the Hershey, Pennsylvania finals. We didn't win any trophies at Honolulu.

We left Indianapolis at 7:00 A.M. from Weir Cook Airport, after the sun was up and arrived in Honolulu at 7:00 P.M., just as it was sinking, sixteen hours later. Nine hours of this was flying, and seven hours layover. The jet age is speedy! We flew over Fort Laramie, Great Salt Lake and Salt Lake City, Las Vegas, and the Donner Pass. We crossed the Oregon Trail, taking four hours from Chicago to the coast, a journey which used to take six months by ox train, or longer. Scooting along at 600 to 650 miles an hour hustles the sun to keep ahead, as it only travels 1000 miles an hour around the earth (the earth does the spinning).

Well, we all landed, got a lei of flowers and were kissed by a dusky maiden (who seemed pretty bored about it, but still earning a living). I have had more voluptuous smacks. Then we rode a bus to the Waikiki-Biltmore Beach Hotel, where it all happened again.

When we got into Hawaii, it was 86° above, hot and sultry, and everybody sweating and sticky, just like a good hot July night in southern Indiana. I asked the locals, "What's Wrong in Paradise?" (That is what the Honolulu Chamber of Commerce calls it). They assured me it was just "unusual weather"—a "kona" wind or south wind, and they had lost the Trade winds. Every time I go anywhere in the United States it is "unusual weather." In the spring of 1959 I went to Florida, and it rained ten days and nights, the worst flood in forty-five years, they said.

Anyhow, the next day, the Trade wind was back and it was truly delicious in the shade in the islands. The sun and wind will burn you in a hurry though, and many of the golfers and swimmers suffered some.

When we got in, we went to a Chinese dinner. Then on Friday night we went to a formal Chinese dinner—nine courses, including boiled octopus, raw fish, chicken chopped into chunks with a cleaver, rice, shrimp boiled in sorghum molasses, bean sprouts, and other things. The chicken was about half done. There was no bread or butter, no jelly or preserves, sugar or cream, or salt or pepper on the table. No self-respecting Hoosier, let alone a country boy like me, can get started on a meal without them. No catsup, either, or fried potatoes.

Then on Saturday we were all guests at a luau, a Hawaiian feast, where they roast a pig in the earth with vegetables, and serve poi, roast bananas, and other dishes. Much festivity and elbow bending is participated in by non-teetotalers while the pig is being done, sort of a backyard cookout in a big way. In the old days the luaus were had at weddings, funerals, or special days, and lasted two or three days until the host was bankrupt and everything cleaned out.

We were the guests of Francis Hyde II Brown, one of the Islands biggest landowners, descendant of chiefs and missionaries and the island's leading amateur golfer in the 1920's and 1930's. He is a graduate of Yale University. His great-grandfather was Prince II, Prime Minister under Kamehameha II and did well when the great land division was made in the early 19th century. "II" is pronounced "ee-ee."

Most of the good land is owned by descendants of the missionaries and whalers. The saying is: "When the missionaries came, they had the Bible and the natives had the land, but it wasn't long until things were reversed." It really wasn't the missionaries, but the second generation. The lady missionaries introduced the Mu Mu, or Muu Muu, a colorful Mother Hubbard, because to their horror, the female natives wore very little clothing. The Mu Mu became the fashion.

Hawaii is our newest state. It is not very large, eight islands and a population of less than Marion County, Indiana, and the people are a polyglot of races. When these islands were discovered by Captain Cook, an English sailor, about 1775, they were inhabited by a dusky race of Polynesians, and each island had its own ruler or king. There was a strong priesthood and nobility.

The nobility and royal family of Hawaii evidently were fed better or were selected as marriage partners for physique, as they were huge people, tall and heavy, much larger than the mine-run of natives. Any extra tall Hawaiian of native extraction today will claim noble descent. Many things were "Kapu," or forbidden, to women, including many foods and eating with men.

Captain Cook was killed in a scuffle with natives led by the nephew of the king of Hawaii, the big island, a youth seven feet tall, who weighted 400 pounds in maturity. He became King Kamehameha I, conquering all the islands. Cook's body was never found and the English accused the natives of eating him. Present day natives know the story, too. Sam Kapu, a full blooded Hawaiian, who is starter at Ala Wai golf course, gave me a beautiful Hawaiian shirt. I said, "I see King Kamehameha I's picture on this. Where is Captain Cook?

Sam said, "He there. You can't see him. He in the king."

One of the boys on the Honolulu golf team in 1960 was Fred Farr, whose father is half Hawaiian and half Welsh. His mother was Portuguese. At the Japanese Sayonara (farewell) dinner given us on Saturday night he introduced me to his wife, a beautiful olive colored girl of about twenty-five. Inquiring about her genealogy, she said her father was a German from Hamburg and her mother half Chinese and half Hawaiian. They have two children who are really a mixture of races, being one-fourth Hawaiian, one-fourth German, one-fourth Portuguese, one-eighth Chinese and one-eighth Welsh, the latter furnishing their name. Farr is a graduate of Tri State College at Angola, Indiana. Being a veteran of Korea, he came over there to study on the G.I. Bill. Some Hoosier in his company in the war had attended Tri State. He was employed in the City Engineer's Office.

Joe Guerrero, the ground's keeper at Ala Wai, was Spanish and Hawaiian, and his wife Chinese, English and Hawaiian. Guinea Kop, the Pro, was Chinese and Hawaiian and his wife the same. Their beautiful daughter Linda was a sophomore at the University of Hawaii and had just returned from a tour of western United States. Hung Soo Ahn was a pure blooded Korean on their team, Henry O'Sullivan Irish, English, Hawaiian and Chinese; Akiro Hashimoto pure Japanese, and Loio Palenapa pure Hawaiian.

The Japs form the largest element on the islands. Then came Chinese, Americans, Portuguese, and so forth. There are many Filipinos, but no East Indians. I did run into a quarter Choctaw Indian, but she was the wife of an USGA official from California and was born in Oklahoma.

Incidentally, the Hawaiian tongue pronounces each letter and vowel distinctly. The "a" sounds as in "arm", and the "i" as in "machine". The "h" is definitely pronounced, unlike in Cockney English and Spanish where it is silent. The native can't say "r"—a good deal like the Jap—but substitutes "l": "Melly Klistmas."

On my last Sunday in Hawaii I went to the Kawaiahao Congregational Church on Punch Bowl Street downtown by the State House, which formerly was the royal palace of the kings of Hawaii.

This was the first church established in the islands and was founded on April 24, 1820, by missionaries from Connecticut. The church was founded in response to a plea by a native youth, Opukahaia (Henry Obookiah), the first Hawaiian Christian, who fled to the beach to escape when Kamehameha I invaded Oahu, and the rest of his family was slain. He asked a Yankee skipper to take him on board and wound up in New England. Henry died there at the age of 26, in 1818, about the time he finished his education, and by his life and death inspired the coming of the first missionaries to Hawaii. There is a plaque on the church wall for him.

Church services are in Hawaiian and English. The Reverend Dr. Abraham K. Akaka, D.D., L.H.D., a full blooded Hawaiian, was pastor. He had just returned from lecturing at Auburn College in New York State.

The church holds 2,000, and there were about 1,000 of us present, seventy percent being tourists. It was built of coral rock in 1840 and is severe white within and out. Following the Puritan New England style, there are no stained glass windows, statues, pictures of Jesus nor saints, just a plain white cross ten feet tall, part of the rear wall, and seven candlesticks back of the pulpit. The only color visible was the green of the palm fronds whispering in the trade wind blowing just outside the open windows, and the blue sky beyond. There were small signs on the posts "E Hamau," and "Be Quiet." There were plaques on the walls in memory of the preachers, and pictures of royalty in the vestibule, including old King Kamehameha I, a pencil drawing. The later monarchs belonged to this congregation, but not Kamehameha I. He lived and died in the old religion of his ancestors, worshipping the old gods to the end. On his death in 1819 they fled the island and have been seen or heard no more in those parts. He was buried in a secret cave on the big island with pagan rites, and his burial place is unknown to this day, like another famous man, Moses.

Royalty built rich pews in the back of this church, but they have been roped off since the death of Queen Liliuokalani, last of the dusky monarchs of the Isles. She wrote the famous song "Aloha" and also the prayer response sung by the choir that Sunday: "Ka Mele Pule O Ka Papa Himeni." There were thirty in the choir with white robes trimmed in green. Deaconess Nora Kama preached in Hawaiian for fifteen minutes, and Dr. Akaka in English for thirty minutes more. Some songs were in English and some in native. Dr. Akaka was forty years old, stocky, dusky, with the straight, raven blue-black hair of the native. Mrs. Akaka was also a full blood of the old race, and they had a large family. The congregation is almost entirely native or part Caucasian. I saw no Japs or Chinese.

Full blood Hawaiians of the original native race are now comparatively rare, and they are mighty proud people. Loio Palenapa, above mentioned, the golf pro at Hilo, whom I have known many years was one and he was no exception. He had ten children, he told me.

"That's fine, Loio! Ten more pure bloods," I congratulated.

"Oh, no, Judge!" he said, "they half Chinee. Judge, when you young, you not think of ancestors, you just see pretty girl and want to marry!"

One part of the church service I understood well was the collection. That announcement was made in English. The ushers had velvet bags on long poles they poked down the rows. I guess this is a hold over from the old days when they didn't trust the congregation to handle the plate themsleves. Maybe they didn't trust us haoles (whites).

After service I ate a thirty-five cent church lunch in the basement that would have cost me $1.50 at Waikiki, being Hawaiian stew, plus watermelon and coffee. Some twenty-five natives—all older people, held a song and prayer service in the corner near me, singing the old familiar hymns in fine melodious voices and harmony, some in English and some in Hawaiian. Well, having sung in the vested choir of the Bloomington Methodist Church when I was in I.U., I moved over and listened, and soon the leader pressed me into singing, too, so we had a real good time. Reminded me much of the prayer meetings I attended long ago in the little Methodist church down home. They also sang some native songs I did not recognize—melodious, but in a sad minor key—sort of a lament of a vanishing race, I guess.

I took pictures of the church, got on the bus and rode back to Waikiki and watched a new load of tourists come in.

"Kawaiahao" and "Waikiki" both contain the Hawaiian word for water, "Wai". The former means "Queen's Fountain," and the latter "Dancing Water."

One thing about going a fourth of the way around the world in one day is the effect on the time clock a person's body contains. It took me three or four days to get used to new hours. As Honolulu is five hours slower than Indianapolis, along around 6:00 P.M. each evening I would get so sleepy I could hardly stay awake.

Honolulu is a city of churches. Here is a partial list from a phone book, quoting from memory: 20 Catholic parishes; 20 Buddhist temples; 3 Shinto temples; 18 Congregational churches; 14 Baptist; 13 Methodist; 4 Seventh Day Adventist; 10 Community; 7 Christian; 10 Nazarene; 4 Apostolic; 16 Episcopal; 16 Latter Day Saints (Mormons); 7 Lutheran; 1 Great I Am Temple; one synagogue; 1 Christian Science; and 1 Presbyterian, the latter one year old. The Presbyterians kept out of there since 1820 under a treaty with the Congregationalists, I was told, till now. I have left out many other sects and churches, but Heaven and the telephone company of Oahu know what and where they are.

We went up on Punch Bowl mountain where the National Military Cemetery overlooks the vast Pacific ocean. There many thousands of American boys are sleeping the long sleep, far from home, with the wind and the surf their requiems, all victims of the Japs at Pearl Harbor, Tarawa, and other places. The long rows of flat head stones show New Jersey, Indiana, Texas, California, and all the other States. Ernie Pyle, whom I knew in my college days at I.U., is buried there, too. He and I, and Spaz Tolle of the News, Congressman Charlie Halleck, and Professor John Stemple of I.U., put out the Daily Student with some others.

Ernie was a sort of lone-wolf fellow, good natured and amiable, but a born wanderer. The University refused him permission to go with the baseball team to Japan, so he went anyway, and was refused his diploma. I. U. was mighty proud to grant him one twenty years later. Well, it's been many a year now since I saw him, and as the poet Fitz-Greene Halleck said:

"Green be the turf above thee,
Friend of my better days!
None knew thee but to love thee,
Nor named thee but to praise."

Ernie was a famed World War II correspondent.

We took the Pearl Harbor Cruise on a Navy launch, and saw the American flag flying top mast over the sunken battleship Arizona. Down in her twisted hull are 1102 American officers and sailors. All warships of battleship class have been retired except the Arizona. She is still carried as on active duty at sea and will never be retired, they said, but will remain in service forever, manned by her ghostly crew, ranging in rank from a rear-admiral to apprentice seaman. That's the reason the flag does not fly half-mast over her.

The narrative of December 7, 1941, aroused some bitter memories in me, and I wondered again why some of our subs or scout ships were not outside on sentry duty that day. Even a flock of crows at home have a couple of scouts posted on a high tree. The Jap carriers had been at sea two weeks before that, whereabouts unknown.

Pearl Harbor was empty of war craft, all gone somewhere.

Hawaii sure has lots of military bases, and if they were abolished half of the people there would have to go back to eating fish and sugar cane.

293

The Indianapolis golf team and I (and all other contestants and officials) stayed at the Biltmore Hotel on Waikiki Beach. The beach is fenced in and at its entrance is a huge banyan tree, said to be one of the largest in the world. It is a far cry from a desert island —more like Miami Beach now. Each room is an outside one, and has a balcony and table for two, with a refrigerator and electric coffee urn. I could sit on mine with Diamond Head at my left and look out over approximately 300 tourists doing belly flops on surf boards and strangling on salt water every day. Some of them paid to ride in outrigger canoes and had to row two big fat Hawaiians around. The surf was so crowded there was hardly a day someone wasn't injured. One boy had his teeth knocked out by a surf board, and another's head was gashed. However, nothing dismays the American tourist.

They came to the island in droves, on tours, singly, and to conventions. The national Shrine Convention had just been there, and Waikiki Beach was still talking about it.

I went down on steamer day and watched the Matsonia (27,000 tons) come in. A lot of sail boats, outriggers, etc., met her off our hotel and took her in. All the tourists lined the rails, decorated with leis, colored shirts and whatnot as they pulled in. The Royal Hawaiian band played "Aloha" and the magnificent "Song of the Islands" as she docked, and a brown lady in a yellow MuMu did the Hula, and everybody cheered and took pictures like mad, including me. All the islanders rubbed their palms in joy at so much new money coming in.

At the Luau we were served Poi, a grayish white gruel made of a native root, and I jokingly asked our team if they knew how it was made. Nobody did, so I gave them the old island recipe for native beer—kasava. The young women chew up the root and spit it in a bucket, and pour on water and let ferment. Ronnie Atwell and Chuck Farrington and the rest refused to eat any Poi after that. As a matter of fact, it tasted pretty flat to me, too.

We officials were invited to the Chinese home of Mr. Tin S. Goo, and his wife, Violet, to dinner up on the mountain overlooking the harbor. It was a beautiful scene at sunset, and after when the lights came on. Goo was president of the local public links association. Among those present were John G. Clock, president of the

294

United States Golf Association, who was from California; Charles Clare of Connecticutt; Fred Brand of Pittsburgh, and P. J. Boatwright, assistant Secretary of the U.S.G.A., which body stages the U.S. Open, the Amateur, the Junior, and the Womens' National Golf Tournaments, as well as our Public Links tournaments.

The Goos had two huge mango trees in their yard filled with delicious fruit, and they kept us supplied during our stay. Mangoes taste like peaches with a hint of pineapple and yellow paw-paw. They are so juicy and squirty the best way to eat them is to undress and sit in the bathtub.

The islands are volcanic and supposed to be comparatively new, as such things go. They are still building from active volcanoes. I flew over to Hawaii, the big island, with Mr. and Mrs. Brand, and we got a car to tour the place. It is very sparsely settled, and has the world's highest mountains, Mauna Loa and Mauna Kea, twin peaks, the latter 13,796 feet above sea level. These mountains are in 30,000 feet of water, so Mauna Kea is 44,000 feet high. Mrs. Brand gathered a big bouquet of beautiful wild orchids. There are many cattle ranches and cowboys there, too.

We went to another active crater, Kilauea, which is only 4,000 feet up. It is a hole about two or three miles across, about 1,000 feet deep and smoking from all over its floor. It erupted in December and January before we arrived and the lava flowed thirty-five miles to the ocean, making the island longer at Kapoho point. We drove there and saw where a native village had been wrecked. We ate lunch at the Volcano House which perches on the rim of the crater. It was owned by a Mr. Lycurgus, who was 102 years old, a spry old gent, who sat in the lobby listening to his Hawaiian string band and singers. It sure was filled with tourists.

Right here I might say there is no tipping in Hawaii, Japan, or Okinawa. They add on ten percent.

Nothing apparently was native to these islands except some small birds and plants and palm trees. When Captain Cook came, there were natives who had pigs. There were no flies, mosquitoes, roaches, snakes or contagious diseases. Everybody, married or single, believed in free love and practiced same. Nobody worked much and the weather was just right, and nobody wore much clothing.

The white man soon fixed that. He brought measles, small pox, venereal diseases, typhoid, cholera, mosquitoes, flies, Christianity, long clothing, English sparrows, Mynah birds (first cousin to starlings), sugar cane, pineapple, autos, cockroaches, and many other drawbacks, comforts, and adjuncts of civilization. He also appropriated the land, put the natives to work, and abolished free love (except on the sly, as on the mainland). So far no ass has brought in starlings or snakes, but give them time. Mongooses (or mongeese) have also been brought over and are a nuisance.

I might add that the Hawaiians of today never tire of talking about their "melting pot" and giving their bloodlines. They don't realize that we have had a melting pot on the mainland for 300 years. I myself am English, German, French, Danish and Scotch as far as I know, and maybe some other.

Emmanuel Lopez and his buddy, representing Arizona in the golf tournament, had the hotel room just above mine. In common with quite a few young bloods in the tournament, Emmanuel adopted a native brown gal who was one-half Hawaiian, one-fourth Portugese and one-fourth American Negro (a rare combination even in Honolulu) who wore a red MuMu and lived in their apartment and was his gallery on the golf course. One night he and his roomy and lady friend threw a big party for about thirty boys and gals, whooping it up and throwing beer cans down on King Kalakaua Avenue until 1:00 A.M. Someone called the Oahu police and five cops of various races responded, only to join the party and make merry until 4:00 A.M.

"I didn't qualify for the finals, Judge," Emmanuel confided later, "but I sure in Hell had a fine time!" The American tourist in Hawaii, male and female, comes from every state in the Union, and contrary to ship cruises in the Caribbean, which are a kind of floating rest home, there are as many, if not more, young people touring here than older. Organized tours of office secretaries and working girls from New York City, Philadelphia, and other eastern places are common. A lot of them are "on the loose" and favor the brown-skinned beach boys.

There was one tour of school teachers from New Mexico and another from California. I ran into many tourists from Florida. Then there are the elderly tourists, attired in walking shorts with their pot bellies and knobby knees, wishing they were home.

The first thing the tourist does on arival is to get into costume and get out on King Kalakaua Avenue or Waikiki Beach. By costume I mean anything in the way of short shorts, colored nightgowns, pajamas, bathing suits, bikinis, shirts, or what have you. The early missionaries clothed the native ladies in Mother Hubbards, and it is the rage now for native and tourist. They call them Muu Muu's (Mu Mu for short) and they are really striking in violent and vivid colors. They start at the lady's chin and sweep to the sidewalk. Like the political platform, a MuMu covers everything and touches nothing. The male tourists grow beatnik beards and smoke pipes. Everyone, except me, bought sandals. The island is full of rubber-neck buses, autos, airplanes, and launches, and camera shops are booming.

Local folk are mighty proud of being the 50th State. When they raised the United States Golf Association tournament flag over Ala Wai Golf Course with the American flag over it, someone noticed the latter had only 48 stars, much to the horror of all loyal Hawaiians of 47 races and mixtures. I'll tell you the park superintendent nearly lost his job.

Back home a favorite fishing lure is a Hawaiian Wiggler. I will have to say I saw more Hawaiian wigglers than any sporting goods stores in Indiana ever had. Also, belly dancers, hula chorus lines, and aloha girls. They are all mighty supple and lithe from all appearances. No night club nor private entertainment is complete without a few Hawaiian or Tahitian toe dancers. They also have Chinese drum dancers, Korean flower dancers, and Filipino cocoanut dancers, all mighty pretty and very nimble.

Mr. George Teshima (pure Japanese), chief of the entertainment committee, took us to a dance under the stars at the Royal Hawaiian Hotel, a beautiful pink castle on the ocean. The floor show was really good. The singer was a tall Hawaiian gal of about six feet one inch, with a powerful contralto voice. I would like to back her as my entry in a Hoosier hog calling contest. Those piggies could hear her five miles on a quiet day. Her name was Princess Alekana, and she claimed royal descent.

Lt. Col. Robert E. Brown, of the Army Judge Advocate's Office, and his lovely wife, Helen, took me out to play golf, to dinner, and put me on the airliner for Japan. Robert was Deputy Prosecutor under Judson L. Stark, and was Marion County Young Republican Chairman in 1940.

So Aloha to Hawaii! Next about a thirteen hour trip to Japan.

Trip to Okinawa

After a couple of weeks in Hawaii in July, 1960, attending a U.S.G.A. golf tournament as an official I decided to go on to Okinawa where my younger daughter Susan and her husband, First Lieutenant Linn Goldsmith of the Air Force, were living. He was stationed at the Naha Air Force Base, and they had a nice house in a government compound.

Col. Brown got me to the Honolulu airport at 10:00 P.M. on a Monday. It was filled with tourists heading home, clutching their duffle bags, and dressed in MuMus, shorts, and so forth. I tried to imagine the lady ex-tourists trudging down main street at home dressed in a bright green, loud purple, or blazing red Mother Hubbard gowns.

I got on the Japan airliner at 11:30 P.M. The schedule said we were due in Tokyo the next morning at 8:30 A.M. The first thing we did was set our watches back to 6:30 P.M., as there is five hours difference to Tokyo from Hawaii. It was a propeller plane, turbo-jet type with 13,600 horsepower, the "City of Los Angeles." The plane weighed 71½ tons, and we had fifty-six passengers. We took off with a roar and flew 3884 miles non-stop over the Pacific—thirteen hours flying time.

Californian Jack Brissey was Captain, and the co-pilot was another American, Charles Smith. The third pilot was Captain Mita, a Jap. Because of so long a flight, there were twelve in the crew: 3 pilots, 2 navigators, 2 flight engineers, two pursers and three stewardesses. All except Brissey and Smith were Japs. Our stewardess was a Jap girl of 24 named Miss Kauru Kuriyama. Her title was "Cherry Blossom," while the rich folks who rode first-class in the middle of the plane had the "Kiku," or "Chrysanthemum" service. (No difference, only $150.00 more)

There were six of us in the little forward tourist cabin just back of the pilot room: two Chinamen, a Spaniard, a German, an American (me) and a half Chinese-half Spaniard. It was powerful hot before we took off, so Cherry Blossom brought us each a big towel dripping with scalding water, and stood over us while we used them to cool our brows.

Having been a widower since 1951, I was traveling alone, and my seat-mate was a Chinese laundryman from Los Angeles named Chang, who said he was also a widower, and was going back to Hong Kong to get a new wife. He was very cheerful about it, and volunteered that he was sixty years old, had property, and his cousin in Hong Kong would help him select a bride. He had no prospects as yet. All of us in the compartment were sympathetic with his aims, and everyone, including Miss Cherry Blossom, gave him lots of advice, of which he made due mental note. He stated he had no children by the first marriage, and thought he should have two sons now, so the New Mrs. Chang must not be over 35 years old.

"Real young girl too much trouble to old man, and old woman no good," he confided.

I asked Mr. Chang how he would go about finding a new bride since he had no prospects.

"My cousin, he help find. Plenty girl like marry me and come to Amelika," he said.

"You pay money for new bride?" I asked, having some knowledge about such things.

"Yeh! Heh! I pay money. I pay one Hunda Dolla, maybe," he said.

"You pay two hunda dolla for new bride," I asked in my best pidgin English.

"Ya-ah! I pay two hunda dolla," he replied hesitantly.

"You pay three hunda dolla?" I inquired further.

"Hell, No! No woman worth Three Hunda Dolla," Uncle Chang snorted.

His new bride was going to work in his Chinese laundry, as well as bear male heirs, so Mr. Chang told me. The two sons were to pray at his tomb, he said.

"What if you only have daughters?" I asked.

"Oh! My God! No! No!" he exclaimed, at such a startling thought.

Mr. Chang had five huge flower leis, given him at a farewell party of relatives at Honolulu, and three large mangoes. Cherry

300

Blossom gave him some cellophane bags to put his leis in. We told him they would not let him take fruit in, so he was pretty cunning— he hid them in the flowers. The last I saw of him in customs the Jap officials were confiscating his fruit and flowers, too, while he waived his arms and shouted in Chinese.

The other Chinese was a lady native of Hong Kong, a welfare worker in the United States, traveling with her husband, a native of Cadiz, Spain, and their two year old son. The husband was a professor at Chicago University, and that is where they first met. The sixth passenger was John Berg, a blond German youth of 22, who had been selling sewing machines in Canada for two years, and who was going on home to Hamburg traveling West and touring, living at Y.M.C.A.'s. He had a horrible sunburn from two days in the sea at Waikiki. He spoke fair English and wanted to learn more, so he practiced his English with me. The professor was learning German, so he practiced that on Mr. Berg. I kept the Spaniard busy practicing my college and Mexican Spanish, and Mr. Chang bored the welfare worker, who thought he was low class, by rattling off Cantonese at her. Thus we improved every shining minute, slept seven hours apiece, and soared gracefully down to Tokyo at 8:30 A.M., on Wednesday, having lost one whole day, plus five hours.

Typhoon Polly and I arrived at Susan's home on Okinawa at the same time, except Polly had been hanging around a couple hundred miles southwest. We were on alert, called "Condition Two," several days with every day a stiff wind from the East and increasing cloudiness. It started to rain, and the wind got up to fifty-four miles an hour, and the military put us in "Condition One." The wind blew the rain in level sheets and the house creaked and groaned as the edge of the typhoon howled around the eaves like a bunch of lost souls. It was not a very big typhoon, and sort of lazy, and the eye was about one hundred miles west and south. All activities were cancelled, including the morning newspaper, and all the military were glad, as they didn't have to go to work, except emergency crews who were typhooned in.

The Okinawans were glad, too, as their quarter acre to an acre farms were suffering from drought. There are a million people on an island seventy miles long and from three to twelve miles wide.

The giant African snails were glad, too. I went up the street and saw thousands of them, ranging from one inch up to four and five inches long, migrating from one draw to another. The rain brought them out. I took some pictures of these snails, and also of two Okinawans who were crushing their heads on the pavement with hammers. They don't like them because they eat crops. Some misguided Jap introduced these giant snails some years ago for the natives to eat, as there is a perpetual scarcity of food here. However, the natives won't eat them (I wouldn't either), and they are a plague. When you run over them on the pavement with an auto, it sounds like shotgun explosions. This individual must have been a cousin of the fellow who brought English sparrows and starlings to America to help us out.

The Okinawans are cousins to the Japs, who took over the islands eighty-five years ago by conquest and made them learn Japanese, although the old folks prefer their native dialect. The military has brought comparative wealth here. Everyone has an efficient maid who is paid $15.00 a month with board and room, or a little more by the day.

I wasn't able to do a thing for a while because of the weather except visit my folks, read, and sleep. I might add that in Honolulu I met the Attorney General of our new state, Honorable Shiro Kashiwa, a Republican, and former classmate of Attorney Erle Kightlinger at Michigan University. I also met K. J. Luke, president of Hawaii National Bank, a graduate of Harvard, who recently had visited classmates at Indianapolis.

Nearly a week was taken up fooling around with the typhoon, and everybody stayed in the house. It finally went away, up the China Sea, but not before leaving several inches of welcome rain. The natives eat a lot of sweet potatoes and rice. They were praying for a typhoon which is the only time rain comes in summer. They seem to be about ¾ Mongolian and ¼ Filipino.

Many rocky hills and small mountains have large tombs partly dug in and partly built outside, "U" shaped with flaring abuttments. Some are centuries old. Here are deposited in the ground outside the honorable corpses of the honorable males of the family, and when time has elapsed, all the females of the family go and dig up and scrape grandpa's bones and put them in an urn. The ladies are not allowed burial inside honorable tomb, as being too good for them.

302

Bernie Fisher, of Fisher Brothers' garage on East Market Street, who was in the First Marine Division which conquered this island, had told me that the Japs holed up in some of these big old tombs, and came out at night to murder people, so they had to blow up the tombs to get the Japs, and Grandpa's bones were casualties, too. Once a year each clan has a family reunion in the cave, gets drunk on hot rice beer, and honors honorable ancestors' bones and dusts them off.

I was informed that the divorce rate was low. Someone said there was a small islet just off the coast, which at high tide has only about a few square feet left at the top, so the village elders row an estranged young couple out to the place as the tide is coming in and leave them there with one blanket, as the nights are somewhat chilly. Many reconciliations are thus affected. Maybe the Water Company should build us one in Geist Reservoir. It would save divorce fees.

I went over to White Sands Beach where the 7th Fleet rides at anchor when it is in. Nobody was there, except one supply ship. The officers' club was deserted, and so were the enlisted men's clubs —there being about a hundred Okinawan bars and cabarets jammed side by side along the road outside the station. About two hundred and fifty taxis have their station there, too, when the fleet arrives.

I went to a reception party for Lt. Col. Anthony Richard (pronounced "Ree-shar" on account of him being Louisiana Cajun French), Linn's new unit commander. Colonel had been teaching in the Air Force School in Montgomery, Alabama, for four years. He was a graduate of West Point, class of '43. There were two young lieutenants from Annapolis in the unit. Officers for the Air Force up to 1960 came from those institutions, but from then on were from the Air Force Academy.

Susan and I drove down by the sea shore on a later day and there in the bay was the biggest warship I ever saw, riding at anchor, attended by eight or nine destroyers and a couple of supply ships. It was the U.S.S. Hornet, an aircraft carrier, and the scene reminded me of an old sow with her litter of pigs. Hornet had her steam up, ready to sting! People said there was another carrier lying off about one hundred miles, and a third about two hundred miles away, and they would alternate coming in port—standard

303

procedure since Pearl Harbor. Would they had done it before!

We met taxi after taxi filled with sailors coming in for shore leave. There were about five thousand men in this unit, a part of the 7th Fleet.

We drove around to the Navy Officers' Club at White Sands Beach, went in, and had a lemonade with gin and left. It was very picturesque on a high bluff overlooking the harbor and the fleet. I took some very nice pictures of the fleet.

I had with me my military pass from the Pentagon to visit Okinawa, which took me five weeks and a letter from cousin Senator Homer Capehart to wangle, and I expected any minute an armed sentry to jump out, stick his bayonet against my teeth, and want to see my pass. No such luck! The only one out of a million natives and forty thousand military who asked for it was a little native clerk in customs at the airport, who stamped the permit. I finally figured out the reason no one asked to see my prized permit was the honest Niblack face that runs in the family. Anyhow, I showed it to a Colonel at a party.

One night I met Lt. Com. (J.G.) Kenneth Robinson, of South Bend, Indiana, class of '58, Notre Dame, who was an engineer on the U.S.S. Evans, a destroyer with the unit here. He was commissioned after going through the R.O.T.C. unit at Notre Dame. Somehow, he mentioned his father was Will Robinson from Vincennes, and his mother was from Terre Haute, and his grandfather was from Bicknell. Shades of old Wheatland, all in good old Knox County, except Terre Haute! A small world!

The occasion of meeting Lt. Com. Robinson was this: The military authorities here thought that as a Judge from home I should see how the local police and courts operated. So one night at 8:00 P.M., a squad patrol car of R.A.S.P. (Ryuku Armed Service Patrol) came by and picked up myself and Linn, and we went with Captain John Hammer, commandant of the 199-man force and his driver, Corporal Lee Briley, a Marine. Capt. Hammer was an air force man, and a native of Enid, Oklahoma, and one-eighth Cherokee Indian. (He said all self-respecting native Oklahomans are at least one-eighth Indian). The Corporal was from Pittsburgh, Pennsylvania, and looked fiercer than any Indian.

We toured the night spots of Okinawa until 1:00 A.M. After

we were out about an hour, they radioed our car to pick up a navy officer on shore patrol, and he was Lt. Robinson. The fleet had assigned fifty officers and men as additional guards. We drove the main streets of all the villages and towns in the central part and went up alleys that made me shudder. If I saw one "Lady of the evening," I will bet I saw three thousand.

There were 2500 licensed bars on this island and 500 unlicensed. Each was owned by a native woman—"a mama-san," who had at least two naisans (girls) as barmaids and waitresses. No men owned bars or served as bartenders. Capt. Hammer said the girls belonged to mama-san, who had bought them from the parents for a couple hundred dollars, or some had come in from the hills to get a job and never could get out of debt to mama-san.

The licensed bars were rated no.1, no.2, or no.3. The no.1 bars were on a main street, well lighted, with running water, and were clean. No. 2 bars had no running water, and No. 3 bars apparently didn't use water. The bar maids were mostly young and cute, and were all dressed up for the fleet. The military police kept diving in these joints, and believe me, I dove in right after them, as I didn't want to be left alone. All these places had a juke box, a bar, and had little bedrooms in the rear, where tired customers could take a nap, or whatever. Capt. Hammer said that without exception these bars were houses of prostitution.

It was a very quiet evening, as only ten percent of the sailors came ashore. Lt. Robinson said they were only nine days out of Kobe, Japan, and would be in Hong Kong in another week, and the men preferred both places to Okinawa. He had in his wallet five shore leave passes of the crew who gave them to him so they couldn't come ashore here. He said they were playing baseball on the Hornet deck, or just catching up on sleep and relaxing.

By unwritten agreement among the men, pretty well kept, the colored troops had reserved Old Koza; the white ones New Koza, and the Okinawan sports Yoshihara as their respective night life spots. The natives murdered a Major who went in the latter town on pleasure bent and dragged another American behind an auto on a rope, but he recovered. The High Commission got a sort of USO going on the military bases in services clubs, whereby decent young Okinawan ladies came in under chaperonage as dancers, and dinner partners, but an article in Time magazine describing the luxurious life of the G.I. here blew that up, and the unmarried men, being about 30,000 out of 40,000 troops, resumed outside social life, visiting the bars. Mamas in the U.S. have not the faintest idea of son's army life in a foreign land.

We had a very quiet night. One G.I. got drunk and fell into a dry 32-foot well. He was reported dead, but only had a scratch on his back. Lt. Robinson said naval officers wear their civvies ashore, except when on duty, as American haters would pick on them, and frisky non-commissioned sailors on shore leave sometimes wanted to pop an officer. The 199 police officers were furnished by each branch of the armed service in proportion to its numbers there, being 48% Marines, 6% Navy, and Army and Air Force about even. Marines can't bring wives over there, as they must be ready to fight right at command.

We drove down one alley in the white "reservation" about 11:00 P.M., and stopped in front of a "bar," where a large mama-san was sitting on the well-lighted porch. She came out on the step, lifted up her sole garment—a dress—to her chin. It was quite a sight.

"You like come and fox me, Cap'n?" she asked demurely.

"You go to Hell! Mary!" growled the Captain and we drove on while Mary cackled in glee.

The Okinawans were a friendly people, short and stocky. The women won't average five feet in height. Both sexes work in the fields from dawn to dark for a living, much to the marvel of the Americans here. When I was a boy down in Southern Indiana we did the same on the farm, and I can remember many a morning in June driving five cows up from pasture at 4:00 A.M. just before sun up, so we would get them milked before the day's work started.

There were very few birds. I noticed a species of wren, some English sparrows, some doves, and some large crows. The ocean was teeming with fish and lobsters, but the natives had lost the art of fishing. The U.S. Government bought a lot of fishing boats and equipment for them, but they rotted at the wharves. The natives prefer rice and sweet potatoes and raise a little pork.

The tuberculosis rate was high, and so was venereal disease, about 25%, some people thought. Inside plumbing was scarce.

Most of the natives are a moral family type people, and the maids who work for army wives are an attractive class of young women, who take their wages home to papa-san to help support the family and the tomb fund. There are so many desperately poor families, it encourages exploitation of some young girls.

Okinawan prices were low. There was a strike at a Chinese laundry by native workers, who wanted 12¢ an hour instead of 10¢, but the owner said he couldn't afford it. My daughter worked half days at the Post Golf Driving Range and golf course, keeping books. She was paid $35.00 a week, while the native manager, a full time employee and a graduate of the University of Ryuku, got $75.00 a month. The Army couldn't give equal pay. It would have upset the native economy, it was said.

Trip To Japan

I left Okinawa on August 5, 1960, on a Ryuku Lines prop plane and flew into Japan, landing at the International Airport. We rode downtown to the Imperial Hotel in an airconditioned bus with radio blaring, one piece being a trio of Japanese girls singing Rudy Vallee's "Whiffenpoof" song in Japanese, sounding mighty curious. All I recognized was the tune and "Baa Baa Baa." The bus driver was very courteous, coming around and making everyone comfortable before we started by putting our chairs in reclining position, whether we wanted it or not. Just said to me, "Thank you too much." When he got busy driving, I sneaked it back up.

The Imperial Hotel is about three blocks from the Imperial grounds, where Emperor Hirohito lives. I went over there one evening and took some pictures. It has a big moat around it, about one-hundred yards wide, and the grounds probably contain six hundred acres of the heart of Tokyo. I didn't see any of the royal family, but did see some wood smoke coming out of a chimney, so I presumed the Empress was in residence and was starting to cook supper.

The hotel was long and low, a long narrow horseshoe in two wings, three stories high, with one thousand rooms. My room was the very front room on the top floor facing Avenue "A." I took a picture of the entrance back there. It used to be the main entrance, and is now the rear one, as there is a new addition and front office about an eighth of a mile away at the other end. There are at least seventeen different ways of getting lost in the maze of rooms, and I used all of them. I finally solved it by just holding out my key, No. 303, and walking and showing it to all hands (and there are dozens of help all over the joint—male and female) and they would work on the problem with me, until pretty soon I would arrive. Hardly any of them spoke English. I talked, they waved hands, then they talked, and I waved my arms. The elevator girls on the night shift wore kimonas and obis. When these Japs talk on the phone it sure is a marvel. They keep yelling "Hi-hi! Hi-hi!", and all the time they are listening. I don't know what it meant, probably nothing.

It was hot in Japan, about 90 degrees in the sun, just like home on a good warm day. I went on the street on a Saturday taking pictures. Everybody was very friendly, and all the little kids said "Haroo," meaning "hello," and high school and college student boys in their white shirts and cadet caps came up and introduced themselves and asked if they could practice talking English, which was okay by me, as all the Japanese I had learned was "Inu" for dog, "Naisan," a girl (my granddaughter), and "Buta," pig (pork). Professional men and business leaders all speak English rather well.

Tokyo was quite large, about nine million people, one-tenth of all Japan, and it was a very modern city. The hotel was very nice. I had a room about twenty feet long and twelve feet wide, air-conditioned, with a large closet, and a bath and shower room, for $7.00 a day, which was 2500 yen. There was no tipping. General McArthur gave names to fifteen or twenty main streets but the rest are nameless. The blocks are numbered, and in each block a group of four or five houses has a number. When you get down that far, anybody in the neighborhood can point out the right house.

They had sewers downtown and running water and were trying to get every one to put in modern plumbing. However, it seems Utopia is hard to come by, as there was a letter to the Editor in the English language newspaper by an irate householder who said his water supply was off half the time and he was worse off now than before he put in flush toilets. The paper had a story about housewives lining up at the Municipal water wagons. Seemed there may have been plenty of water in the reservoir (at least the city fathers claimed so) and people had the facilities, but somebody failed to install sufficient pipes. Probably the contractor was a cousin to city hall, and there might be a grand jury investigation. I found the big problem in front of the Japanese was the same as in Indianapolis, Memphis, New York, London, and several other places. It was not the atom bomb, but what shall we do with our offal?

The taxi drivers here are called "Kamakazi" drivers, for the manner in which they charge down the street. Kamakazi, a name familiar to World War II vets, means "Death Wind". You could ride five miles for $1.50, and a half mile for seventy yen (20 cents). A taxi driver would hurtle down the street at 35 to 50 miles an hour, crossing the center line, running red lights and charging into a seemingly impenetrable oncoming traffic jam, which somehow would open up at the last second. It seemed there was no speed limit. I could bring a Tokyo taxi driver over home, and he could give our jalopy and stock car racers cards and spades and still beat them a mile. I just shut my eyes and hoped to be able to dive to the floor in time, but we always escaped.

I got a hair cut, shave, moustache trim and shampoo from a male barber right downtown in a nice shop for 400 yen ($1.15). I had a lady Chinese barber in Hawaii who used to live in Indianapolis and knew the Frank McKinneys, and in Okinawa, I had a lady barber. All oriental barbers male or female have one bad habit in common. They like to beat you on the back of the neck with rabbit punches for some reason. Everything is small in Japan. The barber chairs were too close to the wall for a six-foot American to stretch out, and in a tea room down the street, the tables were two and a half feet high and the chairs eighteen inches, and I used a chair and a half. Of course, I am not as thin as I once was.

One Sunday morning at 6 a.m. I got on an electric excursion train of eight cars and went on a rubberneck tour to Nikko National Park, about eighty miles north of Tokyo. Seven and one-half of the cars were filled with Japanese tourists, all in a happy holiday spirit and dressed Western style, beaming toothily and clutching the ever present camera. One half car was full of "Westerners" or Caucasians. The train sped along smoothly and quietly at eighty miles an hour.

It is a small world! The lady who sat just in front of me was a second secretary in some U. S. Legation, Rangoon or Bangkok, I think. I asked her where she was from and she said "the Midwest". Her name was Pea and she said she was born in a little Indiana hamlet which I probably had never heard of, and it turned out to be Decker, Knox County, Indiana. I said, "Yes, I had heard of it. That I had been born in the second township from it and had played baseball there on the Fourth of July in 1921, with the Wheatland sandlot team." My seat mate was a man who was a traveling auditor for the State Department who had been in twenty seven countries. The gist of his duties, I gathered, was to see what clique of politicans converted our foreign aid to its own use the fastest.

At Nikko is the sacred mountain, Nantai San, and it and the

surrounding premises constitute one of the scenic wonders of the world. When we unloaded from the train on a bright sunny morning, our group guide, a bespectaled young Jap, held up a banner on a long stick and we all rallied around with others not to get lost as there were a lot of other folks. First we were conducted to a hostelry in the town where we were given a half hour to drink gin slings or boiler makers and to play the slot machines.

At the foot of the mountain is a large collection of many and beautiful Buddhist and Shinto shrines, and a couple of great shoguns of the 1600's are buried there, too. One left the shrine an annual endowment of fifty thousand, yes 50,000 bushels of rice. It sure feeds a lot of more or less holy men, monks, and whatnot around there. You have to pay a few yen to get in the grounds and then to get into the second holiest place you have to pay again and also take off your honorable shoes. To get into a Holy of Holies you have to pay more, some 30 yen, but I balked on this as too much, as I had sneaked a free peep through the door and it was just another room with more figures and some young priests chanting the glories of someone—the rice endower, I suppose. Then there was the Holiest of Holies, sort of a behind the veil of the Tabernacle, it seemed, where only a very few Japs and no atheist dogs of unbelievers at all were allowed in. This was very expensive, I was assured.

The mountain of Nantai San is very sacred for reasons no one could explain, and during the first eight days of August it is most sacred of all. I found that by accident I had arrived in the holy season when pilgrims from all over the Japanese Empire make a pilgrimage to get sanctified. If you walk up the holy mountain you get sacred yourself, at least to a degree, like going to Mecca, I suppose. There are three degrees of sanctity to be had, it seems, something like the lodge back home maybe. In Japan holiness doesn't come cheaply. (They tap your pocket book in other religions, too). You pay your fee at the first station at the foot of the mountain and receive the first degree, pay half way up and get the second degree and are thrice blessed and sanctified on paying the final fee after walking up to the summit. Thousands were struggling up the mountain the day I was there.

However, the oriental mind is such that if you are too old, or too fat or too tired or too political or too lazy to walk up Nantai

311

San you may get all the sacredness by just stopping in at the foot of the mountain and paying your respects and a fee at a copy of the top of the mountain shrine.

Our group went up on a bus by a new road. The mountain is 8900 feet high, but we only made it half way to where there was an amusement park and rest station, which was plenty for me. There was also a large lake up there at 5,000 feet, in an old crater between Nantai San and a twin mountain, and it was dotted with scores of rented fishing canoes filled with earnest pilgrims trying to catch six-inch trouts. There are thirty hairpin turns. The grade is about 25 percent, and it seemed all Japan was either going up or down that road.,

Dizzy precipices on one side, sheer cliff on the other, and a multitude of maddened Japanese motorists, buses, autos, motorcycles, careening wildly in and out in both directions and on both sides of the road. What really was a great sight was the motorcycle crowd. Gentlemen Japs of all ages from seventy down to fifteen were threading the traffic with mama-san or girl friend on behind, sitting side saddle and holding on with one hand, and every where brakes smoking. Our little one-hundred-ten driver would charge at a turn and I would swear he would never make it, but we got there. I came back down on the cable car and, terrifying as that was, suspended on a thread over a chasm two-thousand feet deep, it seemed very safe by comparison.

I took a picture of the road from the cable car station, and you should see it. The Japs call this highway the "Alphabet Road" because from above it looks like the Jap alphabet strewn around. I don't want any more of that. There was one fat tourist, from Cleveland, I think, who got drunk on boiler makers at 10:00 A.M., at our first stop and he snored all the way up on the back seat. The rest of us wondered why we hadn't had that much foresight. There is a sacred bridge down in the heart of the town which would sure be a traffic help, but it is so sacred it has been blocked off for two hundred years, so everybody had to detour.

All of us pilgrims assembled back on the train at the appointed time and arrived home in Tokyo without mishap. The whole car load, Japanese and Westerners, joined in singing American songs.

312

It was a little difficult, as they sang in Jap and we in English, but the tunes were the same.

My letter of recommendation from Adjutant General Bob Brown of the Army at Honolulu in going through channels to Okinawa to Tokyo caused me a little embarrassment in Japan. I was slated to get into Tokyo on Thursday, but arrived Friday and never called the Army until Monday. It turned out I was quite a guest, supposedly on the Supreme Court of the United States instead of a mere Circuit Court Hoosier Judge. The Army said, "Where have you been?" and sent an auto, chauffeur, and interpreter to squire me around. Monday I was escorted on a tour of the Japanese Courts, beginning with the Supreme Court of the Empire. There I met the Honorable Katsumi O Moto, court secretary to fifteen Justices. The Court had gone into vacation, as the Chief Justice had left the day before for Buenas Aires to represent the Emperor in the Sesquicentennial celebration of Argentina. The Supreme Court is housed in a handsome building not too far from downtown Tokyo.

"Where were you last Friday?" O Moto inquired. "You were to be a special guest of our Chief Justice at a garden party." I shuddered inwardly at the thought of such a breach of protocol, and wondered how the party went off. I merely told the good secretary I was sorry, that there must have been some mistake, that no one had informed me and I left my apologies to the Chief Justice and his fourteen cohorts. It was a far, far better thing I didn't make the party at that. I don't know what the penalty would be for impersonating, say Honorable William Douglas, at a Japanese Supreme Court garden party.

Mr. O Moto was a fellow Methodist, a graduate of O Gama University which is maintained by our church. He spoke excellent English. He took me and the Army chauffeur and interpreter on a tour of the lower courts, winding up in a city police court, where I listened to two trials. A bench of three Judges tried one man for forging a driver's license and then tried a Chinaman, a restaurant owner, for trying to bribe a health official.

There are no juries in Japan. A man charged with crime is presumed to be guilty unless he proves himself innocent. The trial consisted of the defendant standing at a podium in the middle of the court room facing the three robed Judges who sat on an elevated platform with a three foot high wall in front of them. The crown prosecutor sat on the left in a waist-high enclosure and the defendant's attorney on the right in a similar one. We spectators were on chairs at the rear.

The trial began. The crown prosecutor called the first witness, who was the health official. Then they called the next witness who was the Chinaman defendent. The three Judges took turns interrogating and berating him and the culprit, who was rather fat, began to squirm and perspire. Next the prosecutor took a few shots at him and finally his own attorney asked him some questions, whereupon, the three justices put their heads together briefly and sent the unhappy wretch to the pokey.

Court recessed, and I was introduced to the Judges. One of them asked me how such a trial would go in the United States.

"We wouldn't try the restaurant owner over there for bribery. The official would take the cash, and that would end it," I said, half in jest. The Judges sucked in their breath in astonishment, though I have been told that bribery is much more common in the Orient than in America where it is bad enough in big cities.

I asked about abortion. It is against the law, being a misdemeanor, they said, but it is very common at $5.00 a job at any reputable doctor, and he is hardly ever punished. The divorce rate is low.

Another day my chauffeur and interpreter took me down toward Kyoto to see the great Buddha, a bronze statue about sixty feet high sitting out in a wooded pasture or park. It was cast in segments about 1100 A.D. and once was in a temple or barn, or some kind of shed, but the building burned down long ago. I took a picture of Buddha with some pigeons sitting on his head about at the part of his hair.

The Japanese interpreter, a personable young fellow about 28 years old, for some reason took the occasion to describe how the rich Shoguns and Samurai went fishing. Seems the great man is rowed along by a yokel while reclining on cushions under an awning, and is fanned by a beautiful Geisha, who hands him soothing drinks of one kind or another, principally Saki, hot rice wine. Another flunky drags a net fishing for a transparent sardine, and when one is caught, the maiden forces red soya sauce down its throat, and the

314

noble swallows it head first—like our college boys in the Roaring Twenties did goldfish. At that it saves a lot of skinning, scaling and gutting, and getting that old fishy slime all over your hands.

One evening seven men of us and two old widows from San Francisco went on a five dollar tour of Tokyo night life. There was a tourist named Peter from Germany; two Frenchmen; an Indian from Nehru's country; a Rotterdam Dutchman; and a bully Englishman who viewed the rest of us and everything else with some disgust. I didn't know why he came along.

First we went to the Kabuki Theater, where an all male cast (some representing ladies) presented a four centuries' old drama about a Samurai who had lost his sword and was in one awful fix, hiding in a small inn. A lot of people were killed, many long messages were read, (all bad news) and there was much talk. It dragged a little more than the next show we attended, the Queen Bee Night Club, where they had a floor show and everyone was furnished a beautiful girl hostess to dance with, including the two elderly ladies from California, whether you wanted a hostess or not. They wore ankle length white silk gowns, slit at the knee to show some calf and thigh. My partner was named "Micky," and she spoke fair English.

We escaped from there and drove off in our bus through a street parade of Anti-Communists who were tailed by police cars, small boys, and half a dozen Japanese dogs. They were the extreme Fascist rightists and are as bad as Commies. The last stop was a Geisha House, which is a high class restaurant where girls in traditional costume of wig, kimona, and obi wash your face and hands, feed you with fork or spoon, and put on entertainment of yelling and squalling and slow dancing while an old lady Jap twangs a samisen, which is something like an out of tune banjo. She picks it with a little butter-paddle like board.

Geisha houses are not houses of prostitution, as many Americans think. There are plenty of the latter in Japan, but they are not staffed by Geisha, who are beautiful young girls trained from chilhood for the ceremonial and stylish calling of entertainer. Many marry well. Another institution "manned" by women is the ever prevalent public bath house. The Japs are very cleanly and love to almost scald themselves in hot water. I was invited by fellow travelers to go for a scrubbing, but modestly refused, as I didn't want strange ladies fooling around with my nakedness, as I understood they wash you all over. The baths are not bad houses either, people said.

I also went on my own to "Miss Tokyo," a night club or cabaret about three blocks from the Imperial Hotel, which was a huge affair with a thousand hostesses, so they said. There was a floor show with some nearly six feet tall, nearly white, Japanese girls from the north end of the North Island of Japan, who put on a sort of strip tease act, stripping to the waist and maneuvering around in a very lively fashion. The act was well received.

The bus trip to the Queen Bee Night Club had a sequel, or near sequel. After I got back to the Imperial Hotel and was in bed, the telephone brought me out of a sound sleep.

"Mr. Neeblock, dees ees Micky. You want I should come up your room and make joy with you?"

Somewhat startled, I replied, "For God's sake, Micky, you go to bed. It's 1:00 A.M. and, anyhow, I got here twenty years too late for joy. You better call that young Dutchman."

I was sure most of my young people's Sunday School class at the Broadway Methodist Church would have approved of my precipitant action, whether prompted by virtue or cowardice.

Saying goodbye to Japan, I went out to the International Airport to leave on the JAL at 11:00 A.M., on Wednesday, August 10, 1960. The far isles of the Pacific and the wonders of the Orient were fine, but I was beginning to yearn for the flesh pots of good old Indiana. At the airport I got acquainted with two men sitting by me, William Cox of Chicago of the International Harvester Company, and Dr. William Siffin of Indiana University. Cox was born and raised at French Lick, Indiana, and Siffin at Frankfort. They were returning from India and Siam respectively. It turned out we all had graduated at Indiana University, and we jointly bemoaned the fact our football team for a dozen years hadn't beaten Purdue.

We didn't leave until 1:00 A.M., Thursday, August 11th, as they had to repair the plane's motors. This made me nervous, as I just love to start out over the Pacific Ocean at midnight with a typhoon coming over the horizon in a plane which just had been repaired. Well, we took off in a forty-mile wind and a heavy rain

316

and flew east to Wake Island where we stopped for lunch. It is a tiny speck on the broad blue Pacific about five miles across, a circle of land surrounding a huge lagoon of shining green water.

On crossing the International date line going east nine hours out of Tokyo, I found I was back in Wednesday, August 10, again, a sort of weird-like feeling. We got to Honolulu at 9:30 P.M., and it being a port of entry, everyone had to expose his clean and dirty underwear, and what have you, to the customs.

On this trip I shared a seat with a 26 year old Japanese wife and four month old baby who were going to New York City where her husband was an employee of the Tokyo Bank. The seats just in front were occupied by a Japanese woman and her three Eurasian daughters, ages five, three and one, who were going to her husband, an American Army sergeant at Honolulu. The man across the aisle was from Texas. He had been in the Merchant Marine in the Persian Gulf and was being sent home to take the alcoholic cure. His midnight lunch, breakfast, and lunch were sips from a quart bottle of bourbon whiskey, and he kept us passengers and the stewardess up all night hollering for digitalis, and telling his troubles, and discussing world affairs in a silly way. I had the window seat, but the Japanese wife got me to change so he couldn't reach her knees.

Changing planes at Honolulu, we started East again at 11:30 P.M., Wednesday, August 10, 1960, and Lo and Behold! as they say in the Bible, in one-half hour at midnight, I ran head long into an old friend: Thursday, August 11th 1960, going around the world heading West. I had been in Wednesday twice and Thursday twice.

The big jet landed in Los Angeles as smoothly as a cob web floating down, and I felt something like Magellan's crew when they got back to Spain after being the first people to circle the world. They thought the home folks had lost their minds when they said "today was yesterday."

Police Court Reform Comes to Indianapolis

As a result of five years on the bench of Municipal Court no. 4, and three sessions as legislator, I was in the position of being able to help implement the Municipal Court Reform Acts of 1969 and 1971, when a set of circumstances coincided to make it possible.

These two acts provided, among other things: (1) a Presiding Judge; (2) non-political appointments of the Presiding Judge and his fourteen associates; (3) simplified appeals on the record from police court to Criminal Court on the taped record of the trial below instead of trial de novo (complete new trial); (4) to establish a small claims Court for petty civil cases where parties could act as their own attorneys; (5) establishment of a nine member nonpartisan nominating commission to sift and recommend nominees to the Governor; (6) tenure for good Judges; and (7) ended the Special Judge and Pro Tem Judge abuse.

About three thousand years ago, Moses, the law giver, received some advice from his father-in-law Jethro on how to set up a good judicial system:

"Get stout hearted men of virtue to be the Judges over the people, men of truth, God-fearing men, who abhor avarice and greed," he admonished the leader of the Israelites, according to the 18th Chapter of the Book of Exodus of Holy Writ. No one has ever improved on Moses' recipe.

That was in the dawn of history. Ever since then civilization has been trying to find a good judicial system. It has made some progress. The early Anglo-Saxons used trial by combat. God would be on the side of Justice, they thought.

It did not always work.

The administration of justice in the big city Police Courts in America has always been a problem, and Indianapolis was no exception. To a large extent the underworld—the gambler, the madam; the bipartisan political machines, political bosses, and the monied men of influence, have joined hands to control such Courts. The professional bondsman and the police court lawyers, "The Alabama Street Bar Association," were the powers behind our bench. The Municipal Judges, seventy-five percent of the time, were political prisoners of the system, and had to "go along" as best they could.

Most of the Police Court Judges in Indianapolis have been good family men, good church members, and have paid their taxes in full, especially since Uncle Sam keeps such a keen eye on a citizen's income. There are three great aids to virtue and honest living: Old age, poverty, and the fear of getting caught.

The main flaw in our police court system for a hundred years was the fact that the big city Judges were politically selected, most of the time by the Republican or Democratic County Chairmen— not an unexpected result—as this County is run by political parties. County Chairmen as a rule are stout-hearted men who like to see good government and who like to handle "soft money"—lots of it and in large denominations.

Until 1925 our Police Court Judges were elected. Things had gotten so out of hand by then, what with ticket fixing, favoritism, fee-splitting, polite extortion, money gouging by bondsmen and police court attorneys on families of arrested persons, bribery and worse, that the Indianapolis Bar Association had the Indiana Legislature pass the 1925 Municipal Court Reform Bill, whereby the Governor would appoint the Judges, half from each Party.

It was hoped that the Governor, being from some other city, would give Indianapolis some non-political Judges, at least ones who would be independent. That didn't work either, as the Governor usually was in heavy debt to our Marion County political chairman for his own election. Now and then, when the Governor was angry at both local County Chairmen, he would appoint his own man—a sort of political accident. I was one of those accidents, having been appointed by Governor Schricker. There were some others.

The average citizen who pays his taxes, who does not interfere when a policeman makes an arrest in his neighborhood, and who never goes to police court, has not the remotest idea of what went on there, or did go on there until the Municipal Court Reform Acts of 1969 and 1971 passed the Legislature and were approved by Governor Edgar D. Whitcomb.

In the past, some Judges left their names on the door of their law office during their terms, and their former partners were retained in eighty percent of the drunken driving cases in such courts, which was where the big fees were. Round trip tickets to Florida, free apartments down there, maybe use of a yacht, financial loans, expensive gifts such as automobiles, etc., were only part of the fringe benefits of such arrangements. If not a former partner, generally one favored attorney, or one firm, had the right-of-way. Other attorneys referred to such arrangements as the "Syndicate." It usually included a couple of professional bondsmen and maybe a ranking police officer or two as silent partners. After four to eight years the fortunate attorney could retire with a nice nest egg of $100,000.00, or more, and devote himself to corporation practice or real estate development, or just plain retire. Some of such Judges also retired well off, but others lived to rue the day their term expired as fair weather partners shut off their tap.

When I was practicing law in the 1930's, a fraternity brother had a couple of drinks at his Legion meeting and failed to stop at a red light, and was arrested. He was frightened stiff. He came to see me, and I entered an appearance in the case. A few days later he informed me:

"My boss says he got a phone call that you are a Republican and the Judge is a Democrat, and I had better get a Democrat lawyer or I will get the works. They gave him the name of a lawyer who is Democrat."

"Who gave him the name?" I asked.

"Someone who said he was from the Court!" he replied.

"Nuts! It is true I'm a Republican, but I can take care of the case just as well. No one was injured, and you have never been arrested before. It will be a fine of $25.00 or $50.00, and a ninety-day suspension of your drivers license, I just know." I told him.

"No, John, I can't risk six months on the farm. You keep the hundred dollars I paid you, and I'll get this other fellow," he said.

He did so and paid him a fee of $400.00. About three months later he came in to see me again and said, "Well, I'm free!" He looked a little "shook-up."

"How did you come out," I asked.

"Well, I want to ask you something. Does that kind of thing go on much at Police Court? If I wasn't the defendant, I believe I would go to the newspapers and expose the whole thing," he said.

"Go on, tell me about it!" I said.

"Well, we got two or three continuances, and one afternoon I was the only one left. The regular Judge says, 'I have to do some office work and Mr. Blank here will be Special Judge,' naming my lawyer, and he went in his office.

"I grabbed my attorney's arm and says, 'Say, who is going to defend me?,' and he says, 'Shut up, you silly bastard, you'll be O.K.' He got on the bench and called my case. There was no one there except the young deputy prosecutor, the policeman, my attorney-Judge, and me.

"So the policeman started testifying, and when he was about half-way through, my attorney rapped the gavel and says, 'I can see you don't have any case on this fellow', and he discharged me."

This particular attorney retired and went to Arizona to live after the above mentioned Judge's term expired. The Judge also built a fine new home in an exclusive neighborhood.

One time a motorist, a drunken ex-soldier, ran up over the curb and hit a lady pedestrian, breaking her leg. He appeared before another Police Court Judge, after his father had retained an attorney who was an ex-partner of the Judge. When the case came up before the Judge, he threw the book at the defendant.

"I'll give you six months on the farm. I wish it could be two years. You are fined $100.00, the maximum. I wish it could be $1,000.00. Your drivers license is suspended for one year, the maximum, and if the law allowed, I would make it for life. Take him away!"

The story drew a four column headline on the front page of the Indianapolis News. A couple of days later, after the newspaper reporters had lost interest, the Judge's stamp went across the face of the docket "Sentence suspended!" The Court watchers of the papers, all earnest women doing good works, never knew of the suspension.

Professional bondsmen who had a lawyer's license often sat as Judges Pro Tem or Special Judges in cases where they had got a fee for writing the bond, part of the attorney's fee by brokering the case to a silent attorney partner, and a day's pay as Special Judge. This particular abuse was ended by the 1969 Reform Act.

321

Every morning during most of the past fifty years, a special messenger would go to the Police Courts with a bundle of traffic tickets from the offices of both County Chairmen. These had been brought in or mailed in by the faithful political henchmen. They were to be and were "fixed." Sometimes the Judge, the bailiff, the deputy prosecutor, a clerk or a police officer took care of them. It was a custom. Only the poor ignorant sap who didn't know anybody had to pay a traffic ticket.

Along this line the public or the smart part of it, including newspaper men, knew of the practice and expected their precinct committeemen or anyone else they know in public life to "fix" a ticket. I still get phone calls from acquaintances who naively inform me they have got a speeding or parking ticket, and what can I do about It? I have one sure answer, as I know many others in public life have: "I got an overtime parking ticket last spring, and I had to pay it, so I guess you will have to pay yours, too."

One professional bondsman took a drunk out on bail, and took him to his house where, incidentally, he made him paint his garage over the weekend. The bondsman pretended to call me on the phone, when he really was talking to his attorney partner, a police court shyster.

The frightened fellow listened to the bondsman argue the case on the phone, and finally heard him say, "All right, Judge, a $300.00 fee is too much, but if you say so, he'll pay it, and you say he will get a suspended sentence? O.K., Judge, and he has to have Attorney Blank as his attorney?" (naming the lawyer he was talking to).

These are only a few samples of Alabama Street Justice in former times.

The fact that many criminal lawyers were former County Chairmen, or were presently serving as Ward Chairman, or other party officials, and that many of the Judges had held similar positions, had much to do with abuse of suspended sentences, judgments withheld, findings of not guilty, or inadequate sentences. An occasional Judge even doubled as a political Ward Chairman while serving on the bench. It was improved some now under the 1969 Reform Act which provided a Presiding Justice for the Municipal Court, and competent men have been appointed to its bench.

In the summer of 1969, Mayor Richard G. Lugar asked me if

322

I had any suggestions for proposed legislation. I did—Municipal Court Reform. I had helped the Honorable Keith Bulen become Republican County Chairman and had some influence with him; had helped Lugar become a school board member and Mayor; and was of some assistance to Governor Edgar D. Whitcomb. Judge William Sharp of Municipal Court Room Four (where I had served) was a fine honest Judge, who was also a political accident on the bench, and what was more important, he was a close friend and political ally of Governor Whitcomb.

Lugar, Sharp and I enlisted the aid of the Honorable Paul Buchanan, President of the Indianapolis Bar Association, and his successor John Kitchen. I drew up the bill for the '69 Act and it went through the Legislature and the Governor signed it. Brother Bulen, a good Sigma Nu, wasn't too happy with the whole thing, but he honored his promise to me not to kill the bill, which he easily could have done. Anyway, he and Richard wanted my influence with the Marion County delegation, a very superior one that year, to pass "Unigov," so we swapped work. Judge Sharp persuaded the Governor to sign it, and was appointed the first Presiding Judge, and he started the new court off in the right direction.

The 1969 Bill had a provision for a non-partisan Board of nine which would nominate three good qualified men for each vacancy on the court to submit to the Governor for him to choose from in appointments. I went to Arizona in an ill advised moment on a vacation in February, and some politician had this provision deleted in the Senate. "When the cat's away, the mice will play" was surely true in that case.

However, we stuck to our guns and in 1971, I prepared a new Bill to provide the nominating Commission and it sailed through after some blood, sweat, and close attention, and Governor Whitcomb again came through. It also provided that if seven of the nine members voted to retain an incumbent Judge, his name would be the only one submitted, thus providing tenure for a good conscientious Judge. The first test of this law came in 1971, when Judge Joe Myers, a Democrat, who had served ably and honorably for twenty years on the bench, came up for re-appointment. He was unanimously recommended and is now serving another term.

By law an Appellate Court Judge is Chairman (now being

Judge Buchanan); the Circuit Judge is Secretary (no coincidence); two members each are appointed by the Governor and the Mayor; one is elected by Superior Court; and two by the Indianapolis Bar Association. No more than five can belong to the same political Party.

I believe Marion County now has the finest police court or Municipal Court system in the United States. It is under the direction of Chief Judge William Cramer at present. The professional bondsmen-attorneys are no longer eligible as Special Judges, and Kramer recently informed the Nominating Commission that appeals are at a record low, being about one-tenth of what they used to be.

The small claims court has not yet been implemented, but I believe that under the supervision of the Bar Association, which keeps close watch on the Court, that it will be put into operation before long.

Politics

They say that Politics makes strange bedfellows. It also creates amusing situations now and then. One time in 1928, I was deep in an anti-Republican political machine struggle, as usual. One of our fellows was Asa J. Smith, the attorney who took Madge Oberholtzer's dying declaration in the D. C. Stephenson case. We were going to elect him County Chairman to unseat George V. Coffin, Steve's crony. County Chairman were elected by precint committeemen and vice-committeemen in county convention the Saturday following primary.

We printed cards decrying "Bossism," "Stephensonism," and "Coffinism" and painting ourselves as the guys in the White Hats. I persuaded three or four business men to run for precinct committeeman on our reform platform. One was Ralph Root who lived out by Butler University in the same precinct with the Honorable William E. "Duke" Bain, an attorney and a hench-gentleman of Coffin. Duke was also precinct committeeman and Washington Township Chairman, pretty high up in the hierarchy.

"How do you do this running for precinct committeeman?" Ralph asked.

"Just knock on every door in your precinct and say you are running for Precinct Committeeman and are going to vote to throw that old crook Coffin out and restore good Government," I told him. "Here are your cards."

Well, Mr. Root was elected two and one-half to one over Bain. I didn't see him until the next Tuesday night at our corner drugstore—Scott's Pharmacy at 16th and Illinois, near where I roomed. Root used to live around there and stopped in frequently. I spoke to him.

"Niblack, you and your reform movements! Ouch, Oh!" he groaned, grasping his back.

"What's wrong with you?" I inquired in alarm.

"Hell, my tail bone! I didn't even get to go vote." he said.

"Ouch! I went down to the convention at the K. of P. building on Saturday, and rode up to the 9th floor. The operator says, 'Every one out.' I told him I wanted the 10th floor, but we all had to get out and walk up.

"At the foot of the stairs two big fat deputy sheriffs blocked me off with their stomachs. 'Let's see your letter from Cap Coffin. No one gets in with out a letter from Cap', they said.

"Shoot! I don't need a letter from that old crook, I'm going to vote against him. Here's my certificate of election as committeeman. 'Like Hell you are', they said, and gave me a push and I fell backward down two steps, and Oh! Oh!—damn near broke my tail bone. And as I lay there who should pass by but the Honorable Duke Bain, waving a letter from Cap."

We found out later that under the State law, Cap had replaced Root with Bain as Committeeman "For the Good of the Party",— election or no election. That was the law then, and incidentally, it still is. Precinct committeemen can be and are elected by the party voters, but a County Chairman can depose them and fill vacancies at will.

Cap had another ward chairman in the downtown district, a genial red-faced Irishman named Joe Quinn, who was also precinct committeeman. About every election a man named Lain who ran a business school there, also a reformer, would run against Joe and caused him no end of trouble as now and then he would get elected, and then came the old business of "for the good of the party." One day Mr. Lain passed on, and Joe was a pall bearer. On returning from the cemetery Joe remarked, "I never was so glad to help bury a feller in all my life."

It seemed like Cap's ward chairmen, about 35 of them in all, looked like the professional politician, fat and well-fed. One day Bill Remy, my former prosecutor boss, came in the office and said he had just witnessed Cap and his chairmen going down the street en mass.

"Reminded me of Ali Baba and his Forty Thieves" Remy remarked. He despised political machines. He thought the boys were all crooks, and some of them were. It has been a curious phenomenon in American politics from Tammany Hall and Boss Tweed on down that many men who would not steal a dime in private life

326

believe they are elected to feather their nests. Some United States Senators have become millionaires many times over on their salaries. I guess their wives didn't peel the potatoes too thick.

Another of Cap's precinct committeemen was a one-eyed old boy named William Law. He lived down in Quinn's territory on North Delaware in a rambling old house where he had been born, and which he had cut up into apartments. William had been arrested on a false charge arising out of his mother's estate, and on investigation I found the true facts and as Deputy Prosecutor dismissed the charges. Mr. Law became my sworn friend. About a year later I ran for State Senator with Remy's endorsement and that of Brother Walter Esterline, a Sigma Nu brother and head of the City Manager League, a reform movement. Our slate in the primary that May in Quinn's ward received about 10 votes in each precinct to 165 to 200 for Cap's boys, headed by the Honorable Russell B. Harrison, the president's son.

I was standing in Superior Court Room No. 1 idly listening to the returns as they were read off publicly, as was the custom in those days, when all of a sudden, Mr. Law's precinct reported:

"Niblack, 175—Harrison, 10," the clerk intoned. My five colleagues only received 10 votes.

I saw Mr. Law in the hall and I asked him how come I did so well.

"Johnny, I just went around and asked the neighbors to vote for you and they did." he replied.

"Now, Bill, are you sure you didn't switch the figures on me and Colonel Harrison?"

"Shut up, you damn fool! You know Old Bill wouldn't do anything crooked at any election. Can't you be satisfied with the vote?" he snapped. I subsided.

Mr. Law was a character. He wore a black patch over one eye, looking a little like a pirate, but he had a sentimental side few people suspected. Now and then, in different primaries, I had occasion to go to his apartment at the end of a long dark hall upstairs—sometimes at night. After he passed away the body of his second wife, a beautiful woman much younger than Law, was found neatly dressed in her coffin under some lumber in the attic. Bill had arranged for burial somewhere in southern Indiana and, I suppose, by bribing an undertaker, had smuggled the body into his house. Some of his former tenants remembered hearing moans and sobs in the attic now and then late at night, presumably from Mr. Law viewing his dead wife. If I had known all that, I believe I would have gone there by daylight.

About that same time Francis Brosnan, who lived in the 1500 block of North Delaware Street, a colleague of mine at I.U., where he was a Beta, took part in one of our efforts to throw Cap and his men out of control of the Party. Fran ran for precinct committeeman and had his 21 year old brother Kevin, a Junior at Indiana University and editor of the Daily Student there, come up and be official watcher at the polls. It was the day of paper ballots. Kevin sat up all night while the election board counted the votes. Of course, they were all appointees of Cap's machine—maybe not dishonest people but public employees whose jobs were at Cap's disposal.

About 6:00 A.M., Fran was ahead by 20 votes and the precinct committeeman, his rival, adjourned the session for breakfast. There were only 22 ballots left to count.

"Everybody be back in on hour and a half" he said.

Kevin ran home, a block, took a shower, shave and a hasty breakfast and got back in about an hour. He met the board closing up and going home, and inquired what was up.

"Well, we decided, after you left, that as there were so few ballots left we would just finish up and then have breakfast," Cap's man told him.

"Who won the precinct committeeman's vote?" the hapless Kevin asked.

"Son, your brother lost by two votes," he was informed. The ballots had already been sealed up and the returns duly certified.

Apropos of Kevin, he became one of the first bearded editors of the Daily Student, resulting from a vow to grow a beard until I.U. beat Purdue at football. He stayed hairy for several years.

The political bosses like to have control of the clerical offices and the County Commissioners, who most of the time were wheelers and dealers deluxe. One of our best Republican examples of this was the genial "Bull" Durham, plumber at the county poor farm, who filed for Republican nomination against Jesse Hutsell, the well-esteemed and honest president of the board.

"You are crazy. You can't beat Mr. Hutsell," some one told Bull (pretty nearly all men named "Durham" forty years ago were nicknamed "Bull" because of Bull Durham cigarettes).

"You never can tell. Maybe the old bastard will drop dead after filing time and before primary day, and I will be the only one left," Bull retorted. He didn't really mean Mr. Hutsell was a bastard—it was just Bull's genial way of talking.

Mr. Hutsell did just that and Bull went in that fall on a Republican landslide. It finally got so bad down there in the commissioner's office that a tax payer filed a malfeasance suit in Circuit Court where I presided against Durham and his Democratic cohort, Eph Virt, and after proof, the Court removed them from office. I appointed William A. Boyce and French Elrod, two Republicans of good repute to fill out the terms. They told me later on that some contractor came in to see them one day and said "I have $10,000 here that belongs to the Commissioners for letting me have that paving contract down in the county in Perry Township. Who shall I pay it to?"

They told him to go and pave a little more of the road with the money. Along this line, one County Commissioner retired—by request of voters—and at a going away party where the cup flowed freely, one of the remaining board members gave him a toast:

"Here's to Mr. Comish! He's one of the honestest fellers I ever seen. He never got no money under the table on any contract or nuthin', but what he split it fair and square among all three of us!"

It was mighty hard to unseat a political County Chairman in those days, and it still is. He holds the gavel at the conventions and can rule anyway he wants. I have seen him gavel down four-fifths of a convention. He rules by voice vote, denying request for standing votes or secret ballots. There is no appeal except to the State Committee which is ruled by his buddies. Only a series of defeats in the fall will cause a change in leadership.

The only successful upheaval I ever participated in was when our County Republican Chairman, Herman Dale Brown, an ex-coffin salesman and an ex-county clerk, suffered three consecutive losses of the Mayor's office in 1955, 1959 and 1963. People wanted a younger and more virile herd-bull to lead us to greener pastures, but H. Dale, a convivial soul, naturally hated to lay down the reins of power. He enjoyed the fringe benefits of the office to the fullest, such as appointing liquor board members, going to horse tracks and mingling with the great and near great at beefsteak dinners, cocktail parties and weekend outings. He just plain couldn't give up, and I don't blame him. It was the good life.

However, I asked Prosecutor Noble Pearcy to my office and we called a meeting of the Republican elected office-holders, twelve of us, including County Recorder Marcia Hawthorne, Auditor John Sutton, Councilman Beurt SerVaas, County Commissioner Lewis Ping, Judges Frank Symmes and Addison Dowling, Sheriff Robert Fields and councilmen James A. Buck, Edwin J. Koch and Ronald E. Bingman.

SerVaas suggested the name Republican Action Committee and I suggested a non-politician, but a good money raiser, Insurance Tycoon John Burkhart, president of the College Life Insurance Company, as Chairman, reserving for myself the title of Chairman of the Board of Directors. A young attorney and ex-legislator, L. Keith Bulen, a Sigma Nu brother of mine from Beta Eta Chapter at I.U., was put on the board of directors, and began campaigning to be our candidate against H. Dale. We got so well organized, largely through the efforts of our co-office managers, W. W. "Dub" Hill, Mrs. Hawthorne and Bulen, that Mr. Brown never went to the post on County Convention day. L. Keith has gone on to victory and to associate with presidents and foreign potentates, such as Emperor Haile Selassie of Ethiopia. It was just a co-incidence that he and Brown used only the initial of their first names.

However, it was no co-incidence that Charles Applegate, now Judge Applegate, but then president of the Republican Victory League, a group of some power, and County Clerk Edwin McClure, an H. Dale Brown ally with 75 deputy precinct committeemen and vice-committeemen in his office, swung over behind our Action Committee. My Court had at its disposal then two refereeships in a multi-million dollar Insurance Company dissolution for which I fixed a salary of $100.00 a week. Sometime before the County Convention my two referees saw fit to resign, and Mr. Applegate and Mr. McClure were appointed, and became enthusiastic supporters of brother L. Keith Bulen. The refereeships lasted about two years.

Some folks might have thought the Circuit Judge was playing

party politics. I'd say they were right. Since 1816 the Judges in Indiana have been elected on a political party ticket, and if you want to succeed in being a judge you had better know how to participate in politics. You don't have to be crooked to be a successful politician, but you have to know how to help things happen.

To be a Judge in Indiana you only have to know one thing: How to get elected or appointed. Then you are a judge willy-nilly. I prefer the Indiana system of electing major judges. In most counties, if a judge makes an honest, impartial record, he will be re-elected as long as he runs. Russell Gordon was the only democratic attorney in Monticello, White County, a rock-ribbed Republican community. He was appointed by a Democratic Governor to fill a vacancy in Circuit Court, and did so well he served thirty years until he died, in latter years with no opposition. In Knox County, Indiana, a Democratic County as a rule, Democrat Circuit Judge Ralph Seal and Republican Superior Court Judge Sidney Gelb were elected and re-elected for many years as long as they wanted.

A bad State judge can be turned out by the people every four to six years in our State Courts. However, our Federal judges are appointed for life and many of them become autocrats and irresponsible, but are not subject to recall. It is a sad thing, as the United States is in the grip of an oligrachey of 300 Federal judges who believe in a government of men and not of written laws, and are doing away with elected grassroots self government. Federal judges were never elected by anybody, but they are making laws to make people do what the judges think is right, under the guise of "equity."

I eased into another political arena, this one non-partisan, in 1929 when I became the paid executive secretary of the Citizens School Committee, which had been organized by a coalition of leading Catholic, Jewish, Negro, and Protestant community leaders to improve city and school government in Marion County, and do away with Ku Klux Klanism and political boss corruption. From 1934 to 1964, I was either the unpaid executive Assistant Chairman or Chairman of the Committee, which had as its aim the drafting of leading men and women of the city, parents of public school children, to run for the Indianapolis School Board, and to serve only one term. We were successful in each election. Our motto

331

was to nominate, help elect and forget them. In other words, to let them strictly alone. It worked fine. During that time there were 13 high schools of 700 in the state who rose to the highest rating by the State Board of Education, that of "A-1 Special." Ten of these were in Indianapolis. Our grade schools also had the highest rating in the state.

All this was too much for the Indiana Civil Liberties Union and the proponents of Federal control of our children's minds. The ICLU organized a "Non-Partisan For Better Schools Committee, succeeding in electing no one in 1959, and one member of seven in 1964 and 1968, the latter a Negro, the Honorable Robert DeFrantz. In an effort to be fair to the black population of Indianapolis, being about 25 or 30%, our Citizens Committee endorsed two Negroes in 1968, who immediately joined with DeFrantz and a white attorney, also a Citizens Committee endorsee, to form a majority on the board. Pretty soon chaos among teachers set in as a result of racial reshuffling and favoritism on a grand scale. The president of the student body of Crispus Attucks, our all colored High School which had brought fame to the city, a lad named Crenshaw appeared before the board to protest transfer of 38 Negro teachers of long standing out of Crispus Attucks, to be replaced by 38 white strangers. The board cut the number of 12 for the time being. Discipline flew out the window as our liberal left wingers took charge of the schools.

I had very little to do with the 1968 election as Henry Schricker, Jr. was general chairman of the Citizens Committee and what with a failing business and illness at home our committee accepted and endorsed without investigation two or three people who belonged in the Indiana Civil Liberties Union Camp.

A new board was to be elected in 1972, and our Citizens School Committee was in bad shape. Dead and gone were Rabbi Maurice Feuerlicht, Sumner Furnis, head of the Negro Shrine, Henry Dithmer, a leading Democrat, Walter Esterline and others who had been the backbone of the good government group. Dead of old age, and their good works had fallen on changing times. Some people. wanted to bus children to schools across the county to provide forcible mixing of races, and the Federal Court said, "It's a good deal, go thou and bus. Don't mind the Civil Rights of parents who want their children to attend the nearest public school. It was wrong to force children to attend certain schools because of their race and color, so we will order that stopped. Segregation must end. So now let's force children to attend certain schools because of their race or color. That's O.K. because it will have a new name — Integration."

Regardless of what the Federal Courts thought in defiance of the 1964 Civil Rights Law passed by Congress, which forbids busing because of race or color, I believe if forcing children to attend a certain school because of race was unconstitutional in 1954, it is unconstitutional in 1972. In 1957 President Eisenhower sent the U.S. army to force Arkansas to let Negro children attend their neighborhood schools.

Therefore I suggested we get up a coalition of the Citizens Committee and the Committee for Quality Schools a group of anti-busing parents and call it the "Committee for Neighborhood Schools." The idea was accepted, and our ticket which included a Negro swept the election, showing what the people think of forcible integration of races. Our group had no opposition to integration of any school if accomplished by people moving into new neighborhoods.

I might add in passing that in 1964, one of my endorsees for school board was a young man who was in the same Sunday School Primary class with my daughter Nancy—one Richard Lugar. Brother Bulen called on me pretty heavily to get Lugar endorsed by his ward captains in 1967 for Mayor, and I spoke right out in a turbulent meeting called for that purpose. Jimmy Redmond, a ward chairman, declared that it "would make him puke" to swallow poor Richard.

About the last time Brother Bulen called on me was to preside at the Atkinson Hotel at a meeting of the Marion County delegation to the 1969 Legislature to sell "Uni-Gov," an idea for a law to make the city include the whole county. I thought it was a good idea, if county government such as courts and sheriff were protected, so I presided, and the bill became law.

Richard Lugar has made a good Mayor. He is an honest man,

the prime qualification for any public servant. Then he has three added assets a lot of us don't have, at least not all three: a silver tongue, a keen mind and a good T.V. presence. He will go far.

As for me, I am glad I had some small part in helping forge our destiny in Indianapolis.

Church In The Wildwood

On Sunday, October 6, 1963, the congregation of the Upper Indiana Presbyterian Church celebrated the 50th Anniversary of their "new" church building, a beautiful little brick country church halfway between Vincennes and Bruceville in Knox County, Indiana. It was one of the three preaching places, or "stands" of the first Protestant church in the new Territory of Indiana. I made a short address on the occasion and have seen fit to set out here part of it, as follows:

My friends, neighbors, and relatives: More than fifty years ago, as an orphaned lad of four, who had come to live with his maternal grandfather, John R. McClure, over there on the home farm, a mile and a half east of this spot, I entered the Sunday School of this Church in the old brick building which was replaced by this one.

Here my mother, then Miss Nannie J. McClure, had been organist, and her father was ordained deacon in 1884. Here his father, Alfred McClure, was a member, as was his grandfather, John McClure; and my third great-grandfather, Daniel McClure, was a founder of and first secretary of this church.

They are, with the exception of my mother, all buried out there in the old churchyard, as well as other ancestors I had in this township, including Purcells, Hogues, Elliotts, Deckers and McCords.

In the churchyard here I have twenty-three direct ancestors. This Presbyterian church, as you know, is the oldest Protestant congregation in Indiana, and the graveyard antedates the church by some years. I am cousin to more than half of the people resting from their labors out there under the pines, and probably some kind of relation to a majority of you folks sitting in this sanctuary.

The explanation is easy. When an elderly widow woman, Mrs. Jane McClure, a Presbyterian Scotch-Irish lady originally from Ulster, Ireland, and her four grown sons and one daugher moved here from Kentucky in a group with their families in 1802, one hundred sixty years ago, she left approximately forty grand-children here who, as the Old Testament says, "begat" numerous descendants. There were fifty-nine McClures buried out here before 1872; I don't know how many since. I am a freeholder and taxpayer of this Palmyra Township, as I now own the old John R. McClure farm.

As nearly as can be ascertained, the Indiana Presbyterian Church, of which this was one part, was founded in Knox County in 1806. The first church records have been lost, the earliest minutes being dated 1812. There were three preaching places with one preacher the Reverend Samuel Thornton Scott. One preaching place was in a log church at Sinking Springs (or Upper Indiana), located two miles south of Bruceville on the farm of Daniel McClure, who donated one acre in 1815 for a church site. The second was at the Lower Indiana site, where it now is and the third was at Vincennes, where they had no building of their own, but started out in the barn of Colonel Small, and later used the old courthouse at 4th and Buntin. In 1831, the entire congregation built a brick church for the Vincennes, or Town, part of themselves, and it was split off as a separate church in 1834.

A brick church was built here in 1836 on land donated by Mr. Samuel Thompson for the Upper congregation and was first known as the Center Meeting House. The Sinking Springs log church was abandoned shortly thereafter. Later a brick edifice was built for the Lower Indiana, and in 1847 it became an independent church.

This Indiana Presbyterian Church was founded by Mrs. William Henry Harrison and, among others, my third great-grand-father, Daniel McClure. From the first it was anti-slavery, despite the fact that several large landowners in Palmyra Township from Kentucky and Virginia were slave owners and kept their slaves until the state was admitted to the Union in 1816. The Northwest Territory, under the Ordinance of Congress of 1787, was free soil, but Governor William Henry Harrison (an Episcopalian) was from Virginia and winked at slavery here. Maybe he used a few slaves in his own family. Among those who brought slaves here and freed them were the original Purcells, who owned a thousand acres around Frichton; two of the brothers of Secretary Daniel McClure, John and William; and Patrick Simpson. There were others. Mr.

Simpson was a member of this church and was expelled in 1812 on a charge of "using slaves in his family," and it took him two or three years to get back in. The others above mentioned were not members. I have read the wills of those who died before 1816 whereby they devised their slaves, cattle, and horses. Two of the names of such Negro slaves so devised appear in the 1828 and 1839 census of this church as members, along with the names of Charles, an Indian youth, and Hannah, an Indian maid. So the first Protestant church in Indiana was fully integrated.

The old church business records show that Charlotte and Abraham, former Negro slaves of William McClure, who died in 1811, were members of this church in 1828 and 1839, as were several of Mr. McClure's children.

The record further shows that on July 2, 1832, Lucy, a woman of Color, was received into the congregation at the Lower Meeting House; that on August 1, 1836, Judy, a woman of Color, presented one infant and he was baptized by the Reverend Samuel R. Alexander; that a few years later Isaac, a man of Color, slipped from grace and was expelled from the congregation for stealing corn. Number 104 of the 1828 census was Mariah, "a woman of Color." These names are preserved in the Old Record Book of the church. There were 176 persons named as members, set down by Reverend Alexander. Of these, thirty lived in Vincennes.

The elders listed were: James Scott, Isaac Westfall, Cornelius Merry, Abraham Westfall, William Williams, James Denny, Samuel Kuykendall, J. D. Wray, A. S. Smith, Samuel Thompson, David McCord.

Two men were responsible for the early growth and spiritual welfare of the Indiana Presbyterian Church. The Reverend Samuel Thornton Scott was its first regular minister. He taught school in Vincennes in 1802 and returned as a Presbyterian minister to this church about 1806 or 1807. He was president of Vincennes University here from 1807 to December 30, 1827, when he died, serving the same time as your pastor. He was a graduate of a Presbyterian Seminary, an educated man, and held many meetings or camp meetings in the woods, sometimes preaching to 1000 people, many person being called into a state of grace by his learned and enthusiastic efforts. When you stop to think that the entire white population of Indiana, Illinois, Michigan and Wisconsin was only 5,000 persons in 1800, and only 200,000 for Indiana and Illinois combined in 1820, this was a notable feat.

I must digress here a moment to review a little history. The land on which you sit originally belonged to Indian tribes. Next the French flag flew over it, then the English. In February, 1779, George Rogers Clark captured Vincennes from the Red Coats and sent Governor Hamilton, the "hair buyer," to Virginia in chains. In May that year this Northwest Territory became a county of Virginia—"Illinois County," now five states. About 1794, the Northwest Territory was divided into three counties: Hamilton on the East; Knox County in the center, being a thin slice of West Ohio, all of Indiana and Michigan, and Eastern Illinois and Wisconsin, including the sites of Milwaukee and Chicago; and the third being Illinois and Wisconsin on the west.

In 1800 William Henry Harrison was appointed Governor of Indiana Territory; in 1804 Michigan was split off; in 1809 Illinois was split off, and Knox County was reduced in size to the present state of Indiana. It continued to be reduced to the present size.

Reverend Scott continued to cultivate the vineyard of the Lord until his death, watering the roots, reaping the harvest, and pruning out the diseased sprouts. His territory knew no bounds and included at least all of present Knox County. He preached in the three "stands" of Upper, Lower, and Vincennes, and held preachings and communion and baptisms at homes over the county, including that of Richard Steen at Wheatland, and Robert McClure at Frichton.

He was succeeded in 1828 by his son-in-law, the Reverend Samuel R. Alexander, a graduate of Princeton Theological Seminary, who continued until 1857. The Reverend Alexander's first action was to set down the names of all members in the official session records. He retired in 1857, though he continued to serve Smyrna Church at Wheatland and Royal Oak Church, two sprouts off the old Indiana Church tree. He was the last preacher to serve jointly Upper and Lower Indiana when they were one congregation. He died in 1884.

Reverend Alexander is buried out there in this churchyard, his funeral services being conducted by the Reverend E. P. Whallen, Pastor of the 1st Presbyterian Church at Vincennes, from whose

"History of the Presbytery of Vincennes," written in 1888, I have gleaned some of this paper.

I might add that Daniel McClure, who donated the acre for a church at Sinking Springs, was the first clerk of the church board. He never missed a meeting and evidently, both as a founding father and elder, was a powerful influence in the church. He owned 800 acres of land, 400 of which he got as a Revolutionary War veteran, and 400 more he bought for $1.25 an acre. He was a justice of the peace and county commissioner, and lived about where the Dan Steffey home is located. At his death the board adopted the following resolution:

"Whereas, it has pleased the all wise head of the church to remove Daniel McClure, Clerk of our Session, this is expressive of our sincere regret for the loss of him and also of our cordial appreciation of the manner in which he kept our records. Mr. McClure departed this life on the 24th of December, 1825."

He was 71 years old, and was a native of Londonderry, North Ireland.

When I was a boy, there was a huge pine tree and a little round sandstone tombstone at the head of his grave out there in the old part. Both are now gone, though a Federal Soldier's stone marks the spot, likewise the graves of his brothers George, William, and John.

I must not fail to discuss some of the early trials and tribulations of the early Presbyterians of Knox County—all members of this church, especially the trials.

The early Presbyterian Church of Knox County was a working church, a community center. While it was fully integrated, opening its arms, altars, and communion tables to one and all—Red Indian, black Negro, or white settler—the fathers of the church, the Reverends Scott and Alexander and the elders, believed that members should abide by their vows, and with support of the congregation, enforced compliance with the laws of God and man. Woe betide the luckless member of the Upper Indiana congregation in 1812 or 1840 who slipped off the straight and narrow path. Charges would be brought against him and a public trial held, with suspension and expulsion from the church and its holy communion services if found guilty. The unfortunate wretch so condemned, having been brought up on the stern doctrines of Knox and Calvin, and believing himself foredoomed to a lake of brimstone and fire in the hereafter if the door to Heaven was thus closed for his sins, quite often reformed himself, made due public penance, and was received back into the fold with much rejoicing as a brand plucked from the burning.

Our ancestors here in Knox County were no milksop weaklings. They were strong and sturdy both of body and mind. Many were veterans of the Revolutionary and the Indian Wars and were accompanied by women who helped conquer the West. Sickness, wolves, bears, Indians, and British might kill and terrify, but never conquer. The secretary Daniel McClure and a brother had been with Clark at Sackville, and numerous sons of all families here had gone to Tippecanoe to fight Tecumseh's warriors. People of this atomic age are not the first Americans to face an uncertain future. The Redskin war whoop at midnight around the lonely cabin in the forest was often the trump of doom to the settler, his wife, and babies.

So it was not too unusual when some character "back slid" and whooped it up, or otherwise got in trouble. I have examined the old church record, and in the very first minutes of the church, being August 13, 1812, there is the trial of John Small, as follows:

Trial #1—August 13, 1812

"The Session of the Indiana Church met at Vincennes. Members present, Reverend Samuel F. Scott, moderator. Elders present: Samuel Adams, Isaac Westfall, Cornealous Merry, and Daniel McClure.

"John Small, a member being summoned, appeared before the Session, being charged with unbecoming conduct: acknowledged his fault, which acknowledgement was read openly in the congregation."

Trial #2

"John Hummer, a member, being summoned, appeared before the Session charged by John Welton for taking corn out of Joseph Rodarmer's crib. After hearing alligations (*sic*) on both sides, the Session came to the following order that Hummer should stand suspended from privileges until Jos. Rodarmer returns from Kentucky."

54 communicants were present that session.

I made some notes of later trials on charges of keeping slaves, public intoxication, unbecoming conduct, stealing corn, stealing hoggs (sic) and breach of promise by a lady, as follows:

Trial #3—Patrick Simpson—February 13, 1813 (Territorial Days)

"Patrick Simpson, a member, being summoned, did appear before the Session being charged of using slaves in his family. After deliberation on the question the Session came to the following order that Mr. Simpson is guilty of this charge, and is suspended from further privileges in the church until he evidences repentance and reformation."

Then came the following entries on Mr. Simpson, who had applied for re-admission:

"November 16, 1813—Mr. Simpson case being taken into consideration (for review) and Mr. Simpson being examined, the Session gives little hope of his reformation; and his own conduct in the presence of the Session was sufficient grounds to continue his suspension."

Evidently being unable to stand the pressure as a lost soul, Brother Simpson must have freed his slaves, because on July 29, the next year, we read:

"Mr. Simpson being suspended from church privileges for some time, applyed (sic) in and through Isaac Westfall (an elder). Session deliberating on the question, ordered Mr. Simpson be admitted."

Also this entry in re: Mr. Hummer, who had been suspended the year before about Joseph Rodarmer's corn:

"Mr. Hummer applyed for relief from his suspension. No relief granted."

Trial #4—November 5, 1813, Samuel Adams, elder.

One of the most famous trials was that of Samuel Adams, an elder of the church, charged with being intoxicated with spirits at the working of two bridges near Sugar Loaf, and also with brawling about whether his horse ate some corn belonging to Mr. Ephiram Gilmore. There was a finding of guilty and sentence:

"Mr. Adams be and is suspended from any further privileges in the church until he gives evidence of his temperance and reform."

Mr. Adams did not take his suspension lying down. He later asked a new trial, which was denied. But five years later at the Sinking Springs meeting house he had a new trial, which had been ordered by the Kentucky Presbytery, to which this church belonged. To insure impartiality, the Reverend John Dicky, pastor of the new church at Washington, Indiana, presided, and two o. his deacons came also. He was found guilty again, but was "turned over to the moderator for private examination to see if the brother is repentant, and if he is, he shall be readmitted." There the record ends, so I assume he was readmitted. The session record of 1840 states that "The Reverend Alexander preached the funeral service of Mr. Samuel Adams, a member, said to be upwards of 90 years of age."

Trial #5—Stealing Hoggs (*sic*) and Breach of the Sabbath

On July 29, 1814, Abraham Westfall, brother of Elder Isaac Westfall, came afoul of the good church fathers as follows:

"Session met at Old Presbyterian Stand (in Vincennes). A report being in consideration that Abraham Westfall, a member, had in the course of last summer killed some hoggs not his own, Mr. Westfall applied for relief. The Session taking into consideration the whole matter, was of the opinion Mr. Westfall was not guilty of this charge of stealing hoggs, the report being it was at his brother Cornealious Westfall's near White River, as he states he gave his brother Abraham leave to kill his own marked hoggs that was running with his (Cornealious') marked hoggs."

But, alas, the "hogg" killing was on a Sunday, almost as bad as stealing, and Abraham was found guilty of breaking the Sabbath, and forced to make public confession of sin next Sunday in open church "to the satisfaction of the board," and then was admitted to communion.

Trials #6 and #7—January 5, 1830

Intemperance was the most common of grievous errors into which otherwise godly brethren would fall. The good preacher, Rev. Alexander and his elders had double duty on account of the Demon Rum on January 5, 1830, at the Upper Meeting House.

"The case of James Neal was taken up on a charge of Intemperance and a committee consisting of James Scott and John McCord was appointed to notify him to appear for trial.

"The case of Joseph Scroggin, a member," was taken up, and Jacob Kuykendall was appointed a committee to talk to him and inform him that if he does not desist from intemperance he will be cut off from the church."

This brought things to a head and caused the adoption that very day of the following temperance resolution:

Quarterly Sessions Temperance Resolution January 5, 1830

"The subject of intemperance was taken up, whereupon it was resolved 1st: That the Session of this church consider the increasing use of ardent spirits in producing intemperance, a great evil;

Resolved 2nd: That the Session of this church do what they can to suppress intemperance by discountenancing, both by precept and example, the use of ardent spirits;

Resolved 3rd: That the Session of this church highly approve the humane and benevolent purposes of the Knox County Temperance Society, and do hereby agree to do all in their power to forward the good cause which is alike for the glory of God and the good of man."

Six years later, on June 12, 1836, at the new center meeting house I found the following entry in reference to Mr. Scroggin, who had finally wrestled old John Barley Corn into submission:

"The committee appointed to talk to Mr. Scroggin reports that Mr. Scroggin whom they visited professed a desire to return unto the church and live, God assisting him, as a Christian."

He was readmitted. Evidently the temperance resolution thus bore one fruit, even though it took six years to ripen.

Trial No. 8 was that of a man of color, Isaac, who was expelled from the congregation for stealing corn.

Trial No. 9—On June 11, 1832, the Reverend Alexander and his board met in Quarterly Session at the Lower Indiana stand and took up a case involving three prominent members of the Indiana congregation, which must have caused much heated discussion in the congregation, all revolving around the pangs of unrequited love of Elder Abraham Westfall. He, one John McClure (there were at least a half-dozen John McClures around at the time), and a Miss Patsy Seaton were summoned before the church fathers on charges and counter-charges involving slander, breach of promise to marry, and contributing to said breach of promise. The formal charges are stated as follows:

"Case of Mistress Patsy Seaton, Abraham Westfall & John McClure, viz: Abraham Westfall had stated, 1st) There was a firm marriage contract between him and Mistress Patsy Seaton; 2nd) that she said he would forget his promise, or don't forget his promise; 3rd) that John McClure had broken off the contract."

Miss Seaton appeared and filed cross-charges of slander. Mr. McClure entered a general denial and a disclaimer of being a love pirate. The testimony is preserved in the old record book in the handwriting of John D. Henry, Clerk of the Session, as follows:

"Thomas Westfall testified that Abraham Westfall told him there was a marriage contract between him and Mistress Seaton, and that John McClure broke it off, and that when he was going away she told him that he would forget his promise. Also she believed she would never marry anyone as there has been such a fuss about this.

"Mistress Seaton being called and asked as to the truth of the above reports denied the truth of them, and considers them as slanderous and injuring her character, causing the Session to enter upon a judicial investigation of them.

"John McClure being called, testifyed (*sic*) that he never heard Mistress Seaton say there was a contract between herself and Westfall, also that Westfall solicited him with tears in his eyes to solicit Mistress Seaton in his behalf, and that he refused to interfere and told him that she was of age and could use her free will; and that he never broke off any marriage contract between Mistress Seaton and Mr. Westfall."

Brother McClure did admit to having talked to the young lady as "Mistress Seaton told him that Westfall was after marriage, but that she had given him the 'flat.' " The church record does not state what "the flat" was, but the record goes on:

"It was then put upon Mr. Westfall to prove the truth of his statements, and he called two witnesses who knew nothing on point. Mr. Abraham Westfall testifies that there was a marriage contract between himself and Mistress Seaton. Also that he believes John McClure broke it off. That he told her when he came back that he had not forgot his promise.

"Mistress Seaton being called (again) stated that there never was a marriage contract between herself and Westfall and that she

344

never told Mr. Westfall she was afraid he would forget his promise, or not to forget his promise, and that she had acted in the matter perfectly and on her own responsibility and with her own free will."

The verdict was as follows:

"After some conversation the Session decided that Mr. Westfall had utterly failed to establish the truth of these reports which he had made about Mistress Seaton, and there was not sufficient evidence to convict Westfall of falsehood, two witnesses being necessary to establish a fact, but that Westfall be rebuked and contemned for having circulated the above named things."

Then this entry follows:

"July 11, 1832. Dear Brethren, I hereby decline acting as elder for reason known to Session which is not necessary I should now specify. You will please accept this and oblige. Yours, Abraham Westfall."

"The above resignation being presented to the Session was accepted by the same. John D. Henry, the Clerk."

There were numerous other trials, but you will have to read the record yourselves for them. Enough of trials.

As the population grew, the parent church divided. First to split off were the Wheatland folks, forming the Smyrna church there on July 30, 1832, sixteen years before Wheatland was founded. Next was West Salem, down toward White River in the southern part of Knox County, where the Westfall brothers ran their "hoggs." The Vincennes portion split off in 1834 as the 1st Presbyterian Church of Vincennes, having had a new brick church in 1832. Reverend Alexander collected $2,000 for it on a trip through the East, and the Upper and Lower people gave $200.

In 1842 the Bruceville members withdrew and founded a church, and in 1871, just after the Civil War, the Royal Oak Church was founded from the Wheatland Smyrna Church. When the Upper and Lower congregations first split, the Old Vincennes and Wheatland Road was taken as the dividing line.

As to the churchyard here, there are at least twelve Revolutionary War soldiers buried in it, including two veterans of George Rogers Clark's campaign. There are veterans of the Tippecanoe battle of November 7, 1811, as several companies of Indiana Territorial militia were raised around Vincennes. One of them was named "Benjamin Parke's Brigade of Light Mounted Dragoons of the Indiana Territorial Militia," in which marched my double great grandfather, John McClure, to do battle with Tecumseh's warriors near Lafayette, Indiana.

There are veterans of all wars, but especially the Civil War, buried here. I can remember Decoration Day here in the first years of the century, with many old soldiers in their G.A.R. hats; grandfathers and great-grandfathers of you people, having a service with speaking and decorating the graves. I remember the fife and the snare drums, and the male quartet singing, "Tenting Tonight on the Old Camp Ground," and "Marching Through Georgia." Now they are all out there themselves beneath the sod and the dew, awaiting the Judgment Day.

I want to congratulate and commend my friend, Mr. Derrel Cazel, and the others on the board for preserving and keeping the cemetery so well and making it look so nice. Theirs is often a thankless job.

It was a pleasure to be here and I have thoroughly enjoyed everything. I cannot return to these precincts without calling to mind the lines of the old song: "How dear to my heart are the scenes of my childhood." It is an emotion common to all mankind, if they are normal. I like to think sometimes of these old folks buried here, your ancestors and mine, as our links to the unfathomed past of Eternity, and without whom you and I would not be here in this church. We are their heirs—heirs to these broad, smiling, fertile fields, hills and valleys, to this church, and to life itself. Would that we could maintain the ideal set out by them in their church record of 1830 "to do all in their power for the Glory of God and the Good of Man."

So, on the 50th anniversary of the building of this "new" church, and of the 157th of its founding, I will close by reciting the epitaph you will find on the tombstone of its first pastor and father, the Reverend Samuel Thornton Scott, who died December 30, 1827. The inscription over his grave in the Vincennes Cemetery is from Revelations xiv:13, and reads:

346

"Blessed are the dead which die in the Lord from henceforth: Yea saith the Spirit, that they may rest from their labors and their works do follow them."

NOTE: In the Indiana State Library at Indianapolis is a microfilm copy of the original church record and minutes of the Quarterly Session of the Indiana Presbyterian Church at Vincennes, Indiana. It was copied from the original in the possession of some of the descendants of the Rev. S. S. Alexander. These notes are in the original longhand of the church secretaries. From them I have gathered most of the information about this first Protestant Church in Indiana.

Also in the State Library is a little book, *History of the Presbytery at Vincennes,* by the Rev. E. P. Whallen, pastor of the 1st Presbyterian Church of that city in 1888. This I consulted, as well as other histories of the Presbyterian Church in Indiana, including the memoirs of the Rev. John Dicky, Washington, Indiana.

EPILOGUE

Being Judge of a big city Court for thirty-two years is a rare experience. This Judge tried to go down the middle and do what he could to further the administration of justice, mindful of the fact he was speaking for half-a-million people, ninety-nine percent of whom had not the slightest idea of what goes on in the Circuit Court. This includes appointment of the County Welfare Board, who make policy for welfare; appointment of two members of the Board of Tax Review; of the Jury Commissioners; members of the Public Library Board, among others; insanity inquests; disputed child custody—that Solomon couldn't decide; habeas corpus, jury trials, and divorces. I estimate I have tried 12,000 divorces. There is no use to deny a divorce—papa files in another court, or goes to Reno.

An effort to make the Orders of the Court mean what they say sometimes gets a Judge some criticism. One day in the old Courthouse at morning recess I went down to the coffee counter, when a young man rushed in, sat down and gulped a cup of coffee. He turned to me and said, "I have to be in Judge Niblack's Court in a minute. Where is his Court?" I told him and he added "What kind of a judge is he? They tell me he's a mean old Son-of-a-Bitch!"

"O, I think you'll find him fair," I replied. The young man rushed up the stairs, and in a few minutes I went in the back door, donned my robe and mounted the bench. I had to laugh inwardly when I saw the poor fellow stretching his head above the crowd, a look of horror on his face. He got probation, as a person has it made in Court if he gets the judge amused.

Another time a member of the Jehovah's witness sect, a most stubborn crowd, told me, "I'll stay in jail until Hell freezes over before I'll pay $8.00 a week support for my two boys as I don't like the way she is raising them"—referring to his divorced wife. It seems "she" was rearing them Presbyterian.

"Well, brother, you have just pronounced yourself a sentence. If you believe you are bigger than the people of this county, you are mistaken. You will be committed to the State Farm until you tell the Warden you will obey the Order of the Court."

The young man stayed there two and a half years until he decided to go along with the court. He learned the baker trade while there and is doing well now.

Incidentally, some Associated Press reporter went out to the farm during his stay and took a picture of Quentin looking from behind prison bars (they were hard to find on the State Farm—an honor system) and wrote a story entitled, "Man sentenced for Life because of Religion." I got letters from forty-three states cursing me out. The AP, under threat of libel and contempt of court, ran a retraction, which was run in all the same papers.

Then there were the strikes, legal accompanied with violence, and illegal, as against public policy. Because Circuit Court enforced its orders, there was an unhappy result—for me. All the strike cases wound up in Circuit Court. It never seemed to affect re-election.

In closing this book, which started out as a little treatise to give my nine grandchildren an insight into how their ancestors lived, I state that the main problems in the United States is not the atomic bomb, but 1) how to dispose of our offal and sewage; 2) how to bridle the Federal Judiciary, who are elected by nobody and responsible to nobody. It has taken over our country and reduced our United States Constitution to the 14th Amendment. We are witnessing a government of men, and not of law; and 3) the biggest problem of all, the Negro question—which caused heated discussion in 1787 at the Constitutional Convention, caused carvings and sword play in Congress and a Civil War in the 19th century, and riots and ill temper in the 20th century—will be solved in time completely— say anywhere from 200 years to a thousand years—by Mother Nature, when all our descendants will be of one hue—a light coffee color, flavored with cream. It will be a superior race, of sinew, brawn and mentality.

Someone said a good Judge should have the wisdom of Solomon, the patience of Job, the hide of a Rhinocerous, the compassion of a mother, the stubbornness of a mule, the ideals of Lincoln and the energy of a dynamo. In the present instance, we fell far short, but we tried.

JOHN L. NIBLACK, Judge
19th Judicial Circuit of Indiana

A Wheatland Album

Second Edition

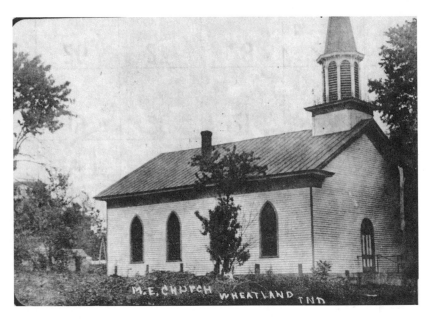

L - R Caroline Nicholson, Mary Commer Nicholson, Esther Nicholson, Maude Sechrest

The above photos are from the Wheatland calendars, courtesy Byron Lewis Histori-
cal Library, Vincennes University

From the 1941 Life Account of John H. Niblack of Wheatland, Father of the Hoosier Judge

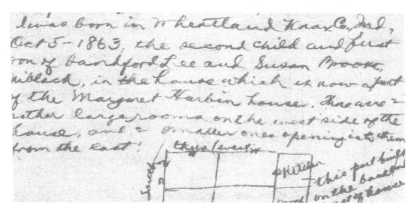

The Niblack family home in Wheatland, Indiana.

...I was married October 22, 1896 to Nannie Jesup McClure, the second daughter of John R. and Frances Purcell McClure. . . We were married in the presence of about 100 guests by Rev EW Fiske, a Presbyterian minister who was preacher at Upper Indiana and Wheatland at different times. . . In August of 1897 John and Martha were born and my delight over our first babies knew no bounds. . . How happy we were in our first cottage with our twin babies. It was too good to last: when dear son Herman was born, it was found that his mother had an abdominal tumor of exaggerated proportions so far advanced that her life was taken when it was removed, and in spite of my tears and prayers she breathed her last

at 8:55 July 30, 1900 in the Union Hospital in Terre Haute. Only those who have trod their "via dolorosa" as I have can appreciate the heart rending grief and despair that was mine. Everyone was so kind; I did not lack for friends or sympathy, but the light of my life had gone out.

Grandpa and Grandma McClure took John and Martha and I took Herman and went to Grandpa and Grandma Niblack's. Then February 25, 1904 I married Anna Scroggins. . .On our return to Wheatland we went to Father and Mother's for dinner. When I told Herman there was "Mama," he immediately took up with her and stuck right with her. . . That day we went to Uncle Willie's for dinner, we took Hermie with us and he never went back to Mother's after that except to vist briefly.

. . . In June of 1906 our dear son Griffith was born and our married life seemed rounded out. The older children welcomed him joyfully and were ever afterwards often his greatest guardians. *Baby Herman*

Baby Griff Niblack and his mother, Anna Scroggins Niblack. Photos on this page courtesy of Tom Niblack, Redlands, California

It was tempting to leave Wheatland, looking for a larger town, more opportunities, but the road always seemed to lead back home. . .

[The Life Account of John H. Niblack continued]

In 1906 we moved to Coalmont, where I had a clothing store with Uncle Herman as partners. Not a very successful venture, so I went on the road with Miller Parrott company, moving to North Vincennes . . . then we moved back to W. [Wheatland]

[This October 26, 1906 letter is to Susan Brooks Niblack in Wheatland from nine-year-old John L. Niblack, as the family prepared to move after trying to keep the store in Coalmont near Terre Haute. An explosion had happened at the mines, damaging tracks. Alum Cave was a small mining town, now gone.]

Dear Grandma: It is very near supper time. We took our dinner to school today. Herman's school room let out at noon, all of them had to take their dinner and ate it out in the woods. They stayed out in the woods till four o'clock. They went to Alum Cave and the cars shop. They seen the reservoir. They seen the E and GH switch part of the track was torn away. Papa had 24 dollars sale yesterday and 17 or 18 today. . . Papa has been so busy manning the store this week. We are going to move in a few weeks. I got a letter from Aunt Helen. Griffith is not well, he has got a bad cold. Herman is writing a letter to Fannie. Mama and I are going to pick some chickens dreckly.

It is after supper now and Papa has gone to the store for a little while. Martha is singing to Baby now. There is going to be a show in town tonight. Papa has brought gasoline lights for the store now. Baby does not like onion tea now; he has took so much. Aunt Helen is going to subscribe to The Companion for us children for a Christmas present and it will be for a year.

I brought the bicicle down to the house the other day. When we move we are going to take in boarders. We brought a bushel and a half of apples today from the house to the barn. We will get eight dollars a week for we are going to keep two boarders. We are all right how are you. I found a ball and put some more twine on the outside. Well I guess I will say goodbye, write soon.   Your grandson John Niblack